RESEARCH HANDBOOK ON DIRECTORS' DUTIES

RESEARCH HANDBOOKS IN CORPORATE LAW AND GOVERNANCE

Elgar *Research Handbooks* are original reference works designed to provide a broad overview of research in a given field while at the same time creating a forum for more challenging, critical examination of complex and often under-explored issues within that field. Chapters by international teams of contributors are specially commissioned by editors who carefully balance breadth and depth. Often widely cited, individual chapters present expert scholarly analysis and offer a vital reference point for advanced research. Taken as a whole they achieve a wide-ranging picture of the state-of-the-art.

Making a major scholarly contribution to the field of corporate law and governance, the volumes in this series explore topics of current concern from a range of jurisdictions and perspectives, offering a comprehensive analysis that will inform researchers, practitioners and students alike. The *Research Handbooks* cover the fundamental aspects of corporate law, such as insolvency governance structures, as well as hot button areas such as executive compensation, insider trading, and directors' duties. The *Handbooks*, each edited by leading scholars in their respective fields, offer far-reaching examinations of current issues in corporate law and governance that are unrivalled in their blend of critical, substantive analysis, and in their synthesis of contemporary research.

Each *Handbook* stands alone as an invaluable source of reference for all scholars of corporate law, as well as for practicing lawyers who wish to engage with the discussion of ideas within the field. Whether used as an information resource on key topics or as a platform for advanced study, volumes in this series will become definitive scholarly reference works in the field.

Titles in this series include:

Research Handbook on Executive Pay
Edited by Randall S. Thomas and Jennifer G. Hill

Research Handbook on Insider Trading
Edited by Stephen M. Bainbridge

Research Handbook on Directors' Duties
Edited by Adolfo Paolini

Research Handbook on Directors' Duties

Edited by

Adolfo Paolini

Senior Lecturer in Commercial Law, University of Buckingham Law School and Consultant, DACBeachcroft LLP, London, UK

RESEARCH HANDBOOKS IN CORPORATE LAW AND GOVERNANCE

Edward Elgar

Cheltenham, UK • Northampton, MA, USA

Published by
Edward Elgar Publishing Limited
The Lypiatts
15 Lansdown Road
Cheltenham
Glos GL50 2JA
UK

Edward Elgar Publishing, Inc.
William Pratt House
9 Dewey Court
Northampton
Massachusetts 01060
USA

A catalogue record for this book
is available from the British Library

Library of Congress Control Number: 2014947027

This book is available electronically in the ElgarOnline.com Law Subject Collection, E-ISBN 978 1 78100 441 8

ISBN 978 1 78100 440 1

Typeset by Servis Filmsetting Ltd, Stockport, Cheshire
Printed and bound in Great Britain by T.J. International Ltd, Padstow

Contents

Contributors

Carlo Amatucci, Professor of Law, The University of Naples Federico II, Italy

Carlo Amatucci is Professor at the Department of Political Science of the University of Naples Federico II, where he currently teaches Commercial Law and Comparative Corporate Law, and Director of the Departmental Course in Sciences of Administration and Organization.

In past years he has also taught the Law of Financial Markets. His primary research interests deal with corporate governance and financial markets. He is a member of the Research Doctorate Board in Commercial Law at the State University of Milan and a member of the regional editorial board of Giurisprudenza Commerciale and of the editorial board of Vestnik, the Law Faculty Journal of Saint Petersburg State University.

Anita Anand, Professor of Law, University of Toronto, Canada

BA (Hons) (Queen's) 1989, BA (Hons Juris) (Oxon) 1991, LLB (Dalhousie) 1992, LLM (Toronto) 1996, joined the University of Toronto Faculty of Law from Queen's University in 2006. She is a Professor at the Faculty of Law at the University of Toronto and served as Associate Dean (JD Program) from 2007–09. She is the Academic Director of the Centre for the Legal Profession including its Program on Ethics in Law and Business. She is also Senior Fellow, Massey College and is cross-appointed to the University of Toronto's School of Public Policy and Governance. During the 2009–10 academic year, Professor Anand was a Visiting Scholar at the Bank of Canada in Ottawa and a Herbert Smith Visitor at the University of Cambridge.

In 2006, she was a Canada-U.S. Fulbright Scholar and Visiting Olin Scholar in Law and Economics at Yale Law School. During Fall 2005, she was a Visiting Lecturer in Law at Yale Law School where she taught comparative corporate governance. She is the recipient of research grants from the Social Sciences and Humanities Research Council of Canada (three awards), the Foundation for Legal Research (three awards), the Connaught Foundation as well as the Canadian Association of Law

Teachers' Scholarly Paper Award (2003). In Fall 2004, she received the Queen's Law Students' Society Award for Excellence in Teaching and in Fall 2006, she and co-authors Frank Milne and Lynnette Purda were awarded the Best Paper in Managerial Finance by the *International Journal of Managerial Finance* for their empirical research relating to corporate governance.

Professor Anand has conducted research for the Five Year Review Committee, the Wise Person's Committee, and the Task Force to Modernize Securities Legislation in Canada. She was the inaugural Chair of the Ontario Securities Commission's Investor Advisory Panel from 2011–12, the Editor of Canadian Law eJournal, published by the Legal Scholarship Network, and the past President of the Canadian Law and Economics Association. In 2012, she was appointed to the Bertha Wilson Honour Society by the Schulich School of Law for service to the legal profession. Since 2010, she has served on the Chief Justice of Ontario's Advisory Committee on Professionalism. Her main research areas relate to the regulation of capital markets and include a focus on corporate and securities law as well as ethics and the corporation.

Vivienne Brand, Senior Lecturer, Law School, Flinders University, Australia

Vivienne Brand researches and teaches in the Law School at the Flinders University of South Australia, with a research focus on corporate law and ethics. Vivienne's doctorate was undertaken in the area of business ethics and considered cross-cultural issues in that context; she also holds a Master of Laws from the University of London, majoring in commercial law and a Masters degree in Education. Vivienne has published nationally and internationally on topics related to corporate law, business ethics and legal education. Recent publications have dealt with whistleblowing and the use of bounties to encourage whistleblowing activity, class actions and litigation funding in Australia, and enforcement of liquidator obligations. Developments in corporate whistleblowing are a particular focus of Vivienne's current research work. Vivienne teaches principally in the area of corporate law and her current teaching responsibilities include a compulsory undergraduate corporate law subject in which ethical issues related to companies and to corporate legal practice form a compulsory element. Before commencing an academic career Vivienne worked in private legal practice for a number of years, with an emphasis on banking and finance and general commercial work, as well as in-house within the treasury operations of a banking corporation.

Theresa A. Gabaldon, Professor, George Washington University, USA

Theresa A. Gabaldon is the Lyle T. Alverson Professor of Law at The George Washington University Law School. She also serves as the Director of Academic Programs and Administration for GW's Center for Law Economics and Finance, and is the Co-Director of GW's LL.M. in Business and Finance. Professor Gabaldon specializes in accounting, corporate and securities law and professional responsibility. She is the author or co-author of multiple books and articles in these fields. Some of her recent scholarship has focused on the regulation of municipal securities and on the importance of math for transactional lawyers. Before joining the faculty of the Law School in 1990, Professor Gabaldon was a member of the law faculties of the University of Colorado and the University of Arizona (and was the first Professor of Latino Heritage at each). Before entering academia, she was an associate and then a partner with the law firm of Snell & Wilmer in Phoenix. She is a graduate of Harvard Law School and the University of Arizona School of Business and Public Management. She is a member of Latino Law Professors and has served as a member of a number of committees and task forces, including the Colorado Supreme Court's Task Force on Gender Bias and the committee responsible for drafting the Association of American Law Schools' Statement of Good Practices by Law Professors.

Michelle M. Harner, Professor of Law, University of Maryland Francis King Carey School of Law, USA

Michelle M. Harner is a Professor of Law and the Director of the Business Law Program at the University of Maryland Francis King Carey School of Law. She teaches courses in Bankruptcy and Creditors Rights, Business Associations, Business Planning, Corporate Finance, and Legal Profession. Professor Harner is widely published and lectures frequently on various topics involving corporate governance, financially distressed entities, risk management, and related legal issues. Her most recent publications appear or are forthcoming in the *Vanderbilt Law Review, Notre Dame Law Review, Washington University Law Review, Minnesota Law Review, Fordham Law Review* (reprinted in *Corporate Practice Commentator*), *Washington & Lee Law Review, University of Illinois Law Review, Arizona Law Review* (reprinted in *Corporate Practice Commentator*), and *Florida Law Review*. Professor Harner currently is serving as the Reporter to the ABI Commission to Study the Reform of Chapter 11. She previously was in private practice in the business restructuring, insolvency, bankruptcy, and related transactional fields, most recently as a partner at the Chicago office of the international law firm Jones Day.

Jennifer G. Hill, Professor of Corporate Law, Sydney Law School, Australia

Jennifer Hill is Professor of Corporate Law and a Director of the Ross Parsons Centre of Commercial, Corporate and Taxation Law. She is known for her work in comparative corporate law and governance. A graduate of the University of Sydney and Oxford University, Jennifer has been a Visiting Professor at several international law schools, including Vanderbilt University, University of Virginia, University of Texas and Cornell.

Jennifer is a Research Associate of the European Corporate Governance Institute (ECGI) and a Fellow of the Australian Academy of Law (AAL). She is a member of the corporations law editorial board of Cambridge University Press, the Advisory Council of the Centre for International Finance and Regulation (CIFR) and the External Advisory Panel of the Australian Securities and Investments Commission (ASIC).

S.H. Goo, Professor of Law, The University of Hong Kong

Say H. Goo is Professor and Director of The University of Hong Kong, Faculty of Law's Asian Institute of International Financial Law (AIIFL) and Japan and Korea Programme, and Deputy Director of HKU's Ronald Coase Centre for Property Rights Research (RCCPRR). A graduate of the University of Leicester (LLB) and the University of East Anglia (LLM), he joined HKU in 1995 after over five years of teaching at the University of East Anglia and the University of Exeter. Over the years, he has taught many subjects including Contract Law, Land Law, Company Law, Insolvency Law, Trust, and Corporate Governance. At HKU, he has also served as Deputy Head of Department of Law, Admissions Tutor, Founding Director of AIIFL and Founding Director of the LLM (CFL) Programme. He is currently Honorary Visiting Professor at the University of Exeter Law School.

He is on the editorial board of the *Journal of Business Law, Hong Kong Law Journal, Company and Securities Law Journal* (Australia), *Property Law Review* (Australia), and has acted as reviewer for Cambridge University Press, HKU Press, Ashgate Publishing Ltd, Cavendish Publishing Ltd, *Journal of Corporate Law Studies* (UK), *Hong Kong Law Journal, Company and Securities Law Journal* (Australia), and *Journal of Business Law* (UK), and some universities' promotional exercises.

Marcos Jaramillo, Professor of Law, Pontificia Universidad de Chile

Marcos Jaramillo, Ph.D. in Law from Kobe University in Japan. He is an Attorney-at-Law, Professor of Asian Laws and Public International Law, Director of the Asian Studies Center CEA-UC of Pontificia Universidad Católica de Chile. He has been appointed as one of the Directors of the Confucius Institute of the same university. He is also a Member of the Chilean National Commission for Scientific and Technological Research, Advanced Human Capital Formation, Law Committee, and a Member of the Chilean Bar Association.

Professor Jaramillo has been teaching Chinese Law and Japanese Law at Pontificia Universidad Católica de Chile as a regular course since 2005, the first of its kind in Latin America. He has also organized two summits on Chinese Law and Practice with famous speakers such as Donald C. Clarke and Daniel Harris.

Professor Jaramillo has conducted legal research in Chile, China (Tsinghua University and Shanghai Jiao Tong University) and Japan (Kobe University and the Institute of Development Economics Ide-Jetro), writing on topics ranging from Criminal Procedure Law to Corporations. He is the author of the Spanish version of a book on Japanese Criminal Procedure. He has also authored several articles on various law topics, such as the Legal Bridge between China and the West (in Chinese), the Japanese Corporation (in Spanish) and the Chilean Banking Corporation (in Japanese). He also has translated into Spanish an article in English about the Chinese State Owned Enterprises (SOEs), and he regularly writes on newspapers and appears on Chilean TV as a specialist on China news.

Désirée Klingler, LLM Corporate and Financial Law, University of Hong Kong

Désirée is currently working as a junior associate at a leading Swiss corporate law firm in the practice groups banking and finance, mergers and acquisitions, as well as arbitration. Her main research interests lie in the areas of corporate finance, corporate governance and securities law, as well as international commercial arbitration and financial markets law. Désirée has previously worked as a research assistant at the Chair for Private, European and Economic Law at the University of Zurich where she has co-authored a textbook on Swiss contract law (2012) with Prof. Dr. Huguenin. She is further co-author of a commentary on the UN sales law (forthcoming) edited by Dr. Brunner, Adj. Prof. of the University of Bern. Désirée is a graduate of the University of Hong Kong (LLM in

Corporate and Financial Law) and the University of Zurich (Bachelor and Master of Law). She is pursuing her interest in arbitration, participating in the Willem C. Vis Commercial Arbitration Moot in Vienna where she achieved the Pieter Sanders Award for the Best Memorandum for Claimant.

Andrea Lista, Associate Professor in Commercial Law, University of Southampton, UK

Andrea Lista, Dott. Giur. LL.D. (Italy), LLM (Soton), PhD (London). He has notably worked as a legal adviser to a multinational enterprise leading in underwater technology and has been a legal consultant to the European Parliament. He has lectured for several years in various areas of commercial law (international trade, competition law, international commercial arbitration, internal market law and corporate law) in Southampton and London, and he is a very active legal consultant. Andrea has vast experience in international commercial law, and he is a legal consultant to companies and law firms.

Jeff MacIntosh, Professor of Law, University of Toronto, Canada

Jeff MacIntosh holds the Toronto Stock Exchange Chair in Capital Markets at the Faculty of Law and is a past Associate Director and Director of the Capital Markets Institute at the University of Toronto. He holds law degrees from Harvard and Toronto, and a Bachelor of Science degree from M.I.T. He was appointed a John M. Olin Fellow at Yale Law School in 1988–89. He also served as a member of the Ontario Securities Commission Task Force on Small Business Financing in 1996.

Professor MacIntosh is the author (with Chris Nichols) of a textbook on securities regulation. He has also authored numerous articles on a variety of corporate and securities law topics, including directors' fiduciary duties, controlling shareholders' duties, corporate governance, minority shareholders' rights, takeover bids, insider trading, the legal mandate of the Ontario Securities Commission, the role of retail and institutional investors in Canadian capital markets, prospectus disclosure, continuous disclosure, the oppression remedy, shareholders' dissent rights, and whether Canada should move to a national securities regulator. His recent research has focused on the law and financial economics of funding small technology start-ups, with an emphasis on venture capital. He has taught a finance-based course in venture capital financing for the past 15 years, and has also been closely involved in spinning off a start-up company from the Chemistry Department at the University of Toronto. Professor MacIntosh (with Douglas Cumming) was awarded the Iddo Sarnat Annual Memorial Award for the best paper published in the *Journal of Banking and Finance* (an international finance journal) in 2003 (for a paper on venture capital exits).

Adolfo Paolini, Senior Lecturer in Commercial Law, University of Buckingham and Consultant, DACBeachcroft LLP, London, UK

Adolfo Paolini, PhD (Southampton) LLM (Cardiff) LLB (UCAT Venezuela), is Senior Lecturer in Commercial Law and LLM Director in the University of Buckingham. His area of expertise, research and practice includes Banking, Company and Insurance Law. His PhD thesis on the nature of Directors' and Officers' Liability insurance was published by Informa Professional in London UK and in 2009 the British Insurance Law Association awarded Adolfo and his co-author the BILA book prize 2009 for their formidable contribution to the area of insurance law. Adolfo is also the vice chairman of the civil liability working party in AIDA (Association Internationale de Droit des Assurances). He is consultant to the DACBeachcroft LLP, a law firm based in London with offices in more than 14 jurisdictions, where he advises on issues regarding D&O Insurance, Financial Lines, Comparative Insurance Law and Latin America Legal Disputes.

Pedro Pais de Vanconcelos, Professor of Law, University of Lisbon, Portugal

Pedro Pais de Vanconcelos is a Professor of Law in the University of Lisbon with extensive experience in the fields of Civil Law, Commercial Law, Banking Law, Companies Law, Intellectual Property Law and Bioethics Law. He is a member of the Project Group 'Restatement of European Insurance Contract Law' – Principles of European Insurance Contract Law (PEICL). Member of the Roberto Schlessinger Association and participant on the 'The Common Core of European Private Law' on Commercial Trust and Administration of Property and on Personality Rights in European Tort Law. Member of IVM – Instituto dos Valores Mobiliários da Faculdade de Direito de Lisboa (Institute for Financial Services of the Faculty of Law of the University of Lisbon). Chairman of the AIDA-International Association of Insurance Law – Portuguese Section and a member of the Institute for Securities Law of the Faculty of Law in the University of Lisbon.

Susan Watson, Professor of Law, University of Auckland, New Zealand

Susan Watson is a Professor in Law, who writes, teaches and consults in the areas of company law, in particular the nature of the company, and directors' duties and liabilities. She has published widely in these areas both locally in publications such as the *New Zealand Business Law Quarterly*, and the *New Zealand Universities Law Review* and internationally in publications such as the *Law Quarterly Review, Journal of Business Law*, the *Journal of Corporate Law Studies* and the *Company Lawyer*. She is also an editor and chief contributor to the text *The Law of Business Organisations* (now in its fifth edition), and an author and editor J Farrar and S Watson (ed.) *Company and Securities Law in New Zealand* (second edition). Susan is the New Zealand editor for the *Journal of Business Law* and is the joint editor of the *New Zealand Business Law Quarterly*. She is a member of Global Women New Zealand and is a visiting Professor at Vanderbilt Law School and Tilburg University.

Within her areas of specialisation, Susan is particularly interested in the legal relationship between shareholders and boards, the role of the board, corporate governance and the liability of company directors and professionals. She is currently part of a research project looking at the relationship between leadership and governance. Her own research is currently focused on the development of internal rules in companies.

Before joining the University, Susan worked as a staff solicitor and associate in two city law firms. Before joining the Law School she was Professor of Commercial Law in the Business School where she was Head of Department from 2008 to 2011 and Associate Dean Academic Faculty in 2011. She is currently Deputy Dean of the Law School and joint Director of the Research Centre for Business Law.

Introduction

Adolfo Paolini

Company directors have been the centre of attention for a number of years, following the financial crisis that affected and still affects worldwide economies. The role of directors is increasingly becoming a very demanding one and it is safe to say that it encompasses duties which go beyond the corporate body, of which they are in charge. This is why corporate governance authors always talk about directors and corporate social responsibility, and to some extent, these authors are right.

Public limited companies benefit from the fact that they can raise capital from the general public; thus, anybody can become a shareholder in a company, which could grow well beyond one's imagination. Such large entities also usually have a number of customers, suppliers and stakeholders who can be measured in hundreds of thousands. It is not difficult therefore to think and realise that in discharging office directors should and must take into consideration the damaging social effect that their misconduct could cause. For an example, let us use banks, which adopt corporate structures to perform their business (in fact in most jurisdictions, banks can only operate as private or public companies) and remember the long queues that formed outside some at the end of 2007 and 2008. People wanted to withdraw the little they had in their bank accounts before the bank shut its doors. Those forming the queue were not the bank's shareholders, they were the bank's customers wanting to recover the fruit of their labour, their life savings, their pensions and the like. Is it true then, that those who suffered the effect of a company going into financial distress were not only company shareholders but also society at large?

The same could be said about any company whose main business is that of providing members of society with basic services: telecommunications, utilities, transportation, etc. The idea of making company directors potentially liable to outsiders (stakeholders) when they infringe their duties to the company is not therefore groundless.

Consequently, the problem we face is that making directors potentially liable to an undetermined number of potential claimants may deter good and diligent people from accepting managing or directorial positions. How can we then encourage actual or future directors to accept or remain in such demanding jobs? This can be done by making them aware of what the law is, what it entails and what liabilities are to be avoided. This is precisely the purpose of this collection of essays *Research Handbook on Directors' Duties*.

The book has been conceived with the purpose of bringing together academics of international dimension whose reputation and expertise in this field will produce ground-breaking ideas, which no doubt are going to motivate other's research and interest.

The book is divided in four parts. The first part generally focuses on directors' duties and liabilities in the common law legal system.

Comparing legal principles in Australia, Canada, New Zealand and the UK is far from being an easy task, nevertheless, the authors have managed to clearly underpin the basic features that make these legal systems so solid and attractive. From the business judgement rule through the new structural conflict of interest duty and the effect of codifying directors' duties in New Zealand and the UK, this part has managed to achieve the clear objective of showing that in the common law system the law rapidly adapts to the circumstances.

Part II on the other hand focuses on the Civil Law legal system, trying to explain (and indeed it does explain) the Italian, Portuguese and Chinese approach to directorship. The contrast between well-established systems and fast-evolving economies happens to be very interesting. Albeit the ultimate objective is to inform directors as to what they should do and the repercussions of not so doing, it is very interesting to see the different angles and views taken by these three jurisdictions, including the possibility of directors incurring liability to third parties.

Part III proves that directors' duties go well beyond the boundaries of the company. In fact, there is now a strong ethical content in what directors must do and the need to bear in mind that not only human rights in general but also consumer rights in particular have to be protected and most importantly respected.

Part IV takes us to a new dimension; namely, the aftermath of the company and liabilities that may arise once the company faces insolvency. From analysing directors' exposure in times of financial distress, through non-executive directors' standard of care and liabilities to investors and the corporation, this part shows us that directors could effectively experience personal liability when insolvency strikes the corporate body.

Finally, I would like to take this opportunity to thank all of the contributors for your excellent work and commitment to make this project a reality. I would also like to thank my colleagues, Dr Sarah Sargent,

Dr Phil Larkin and Dr Patricia Covarrubia for their help in proofreading the materials and giving useful comments. Last but by no means least, to Edward Elgar Publishing for contacting me in the first place to produce this book, its constant support and especially patience.

PART I

DIRECTORS' DUTIES IN THE COMMON LAW LEGAL SYSTEM

1. Evolving directors' duties in the common law world

*Jennifer G. Hill**

1. INTRODUCTION

Legal scholars have long discussed the gap, or 'acoustic separation', between the stringent standards of conduct ('conduct rules') and the more lenient standards of review ('decision rules') in legal regulation.[1] This gap has been particularly stark in the United States (US) in the area of directors' duties.[2] For example, although the duty of care appears on its face to be a relatively strict doctrine, adjudication by the courts has tended to be generous to directors. The gap between conduct and decision rules is also relevant to the question of whose interests directors should take into account in the performance of their duties.

The goal of this chapter is to explore a range of developments relating to directors' duties across several common law jurisdictions, against the backdrop of conduct and decision rules. The chapter is structured as follows. First, it examines US law relating to directors' duty of care and the business judgment rule, from the perspective of acoustic separation. As US case law, such as the *Disney* litigation,[3] shows, the liability risk to

* I would like to thank a number of people for their help and comments relating to the research in this chapter. They include Carlo Amatucci, Fady Aoun, Elizabeth Boros, Stefan Lo, Joan Loughrey, Louis Chu, Manlio Lubrano and Julian Velasco. Thanks also go to Alice Grey, Leonor Cagigal and Jerome Entwisle for excellent research assistance. Funding for research in this paper was provided by the University of Sydney and the Australian Research Council.

1 See Dan-Cohen, 'Decision Rules and Conduct Rules: On Acoustic Separation in Criminal Law' (1984) 97 *Harv L Rev* 625; Eisenberg, 'The Divergence of Standards of Conduct and Standards of Review in Corporate Law' (1993) 62 *Fordham L Rev* 437; Smith, 'A Proposal to Eliminate Director Standards from the Model Business Corporation Act' (1999) 67 *U Cin L Rev* 1201.

2 See Velasco, 'The Role of Aspiration in Corporate Fiduciary Duties' (2012) 54 *Wm & Mary L Rev* 519.

3 See, for example, *In re The Walt Disney Company Derivative Litigation*, Del.

directors, particularly non-executive directors, for breach of the duty of care is negligible.[4]

Secondly, the chapter discusses some contemporary Australian case law on directors' duty of care and diligence, which highlights the ongoing tension between conduct rules and decision rules, yet diverges from US law in many respects. Under Australia's regulatory model, the corporate regulator, namely the Australian Securities and Investments Commission ('ASIC'), operates as the main enforcement mechanism for breach of directors' duties.[5] This section of the chapter provides a detailed examination of three important recent cases brought by ASIC in the context of the duty of care and diligence – the *James Hardie* litigation,[6] *ASIC v Rich*,[7] and the *Centro* litigation.[8]

Finally, the chapter assesses some recent developments in the common law world on the perennial issue of to whom directors owe their duties, and the extent to which stakeholder interests can, or must, be taken into account in board decision-making. This is by no means a new topic in corporate law. It dates back at least to the 1930s, when Professors Berle and Dodd engaged in their seminal debate on the subject.[9] However, corporate scandals at the turn of the last decade, such as Enron, gave the issue new momentum, and this has continued through the global financial crisis. Developments in this regard include the introduction in 2006 of a controversial statutory duty for directors in the United Kingdom (UK), two Australian Government reports on corporate responsibility, and some

Ch., 907 A.2d 693 (2005); *In re The Walt Disney Company Derivative Litigation*, Del.Supr., 906 A.2d 27 (2006).

4 Black, Cheffins and Klausner, 'Outside Director Liability' (2006) 58 *Stan L Rev* 1055; Armour, Black, Cheffins and Nolan, 'Private Enforcement of Corporate Law: An Empirical Comparison of the United Kingdom and the United States' (2009) 6 *J Empirical Legal Studies* 687.

5 See Jones and Welsh, 'Toward a Public Enforcement Model for Directors' Duty of Oversight' (2012) 45 *Vand J Transnat'l L* 343.

6 See *ASIC v Macdonald (No 11)* (2009) 256 ALR 199; *Morley v ASIC* (2010) 274 ALR 205; *ASIC v Hellicar* (2012) 286 ALR 501.

7 *ASIC v Rich* (2009) 75 ACSR 1.

8 *ASIC v Healey* (2011) 196 FCR 291.

9 Berle, 'Corporate Powers as Powers in Trust' (1931) 44 *Harv L Rev* 1049; Berle, 'For Whom Corporate Managers Are Trustees: A Note' (1932) 45 *Harv L Rev* 1365; Dodd, 'For Whom Are Corporate Managers Trustees?' (1932) 45 *Harv L Rev* 1145; Weiner, 'The Berle-Dodd Dialogue on the Concept of the Corporation' (1964) 64 *Colum L Rev* 1458; Hill, 'At the Frontiers of Labour Law and Corporate Law: Enterprise Bargaining, Corporations and Employees' (1995) 23 *Fed L Rev* 204, 209ff; Hill, 'Then and Now: Professor Berle and the Unpredictable Shareholder' (2010) 33 *Seattle U L Rev* 1005, 1006–10.

interesting recent case law in Australia and Canada on directors' duties and stakeholder interests.

2. CONDUCT RULES AND DECISION RULES IN THE UNITED STATES – *DISNEY, VAN GORKOM* ET AL.

Professors Melvin Eisenberg[10] and Meir Dan-Cohen[11] have written about the gap between standards of conduct and standards of review in legal regulation. Their analysis assumes a divergence, or 'acoustic separation', between the messages directed to legal actors as conduct rules, and the messages directed to the courts as legal adjudicators via decision rules. Although this paradigm is not without its critics,[12] it is a helpful way to conceptualise US developments concerning directors' duties where, in many cases, the regulatory bark has been much worse than its bite.[13]

In the US, nowhere has this regulatory dissonance been more striking than in the area of directors' duties,[14] where the law often reveals a divide between legal rules and aspirational standards.[15] Thus, although conduct rules under US corporate law require directors to act with a reasonable degree of care and diligence,[16] the business judgment rule provides

---

[10] Eisenberg, 'The Divergence of Standards of Conduct', note 1 above.

[11] Dan-Cohen, 'Decision Rules and Conduct Rules', note 1 above.

[12] See Singer, 'On Classism and Dissonance in the Criminal Law: A Reply to Professor Meir Dan-Cohen' (1986) 77 *J Crim L & Criminology* 69; and Velasco, 'The Role of Aspiration', see note 2 above, 17–21. Both authors argue that 'acoustic separation' between the rules communicated to the public and those communicated to officials cannot, and perhaps more importantly should not, be maintained. Velasco is particularly critical of the application of the concept in the context of director's duties, because directors can be expected to have obtained legal advice and thus be aware of the decision rules that apply to them: ibid., 541.

[13] See Singer, 'On Classism and Dissonance in the Criminal Law', note 12 above, 83, where Singer describes Meir Dan-Cohen's 'acoustic separation' theory as a '"bark-bite" philosophy'.

[14] Smith, 'A Proposal to Eliminate Director Standards', note 1 above, 1203ff.

[15] See Velasco, 'The Role of Aspiration', note 2 above.

[16] Prior to 1998, the US Model Business Corporation Act (MBCA) § 8.30(a)(2), borrowing from concepts of tort law, required directors to carry out their duties 'with the care an ordinarily prudent person in a like position would exercise under similar circumstances'. Amendments were introduced by the ABA Committee on Corporate Laws in 1998, which altered the wording of § 8.30(a)(2) to require directors to 'discharge their duties with the care that a person in a like position would reasonably believe appropriate under the circumstances'.

protection to directors at the time of any adjudication of their actions.[17] With the notable exception of the famous Delaware Supreme Court decision in the mid 1980s, *Smith v Van Gorkom*,[18] this protection is capacious. The disciplinary effect of the *Van Gorkom* 'bomb'[19] proved to be remarkably short-lived. Delaware responded to the decision, by rapidly enacting § 102(b)(7) of the Delaware General Corporations Law ('DGCL'), which authorised inclusion in the corporate charter of exculpation provisions for this kind of breach.[20]

Liability for breach of duty of care has always been rare in the US and tends to be limited to egregious conduct that also implicates the duty of loyalty.[21] Recent US case law continues this trend.[22] The business judgment rule has been a prominent buffer against director liability.

---

[17] For discussion of the business judgment rule, and traditional justifications for the rule, in the new context, represented by the global financial crisis, see Sprague and Lyttle, 'Shareholder Primacy and the Business Judgement Rule: Arguments for Expanded Corporate Democracy' (2010) 16 *Stan JL Bus & Fin* 1, 14–17; Aman, 'Cost-Benefit Analysis of the Business Judgment Rule: A Critique in Light of the Financial Meltdown' (2010) 74 *Alb L Rev* 1, 3; Rosenberg, 'Supplying the Adverb: the Future of Corporate Risk-Taking and the Business Judgment Rule' (2009) 6 *Berkeley Bus LJ* 216.

[18] Del. Supr., 488 A.2d. 858 (1985). The main focus of *Smith v Van Gorkom* was the process of decision-making. See Stout, 'In Praise of Procedure: An Economic and Behavioral Defense of Smith v. Van Gorkom and the Business Judgment Rule' (2002) 96 *Nw U L Rev* 675, who describes *Smith v Van Gorkom* as providing the classic example of the procedural focus embedded in the business judgment rule (at 696). See also Elson and Thompson, 'Van Gorkom's Legacy: The Limits of Judicially Enforced Constraints and the Promise of Proprietary Incentives' (2002) 96 *Nw U L Rev* 579, 582–7.

[19] See Manning, 'Reflections and Practical Tips on Life in the Boardroom After Van Gorkom' (1985) 41 *Bus Law* 1.

[20] See Elson and Thompson, 'Van Gorkom's Legacy', note 18 above, 583. For a good example of the operation of such exculpation provisions, see *Malpiede v Townson*, Del. Supr., 780 A.2d 1075 (2001).

[21] See Johnson, 'Rethinking Judicial Review of Director Care' (1999) 24 *Del J Corp L* 787, 801; Cary and Harris, 'Standards of Conduct under Common Law, Present Day Statutes and the Model Act' (1972) 27 *Bus Law* 61; Armour, Black, Cheffins and Nolan, 'Private Enforcement of Corporate Law', note 4 above; Furlow, 'Good Faith, Fiduciary Duties, and the Business Judgment Rule in Delaware' (2009) 3 *Utah L Rev* 1061.

[22] In relation to derivative litigation pleadings, see, for example, *In re Citigroup Inc Shareholder Derivative Litigation*, Del. Ch., 964 A.2d 106 (2009). Cf. *American International Group, Inc Consolidated Derivative Litigation*, Del. Ch., 965 A.2d 763 (2009). See also *Lyondell Chemical Co v Ryan*, Del. Supr., 970 A.2d 235 (2009); *In re The Dow Chemical Company Derivative Litigation*, No. 4349, Del. Ch. LEXIS, *2 (2010).

Nonetheless, other factors, including delegation, exculpation clauses in corporate charters and insurances, have also effectively insulated US directors, particularly non-executive directors, either from liability or the financial consequences of liability for breach of the duty of care.[23]

The high-profile *Disney* litigation provided a good example of the gap between conduct rules and decision rules in the US.[24] In 2003, the Delaware Court of Chancery[25] confirmed that a shareholders' derivative action for breach of duty could proceed against directors and officers at the Walt Disney Company ('Disney') who approved an executive contract that resulted in payment of a US$140 million severance package to former President, Michael Ovitz, for a mere 15 months of unremarkable work.[26] Some obiter dictum in this case caused consternation in the US business community, by suggesting that directors would lose the protection of the business judgment rule if their conduct could be characterised as reckless and in conscious disregard of known risks.[27] The 2003 *Disney* decision therefore countenanced a narrowing of the traditional gap between conduct rules and decision rules in these particular circumstances.

Subsequent decisions in the *Disney* litigation, however, restored both 'acoustic separation' to the duty of care, and equanimity to US company directors. In his 2005 decision, which considered whether Disney's directors had breached their duties in approving Mr Ovitz's extravagant termination package,[28] Chancellor Chandler condemned the behaviour of the directors and officers of Disney in approving the package, and identified serious procedural flaws in the pay determination process.[29] Accusing the

---

23 Black, Cheffins and Klausner, 'Outside Director Liability', note 4 above, 1090–5.

24 Hill, 'Regulating Executive Remuneration: International Developments in the Post-Scandal Era' (2006) 3 *Eur Comp L* 64.

25 *In re The Walt Disney Company Derivative Litigation*, Del. Ch., 825 A.2d 275 (2003).

26 For a good summary of the background facts relating to the appointment and removal of Michael Ovitz, see 'Recent Cases' (2006) 119 *Harv L Rev* 923, 923–6.

27 According to Chancellor Chandler, this would occur if the 'defendant directors *consciously and intentionally disregarded their responsibilities*, adopting a "we don't care about the risks" attitude'. *In re The Walt Disney Company Derivative Litigation*, note 25 above, p. 289 (original emphasis). Another matter of great concern to directors arising from this dictum was that such a finding could also deprive them of the protection of exoneration clauses in corporate charters. See, for example, s. 102(b)(7) DGCL.

28 *In re The Walt Disney Company Derivative Litigation*, Del. Ch., 907 A.2d 693 (2005).

29 See ibid., pp. 708, 734, 736–77.

board of 'collective kowtowing',[30] Chancellor Chandler described Disney as a place where CEO, Michael Eisner, had 'enthroned himself as the omnipotent and infallible monarch of his personal Magic Kingdom'.[31] Although some scholars argue that the days of the 'imperial' CEO are now numbered,[32] such imperialism appeared to be alive and well at Disney during this period.

Although Chancellor Chandler considered the actions of Disney's directors to provide 'many lessons of what not to do' as a director,[33] he, nonetheless, drew a sharp distinction between legally enforceable directors' duties and 'aspirational' standards of corporate governance.[34] According to Chancellor Chandler, 'Delaware law does not – indeed, the common law cannot – hold fiduciaries liable for a failure to comply with the aspirational ideal of best practices'.[35]

Chancellor Chandler's 2005 decision, which was approved by the Delaware Supreme Court the following year,[36] reflected a clear gap between conduct rules and decision rules. He considered that, although the defendants' behaviour fell well short of aspirational standards, it did not constitute a breach of legally enforceable duties. In spite of numerous procedural flaws, he held that, since the directors acted in good faith and 'did not intentionally shirk or ignore their duty', their actions were protected by the business judgment rule.[37] Although some commentators consider that the business judgment rule rests upon a rational policy basis[38] for others, the outcome of the *Disney* litigation merely perpetuated what has been described as Delaware's 'elaborate theology of deference' to decisions of the board of directors.[39]

---

30 Ibid., p. 761, n 488.

31 Ibid., p. 763.

32 Kahan and Rock, 'Embattled CEOs' (2010) 88 *Tex L Rev* 987.

33 *In re The Walt Disney Company Derivative Litigation*, note 28 above, p. 760.

34 A leading proponent of the aspirational theory of fiduciary duties in the US was Chancellor Allen of the Delaware Court of Chancery, who stated that the US duty of care was 'essentially aspirational: informing well-intentioned persons of what they should be doing in a general way'. See generally Velasco, 'The Role of Aspiration', note 2 above, 537–8.

35 *In re The Walt Disney Company Derivative Litigation*, note 28 above, p. 697.

36 *In re The Walt Disney Company Derivative Litigation*, Del. Supr., 906 A.2d 27 (2006). In the decision of the Delaware Supreme Court, Jacobs J considered that there were rational commercial justifications for the Disney directors agreeing to the enormous termination payment to Michael Ovitz. See ibid., p. 58.

37 Note 28 above, p. 772.

38 See, for example, Winter J's discussion of some of the policy justifications for the business judgment rule in *Joy v North*, 692 F.2d 880, 885–6 (1982).

39 See Baums and Scott, 'Taking Shareholder Protection Seriously? Corporate

The *Disney* litigation[40] sits somewhat uncomfortably with *Smith v Van Gorkom*,[41] decided more than 20 years earlier, which itself had been described as 'a recital of explicit and implicit do's and don'ts' for directors.[42] In *Van Gorkom's* case, however, the Delaware Supreme Court held the directors liability for breach of the duty of care, noting that mere absence of bad faith or fraud was insufficient to satisfy the duty.[43]

The 2005 *Disney* decision accords with the approach taken in other contemporary US cases, such as *In re Caremark International Inc. Derivative Litigation* ('*Caremark* decision'),[44] which also recognise a divide between aspirational and legally enforceable rules.[45] Although some of Chancellor Allen's rhetoric in the *Caremark* decision suggested the espousal of a more stringent duty of oversight,[46] this was ultimately counteracted in the case

---

Governance in the United States and Germany' (2005) 53 *Am J Comp L* 31, 32. See also Sprague, 'Beyond Shareholder Value: Normative Standards for Sustainable Corporate Governance' (2010) 1 *Wm & Mary Bus L Rev* 47.

40 *In re The Walt Disney Company Derivative Litigation*, note 28 above.

41 Del. Supr., 488 A.2d 858 (1985). It has been suggested that *Smith v Van Gorkom* can be reconciled with the later cases by recognising that *Smith v Van Gorkom* was essentially a takeover case, rather than a case about business judgment: see Macey and Miller, 'Trans Union Reconsidered' (1988) 98 *Yale Law Journal* 127, 128. Nonetheless, Chancellor Chandler went to some lengths in the 2005 *Disney* decision to distinguish the case from *Smith v Van Gorkom*. Some of his points of distinction were transactional, others were not: see generally Hill, 'Centro and the Monitoring Board – Legal Duties versus Aspirational Ideals in Corporate Governance' (2012) 35 *UNSW LJ* 341, 350–51.

42 See Manning, 'Reflections and Practical Tips', note 19 above. For a list of the relevant do's and don'ts for directors in the context of the *Smith v Van Gorkom* decision, see ibid., p. 7, Appendix.

43 *Smith v Van Gorkom*, note 41 above, p. 872.

44 Del. Ch., 698 A.2d 959 (1996). See generally Arlen, 'The Story of Allis-Chalmers, Caremark, and Stone: Directors' Evolving Duty to Monitor', in Ramseyer (ed.), *Corporate Law Stories* (Foundation Press, 2009), p. 323.

45 See Hill, 'Deconstructing Sunbeam – Contemporary Issues in Corporate Governance' (1999) 67 *U Cin L Rev* 1099, 1114–7. See also Nees, 'Who's the Boss? Unmasking Oversight Liability Within the Corporate Power Puzzle' (2010) 35 *Del J Corp L* 199, highlighting the divergence between theory, where directors face potential liability for failed oversight, and practice, where liability exists only within extremely narrow procedural limits.

46 The *Caremark* decision reassessed directors' duties of oversight 30 years after the former leading case, *Graham v Allis-Chalmers Manufacturing Company*, Del. Supr., 188 A.2d 125 (1963), which had previously set a relatively undemanding standard for directors in terms of their oversight duty. According to the decision in *Graham v Allis-Chalmers Manufacturing Company*, the directors were entitled to rely upon the integrity of their subordinates in the absence of grounds for suspicion, and were not required 'to install and operate a corporate system of

by certain procedural limitations and presumptions, including the business judgment rule, which ultimately protected the board of directors from liability.[47]

3. RECENT AUSTRALIAN CASE LAW ON THE DUTY OF CARE – A 'WAKE-UP CALL FROM DOWN UNDER'?[48]

Recent Australian case law on directors' duty of care reflects the continuing tension between conduct rules and decision rules. Whereas contemporary US law tends to be relatively static and predictable in this regard, Australian case law exhibits greater fluidity. Some recent Australian decisions strongly suggest a narrowing of the traditional 'acoustic separation'.

Australia has a distinctive regulatory model for the enforcement of directors' duties. In contrast to the US and the UK, where the primary means of enforcing breach of directors' duties is by way of private litigation,[49] Australia's regulatory system[50] relies heavily on a public enforcement model.[51] Under this paradigm, ASIC operates as the main enforcement mechanism for breach of directors' duties under Australia's civil penalty regime. The goal of the civil penalty regime at the time of its introduction in 1993 was to draw a clearer line between civil and criminal

espionage to ferret out wrongdoing which they have no reason to suspect exists'. Ibid., p. 130.

[47] See *In re Caremark International Inc. Derivative Litigation*, note 44 above, pp. 970–71. See generally Orenstein, 'A Modified Caremark Standard to Protect Shareholders of Financial Firms from Poor Risk Management' (2011) 86 *NYU L Rev* 766, 769ff. See also *Stone v Ritter*, Del. Supr., 911 A.2d 362 (2006), confirming Chancellor Allen's ruling in *Caremark* that directors could only be liable if they had acted in bad faith. See also generally, Arlen, 'The Story of Allis-Chalmers', note 44 above, p. 323.

[48] See Katz, 'For Directors, A Wake-Up Call from Down Under', *The Harvard Law School Forum on Corporate Governance and Financial Regulation*, 4 October 2011 (available at: http://blogs.law.harvard.edu/corpgov/2011/10/04/for-directors-a-wake-up-call-from-down-under/).

[49] See, however, Armour, Black, Cheffins and Nolan, 'Private Enforcement of Corporate Law', note 4 above, highlighting the gap between 'law on the books' and 'law in action' in this regard in the UK.

[50] See generally, Hill, 'Australia: The Architecture of Corporate Governance' in Fleckner and Hopt (eds), *Comparative Corporate Governance: A Functional and International Analysis* (Cambridge University Press, 2013), p. 106.

[51] For a comparison of the Australian and US enforcement models, see Jones and Welsh, 'Toward a Public Enforcement Model', note 5 above.

liability.[52] Since that time, however, these boundaries have become increasingly blurred.[53] ASIC has extensive enforcement powers under the civil penalty regime, including power to enforce breaches of the statutory duty of care and diligence under section 180(1) of the Corporations Act.[54] In the light of these broad powers,[55] ASIC has been described as occupying a 'special role . . . as a regulator'.[56]

In recent years, ASIC has brought numerous cases alleging breach of directors' duty, many of which reflect the shifting balance between standards of conduct and standards of review.[57] A high-profile example of this trend relates to Australia's well-known James Hardie saga.[58]

3.1 The James Hardie Saga

James Hardie Industries Ltd ('JHIL'), a public company with shares listed on the Australian Stock Exchange ('ASX'),[59] was the ultimate holding company of the James Hardie group. Two of its wholly owned subsidiaries were involved in the manufacture and sale of asbestos in Australia until 1987.[60] As

---

52 For background to the introduction of the civil penalty regime, see Welsh, 'The Regulatory Dilemma: The Choice between Overlapping Criminal Sanctions and Civil Penalties for Contraventions of the Directors' Duty Provisions' (2009) 27 *Comp & Sec LJ* 370. See also Golding, 'Tightening the Screws on Directors: Care, Delegation and Reliance' (2012) 35 *UNSW LJ* 266, 272–3.

53 See, for example, *Rich v ASIC* (2004) 220 CLR 129, where, in recognition of the blurring of these boundaries, the High Court of Australia rejected an argument that the civil penalty provisions are purely 'protective' in nature.

54 As the NSW Court of Appeal noted in *Morley v ASIC* (2010) 274 ALR 205, para. [723], ASIC alone is granted authority under s. 1317J(1) of the Corporations Act to apply for a declaration of contravention or for a pecuniary penalty under the civil penalty regime in Part 9.4B of the Corporations Act.

55 For a list of ASIC's general enforcement powers, see *Morley v ASIC*, ibid., para. [725].

56 Ibid., para. [724].

57 For a summary of some of the key cases for breach of directors' duties brought by ASIC in recent years, see Gibson and Brown, 'ASIC's Expectations of Directors' (2012) 35 *UNSW LJ* 254.

58 See generally Haigh, *Asbestos House: The Secret History of James Hardie Industries* (Scribe, 2006).

59 The Australian Stock Exchange became the Australian Securities Exchange in 2006, following the merger of the Australian Stock Exchange and the Sydney Futures Exchange. From 2010, the Exchange became known as the ASX Group. For history of the ASX Group, see http://www.asxgroup.com.au.

60 These subsidiaries were James Hardie & Coy Pty Ltd ('Coy') and Jsekarb Pty Ltd ('Jsekarb'). Coy manufactured and sold asbestos between 1937 and 1987

a result of these operations, the James Hardie group was 'haunted by . . . the spectre of asbestos litigation'.[61]

In 2001, the James Hardie group undertook a complex restructure, which was designed to contain potential asbestos liabilities. The restructure included a 'separation proposal', whereby the two affected subsidiaries would be quarantined from the rest of the group.[62] On 15 February 2001, JHIL held a critical meeting of its board of directors, at which the separation proposal was approved.[63] The proposal included the creation of a Foundation[64] to manage and satisfy asbestos claims, as well as conducting medical research into asbestos-related diseases.[65] Also, a new company, James Hardie Industries NV ('JHINV') would be incorporated in the Netherlands, replacing JHIL as the group's ultimate holding company.[66]

The separation proposal, which effectively limited the funding available to satisfy present and future asbestos claims, was potentially controversial as asbestos compensation had become a matter of public interest and

---

and Jsekarb manufactured and sold asbestos between 1978 and 1987. See *ASIC v Hellicar* (2012) 286 ALR 501, para. [180] (Heydon J).

[61] Ibid., para. [179] (Heydon J).

[62] See ibid., para. [13]; Dunn, 'James Hardie: No Soul to be Damned and No Body to be Kicked' (2005) 27 *Syd L Rev* 339, 339–42; Jackson QC, *Report of the Special Commission of Inquiry into the Medical Research and Compensation Foundation* (2004), paras [2.43]–[2.45].

[63] *ASIC v Hellicar*, note 60 above, para. [13]. The threat of asbestos litigation was viewed as deleterious to JHIL's share price, and possibly the James Hardie group's long-term viability. Ibid., paras [180]–[181]. This problem was exacerbated by the proposed adoption of a new accounting rule which would have required JHIL to disclose, not only known asbestos claims, but also expected future liability, and there was concern that this would negatively affect the company's balance sheet. Ibid., paras [43], [50], [188].

[64] The Foundation was a newly formed Australian company called the Medical Research and Compensation Foundation.

[65] See James Hardie Industries Ltd, *James Hardie Resolves its Asbestos Liability Favourably for Claimants and Shareholders*, 16 February 2001 (available at: http://www.asx.com.au/asx/statistics/displayAnnouncement.do?display=text&issuerId=602&announcementId=645410). Under the corporate restructure, implemented in a Deed of Covenants and Indemnity, JHIL effectively transferred its shares in Coy and Jsekarb to the Foundation, agreeing to pay A$3 million for research and to pay over $100 million over time to the two subsidiaries, which, for their part, agreed to make no claim against JHIL and to indemnify JHIL with respect to any asbestos liabilities. See *ASIC v Hellicar*, note 60 above, paras [13], [49].

[66] The restructuring, under which JHIL became a wholly owned subsidiary of JHINV, was effected by a scheme of arrangement under s. 411 of the Corporations Act 2001 (Cth). See generally Jackson QC, note 62 above, pp. 32–5.

concern.[67] On 16 February 2001, JHIL issued a market announcement to the ASX ('ASX announcement') stating that the Foundation, which had starting assets of A$293 million, was 'fully-funded', with 'sufficient funds to meet all future legitimate compensation claims'.[68] The minutes of the board meeting one day earlier[69] recorded that JHIL's directors had considered and approved a draft of this announcement, although the directors later denied that this had occurred.

It soon became clear that JHIL's assurance concerning adequacy of funding was false. In October 2003, the Foundation announced a massive funding shortfall and that it would soon exhaust the funds allocated to compensate victims.[70] It was apparent that, far from being 'fully-funded', the Foundation would in fact be unable to satisfy any claims beyond the first half of 2007. The funding shortfall, coupled with estimated future asbestos liabilities assessed at A$1.5 billion,[71] prompted the launch in 2004 of a Special Inquiry and Report ('Jackson Commission Report').[72] In 2005, following intense political pressure and public backlash,[73] JHINV and the New South Wales state government entered into the largest personal injury settlement in Australian history.[74]

---

[67] See *ASIC v Hellicar*, note 60 above, para. [186].

[68] See James Hardie Industries Ltd, note 65 above; *ASIC v Hellicar*, note 60 above, para. [17].

[69] These minutes were subsequently confirmed as having been 'signed as a correct record' of JHIL's 15 February board meeting by the chairman at JHIL's next board meeting on 4 April 2001. See *ASIC v Hellicar*, note 60 above, para. [15]; *ASIC v Macdonald (No 11)* (2009) 256 ALR 199, para. [53].

[70] See Dunn, 'James Hardie', note 62 above, 339, citing Edwards, Chairman MRCF, *Media Release: Financial Statements of MRCF* (29 October 2003).

[71] Maiden, 'Court sends message to boards', *The Age*, 4 May 2012, 9; Sexton, 'Hardie asbestos lawyer to be ASIC's first witness in case against board', *Sydney Morning Herald*, 23 September 2008, 19.

[72] Jackson QC, note 62 above. The Special Commission of Inquiry was established in February 2004 and reported in September 2004.

[73] Sexton, 'Unions to view Hardie's new compensation deal', *Sydney Morning Herald*, 20 December 2004, 5.

[74] The original Heads of Agreement signed in December 2004 provided for an open-ended funding agreement for a minimum term of 40 years, under which JHINV agreed to cover an estimated A$1.5 billion, though potentially as much as A$4.5 billion, in future mesothelioma claims. See Higgins and Saunders, 'Deal breathes humanity back into Hardie', *The Australian*, 22 December 2004, 1. After a series of delays due to legal complexities, JHINV signed the final agreement with the New South Wales state government on 1 December 2005. See generally 'Timeline of events in James Hardie compensation saga', *Australian Associated Press General News*, 2 December 2005; James Hardie Industries NV, ASX

In spite of this settlement,[75] in 2007 ASIC announced that it had filed civil penalty proceedings against former JHIL officers and directors.[76] According to ASIC's then-chairman, the regulator's objective in bringing the proceedings, which centred around JHIL's disclosures concerning the Foundation's adequacy of funding, was 'to reinforce the standards of corporate behaviour that are vitally important in ensuring public confidence in Australia's corporate sector and capital markets'.[77]

The *James Hardie* litigation traversed several courts between 2009 and 2012. Key decisions were *ASIC v Macdonald (No 11)*[78] in the Supreme Court of New South Wales, *Morley v ASIC*[79] in the New South Wales Court of Appeal, and finally *ASIC v Hellicar*[80] in the High Court of Australia.

At first instance in *ASIC v Macdonald (No 11)*,[81] Gzell J held that JHIL's non-executive directors, together with the chief executive officer ('CEO'), chief financial officer ('CFO') and the joint company secretary/general counsel, had breached the statutory duty of care and diligence under the Corporations Act. The judge subsequently imposed a five-year disqualification order and a pecuniary penalty of A$30 000 for each of the non-executive directors.[82]

Announcement, *Long-term Funding of Personal Injury Claims against Former Subsidiary Companies*, 1 December 2005.

[75] It is interesting to note that JHINV tried, but failed, in its negotiation of the final Heads of Agreement, to obtain immunity for officers and directors from any civil action brought by ASIC. See Higgins, 'Hardie board bid to desert victims', *The Australian*, 13 August 2005, 4; Heywood, 'Costello fights Hardie civil immunity claim', *The Courier-Mail*, 29 November 2005, 7. In announcing the civil penalty proceedings, ASIC's chairman stated that, while new compensation arrangements 'were very much welcomed, they do not diminish the need for those responsible for the breaches we have identified to be held to account for their actions'. See ASIC, Media Release 07-35, *ASIC commences proceedings relating to James Hardie*, 15 February 2007.

[76] ASIC also commenced proceedings against JHIL and JHINV. See generally ASIC, Media Release 07-35, note 75 above; Priest, 'ASIC seeks bans for Hardie asbestos directors', *Australian Financial Review*, 16 February 2007, 1; Jacobs, 'Case against Hardie board begins', *Australian Financial Review*, 29 September 2008, 6.

[77] ASIC, Media Release 07-35, note 75 above.

[78] See note 69 above.

[79] See note 54 above.

[80] See note 60 above.

[81] *ASIC v Macdonald (No 11)*, note 69 above. See generally Young QC, 'Directors' Duty of Care and Diligence: A Review in Light of the Recent Decision in ASIC v Macdonald (No 11)', in Austin and Bilski (eds), *Directors in Troubled Times* (Ross Parsons Centre of Commercial, Corporate and Taxation Law, 2009), pp. 60, 73ff.

[82] See *ASIC v Macdonald (No 12)* (2009) 259 ALR 116, paras [481]–[492].

Gzell J held that JHIL's issuance of the final ASX announcement to the effect that the Foundation was 'fully-funded' was misleading or deceptive, thereby contravening the Corporations Act.[83] The non-executive directors were found to have breached the statutory duty of care and diligence under section 180 of the Corporations Act[84] on the basis that they knew, or should have known, that unequivocal public statements of this kind could result in legal liability, harm to the company's reputation, and market backlash.[85] The specification of particulars of harm to the company was important, since it countered a possible argument, arising from the earlier decision of *ASIC v Maxwell*,[86] that directors do not have automatic personal liability for breaches of law by the corporation itself.[87]

Gzell J's finding that JHIL's board had approved a draft version of the final ASX announcement at its meeting on 15 February 2001, while consistent with the board minutes,[88] directly contradicted the evidence of JHIL's directors.[89] In what was described as an example of 'collective

---

83 At the time, ss 995 and 999 Corporations Act 2001 (now replaced by ss 104H and 1308). See also *ASIC v Macdonald (No 11)*, note 69 above, paras [628], [638].

84 Section 180(1) states that:

> A director or other officer of a corporation must exercise their powers and discharge their duties with the degree of care and diligence that a reasonable person would exercise if they:
>
> (a) were a director or officer of a corporation in the corporation's circumstances; and
> (b) occupied the office held by, and had the same responsibilities within the corporation as, the director or officer.

85 *ASIC v Macdonald (No 11)*, note 69 above, paras [259], [343].

86 (2006) 59 ACSR 373; [2006] NSWSC 1052.

87 See ibid., para. [104]; Young QC, note 81 above, pp. 60, 91. See also Petrin, 'The Curious Case of Directors' and Officers' Liability for Supervision and Management: Exploring the Intersection of Corporate and Tort Law' (2010) 59 *Am U L Rev* 1661, arguing that the current US liability regime fails to distinguish properly between corporate duties and duties of directors/officers, resulting in an unwarranted expansion of the latter group's risk and potential liability.

88 See *ASIC v Macdonald (No 11)*, note 69 above, para. [53]. ASIC failed in an argument that these minutes should attract a statutory presumption of accuracy under s. 251A(6) Corporations Act, because the minutes had not been recorded in a minute book within one month of the meeting as required by s. 251A(1). Ibid., para. [56]. The minutes were therefore procedurally flawed and deprived of any special evidentiary value. Ibid., paras [69], [72].

89 See ibid., para. [187]. See also Sexton, 'Put to the test', *Sydney Morning Herald*, 27 December 2008, 19; Sexton, 'Secrets of the boardroom', *Sydney Morning Herald*, 25 October 2008, 45.

memory loss',[90] none of the defendant directors who gave evidence in the proceedings recalled the draft ASX announcement being tabled or approved at the meeting.[91] In spite of the lack of 'positive evidence' in this regard, Gzell J considered that such board approval could be inferred from other evidence which suggested that the draft ASX announcement had been brought to the board meeting.[92]

The JHIL directors not only denied authorising the draft ASX announcement,[93] but also asserted that they *would* not have authorised an unqualified announcement, thereby reinforcing ASIC's claim that the announcement was indeed misleading or deceptive.[94] The judge held that approval of the draft ASX announcement was part of the directors' monitoring function, rather than a matter of 'operational responsibility'.[95]

Several possible liability safe harbours were unavailable to the non-executive directors on the particular facts of the case. Since the directors denied approving the draft ASX announcement, they did not seek to rely on the business judgment rule.[96] Reflecting a trend in contemporary Australian corporate law,[97] Gzell J also held that delegation was unavailable to insulate directors from liability. In his view, '[m]anage-

---

[90] Durie, 'Humble release crashes careers', *The Australian*, 24 April 2009, 26.

[91] Five of the seven non-executive director defendants entered the witness box. Two of these directors, Koffel and Willcox, who attended the meeting by phone from the US, swore that they had neither been provided with a copy, nor approved, the draft ASX announcement. Three others, Brown, Gillfillan and Hellicar did not agree that the announcement had been approved. The two other non-executive directors, O'Brien and Terry, did not give evidence in the case. *ASIC v Macdonald (No 11)*, note 69 above, paras [331], [338]; Sexton, 'The suits that turned to dust', *Sydney Morning Herald*, 25 April 2009, 1; Frith, 'Hardie's adverse finding will be closely analysed by corporate Australia', *The Australian*, 24 April 2009, 18.

[92] See *ASIC v Macdonald (No 11)*, note 69 above, paras [187]–[224]; Sexton, 'The suits that turned to dust', note 91 above.

[93] According to Gzell J, '[b]y acknowledging they would have spoken against, or in modification of, the Draft ASX Announcement those directors impliedly conceded that they had a duty to do so'. *ASIC v Macdonald (No 11)*, note 69 above, para. [331].

[94] Ibid., para. [262].

[95] Ibid., paras [332]–[333].

[96] See Blake Dawson (now Ashurst), 'Lessons for directors and officers from the James Hardie litigation', *Company Law & Governance Update*, 8 May 2009 (available at: http://www.blakedawson.com/Templates/Publications/x_article_content_page.aspx?id=55219), 4; Young QC, note 81 above, pp. 60, 81. For an overview of some of the ambiguities and weaknesses associated with the Australian statutory business judgment rule, see Young QC, ibid., pp. 79–82.

[97] See generally Young QC, ibid., pp. 60, 76–9.

ment having brought the matter to the board, none of them was entitled to abdicate responsibility by delegating his or her duty to a fellow director'.[98] In this respect, there was less scope for delegation to operate as a safe haven for directors than, for example, was possible in the US *Disney* litigation.[99]

Several defendants lodged appeals against Gzell J's decision.[100] In *Morley v ASIC*,[101] the New South Wales Court of Appeal reversed Gzell J's decision in relation to the non-executive directors.[102] The Court of Appeal held that ASIC had failed to establish that the non-executive directors had approved the draft ASX announcement at the relevant board meeting,[103] thereby rejecting a central finding of fact at first instance.[104]

A controversial aspect of the Court of Appeal's decision related to ASIC's duties as corporate regulator. The court considered that, in bringing civil proceedings of this kind, government agencies like ASIC owed an

---

98 *ASIC v Macdonald (No 11)*, note 69 above, para. [260].

99 Delegation was an important theme in the decision of Jacobs J in the Delaware Supreme Court decision, *In re The Walt Disney Company Derivative Litigation*, Del. Supr., 906 A.2d 27 (2006). Jacobs J considered that, since Disney's charter conferred exclusive responsibility for pay decisions on the compensation committee, the board of directors as a whole was protected from liability as a result of this form of delegation. Ibid., 41–2. Jacobs J noted that nothing in the Delaware General Corporation Law 'mandates that the entire board must make those decisions'. Ibid., 54.

100 Appeals were lodged by the non-executive directors, the CFO (Mr Morley), the company secretary/general counsel (Mr Shafron) and JHINV, with ASIC filing a notice of cross-appeal. These appeals resulted in two judgments delivered by the New South Wales Court of Appeal in December 2010 – *Morley v ASIC* (2010) 274 ALR 205 and *James Hardie Industries NV v ASIC* (2010) 274 ALR 85. See Jacobs, 'Former Hardie directors lodge appeals', *Australian Financial Review*, 17 October 2009, 7; Sexton, 'Accelerated appeals for banned directors', *Sydney Morning Herald*, 2 October 2009, 2; Hutton, 'James Hardie to appeal', *Australian Financial Review*, 24 September 2009, 16.

101 (2010) 274 ALR 205. See generally Minter Ellison, *Alert – James Hardie in the NSW Court of Appeal*, 22 December 2010 (available at: http://www.minterellison.com/NA_20101222_jamesHardie/).

102 The appeal by Mr. Shafron was partially successful only and the appeal by Mr. Morley failed. See *Morley v ASIC*, note 100 above, paras [871]ff, [1075]ff.

103 Ibid., paras [789]–[792], [804]. The Court of Appeal admitted, however, that there was some basis for a finding that the directors had approved the draft ASX announcement: para. [796].

104 Although acknowledging that the JHIL board minutes bolstered ASIC's case to some degree, ultimately the Court of Appeal thought that a range of factors weakened the reliability of the minutes as a correct record of events. Ibid., para. [791].

'obligation of fairness', arising from its status as a model litigant.[105] The Court of Appeal considered that ASIC had breached its obligation of fairness by failing to call a particular witness, JHIL's solicitor, to help determine the 'true facts' on which the action was based,[106] and that failure to do this undermined the cogency of ASIC's case and its ability to discharge the burden of proof.[107]

Although the Court of Appeal diverged from the first instance decision in terms of its findings of fact, the appellate decision did not depart substantively from Gzell J's analysis of directors' duties. Indeed, the Court of Appeal agreed that had ASIC proved that the non-executive directors voted in favour of the draft ASX announcement they would have breached their statutory duty of care and diligence,[108] and been unable to invoke the protection of reasonable reliance on management.[109]

A final volte-face in the *James Hardie* litigation occurred in 2012, when the High Court of Australia considered the matter.[110] In *ASIC v Hellicar*,[111] the High Court unanimously[112] allowed ASIC's appeal,[113] and

---

[105] Ibid., paras [710]–[713]. According to the Court of Appeal, this is reflected in the special role occupied by ASIC and its enhanced powers in relation to corporate law enforcement: paras [723]–[728]. Cf. D'Aloisio, 'ASIC played by the rules, but the court rewrote them', *The Australian*, 21 December 2010, 22, arguing that ASIC had in fact conducted the *James Hardie* litigation as a model litigant in accordance with legal services directions and had complied with the law as it stood prior to the Court of Appeal decision.

[106] *Morley v ASIC*, note 100 above, paras [775]–[776].

[107] Ibid., paras [777], [796].

[108] Ibid., para. [810]. See generally Minter Ellison, note 101 above.

[109] Ibid., paras [817], [821]. See D'Aloisio, 'ASIC played by the rules', note 105 above, describing this as a 'significant finding for corporate governance'.

[110] ASIC lodged an application for special leave to appeal to the High Court of Australia in January 2011 to seek clarification 'in the public interest' concerning 'the content and scope of ASIC's obligations' in bringing civil penalty proceedings. See ASIC, Media Release 11-07, *ASIC applies for special leave to appeal James Hardie decision*, 14 January 2011 (available at: http://www.asic.gov.au/asic/asic.nsf/byheadline/11-07MR+ASIC+applies+for+special+leave+to+appeal+James+Hardie+decision?openDocument).

[111] See note 60 above.

[112] There were two separate judgments in *ASIC v Hellicar* (2012) 286 ALR 501. A joint judgment was delivered by French CJ, Gummow, Hayne, Crennan, Keifel and Bell JJ (paras [1]ff) and an individual judgment, also allowing ASIC's appeal, was delivered by Heydon J (paras [179]ff).

[113] There were also appeals and cross-appeals in relation to the Court of Appeal's decision concerning Mr Shafron. In *Shafron v ASIC* (2012) 286 ALR 612, the High Court dismissed Mr Shafron's appeal, holding that he had contravened s. 180(1) of the Corporations Act, by failing to discharge his duties as an officer with the requisite degree of care and diligence. See generally Austin, Standen

restored Gzell J's first instance decision that the non-executive directors and company secretary/general counsel had breached their statutory duty of care and diligence.[114]

The High Court's approach differed from the NSW Court of Appeal decision in several critical respects. The High Court held, for example, that the Court of Appeal was wrong in its assessment that ASIC had failed to prove that the JHIL directors authorised the draft ASX announcement at their February 2001 board meeting.[115] According to the High Court, the board minutes, although procedurally flawed,[116] constituted a formal record of the proceedings at the meeting, including the fact that the draft ASX announcement was tabled and approved.[117] The High Court also considered that the Court of Appeal was wrong in holding that ASIC breached its duty of fairness by failing to call a particular witness, and in concluding that this 'diminished the cogency' of ASIC's evidence.[118]

ASIC v Hellicar[119] represented a major victory for ASIC and other government regulators,[120] as well as a cautionary tale for directors. The *James Hardie* litigation as a whole represents a watershed in Australian corporate law. Previously, Australian corporate law, like its US counterpart, tended to maintain a clear divide between conduct and decision rules, particularly in relation to non-executive directors.[121] Although the leading decision on directors' duty of care and diligence, the mid-1990s case of *Daniels v Anderson*,[122] contained strong dicta about the responsibilities of all directors, ultimately these aspirational statements were not matched by liability for non-executive directors. However, by reinstating Gzell J's first instance decision in the *James Hardie* litigation, the High Court in *ASIC v Hellicar*[123] signalled support for a narrowing of the traditional 'acoustic

---

and Reynolds, *Alert – The High Court Decides the James Hardie Case*, Minter Ellison Lawyers, 8 May 2012 (available at: http://www.minterellison.com/Pub/NA/20120504_JamesHardieDecision/).

114 In *ASIC v Macdonald (No 11)*, note 69 above.

115 *ASIC v Hellicar*, note 112 above, para. [6].

116 The board minutes had not been recorded in a minute book within one month of the meeting as required by s. 251A(1). Ibid., para. [56].

117 Ibid., para. [7].

118 Ibid., para. [9].

119 See note 112 above.

120 See Maiden, 'Court sends message to boards', note 71 above, 9, stating that the decision 're-arms all government regulators in civil court cases'.

121 See generally Cheffins and Black, 'Outside Director Liability Across Countries' (2006) 84 *Tex L Rev* 1385, 1433–41.

122 (1995) 16 ACSR 607.

123 See note 112 above.

separation' between conduct rules and decision rules for non-executive directors.

The *James Hardie* litigation provides an interesting counterpoint to two other recent Australian cases in which ASIC has brought civil penalty proceedings based on directors' breach of duty. The first of these cases was *ASIC v Rich*,[124] delivered by Austin J of the Supreme Court of New South Wales in 2009. This decision arguably recognises a higher degree of 'acoustic separation' between conduct rules and decision rules than is apparent in the findings of liability in the *James Hardie* litigation.

3.2 The Surprising Case of *ASIC v Rich*

ASIC v Rich[125] arose out of the collapse in May 2001 of One.Tel Ltd ('One.Tel'), a relatively new player at the time in Australia's telecommunications sector.[126] At the time of the company's collapse, it had claimed debts totalling A$377 million.[127] News Corporation Ltd and Publishing and Broadcasting Ltd, companies controlled by the Murdoch and Packer families, respectively, held a 40 per cent stake in One.Tel,[128] and James Packer and Lachlan Murdoch sat as non-executive directors on One.Tel's board. Following the company's collapse, Lachlan Murdoch swore in an affidavit that he had been 'profoundly misled' about its financial position.[129]

In late 2001, ASIC commenced civil penalty proceedings against four former One.Tel directors.[130] ASIC's central allegation was that these directors had breached their statutory duty of care and diligence under section 180(1) of the Corporations Act by failing to keep the board of directors

---

124 (2009) 75 ACSR 1; [2009] NSWSC 1229. A slightly abridged version of the case can also be found at (2009) 236 FLR 1.

125 Ibid.

126 See Hill, 'Regulatory Responses to Global Corporate Scandals' (2005) 23 *Wis Int'l LJ* 367, 370–73. For general discussion of the One.Tel saga, see Barry, *Rich Kids: How the Murdochs and Packers Lost $950 Million in One.Tel* (Bantam Books, 2002).

127 Jury, 'Chanticleer: ASIC's credibility on the line', *Australian Financial Review*, 19 November 2009, 64.

128 See (2009) 75 ACSR 1, [10]; Barry, note 126 above, p. 359.

129 Affidavit lodged by Mr Lachlan Murdoch, Supreme Court of NSW (Lacey and Hepworth, 'One.Tel: ASIC bombshell', *Australian Financial Review*, 15 June 2001, 1).

130 The defendants to the suit were joint managing directors, John David ('Jodee') Rich and Bradley Keeling, finance director, Mark Silbermann, and non-executive chairman, John Greaves. See ASIC, Media Release 01-441, *ASIC commences civil proceedings against former One.Tel officers and Chairman*, 12 December 2001.

adequately informed of the company's true financial position.[131] The regulator sought disqualification and compensation orders of up to A$93 million.[132] Prior to the commencement of proceedings, two of the defendants[133] entered into settlement agreements with the regulator, under which they accepted disqualification and compensation orders.[134]

There are a number of interesting contrasts between the *James Hardie* and *One.Tel* litigation in relation to both their proceedings and outcomes. First, ASIC set its sights on different targets in these two cases. In the *James Hardie* litigation, ASIC brought civil penalty proceedings against not only the executive officers, but also the non-executive directors. In the *One.Tel* litigation, however, ASIC initially commenced civil proceedings against One.Tel's former officers and its non-executive chairman, but no proceedings were brought against the company's other non-executive directors, including James Packer and Lachlan Murdoch.[135] Justice Austin described this fact as 'noteworthy'.[136] The judge pointed out that one of the non-executive directors, James Packer, was substantially involved in One.Tel's day-to-day business,[137] and that PBL and News executives received frequent briefings on aspects of the One.Tel business.[138]

Secondly, *ASIC v Rich* is a surprising case since, unlike the *James Hardie* litigation where ASIC succeeded in its claims against both executive and non-executive directors, Austin J held that ASIC failed to prove its pleaded case against either of One.Tel's remaining executive defendant

---

[131] *ASIC v Rich*, note 124 above, paras [3], [85]–[123].

[132] ASIC, Media Release 03-068, *Landmark decision on chairman's duties*, 24 February 2003.

[133] The two directors who entered into settlements with ASIC were Bradley Keeling and John Greaves.

[134] Mr Keeling was banned from managing a corporation for 10 years, and found jointly and severally liable for A$92 million compensation to One.Tel. See ASIC, Media Release 03-099, *Brad Keeling settles in ASIC One.Tel proceedings*, 21 March 2003. Mr. Greaves was banned from managing a corporation for four years and found liable for A$20 million compensation to One.Tel. See ASIC, Media Release 04-283, *ASIC reaches agreement with John Greaves in One.Tel proceedings*, 6 September 2004.

[135] ASIC announced, at the time of commencing the civil penalty proceedings, that evidence available to it indicated that the non-executive directors were unaware of One.Tel's '"true financial position" until shortly before the appointment of the administrator on 29 May 2001'. See ASIC, Media Release 01-441, note 130 above.

[136] *ASIC v Rich*, note 124 above, para. [3]. See also Sexton, 'Judge clobbers ASIC case', *Sydney Morning Herald*, 19 November 2009, 1.

[137] *ASIC v Rich*, note 124 above, para. [2].

[138] Ibid., para. [7247].

directors,[139] and awarded the defendants A$15 million in costs.[140] In sharp contrast with ASIC's High Court success in *ASIC v Hellicar*,[141] the decision in *ASIC v Rich*[142] has been described as 'an emphatic victory for the defendant directors and defeat for ASIC as corporate regulator'.[143] Austin J was highly critical of the scope and management of the case by ASIC, contrasting it unfavourably with the far narrower evidentiary focus of the *James Hardie* litigation.[144]

Thirdly, the business judgment rule, which was invisible in the *James Hardie* litigation due to the unusual facts of the case, emerged from the shadows in *ASIC v Rich* and potentially laid the groundwork for acoustic separation. Australia's statutory business judgment rule in section 180(2) of the Corporations Act, was first introduced in 2000.[145] Although based on the American Law Institute's version of the business judgment rule,[146] *ASIC v Rich* shows that the Australia's statutory formulation of the rule

---

[139] See ibid., para. [7318]; Carson, 'One.Tel shock: ASIC loses case against Jodee Rich', *Sydney Morning Herald*, 18 November 2009. Austin J stated that superficially appealing arguments presented by ASIC were ultimately unpersuasive in the light of factual evidence. *ASIC v Rich*, ibid., para. [7319].

[140] See ibid., para. [7324]; Eyers, 'ASIC pursues Rich to the bitter end', *Australian Financial Review*, 18 December 2009, 3; Grigg, 'ASIC to pay record costs for One.Tel', *Australian Financial Review*, 28 November 2009, 9.

[141] See note 112 above.

[142] See note 124 above.

[143] King & Wood Mallesons, *One.Telling Wipe-Out: Decision in ASIC v Rich Finally Delivered*, 23 November 2009 (available at: http://www.mallesons.com/publications/marketAlerts/2009/Pages/One-Telling-wipe-out-Decision-in-ASIC-v-Rich-finally-delivered.aspx).

[144] See note 124 above, para. [65]. Austin J stated that: 'there is a real question whether ASIC should ever bring civil proceedings seeking to prove so many things over such a period of time as in this case'. This criticism related to the fact that ASIC's case required it to prove the financial position of the multi-national group of companies comprising the One.Tel group over a period of four months. Ibid., para. [4].

[145] For background to Australia's statutory business judgment rule, see Byrne, 'Directors to Hide from a Sea of Liabilities in a New Safe Harbour' (2008) 22 *Aust J Corp L* 255. Under s. 180(2) of the Corporations Act, a director is deemed to have complied with the requirements of the duty of care and diligence if the director has made a business judgment in good faith for a proper purpose, does not have a conflicting interest, has adequately informed himself or herself, and rationally believes that the decision is in the best interests of the corporation. See generally Hill, 'Australia: The Architecture of Corporate Governance', note 50 above, pp. 106, 126–8.

[146] See American Law Institute, *Principles of Corporate Governance: Analysis and Recommendations* (1992), [4.01(c)]; Austin and Ramsay, *Ford's Principles of Corporations Law* (loose-leaf service), [8.310.27]. For an early assessment of Australia's then-proposed statutory business judgment rule through US eyes, see

is no simple Antipodean transplant of US law.[147] In contrast to the operation of the US business judgment rule,[148] for example, Austin J considered that Australia's statutory business judgment rule imposes the onus of proving that the preconditions to protection have been satisfied on the defendant directors, not the plaintiff.[149] It seems that ASIC's 'special role' in relation to enforcement of directors' statutory duties played a role in justifying such an interpretation of the provision.[150]

Following its reception into Australian law, some commentators argued that the statutory business judgment rule was ineffectual[151] and mere 'window dressing'.[152] However, in *ASIC v Rich*,[153] the rule took on a considerably more robust aspect. One of the requirements for the application of the rule is that a director or other officer[154] has made a 'business judgment', which is defined in the Corporations Act as 'any decision to take or not take action in respect of a matter relevant to the business operations of the corporation'.[155] In *ASIC v Rich*[156] Austin J

DeMott, 'Legislating Business Judgment – A Comment from the United States' (1998) 16 *Comp & Sec LJ* 575.

[147] For a discussion of some important differences between the US business judgment rule and its Australian statutory counterpart, see generally Redmond, *Companies and Securities Law: Commentary and Materials* (Thomson Reuters, 6th ed., 2013), [7.105].

[148] See Bainbridge, 'The Business Judgment Rule as Abstention Doctrine' (2004) 57 *Vand L Rev* 83, arguing that, rather than operating as a standard of liability by which courts review board decisions, the US business judgment rule in fact functions as a doctrine of abstention, precluding judicial review of board decisions unless the plaintiff satisfies certain demanding preconditions.

[149] See note 124 above, para. [7264]. The issue of who bears the onus of proof in relation to the Australian business judgment rule has been a vexed one, which Austin J recognised will ultimately need to be resolved at appellate level. Ibid., para. [7269]. See also Young QC, 'Directors' Duty of Care and Diligence', note 81 above; Lumsden, 'The Business Judgement Defence: Insights from ASIC v Rich' (2010) 28 *Comp & Sec LJ* 164, 169.

[150] For example, Austin J stated that: 'it would be unusual if . . . ASIC were required to establish . . . that the defendant's business judgment was not made in good faith for a proper purpose, since that would amount to proving a more serious contravention of the law, namely a contravention of s. 181' (citing Santow J in *ASIC v Adler* (2002) 41 ACSR 72). Ibid., para. [7269]. See also Lumsden, ibid., 169.

[151] See, for example, Young QC, note 81 above, pp. 60, 79–82.

[152] Young QC, 'Has Directors' Liability Gone Too Far or Not Far Enough? A Review of the Standard of Conduct Required of Directors under Sections 180–184 of the Corporations Act' (2008) 26 *Comp & Sec LJ* 216, 222.

[153] See note 124 above.

[154] The terms 'director' and 'officer' are defined in s. 9 of the Corporations Act.

[155] Section 180(3) Corporations Act.

[156] See note 124 above.

agreed with ASIC's contention that, according to this definition, the business judgment rule would not protect directors in breach of their oversight duties.[157] The judge accepted, however, that the business judgment rule could protect directors in relation to an array of other managerial conduct, including planning, budgeting and forecasting,[158] and applied the rule to provide protection in this regard to the defendant directors' decision to continue to grow One.Tel's business despite certain overdue debts.[159] It seems likely that, following *ASIC v Rich*, the business judgment rule will become an important part of Australian directors' defensive armoury.[160]

ASIC, although originally signalling its intention to appeal Austin J's judgment in *ASIC v Rich*,[161] later reversed its decision, on the basis of '[p]ublic policy considerations, cost and effluxion of time'.[162]

3.3 The *Centro* Litigation – Directors' Duties and the Global Financial Crisis

Australian directors, executive and non-executive alike, were, however, back in dangerous territory in *ASIC v Healey*[163] ('*Centro* decision'). This litigation arose directly out of the global financial crisis, and highlighted potential dangers to boards posed by the crisis.[164] The Centro Group,[165]

---

157 The judge took the view that monitoring the company's affairs and maintaining familiarity with the company's financial position are not in themselves matters that involve a 'decision to take or not take action': see ibid., para. [7278].

158 Ibid., paras [125], [7273]–[7276].

159 Although the relevant debts owed to certain creditors by One.Tel were overdue according to the terms of the contract, Austin J found that the One.Tel directors reasonably held the belief that the debts were not required to be paid immediately: ibid., para. [3766]. See also Lumsden, 'The Business Judgement Defence', note 149 above, 169–71.

160 Jacobs, 'Business judgement rule comes to aid of the parties', *Australian Financial Review*, 19 November 2009, 60. For further discussion of Austin J's discussion of the business judgment rule in *ASIC v Rich* and the implications of the judgment, see Lumsden, 'The Business Judgement Defence', note 149 above.

161 See ASIC, Media Release 09-259AD, *ASIC lodges notice of intention to appeal*, 17 December 2009.

162 ASIC, Media Release 10-34AD, *ASIC not to appeal One.Tel decision*, 26 February 2010.

163 (2011) 196 FCR 291.

164 See generally Hill, 'Centro in the Monitoring Board', note 41 above.

165 The Centro Group comprised Centro Properties Ltd ('CPL'); Centro Property Trust ('CPT'); and Centro Retail Trust ('CRT'): see *ASIC v Healey*, note 163 above, 296, para. [2].

like many other highly leveraged firms at the time, experienced intense liquidity problems when the crisis hit. The group came close to collapse in December 2007, when an announcement signalled the group's difficulty in refinancing A$3.9 billion in short-term debt.[166]

Two years after this corporate funding crisis, ASIC commenced civil penalty proceedings against the Centro Group's former directors and CFO.[167] The action, which related to the board's of consolidated financial statements for the Centro Group for the financial year ended June 2007,[168] merged issues relating to financial disclosure with directors' duties. ASIC claimed that the financial statements failed to comply with relevant accounting standards and regulations[169] and did not give a true and fair view of the group's financial position. This was because the financial statements had been wrongly classified around A$2 billion of debt as non-current liabilities[170] and failed to disclose guarantees of short-term liabilities amounting to approximately US$1.75 billion.[171] ASIC alleged that the defendants had failed to take all reasonable steps to ensure compliance with the Centro Group's reporting obligations under the Corporations Act[172]

[166] See Centro Properties Group, 'Centro Earnings Revision and Refinancing Update' (ASX Media Release, 17 December 2007). See also Harley and Dunckley, 'Credit crisis savages Centro', *Australian Financial Review*, 18 December 2007, 1; 'Tread carefully in volatile times', *Australian Financial Review*, 18 December 2007, 46; Maley, 'The year the financial system snapped', *Australian Financial Review*, 21 December 2007, 32.

[167] The defendants included former Centro CEO and Managing Director, Andrew Thomas; former CFO, Mr Romano Nenna; and former Chairman and non-executive director, Mr Brian Healey: See ASIC Media Release, 09-202AD, *ASIC commences proceedings against current and former officers of Centro*, 21 October 2009. See generally Crutchfield and Button, 'Men Over Board: The Burden of Directors' Duties in the Wake of the Centro Case' (2012) 30 *Comp & Sec L J* 83, 86–9.

[168] The board's approval, which formed the basis that the action, related to financial statements for the Centro Group for the financial year ended 30 June 2007.

[169] Section 296(1) of the Corporations Act requires that financial reports must comply with the accounting standards. The relevant accounting standard for the purposes of Centro was Australian Accounting Standards Board ('AASB') 101, 'Presentation of Financial Statements', which related to the classification of liabilities as current in a corporation's financial reports: *ASIC v Healey*, note 163 above, 302, paras [40]ff.

[170] ASIC Media Release, 09-202AD, note 167 above.

[171] See *ASIC v Healey*, note 163 above, 297, para. [9].

[172] Section 344(1) of the Corporations Act requires a director 'to take all reasonable steps to comply with, or to secure compliance with, Part 2M.2 or 2M.3'. Part 2M.2 of the Corporations Act 2001 (Cth) relates to financial records, which

and had breached their statutory duty of care and diligence by failing to detect these critical errors in the accounts.[173]

Australia was not alone in confronting issues of defective financial disclosure, and such issues are still highly relevant in the Australian corporate governance context.[174] These were also crucial issues in the US during the global financial crisis, and had been on the radar screen of US corporate legislators since the time of Enron's collapse in 2001.[175] However, the merging of directors' duties and financial disclosure issues, such as occurred in the *Centro* decision, would be precluded under US law, given that the two matters are regulated under state corporations law and federal securities law respectively.[176]

As in the *James Hardie* litigation, ASIC's claim in the *Centro* decision focused on approvals given at a specific board meeting,[177] and included both executive and non-executive directors in its enforcement sights. Justice Middleton agreed with ASIC's contention that the defendants had 'failed to take all reasonable steps required of them', and had performed their directors duties without the requisite degree of care and diligence.[178]

---

the corporation is obliged to keep. Part 2M.3 deals with financial reports, including the annual directors' report and audit. See generally *ASIC v Healey*, ibid., 321, paras [125]ff.

[173] See Stevens, 'Centro in line to become ultimate testbed for board behaviour', *The Australian*, 22 October 2009, 21; Eyers and Durkin, 'ASIC's Centro case rattles boards', *Australian Financial Review*, 24 October 2009, 22.

[174] The Hastie Group, for example, was placed into administration in May 2012, following the discovery of a $20 million accounting shortfall. A representative of the group's administrator, PPB Advisory, recently linked issues of financial disclosure with possible breach of directors' duties, stating that '[r]eporting from subsidiaries up to head office level was inadequate and open to manipulation. The board did not have an inquiring mind as to the reliability of financial statements and overall reporting'. The representative further stated that these concerns had been reported to ASIC. See LaFrenz, 'Call for Hastie directors inquiry', *Australian Financial Review*, 31 January 2013, 7. See also Boxsell, 'Hastie class action in Slater sights', *Australian Financial Review*, 22 January 2013, 13.

[175] Enron Corporation ('Enron') filed for bankruptcy in late 2001, following revelation of the scandal in October 2001.

[176] See Hill, 'Centro and the Monitoring Board', note 41 above, p. 345.

[177] The consolidated financial statements of the Centro Group were approved at a board meeting, attended by the defendants on 6 September 2007: *ASIC v Healey*, 296, note 163 above, para. [2]. See Crutchfield and Button, 'Men Over Board', note 167 above, 88.

[178] *ASIC v Healey*, note 163 above, 296–7, para. [8]. See generally Austin and Reynolds, *All Reasonable Steps to be in a Position to Guide and Monitor – The Impact of the Centro Decision*, Minter Ellison Lawyers, 1 July 2011 (available at: http://www.minterellison.com/NA_20110701_centroDecision/).

This was in spite of the fact that, according to the judge, the directors were 'intelligent, experienced and conscientious people', against whom no suggestion of dishonesty had been levelled.[179] The judge's finding of breach of duty of care and diligence by the directors was also despite the existence of an audit committee, and audit sign-off by a major accounting firm.[180]

As in Gzell J's first instance decision in the *James Hardie* litigation,[181] delegation and reliance failed to protect Centro's directors. Although acknowledging that delegation and reliance are permissible,[182] the *Centro* decision emphasised that there are limits to legally sanctioned buck-passing,[183] and that that directors must critically analyse material presented to them and maintain 'an inquiring mind'.[184] According to Middleton J, this had not occurred on the facts of the case. Rather, he considered that the directors had engaged in wholesale reliance on management and external advisers with respect to the financial statements,[185] thereby relinquishing a vital aspect of their duties to the company.[186] Middleton J stated that a 'core, irreducible requirement of directors [is] to be involved in the management of the company and to take all reasonable

---

179 *ASIC v Healey*, ibid., 296, para. [8].

180 See generally Crutchfield and Button, 'Men Over Board', note 167 above.

181 See *ASIC v Macdonald (No 11)*, note 69 above, para. [260].

182 The Corporations Act gives directors explicit permission to delegate 'any of their powers' unless the company's constitution provides otherwise. See s. 198D Corporations Act; see also s. 190 Corporations Act. In relation to a director's reliance on information or advice provided by others, see s. 189 Corporations Act.

183 See also Bird and Hill, 'Regulatory Rooms in Australian Corporate Law' (1999) 25 *Brook J Int'l L* 555, 572–4.

184 *ASIC v Healey*, note 163 above, 298, para. [20]. See also Leung and Webster, 'Directors' Duties, Financial Literacy and Financial Reporting After Centro' (2012) 30 *Comp & Sec LJ* 100, 106–7. This requirement of independent scrutiny is consistent with Corporations Act 2001 (Cth), s. 189(b)(ii), which requires that reliance be made 'after making an independent assessment of the information or advice, having regard to the director's knowledge of the corporation and the complexity of the structure and operations of the corporation'.

185 *ASIC v Healey*, ibid., 427, para. [582].

186 Middleton J states that: '[w]hilst there are many matters a director must focus upon, the financial statements must be regarded as one of the most important': ibid., 426, para. [567]. See generally Lowry, 'The Irreducible Core of the Duty of Care, Skill and Diligence of Company Directors: Australian Securities and Investments Commission v Healey' (2012) 75 *Mod L Rev* 249. The judge suggests that if the directors had taken care to read and understand the final accounts, the errors might have come to light earlier: *ASIC v Healey*, ibid., 427, para. [582]. Middleton J also stated that it was not possible for directors to delegate ultimate responsibility for their declaration regarding the annual financial report under s. 295(4) of the Corporations Act. Ibid., 321, para. [125].

steps to be in a position to guide and monitor'.[187] Commentators have suggested that, since Australian directors appear to have a number of 'core', non-delegable duties, it would be useful to know the precise contours of those duties.[188]

The *Centro* decision reflects the strengthening of the duty of care and diligence in Australia, a trend which is also apparent in the UK.[189] Since the pivotal mid-1990s decision in *Daniels v Anderson*,[190] there has been a significant increase in reported Australian cases in this area, and ASIC has had an 'extraordinarily high success rate' in these cases.[191] The *James Hardie* and *Centro* litigation exemplifies this trend, while *ASIC v Rich*[192] is an outlier in this regard.[193]

From a US/Australian comparative law perspective, the *Centro* decision bears a much closer family resemblance to *Smith v Van Gorkom*[194] than to the *Disney* litigation. The *Centro* decision has been described as 'a wake-up call from down under',[195] just as *Smith v Van Gorkom* was once labelled (at least in the pre-§ DGCL 102(b)(7) era) a 'wake-up call to passive boards'.[196] As in *Smith v Van Gorkom*, 'mere absence of bad faith'[197] did not save the Centro Group's directors from breach of duty. Each of these judgments sharply criticised the board for effectively delegating all decision-making to management, when the directors should themselves have assessed information with 'a critical eye'[198] and 'an inquiring mind'.[199]

---

[187] Ibid., 298, para. [16]. See also *Deputy Commissioner of Taxation v Clark* (2003) 57 NSWLR 113, para. [108].

[188] See generally Golding, 'Tightening the Screws on Directors: Care, Delegation and Reliance' (2012) 35 *UNSW LJ* 266, 278.

[189] Lowry, 'The Irreducible Core', note 186 above.

[190] See note 122 above. As noted earlier, however, the heightened standards identified in this case were not matched by liability for the non-executive directors. For general developments in the area of directors' duty of care and insolvent trading at the time of *Daniels v Anderson*, see Bird and Hill, 'Regulatory Rooms in Australian Corporate Law', note 183 above, 560–72.

[191] See Golding, 'Tightening the Screws on Directors', note 188 above, 273–4, 287–8 (Annexure 1 – Survey of reported Australian duty of care, skill and diligence cases 1990–2011).

[192] See note 124 above.

[193] In spite of the fact that it concerned executive directors, it is one of only two cases, out of 20 reported cases, where the trial judge held that the defendants had not breached their duty: ibid., 273.

[194] See note 18 above.

[195] Katz, 'For Directors, a Wake-Up Call from Down Under', note 48 above.

[196] Elson and Thompson, 'Van Gorkom's Legacy', note 18 above, 583.

[197] See note 18 above.

[198] Ibid.

[199] *ASIC v Healey*, note 163 above, 298, para. [20].

On its face, the *Centro* decision appears to be example of narrow 'acoustic separation'. It should be noted, however, that the decision did not tell the entire story. Another important part of the narrative is found in a subsequent decision by Middleton J, *ASIC v Healey (No 2)* ('*Centro* penalty decision'),[200] which considered the appropriate penalties to impose for the directors' breaches of duty. Whereas, in the original *Centro* decision,[201] Middleton J held that the executive officers and non-executive directors had all breached their duties of care and diligence, in the later penalty decision[202] he distinguished between the defendants for the purposes of punishment. In the *Centro* penalty decision, Middleton J made detailed declarations of contravention against all defendants. He imposed a fine of A$30 000 on Centro's former CEO, and a two-year managerial disqualification order on its former CFO.[203] However, interestingly, no penalties were imposed on the six non-executive directors. Middleton J considered that declarations of contravention, without disqualification or pecuniary penalty orders, were sufficient 'to indicate the Court's disapproval' of the conduct of the non-executive directors,[204] and that a range of factors 'militate[d] very strongly against more excessive penalties'.[205]

Whereas the original *Centro* decision was criticised for the stringency of Middleton J's findings, the *Centro* penalty decision received widespread censure for being too lenient.[206] In spite of the potential incongruity between the two judgments, they can be viewed as complementary parts of holistic determination of directors' conduct, where aspirational standards

---

200 *ASIC v Healey (No 2)* (2011) 196 FCR 430.

201 *ASIC v Healey*, note 163 above.

202 *ASIC v Healey (No 2)*, note 200 above.

203 Ibid., 433, paras [4]–[5].

204 Ibid., 433, para. [6].

205 Indeed, Middleton J considered that imposition of more extreme penalties could be contrary to 'public interest': Ibid.

206 See, for example, Lenaghan and Durkin, 'A fine, a ban and off the hook', *Australian Financial Review*, 1 September 2011, 9; Durkin, 'Investors vent anger at "injustice"', *Australian Financial Review*, 1 September 2011, 9; West, 'Off the hook, with barely a slap', *Sydney Morning Herald*, 3 September 2011, 2. Leniency of penalties was also an issue in the final phase of the *James Hardie* litigation. Following the High Court of Australia decision in *ASIC v Hellicar*, note 60 above, which upheld ASIC's appeal, the New South Wales Court of Appeal considered the appropriate penalties in *Gilfillan v ASIC* [2012] NSWCA 370. The Court of Appeal reduced the penalties imposed on the non-executive directors by Gzell J at first instance. For a comparison of the penalties imposed by Gzell J and the New South Wales Court of Appeal, see Ashurst Australia, *James Hardie – The Final Chapter*, 16 November 2012 (available at: http://www.ashurst.com/page.aspx?id_content=8471).

make a late entry, namely at the penalty stage.[207] Although, when viewed in isolation, the original *Centro* liability decision would suggest that Australia's law relating to the duty of care and diligence is considerably stricter than comparable US law,[208] the combined effect of the two *Centro* judgments is that this jurisdictional difference is ultimately less dramatic than at first sight.[209] However, it is worth noting that there is growing pressure to increase penalties in the Australian corporate law arena, which could itself operate to narrow acoustic separation.[210]

4. DIRECTORS' DUTIES, SHAREHOLDER VERSUS STAKEHOLDER INTERESTS, AND CORPORATE SOCIAL RESPONSIBILITY

The tension between conduct rules and decision rules can also be discerned in the context of the debate concerning shareholder and stakeholder interests. How do directors decide whose interests to promote,[211] and to what extent can their choices result in legal liability for breach of directors' duties?

In the US, the traditional message of legal rules directed to corporate managers was one of profit maximisation for shareholders. This is reflected in the classic case of *Dodge v Ford Motor Co* ('*Dodge v Ford*'),[212] where Ostrander CJ famously declared:

---

[207] See Singer, 'On Classicism and Dissonance', note 12 above, 83–4, who, although generally critical of Professor Dan-Cohen's distinction between conduct rules and decision rules, considers that the imposition of penalties in the sentencing context is one area where the philosophy of acoustic separation resonates strongly.

[208] See, for example, *In re The Walt Disney Company Derivative Litigation*, Del. Ch., 907 A.2d 693 (2005); *In re The Walt Disney Company Derivative Litigation*, Del.Supr., 906 A.2d 27 (2006); *In re Caremark International Inc. Derivative Litigation*, Del.Ch., 698 A.2d 959 (1996).

[209] For a detailed analysis of the interrelation between the *Centro* liability and penalty decisions against the backdrop of US corporate law, see Hill, 'Centro and the Monitoring Board', note 41 above, 353–8.

[210] See, for example, Golding, 'Tightening the Screws on Directors', note 188 above, arguing that the time is now ripe, following the *Centro* and *James Hardie* litigation to consider, from a policy perspective, allowing courts to grant substantially larger penalties in appropriate cases. See also the comments of Finkelstein J in *ASIC v Vizard* (2005) 54 ACSR 394, paras [39]–[40] on the importance of 'formal retribution' as a means of ensuring 'proper punishment'.

[211] See generally Adams, Licht and Sagiv, 'Shareholders and Stakeholders: How Do Directors Decide?' (2011) 32 *Strategic Management Journal* 1331.

[212] *Dodge v Ford Motor Co et al.*, 204 Mich. 459, 170 NW 668 (1919).

> [a] business corporation is organized and carried on primarily for the profit of the stockholders. The powers of the directors are to be employed for that end. The discretion of directors is to be exercised in the choice of means to attain that end, and does not extend to a change in the end itself.[213]

Yet, *Dodge v Ford* was hardly a pin-up decision for a shareholder primacy norm.[214] The case involved a conflict, not between shareholder and other stakeholders, but rather between majority and minority shareholders.[215] According to one commentator, the failure of *Dodge v Ford* to acknowledge other stakeholder interests potentially renders it bad law.[216]

In spite of the lip service paid to shareholder primacy, the US business judgment rule provides directors with considerable leeway to consider non-shareholder interests,[217] including in *Dodge v Ford* itself.[218] Case law permits directors to take into account stakeholder interests in the hostile takeover context,[219] except where the company is up for sale, when shareholder interests will prevail.[220] In addition, US constituency statutes explicitly permit, or in some rare instances require,[221] directors to have regard to a broad range of stakeholder interests.[222] Although sometimes

---

[213] Ibid., p. 684.

[214] Gelter, 'The Dark Side of Shareholder Influence: Managerial Autonomy and Stakeholder Orientation in Comparative Corporate Governance' (2009) 50 *Harv Int'l LJ* 129, 145.

[215] See Gelter, 'Taming or Protecting the Modern Corporation? Shareholder – Stakeholder Debates in a Comparative Light' (2011) 7 *NYU J L & Bus* 641, 675–6; Chander, 'Minorities, Shareholder and Otherwise' (2003) 113 *Yale LJ* 119, 125–6; Smith, 'The Shareholder Primacy Norm' (1998) 23 *J Corp L* 277, 319–20.

[216] Stout, 'Why We Should Stop Teaching Dodge v. Ford' (2008) 3 *Va L & Bus Rev* 163; cf. Macey, 'A Close Read of an Excellent Commentary on Dodge v. Ford' (2008) 3 *Va L & Bus Rev* 177.

[217] See, for example, *Shlensky v Wrigley*, 237 N.E.2d. 776, 778 (1968). See also Henderson and Malani, 'Corporate Philanthropy and the Market for Altruism' (2009) 109 *Colum L Rev* 571, 572 fn 3, stating that: '[t]he business judgment rule . . . insulates firms from judicial review of decisions that do not maximise shareholder value'.

[218] *Dodge v Ford Motor Co et al.*, note 212 above, 681–2. See also Frug, 'The Ideology of Bureaucracy in American Law' (1984) 97 *Harv L Rev* 1276, 1309–10.

[219] See, for example, *Unocal Corp v Mesa Petroleum Co*, 493 A.2d 946 (1985). For a discussion of the social background to the courts' adoption of a stakeholder oriented approach in the hostile takeover context, see Bruner, 'Power and Purpose in the 'Anglo-American' Corporation' (2010) 50 *Va J In'l L* 579, 639–41.

[220] *Revlon, Inc v MacAndrews & Forbes Holdings, Inc*, 506 A.2d 173 (1986).

[221] Over 30 US states have adopted constituency statutes. Only two constituency statutes are mandatory in nature: Connecticut and Arizona.

[222] O'Kelley and Thompson, *Corporations and Other Business Associations: Cases and Materials*, (Aspen Law and Business, 6th ed., 2010), 271–2.

portrayed as exemplifying principles of corporate social responsibility, US constituency statutes in fact operate as anti-takeover devices, and arguably represent another example of legal deference to the board of directors.[223]

Corporate scandals at the beginning of the last decade, including the collapse of Enron, focused greater attention on the plight of stakeholders, particularly employees,[224] and highlighted the underlying tension between shareholder and stakeholder interests in corporate law.[225] In spite of this, the US regulatory response to Enron was largely focused on protecting shareholder interests.[226] The express aim of the US Sarbanes-Oxley Act of 2002, for example, was: '[t]o protect investors by improving the accuracy and reliability of corporate disclosures',[227] which some scholars have viewed as reinforcing a shareholder primacy norm.[228]

The impact of these corporate scandals on debate concerning stakeholders, and corporate social responsibility generally, was arguably much greater in other common law jurisdictions, such as the UK, Australia and Canada. These countries possess strong historical legal ties, and have been described as 'three peas in a pod' in terms of their approach to directors' duties and corporate social responsibility.[229] Although directors' conduct rules in these jurisdictions have traditionally been shareholder-centred,[230] in the post-Enron era, stakeholder interests and corporate social responsibility became major topics of debate. A key issue in this debate, which continued to resonate throughout the global financial crisis, is whether the

---

[223] Baums and Scott, 'Taking Shareholder Protection Seriously? Corporate Governance in the United States and Germany' (2005) 53 *Am J Comp L* 31, 32; Macey and Miller, 'Corporate Stakeholders: A Contractual Perspective' (1993) 43 *U Tor LJ* 401, 405; Springer, 'Corporate Constituency Statutes: Hollow Hopes and False Fears' [1999] *Ann Surv Am L* 85.

[224] Williams and Conley, 'An Emerging Third Way? The Erosion of the Anglo-American Shareholder Value Construct' (2005) 38 *Cornell Int'l LJ* 493.

[225] Choudhury, 'Serving Two Masters: Incorporating Social Responsibility into the Corporate Paradigm' (2009) 11 *U Penn J Bus L* 631.

[226] Hill, 'Regulatory Show and Tell: Lessons from International Statutory Regimes' (2008) 33 *Del J Corp L* 819, 825.

[227] See Preamble to the Sarbanes-Oxley Act of 2002.

[228] See Karmel, 'Should a Duty to the Corporation be Imposed on Institutional Shareholders?' (2004) 60 *Bus Law* 1, 2. Cf. Langevoort, 'The Social Construction of Sarbanes-Oxley' (2007) 105 *Mich L Rev* 1817, 1828ff.

[229] See Pitts, 'Corporate Social Responsibility: Current Status and Future Evolution' (2009) 6 *Rutgers J L & Pub Pol'y* 334, 385.

[230] See Keay, 'Shareholder Primacy in Corporate Law: Can it Survive? Should it Survive?' (2010) 7 *Eur Comp & Fin Rev* 369, describing shareholder primacy theory, including its benefits and downsides.

law should encourage higher levels of 'laudable' and 'enlightened' board conduct, by reframing directors' conduct rules to protect stakeholder, as well as shareholder, interests.[231]

In the UK, this trend was manifested in reforms introduced in the Companies Act 2006. This Act codified UK directors' duties into a number of basic duties. One aspect of the UK reforms that provides an interesting contrast with Australian law is the interaction between the statutory duties and the general law. Whereas the Australian Corporations Act, which also codifies directors' duties, explicitly preserves the operation of general law duties,[232] the UK reforms seek to supplant the general law.[233]

The most contentious of the statutory duties enunciated in the UK Companies Act 2006 is section 172, requiring UK directors to 'promote the success of the company'.[234] Section 172 states:

> (1) A director of a company must act in the way he considers, in good faith, would be most likely to promote the success of the company for the benefit of its members as a whole, and in doing so have regard (amongst other matters) to:
>
> (a) the likely consequences of any decision in the long term,
> (b) the interests of the company's employees,
> (c) the need to foster the company's business relationships with suppliers, customers and others,

---

[231] For a detailed explanation of stakeholder theory, see Keay, 'Stakeholder Theory in Corporate Law: Has it Got What it Takes?' (2010) 9 *Rich J Global L & Bus* 249, 254–64.

[232] See ss 179(1) and 185 Corporations Act 2001 (Cth).

[233] Section 170(3) of the UK Act states that the statutory duties are based on certain common law rules and equitable principles, and operate in place of those rules and principles in relation to directors' duties. However, the statutory provisions which displace the general law also relate back to the general law, and the body of case law comprising it, since s. 170(4) of the UK Act states that the general duties are to be interpreted and applied in the same way as common law rules or equitable principles, and regard must be had to the corresponding common law rules and equitable principles in interpreting the general law duties. This turns traditional statutory interpretation on its head, by directing the adjudicator to look outside the legislator's wording to determine its meaning. For a discussion of the complexity created by this interaction between the UK statutory duties and the general law, see Alcock, 'An Accidental Change to Directors' Duties?' (2009) 30 *Comp Law* 362, 368; Austin, 'Australian Company Law Reform and the UK Companies Bill', in Austin (ed.), *Company Directors and Corporate Social Responsibility: UK and Australian Perspectives* (Ross Parsons Centre of Commercial, Corporate and Taxation Law, 2007), pp. 3, 5–6.

[234] See Arden, 'Clause 173 (Section 172): The UK's Proposed Re-formulation of the Directors' Duty of Good Faith', in Austin (ed.), note 233 above, pp. 20, 20ff.

(d) the impact of the company's operations on the community and the environment,
(e) the desirability of the company maintaining a reputation for high standards of business conduct, and
(f) the need to act fairly as between members of the company.

The goal of section 172 was to introduce an 'enlightened self-interest' approach to UK corporate law.[235] However, not all stakeholders were necessarily better off under this new provision – employees, for example, arguably went backwards.[236] Earlier, under section 309 of the UK Companies Act 1985, directors had been explicitly required to consider the interests of employees, as well as those of members.[237] Under section 172 of the Companies Act 2006, on the other hand, employee interests are just one of a far more diverse set of interests and factors to which directors must have regard. Section 172 remains 'shareholder-centric', particularly from an enforcement perspective, since the directors' duty is owed to the company, and can therefore only be enforced by the company or its shareholders in derivative suit, not by stakeholders generally.[238] The UK Company Law Review regarded section 172 as representing best practice in directors' duties in a modern context.[239]

Section 172 of the UK Companies Act 2006 presents aspirational standards in a new manner.[240] In spite of its worthy goals, scathing criticism of

[235] Ibid., 24; cf. Keay, 'Tackling the Issue of the Corporate Objective: An Analysis of the United Kingdom's "Enlightened Shareholder Value Approach"' (2007) 29 *Syd L Rev* 577; Wen and Zhao, 'Exploring the Rationale of Enlightened Shareholder Value in the Realm of UK Company Law – The Path Dependence Perspective' (2011) 14 *Int'l Trade & Bus L Rev* 153.

[236] See Hodge, 'The Treatment of Employees as Stakeholders in the European Union: Current and Future Trends' (2010) 38 *Syracuse J Int'l L & Com* 91, 159.

[237] Wynn-Evans, 'The Companies Act 2006 and the Interests of Employees' (2007) 36 *Industrial LJ* 188, 190.

[238] See Harper Ho, '"Enlightened Shareholder Value": Corporate Governance Beyond the Shareholder-Stakeholder Divide' (2010) 36 *J Corp L* 59, 79.

[239] Arden, 'Clause 173', note 234 above, pp. 20, 24. It is worth noting that s. 172 applies to non-UK companies that are listed on the UK Stock Exchange. This means, for example, that the provision is applicable to some major Australian mining companies, such as BHP Billiton and Rio Tinto, which have dual listing on the UK Stock Exchange: Kerr, Seminar, 'Corporate Social Responsibility: International Legal Developments and the Global Recession' (Sydney Law School, 7 September 2009).

[240] For an interesting assessment of the perceived impact of the UK reforms relating to directors' duties, and s. 172 in particular, see Infogroup/ORC International, Department for Business, Innovation and Skills, 'Evaluation of the Companies Act 2006, Volume One', 2 August 2010, (available at: http://www.

the section's policy and drafting has been made by some commentators, including one Australian critic who described the provision as 'British folly'.[241] Case law, which to date has been scant,[242] will be needed to determine what the words, 'success of the company', in section 172 actually mean, and whether their meaning is synonymous with 'maximising wealth'.[243]

A particular concern relating to section 172 is the potential gap between motivation and ultimate outcome in law reform.[244] In spite of its goal of promoting 'enlightened self-interest', there is the danger that section 172 will, by specifying such a broad range of factors for consideration, ultimately dilute director accountability.[245] Paralleling similar problems in the context of US constituency statutes, the risk is that the presence of multiple interests may enable management to justify any decision by reference to the interests of a particular stakeholder.[246] Also, early predictions of a spate of legal actions against directors following the introduction of a statutory derivative action in the UK Companies Act 2006,[247] are, as yet, unfulfilled.[248] In the light of these factors, it seems that section 172 reflects

bis.gov.uk/assets/biscore/business-law/docs/e/10-1360-evaluation-companies-act-2006-volume-1), 61–76.

241 Green, 'Should the Corporations Act Require Directors to Consider Non-Shareholder "Stakeholders"? Two Perspectives', in Austin (ed.), note 233 above, pp. 44, 49–50.

242 See Keay, 'The Duty To Promote The Success Of The Company: Is It Fit For Purpose?', University of Leeds School of Law, Centre for Business Law and Practice Working Paper, 20 August 2010, (available at: http://ssrn.com/abstract=1662411), 12.

243 Beerworth, 'Should the Corporations Act Require Directors to Consider Non-Shareholder "Stakeholders'? Two Perspectives", in Austin (ed.), note 233 above, pp. 39, 41. For interpretational difficulties under s. 172 in relation to long-termism and short-termism, see Keay, 'The Duty To Promote', ibid., 23–24.

244 See Keay, ibid. In relation to the gap between law reform motivation and outcome more generally, see Langevoort, 'The Social Construction of Sarbanes-Oxley', note 228 above.

245 See Green, note 241 above, pp. 44, 50; Keay, ibid., 19.

246 See Macey, 'An Economic Analysis of the Various Rationales for Making Shareholders the Exclusive Beneficiaries of Corporate Fiduciary Duties' (1991) 21 *Stetson L Rev* 23, 31ff, 44; Springer, 'Corporate Constituency Statutes', note 223 above; cf. Stout, 'Bad and Not-So-Bad Arguments for Shareholder Primacy' (2002) 75 *S Cal L Rev* 1189.

247 Mirchandani and Huntsman, 'Directors' Cut' (2007) 21 *Lawyer* 31.

248 See Keay, 'The Duty To Promote', note 242 above, 12; Loughrey, Keay and Cerioni, 'Legal Practitioners, Enlightened Shareholder Value and the Shaping of Corporate Governance' (2008) 8 *J Corp L Stud* 79.

an aspirational approach to directors' duties, comparable to that in US case law, such as the *Disney* litigation[249] and the *Caremark* decision.[250]

In Australia, the *James Hardie* saga focused attention on stakeholders and corporate social responsibility in an acute way, after it was announced in late 2003 that the Foundation, formed to satisfy the group's asbestos claims, was dramatically underfunded.[251] JHIL took the view that legally it had no responsibility in relation to the compensation of the tort victims.[252] According to JHIL, such action would be precluded under Australian law.[253] The subtext of this statement was that the JHIL's directors were prohibited from acting to benefit the company's affected workers, since this would conflict with their primary duty to maximise profits for their shareholders.[254]

These events prompted the Jackson Commission Report,[255] and two government reports on the broader issue of corporate responsibility – one by the Parliamentary Joint Committee on Corporations and Financial Services ('PJC Report'),[256] and the other by the Corporations and Markets Advisory Committee ('CAMAC Report').[257]

The Jackson Commission Report agreed with JHIL's assessment that under Australian corporate law, there was no legal obligation to

---

[249] *In re The Walt Disney Company Derivative Litigation*, Del.Ch., 907 A.2d 693 (2005); *In re The Walt Disney Company Derivative Litigation*, Del.Supr., 906 A.2d 27 (2006).

[250] *In re Caremark International Inc. Derivative Litigation*, Del.Ch., 698 A. 2d. 959 (1996).

[251] See Dunn, 'James Hardie', note 62 above.

[252] In a media release issued at the time, JHIL stated that there was 'no legal or other legitimate basis on which shareholders' funds could be used to provide additional funds to the Foundation'. See James Hardie, Media Release, *Possible Asbestos Funding Shortfall Suggests Significant Change in Claims*, 29 October 2003 (available at: www.ir.jameshardie.com.au/public/download.jsp?id=1171).

[253] Ibid.

[254] Ibid.The media release suggested that the 'duties of the company's directors would preclude them' from using shareholders' funds to provide further funding to the Foundation.

[255] Jackson QC, *Report of the Special Commission*, note 62 above.

[256] Parliament of Australia, Parliamentary Joint Committee on Corporations and Financial Services (PJC), *Corporate Responsibility: Managing Risk and Creating Value* (2006) (available at: http://www.aph.gov.au/Parliamentary_Business/Committees/Senate_Committees?url=corporations_ctte/completed_inquiries/2004-07/corporate_responsibility/report/report.pdf).

[257] Corporations and Markets Advisory Committee (CAMAC), *The Social Responsibility of Corporations: Report* (December 2006) (available at: http://www.camac.gov.au/camac/camac.nsf/byHeadline/PDFFinal+Reports+2006/$file/CSR_Report.pdf).

contribute to the shortfall in the Foundation's funding, due to the operation of the principles of separate legal personality and limited liability.[258] However, the Jackson Commission Report considered this legal outcome less than satisfactory, stating:

> . . . . there are significant deficiencies in Australian corporate law . . . In addition, the circumstances have raised in a pointed way the question whether existing laws concerning the operation of limited liability . . . within corporate groups adequately reflect contemporary public expectations and standards.[259]

The two Australian government reports, the PJC Report and the CAMAC Report, considered whether Australia should follow the statutory reforms embodied in section 172 of the UK Companies Act 2006.[260] A major focus of these reports was the scope of directors' duties, and the extent to which the current Australian legal framework permits directors to consider the interests of stakeholders or the broader community.[261] This investigation was a direct response to the argument that existing law required JHIL's to protect and preserve shareholder interests 'at all costs',[262] and that law reform was therefore needed in Australia to provide directors with a 'safe harbour' to consider stakeholder interests without the risk of liability.[263] In relation to James Hardie's argument that the law required the directors to consider only shareholder interests, the PJC Report observed that 'rampant corporate irresponsibility certainly decreases shareholder value'.[264]

---

[258] See Spender, 'Weapons of Mass Dispassion: James Hardie and Corporate Law' (2005) 14 *Griffith L Rev* 280, 286. See also, more generally, Collins, 'Ascription of Legal Responsibility to Groups in Complex Patterns of Economic Integration' (1990) 53 *Mod L Rev* 731.

[259] Jackson QC, *Report of the Special Commission*', note 62 above, [30.67].

[260] It has been suggested that Australian and Canadian legislators keep a close eye on the operation of s. 172 of the UK Companies Act 2006 to assess whether they too should adopt the provision, and the PJC Report and the CAMAC Report are good examples of this development. See Pitts, 'Corporate Social Responsibility', note 229 above; cf. Green, 'Should the Corporations Act Require Directors', note 241 above, pp. 44, 50.

[261] Marshall and Ramsay, 'Stakeholders and Directors' Duties: Law, Theory and Evidence' (2012) 35 *UNSW LJ* 291.

[262] PJC, *Corporate Responsibility*, note 256 above, 47, 181.

[263] JHINV's chair, Meredith Hellicar, argued that reforms were needed to provide greater protection to Australian directors in this regard. See Pheasant, 'Directors need a safe harbour: Hellicar', *Australian Financial Review*, 17 March 2005, 3, cited in Lumsden and Fridman, 'Corporate Social Responsibility: The Case for a Self-Regulatory Model' (2007) 25 *Comp & Sec LJ* 147, fn 14.

[264] PJC, *Corporate Responsibility*, note 256 above, 59.

Nonetheless, both the PJC Report and the CAMAC Report rejected the desirability or need for legislative reform to directors' duties in Australia, comparable to section 172 of the Companies Act 2006. The PJC Report was critical of the UK amendment to directors' duties, on the basis that it was overly prescriptive and would result in confusion.[265] The CAMAC Report considered that a comparable statutory amendment in Australia would provide 'no worthwhile benefit'.[266] Contrary to the arguments of the James Hardie directors that they were straitjacketed by narrow shareholder-centred legal rules, the two reports found that Australian law already provided directors with considerable discretion to consider a range of interests and factors, such as environmental and social interests, in the exercise of their duties.[267]

In undertaking their review of corporate social responsibility, both the PJC and CAMAC Reports revisited the thorny issue of the meaning of 'the company's interests', or the 'best interests of the corporation', in the context of directors' duties.[268] Historically, cases such as the Australian High Court decision, *Ngurli Ltd v McCann*,[269] interpreted the concept to mean the shareholders as a general body, in preference to a commercial entity approach.[270] The PJC and CAMAC Reports appeared to diverge on this issue. While the CAMAC Report followed the traditional view that the corporation is an aggregation of its shareholders, the PJC Report adopted a holistic approach, treating the corporation as a separate commercial entity to its stakeholders.[271] The PJC Report considered that a 'shareholders first' approach to directors' duties was overly narrow and constrained, and denied that acting in the best interests of the corporation was equivalent to acting in the best interests of the shareholders.[272]

The issue of the meaning of 'the company's interests' for the purposes of directors' duties has also been considered in some important Australian and Canadian case law. The 2008 Australian case, *The Bell Group Ltd*

---

[265] Ibid., 54–6.

[266] CAMAC, *The Social Responsibility of Corporations*, note 257 above, 111.

[267] Ibid., 7, 111; PJC, *Corporate Responsibility*, note 256 above, 52–3, 59.

[268] See generally Heydon, 'Directors' Duties and the Company's Interests', in Finn (ed.), *Equity and Commercial Relationships* (The Law Book Company Ltd, 1987), p. 120.

[269] *Ngurli Ltd v McCann* (1953) 90 CLR 425, 438.

[270] Ibid., citing the decision of Evershed MR in *Greenhalgh v Arderne Cinemas Ltd* [1951] Ch 286, 291. See generally ibid., (Heydon J).

[271] Kerr, Seminar, 'Corporate Social Responsibility', note 239 above.

[272] PJC, *Corporate Responsibility*, note 256 above, 52; Marshall and Ramsay, 'Stakeholders and Directors' Duties', note 261 above, 301.

(in liq) v Westpac Banking Corp (No 9) ('the *Bell Group* decision'),[273] a legacy of the 1989 financial crash, diverged from the traditional position concerning directors' duties. In that case, Owen J explicitly accepted an approach in which duties are owed to the company itself as a commercial entity.[274] Adopting a nuanced and highly contextualised approach to directors' duties, the judge stated:

> This does not mean that the general body of shareholders is always and for all purposes the embodiment of 'the company as a whole'. It will depend on the context, including the type of company and the nature of the impugned activity or decision. And it may also depend on whether the company is a thriving ongoing entity or whether its continued existence is problematic. In my view the interests of shareholders and the interests of the company may be seen as correlative not because the shareholders *are* the company but, rather, because the interests of the company and the interests of the shareholders intersect.[275]

In the insolvency context under consideration in the *Bell Group* decision,[276] Owen J considered that the directors, in fulfilling their duty to the company, had an obligation, not merely a discretion, to consider the interests of creditors.[277] The judge accepted, however, that this duty was one of 'imperfect obligation', since it did not constitute an independent duty owed to, and enforceable by, the creditors.[278] The directors were held to have breached the duty by entering into a refinancing transaction and providing securities to a consortium of banks at a time when the directors knew, or should have known, that the company was insolvent. The banks, in turn, were found to have knowledge of the breach of duty and were liable as constructive trustees. On appeal, the Western Australia Court of Appeal upheld, by a majority of two to one, Owen J's first instance decision.[279]

---

[273] (2008) 39 WAR 1; [2008] WASC 239.

[274] Ibid., para. [4389].

[275] Ibid., para. [4393].

[276] Owen J acknowledged, however, that directors might have an obligation to take account of creditor interests in circumstances falling short of actual insolvency. Ibid., para. [4445].

[277] Ibid., para. [4418]. Marshall and Ramsay, 'Stakeholders and Directors' Duties', note 261 above, 298.

[278] *The Bell Group Ltd (in liq) v Westpac Banking Corp (No 9)*, note 273 above, paras [4398], [4401] citing the High Court's majority judgment in *Spies v R* (2000) 201 CLR 603, paras [93]–[95]; Owen, 'Going Broke Ungraciously – Idle Musings on Insolvency and other Irrelevancies', paper presented at the Law Council of Australia (Business Law Section) Corporations Workshop, 13 September 2009.

[279] *Westpac Bank Banking Corporation v Bell Group Ltd (in liq) (No 3)* (2012) 89 ACSR 1; [2012] WASCA 157 per Lee and Drummond AJJA, Carr AJA

The theoretical approach taken by Owen J was not dissimilar to that adopted by Chancellor Allen in the 1991 Delaware Court of Chancery decision in *Credit Lyonnais Bank Nederland NV v Pathe Communications Corp*.[280] In that case, which reflected the trend of taking into account creditor interests when a company approaches insolvency, Chancellor Allen likened the corporation to an autonomous collective entity, representing a 'community of interests'. According to the judge, '[a]t least where a corporation is operating in the vicinity of insolvency, a board of directors is not merely the agent of the residue risk bearers, but owes its duty to the corporate enterprise'.[281] Like Owen J, Chancellor Allen considered that the interests of the 'corporate enterprise' will not necessarily coincide with the interests of any particular group of stakeholders.[282]

Read

The *Bell Group* litigation, while addressing some basic theoretical problems of corporate law, also had a profound commercial impact,

dissenting. Subtle differences in the conceptualisation of directors' duties with respect to creditor interests emerged in the appellate decision. Lee AJA adopted an approach similar to that of Owen J in the first instance decision. Lee AJA stated that; '[o]nce it appears that a company is insolvent, creditors of the company are regarded as having a direct interest in the company . . . in the sense that . . . an obligation will then be imposed on the company not to prejudice the interests of the creditors': ibid., para. [767]. Drummond AJA, the other member of the majority, considered that the court's willingness to intervene to ensure protection of creditor interests was based upon the obligation of directors to exercise their powers for 'proper purposes', rather than simply an aspect of the duty to act in the interest of the company: ibid., paras [2031]–[2032]. This distinction was important, because Drummond AJA interpreted the test for breach of the duty to act bona fide in the interests of the company as a subjective standard only, which was dependent on the beliefs of the directors, whereas the test for breach of the duty to act for proper purposes was objective and therefore subject to stronger judicial scrutiny: ibid., paras [2027]–[2028]. On the other hand, Carr AJA, in dissent, appears to have interpreted the duty of directors to act 'bona fide in the best interests of the company and for a proper purpose' as a composite duty, which should be assessed by a subjective standard, and which would fully protect the board's discretion and autonomy, provided the directors 'bona fide believe that a transaction is in the best interests of the company': ibid., para. [2819]. Carr AJA believed that where there is no allegation of dishonesty or negligence, directors should be given more latitude to make entrepreneurial decisions in the context of insolvency: ibid., paras [3064]–[3066]. He was consequently critical of what he regarded as Owen J's conduct in 'looking over the directors' shoulders and applying a business decision' to assess whether the directors had breached their duty to the company: ibid., para. [2804]

[280] Del. Ch., LEXIS 215 (1991), 108–9.

[281] Ibid., 108.

[282] Ibid. See also Lin, 'Shift of Fiduciary Duty Upon Corporate Insolvency: Proper Scope of Directors' Duty to Creditors' (1993) 46 *Vand L Rev* 1485.

creating significant risks for directors of distressed corporations engaged in refinancing and other material 'work-out' transactions.[283] In addition, the litigation highlighted the associated risks for banks, and other entities, engaged in such transactions.[284] These risks were exacerbated by the global financial crisis.[285]

Canada's courts have also considered the meaning of 'the company's interests' for the purposes of directors' duties in recent times. Section 122(1) of the Canada Business Corporations Act[286] states that: '[e]very director and officer of a corporation in exercising their powers and discharging their duties shall . . . act honestly and in good faith with a view to the best interests of the corporation'. The 2004 Supreme Court of Canada decision, *Peoples Department Stores Inc (Trustee of) v Wise* ('the *Wise* decision')[287] deviated from the traditional approach of regarding the corporation's interests as coextensive with the interests of shareholders, echoing the commercial entity approach adopted by Owen J in Australia's *Bell Group* decision.[288] According to the *Wise* decision, directors at all times 'owe their fiduciary obligations to the corporation, and the corporations' interests are not to be confused with the interests of the creditors or those of any other stakeholder'.[289] The court also accepted that, in determining whether directors have acted in the best interests of the corporation, it may be legitimate, depending upon the circumstances of the case, for the board to consider a broad range of stakeholder interests, including those of shareholders, employees, suppliers, creditors,

---

283 Directors are often in a particularly difficult situation in such circumstances, given that they can be personally liable for corporate debts under Australia's somewhat draconian insolvent trading regime, which has been described by the Chief Justice of the Supreme Court of Western Australia as 'arguably the strictest in the world'. See Martin CJ, 'Official Opening Address' (Speech delivered at Insolvency Practitioners' Association of Australia 16th National Conference, Perth, 28 May 2009). See generally Hill, 'Australia', note 50 above, pp. 106, 123–4.

284 Loxton, 'The Bell Group Litigation – The Lessons Learned', *Allens Arthur Robinson Insolvency & Restructuring*, November 2008 (available at: http://www.aar.com.au/pubs/insol/foinsolnov08.htm).

285 See Harris, 'Director Liability for Insolvent Trading: Is the Cure Worse than the Disease?' (2009) 23 *Aust J Corp L* 266; Sheahan, 'Directors' Insolvent Trading Liability After Collapse of Trading Markets in Debt Instruments', in Austin (ed.), note 233 above, pp. 88, 89.

286 RSC 1985, c. C-44.

287 [2004] 3 SCR 461; 2004 SCC 68.

288 *The Bell Group Ltd (in liq) v Westpac Banking Corp (No 9)*, note 273 above.

289 *Peoples Department Stores Inc (Trustee of) v Wise*, note 287 above, para. [43].

consumers, governments and the environment.[290] In 2008, the Supreme Court of Canada in *BCE Inc v 1976 Debentureholders*,[291] agreed with the *Wise* decision that the duty of directors is to act in the long-term interests of the corporation.[292] This emphasis on the corporation's long-term interests reflects another important theme underlying section 172 of the UK Companies Act 2006[293] and a diverse range of regulatory responses to the global financial crisis.[294]

5. CONCLUSION

The goal of this chapter has been to traverse a wide range of recent developments in the area of directors' duties in the common law world, through the conceptual lens of 'acoustic separation'. The chapter discusses US case law concerning directors' duty of care and the business judgment rule, where directors, particularly non-executive directors, face little risk of legal liability. Against this backdrop, the chapter also considers contemporary recent Australian decisions which arguably send conflicting messages in relation to the duty of care and diligence. Although from a liability perspective, some of the Australian decisions[295] are far more stringent than their US counterparts, to some degree it appears that aspirational standards are reintroduced into Australia at the penalty stage.

The chapter also discusses several recent developments across the common law world relating to the issue of to whom directors owe their duties when making decisions. This issue has gained significance since the corporate scandals, such as Enron, and more recently, the global financial crisis. Some of these developments, such as the introduction of section 172(1) of the UK Companies Act 2006, are aimed at promoting

---

290 Ibid., para. [42].

291 [2008] 3 SCR 560, 2008 SCC 69.

292 Ibid., paras [37]–[38].

293 See s. 172(1)(a) Companies Act 2006 (UK), which requires a director to have regard to '[t]he likely consequences of any decision in the long term'. See also Keay, 'The Duty To PromoteThe Success Of The Company', note 242 above, 11.

294 Long-termism was, for example, a central regulatory theme arising out of the global financial crisis in connection with executive compensation. See generally Hill, 'Regulating Executive Remuneration After the Global Financial Crisis: Common Law Perspectives' in Thomas and Hill (eds), *Research Handbook on Executive Pay* (Edward Elgar, 2012), pp. 219, 232–3.

295 See, for example, *ASIC v Macdonald (No 11)* (2009) 256 ALR 199; *ASIC v Healey* (2011) 196 FCR 291. Cf. *ASIC v Rich* (2009) 75 ACSR 1.

long-termism and ensuring that directors consider a range of stakeholder interests. It remains to be seen, however, whether such reforms will achieve their goals, or will, paradoxically, increase 'acoustic separation',[296] thereby reducing board accountability.

Basically the autor explords that the change expected by introduction of s172 to the companys act is suppressed by this 'acoustic seperation' therefore seeing the impact of the 172 would be slow or lossed as relating to Bank customers (Stakeholders) even in spite of the fact that they are the reason 4 Banks financies.

[296] I am grateful to Jerome Entwisle for pointing out this potential paradox in relation to some of the reforms discussed.

2. Directors' duties in Canada: paintings in a stream?

Jeff MacIntosh

I. INTRODUCTION

The issue of to whom directors' duties are owed is, without question, the most important issue in corporate law, for it defines the end or purpose of corporate existence and thus delineates the function that we wish corporations to play in our society. Shareholders are the only class of residual taker in the corporation; all other constituents are fixed claimants. Particularly as the traditional formulation of fiduciary duties in English and Canadian law is that the duty is owed only to the shareholders, the choice of duties, at the highest level of abstraction, is whether directors' duties should be owed only to shareholders, only to fixed claimants, or to some combination of the two.

In this chapter, I explore the rather abrupt paradigm shift from a shareholder-centric universe of directors' duties to a new duty of uncertain proportions, a shift wrought by two decisions in the Supreme Court of Canada – *Peoples Department Stores Inc. v. Wise*[1] ('*Peoples*') and *BCE Inc. v. 1976 Debentureholders* ('*BCE*').[2] These decisions reject shareholder wealth maximization in favour of a duty to 'the corporation', where '[t]he interests of the corporation are not to be confused with the interests of the creditors or those of any other stakeholders'.[3] This peculiar formulation, which divorces the fiduciary duty from *any* stakeholder interests, whether taken individually or collectively, is the intellectual equivalent of an M.C. Escher impossible figure. It simply defies rational construction, and is likely to tie both boards of directors and courts in knots for many years to come. Only legislative intervention can restore the shareholder primary view (and in my view, rationality) to corporate law.

1 [2004] 3 S.C.R. 461.
2 [2008] S.C.J. No. 37.
3 *Peoples*, supra, note 1, para. 43.

II. THE TRADITIONAL FORMULATION OF FIDUCIARY DUTY: SHAREHOLDER WEALTH MAXIMIZATION

At the dawn of the corporate age in England and Canada, shareholders were thought of as the 'owners' of the corporation. As directors and officers are agents of shareholders,[4] this characterization naturally led the courts to embrace a shareholder primacy view of directors' duties.

This can be seen as early as 1843 in the signal decision of *Foss v. Harbottle*.[5] In *Foss*, the question was whether an individual shareholder[6] might sue (both on his own behalf, and that of all the other shareholders save the wrongdoers) to redress a wrong allegedly done to the company by its directors. The court held that he could not, as the corporation was the proper plaintiff. The court also, however, identified the shareholders as the 'proprietors' of the corporation, and held that a majority of shareholders was competent to decide whether the corporation should sue.[7] In so holding, *Foss* thus effectively defines the body of shareholders as a whole as 'the corporation'.[8]

Another early holding that affirms shareholder primacy is *Hutton v. West Cork Railway Co.*[9] In *Hutton*, the shareholders in general meeting passed a resolution that sizeable payments be made to former managers who were let go as a result of a sale of the company's assets to a third party. The payments were *ex gratia*, since the managers had no legal entitlement to such payments. The English Court of Appeal expanded upon *Foss* by indicating that directors *may* make *ex gratia* payments, but only as long as these payments ultimately benefit the shareholders. The Court stated:

---

[4] See e.g. *Automatic Self-Cleansing Filter Syndicate v. Cuninghame*, [1906;cb] 2 Ch. 34, 75 L.J. Ch. 437 (C.A.).[cm

[5] (1843), 2 Hare 460, 67 E.R. 189.

[6] There were in fact two plaintiffs, but the issue was whether any individual shareholder might sue on his behalf and that of the other shareholders.

[7] The court stated that:

> the majority of the proprietors at a special general meeting assembled, independently of any general rules of law upon the subject, by the very terms of the incorporation in the present case, has power to bind the whole body, and every individual corporator must be taken to have come into the corporation upon the terms of being liable to be so bound.

Ibid., note 5.

[8] This comports with the reading given to *Foss* by subsequent judicial decisions. See e.g. *Hercules Management Ltd. v. Ernst & Young*, [1997] 2 S.C.R. 165, para. 60.

[9] (1883) 23 Ch. D. 654 (C.A.).

> A railway company, or the directors of the company, might send down all the porters at a railway station to have tea in the country at the expense of the company. Why should they not? It is for the directors to judge, provided it is a matter which is reasonably incidental to the carrying on of the business of the company, and a company which always treated its employees with Draconian severity, and never allowed them a single inch more than the strict letter of the bond, would soon find itself deserted – at all events, unless labour was very much more easy to obtain in the market than it often is. The law does not say that there are to be no cakes and ale, but there are to be no cakes and ale except such as are required for the benefit of the company.[10]

As in *Foss*, 'the benefit of the company' means the shareholders as a body.

The court's embracing of the indirect benefit test in *Hutton* is of vital importance in understanding – as many modern critics do not – the nature of directors' duties. Directors are not required to ignore the interests of non-shareholder constituencies in their decision-making processes. Indeed, as a matter of business, they do so at peril. However, to the extent that they benefit non-shareholder constituencies, they can only do so with a view to ultimately facilitating shareholder wealth maximization.

The identification of the company with the shareholders can also be seen in a later holding in the English Court of Appeal. In *Greenhalgh v. Arderne Cinemas (No.2)*,[11] Evershed M.R. held that:

> the phrase 'the company as a whole', does not (at any rate in such a case as the present) *mean the company as a commercial entity, distinct from the corporators* [i.e. the shareholders]: *it means the corporators as a general body*, that is to say the case may be taken of an individual hypothetical member and it may be asked whether what is proposed is in the honest opinion of those who voted in its favour, for that person's benefit. [emphasis added]

And what of Canada? Until 1949, the highest court of appeal for disputes originating in Canada was the Privy Council.[12] While decisions of the Privy Council were not technically binding within the UK, the decisions of the Privy Council in corporate matters prior to 1949 faithfully reflect the extant English common law. Moreover, although decisions of the UK House of Lords (then the highest domestic court of appeal) were not binding within Canada, they were routinely followed by Canadian courts. Thus, the Canadian common law of corporations prior to 1949 was

---

[10] See also *Parke v. Daily News Ltd.* [1962;cb] 1 Ch. 927; ob[1962;cb] 2 All E.R. 929 (Ch. D.).

[11] [1946] 1 All E.R. 512; [1951] Ch. 286 (C.A.).

[12] Somewhat more accurately, the Judicial Committee of the Privy Council.

essentially identical to English law. Indeed, two of the leading corporate cases decided by the Privy Council originated in Canada.[13]

Thus, for example, the Supreme Court of Canada holding in *Royal Guardians v. Clarke*[14] faithfully reflects the extant English common law. The court stated (albeit in *obiter dictum*):

> In the management of its business these officials in the case of mutual-benefit societies represent the members of the society, *who are its owners* and presumably have entrusted the management of its affairs to such officials because they repose confidence in them, quite as much as the directors and high office holders in the joint-stock company *represent its owners, the shareholders.*[15] [emphasis added]

The 1945 holding of the Supreme Court in *Canada v. Montreal Telegraph Company*[16] is similar; the court stated that '[t]he shareholders are the owners' of the corporation.[17]

These principles were carried forward after the abolition of appeals to the Privy Council in 1949. Thus, in the 1990 case of *McClurg v. Canada*[18] in the Supreme Court of Canada, La Forest J. stated:

> The independent legal existence of the corporation means that, while the shareholder *remains a proportionate owner of the corporation*, he does not actually own its assets . . . Management of the corporation is entrusted to its officers and directors with the shareholder's interest protected through the distribution of shareholder votes. Thus, the corporate entity is unique in that it allows the shareholder to alienate ownership of property by placing it in a structure where the ownership of the property is separated from the effective control over that property; see Welling, supra, at p. 81.[19] [emphasis added]

Justice La Forest also endorsed a passage from Wegenast's *The Law of Canadian Companies* giving voice to the principle (reflected in English cases such as *Greenhalgh v. Arderne Cinemas*, above) that 'the benefit of

---

13 *North-West Transportation Co. Ltd. v. Beatty* (1887), 12 App. Cas. 589 (P.C.); *Cook v. Deeks*, [1916] 1 A.C. 554.

14 (1914), 49 S.C.R. 229.

15 Ibid., para. 108.

16 [1945] S.C.R. 669.

17 Ibid., para. 30.

18 [1990] 2 S.C.R. 1020.

19 Ibid., para. 52. It is of no moment that Justice La Forest (and two others) dissented in the result; the three dissenting judges and the four majority judges were unanimous as to the fundamental principles of corporate law to be applied in the case, differing only in the application of those principles to the facts at bar.

the company as a whole' means the benefit of all the shareholders, without discrimination between majority and minority:

> Shareholders may differ as to the wisdom of a particular course of action, but once adopted *it must be carried out without discrimination amongst the shareholders* or, as it is said in some of the cases, 'for the benefit of the company as a whole.'[20] [emphasis added by Justice La Forest]

There are something of the order of 50 other Canadian cases that echo the identification theory; i.e. the view that 'the company' means *the shareholders*.[21] The holding of the Saskatchewan Court of Appeal in *347883 Alberta Ltd. v. Producers Pipelines Inc.*[22] is representative. The court stated, 'Although the duties of the directors are stated to be to the corporation, the authorities say that the corporation cannot be considered as an entity separate from its shareholders.'[23]

It is one of the curiosities of the Supreme Court of Canada decisions in *Peoples*[24] and *BCE*[25] that none of the above jurisprudence is referenced. Indeed, in *Hercules Management Ltd. v. Ernst & Young*,[26] decided only six years prior to *Peoples*, the Supreme Court itself adopted the identification theory. In *Hercules*, individual shareholders who had relied on an allegedly negligent audit report in making their investments sought to hold the auditors personally liable. The Supreme Court held:

---

20 Ibid., para. 64.

21 At least seven of these cases specifically quote the passage from *Greenhalgh* quoted above that states that the company as a whole 'means the corporators [i.e. shareholders] as a general body'. *See 347883 Alberta Ltd. v. Producers Pipelines Inc.* [1991] 4 W.W.R. 577, 3 B.L.R. (2d) 237, 80 D.L.R. (4th) 359, 92 Sask. R. 81 (Sask. C.A.); *Greenlight Capital Inc. v. Stronach* (2006), 22 B.L.R. (4th) 11 (Ont. Sup. Ct.); *Alexander v. Westeel-Rosco Ltd.* (1978), O.R. (2d) 211, 93 D.L.R. (3d) 116 (Ont. H. Ct.); *Re Hillcrest Housing Ltd.* (1998), 165 Nfld. & P.E.I.R. 181 (P.E.I. Sup. Ct.); *Benson v. Third Canadian General Investment Trust Ltd.* (1993), 14 O.R. (3d) 493, 13 B.L.R. (2d) 265 (Ont. Ct. J.); *Palmer v. Carling O'Keefe Breweries of Canada Ltd.* (1989), 67 O.R. (2d) 161, 56 D.L.R. (4th) 128, 41 B.L.R. 128 (Ont. Sup. Ct.); *Nova Scotia Trust Co. v. Rudderham* (1969), 9 D.L.R. (3d) 492, 1 N.S.R. (2d) 379 (N.S. Sup. Ct.). Though not specifically referencing this passage, many (or most) of the other cases adopting the 'company as a whole' principle also clearly adopt the identification theory.

22 [1991] 4 W.W.R. 577, 3 B.L.R. (2d) 237, 80 D.L.R. (4th) 359, 92 Sask. R. 81 (Sask. C.A.).

23 Ibid., para. 26.

24 Supra, note 1.

25 Supra, note 2.

26 [1997] 2 S.C.R. 165.

> Any duty owed by auditors in respect of this aspect of the shareholders' functions, then, would be owed not to shareholders *qua* individuals, but rather to all shareholders as a group, acting in the interests of the corporation. And if the decisions taken by the collectivity of shareholders are in respect of the corporation's affairs, then the shareholders' reliance on negligently prepared audit reports in taking such decisions will result *in a wrong to the corporation* for which the shareholders cannot, as individuals, recover.[27] [emphasis added]

The court also stated:

> This line of reasoning finds support in Lord Bridge's comments in *Caparo, supra* [*Caparo Industries plc. v. Dickman*, [1990] 1 All E.R. 568], at p. 580:
>
>> The shareholders of a company have a collective interest in the company's proper management and in so far as a negligent failure of the auditor to report accurately on the state of the company's finances deprives the shareholders of the opportunity to exercise their powers in general meeting to call the directors to book and to ensure that errors in management are corrected, the shareholders ought to be entitled to a remedy. *But in practice no problem arises in this regard since the interest of the shareholders in the proper management of the company's affairs is indistinguishable from the interest of the company itself and any loss suffered by the shareholders . . . will be recouped by a claim against the auditors in the name of the company, not by individual shareholders*[28] [editing and emphasis by Supreme Court].

Thus, yet again, 'shareholders as a group' are identified with 'the corporation'.

III. THE SUPREME COURT OF CANADA DECISIONS IN *PEOPLES*[29] AND *BCE*[30] *DEBENTUREHOLDERS*

Peoples

The Supreme Court of Canada decision in *Peoples*[31] makes no reference at all to any of the above jurisprudence. Remarkably, shareholder primacy is rejected on the basis of a single *obiter dictum* in a lower court holding, in which the court stated that

---

27 Ibid., para. 60.
28 Ibid., para. 61.
29 Supra, note 1.
30 Supra, note 2.
31 Supra, note 1.

the courts have long recognized that various other factors may be relevant in determining what directors should consider in soundly managing with a view to the best interests of the corporation. For example, in *Teck Corp. v. Millar* (1972), 33 D.L.R. (3d) 288 (B.C.S.C.), Berger J. stated, at p. 314:

> A classical theory that once was unchallengeable must yield to the facts of modern life. In fact, of course, it has. If today the directors of a company were to consider the interests of its employees no one would argue that in doing so they were not acting *bona fide* in the interests of the company itself. Similarly, if the directors were to consider the consequences to the community of any policy that the company intended to pursue, and were deflected in their commitment to that policy as a result, it could not be said that they had not considered *bona fide* the interests of the shareholders.
>
> I appreciate that it would be a breach of their duty for directors to disregard entirely the interests of a company's shareholders in order to confer a benefit on its employees: *Parke v. Daily News Ltd.*, [1962] Ch. 927. But if they observe a decent respect for other interests lying beyond those of the company's shareholders in the strict sense, that will not, in my view, leave directors open to the charge that they have failed in their fiduciary duty to the company.[32]

The purport of this obiter is actually quite modest. It appears to accept the view that the shareholders are the first among equals, but that the directors will not breach their fiduciary duty if they *consider* the interests of other constituencies.[33] Initially, the Supreme Court appears to accept this constrained view:

> We accept as an accurate statement of law that in determining whether they are acting with a view to the best interests of the corporation it may be legitimate, given all the circumstances of a given case, for the board of directors to consider, *inter alia*, the interests of shareholders, employees, suppliers, creditors, consumers, governments and the environment.[34]

However, in the very next paragraph in the judgment, the Supreme Court proffers a radically different interpretation:

> At all times, directors and officers owe their fiduciary obligation to the corporation. The interests of the corporation are not to be confused with the interests of the creditors or those of any other stakeholders.[35]

---

32 Ibid., para. 42.

33 The *Parke* case, supra, note 10, is mis-cited. It does not stand for the proposition that 'it would be a breach of their duty for directors to disregard entirely the interests of a company's shareholders in order to confer a benefit on its employees'. Rather, it stands for the proposition that directors breach their duty if they regard interests other than those of the shareholders.

34 Supra, note 1, para. 42.

35 Ibid., para. 43.

Further:

> In using their skills for the benefit of the corporation when it is in troubled waters financially, the directors must be careful to attempt to act in its best interests by creating a 'better' corporation, and not to favour the interests of any one group of stakeholders.[36]

In this manner, 'the corporation' is effectively viewed as an abstraction divorced not only from the welfare of any individual constituency of shareholders, but from *all* constituencies taken together.[37] The odd result is that, although the directors may 'consider' the interests of constituencies other than shareholders, and not fall afoul of their fiduciary duties, these constituencies have no standing to complain if their interests are disregarded.

The situation is further complicated by the court's comments on the breadth of the statutory oppression remedy in Canadian corporate law, and its interpretation of the remedy. The oppression remedy contained in section 241 of the Canadian Business Corporations Act states:

> (1) A complainant may apply to a court for an order under this section.
> (2) If, on an application under subsection (1), the court is satisfied that in respect of a corporation or any of its affiliates
> (*a*) any act or omission of the corporation or any of its affiliates effects a result,
> (*b*) the business or affairs of the corporation or any of its affiliates are or have been carried on or conducted in a manner, or
> (*c*) the powers of the directors of the corporation or any of its affiliates are or have been exercised in a manner
>
> that is oppressive or unfairly prejudicial to or that unfairly disregards the interests of any security holder, creditor, director or officer, the court may make an order to rectify the matters complained of.

---

36 Ibid., para. 47.

37 In the *BCE* decision, the court reaffirmed the schism between 'the corporation' and its various constituents:

> The fiduciary duty of the directors to the corporation originated in the common law. It is a duty to act in the best interests of the corporation. Often the interests of shareholders and stakeholders are co-extensive with the interests of the corporation. But if they conflict, the directors' duty is clear – it is to the corporation: *Peoples Department Stores*.

Supra, note 2, para. 37. *See also* para. 66. As was the case with *Peoples*, this statement utterly disregards the common law paradigm that 'the corporation' means the shareholders. Indeed, it lacks intellectual content. How can the corporation be divorced from its various constituents?

After noting that the definition of 'complainant' is broadly drawn to include a variety of constituents, including creditors, and highlighting section 241(2)(c) (dealing with the powers of directors), the court stated:

> Section 241 of the CBCA provides a possible mechanism for creditors to protect their interests from the prejudicial conduct of directors. In our view, the availability of such a broad oppression remedy undermines any perceived need to extend the fiduciary duty imposed on directors by s. 122(1)(*a*) of the CBCA to include creditors.[38]

If the oppression remedy 'undermines any perceived need to extend the fiduciary duty' to creditors, then presumably it must pull much or all the same freight as a fiduciary duty, in which case we might as well call it a fiduciary duty. Moreover, the quoted passage hints that this fiduciary duty is owed directly to creditors. However, because the definition of 'complainant' is broadly drawn, it is easy to draw the conclusion that the duty is owed to the complainant of the moment. This time, creditors; the next time, shareholders; the next time, a corporate officer; etc.[39]

The Supreme Court has thus created any number of inconsistent fiduciary duties. On the one hand, pursuant to the duty of loyalty, directors must consider whether what they are doing makes the corporation a 'better corporation', without regard to the effect on any individual constituency or even the totality of all constituencies. On the other hand, under the oppression remedy, they must consider the welfare of individual constituencies – in a manner highly suggestive of a fiduciary duty that extends to each and every possible class of 'complainant'. How it is possible to simultaneously ignore individual constituencies and fix one's attention only on the corporation as an abstraction, while simultaneously paying scrupulous attention to the welfare of each and every individual constituency? This surely requires Orwellian double-think of Olympian proportion.

---

[38] The court also stated, supra, note 1, at para. 53:

> In light of the availability both of the oppression remedy and of an action based on the duty of care, which will be discussed below, stakeholders have viable remedies at their disposal. There is no need to read the interests of creditors into the duty set out in s. 122(1)(*a*) of the CBCA.

[39] The ambit of the oppression remedy is limited not merely by the definition of 'complainant', but by the words of the remedy itself, which states that there just be conduct that is 'oppressive or unfairly prejudicial to or that unfairly disregards the interests of any *security holder, creditor, director or officer* . . .' [emphasis added] It does not appear that the court was aware of this restriction in its discussion of the scope of the oppression remedy.

Peoples thus confuses the situation in a number of ways. The 'accurate statement of law' from *Teck* does not reject shareholder primacy in its entirety, but adds a gloss: that directors may 'consider' the interests of other constituencies and not breach their duties. The Supreme Court then proceeds, however, to summarily reject shareholder primacy in favour of a duty owed to the 'the corporation' as an abstract entity. Finally, the court obliquely suggests that creditors have a complaint against the directors under the oppression remedy that seems to be commensurate with a fiduciary duty. This does not square with the notion that directors' duties are owed only to 'the corporation'.

BCE[40]

The substantive content of the duty of loyalty

In the *BCE* decision, the court gives us, in succession, a number of conflicting views on the content of the fiduciary duty.

In the first instance, the court affirms the schism between 'the corporation' and its various constituents:

> The fiduciary duty of the directors to the corporation originated in the common law. It is a duty to act in the best interests of the corporation. Often the interests of shareholders and stakeholders are co-extensive with the interests of the corporation. But if they conflict, the directors' duty is clear – it is to the corporation: *Peoples Department Stores*.[41]

Then, however, the court makes the following statement:

> There are no absolute rules. In each case, the question is whether, in all the circumstances, the directors acted in the best interests of the corporation, having regard to all relevant considerations, including, but not confined to, the need to treat affected stakeholders in a fair manner, commensurate with the corporation's duties as a responsible corporate citizen.[42]

---

40 Supra, note 1.

41 Ibid., para. 37. See also para. 66.

42 Ibid., para. 82. It is clear from a later comment that acting as a 'responsible corporate citizen' means treating all stakeholders fairly:

> Directors, acting in the best interests of the corporation, may be obliged to consider the impact of their decisions on corporate stakeholders, such as the debenture holders in these appeals. This is what we mean when we speak of a director being required to act in the best interests of the corporation viewed as a good corporate citizen.

Ibid., para. 66.

Earlier, we were advised that '[t]he interests of the corporation are not to be confused with the interests of the creditors or those of any other stakeholders'. The above passage, however, suggests that the interests of various stakeholders is a key component of the fiduciary duty – and that there is a 'need' to ensure that all are treated 'in a fair manner'.[43] The latter view is reinforced by the following:

> However, this case does involve the fiduciary duty of the directors to the corporation, and particularly the 'fair treatment' component of this duty, which, as will be seen, is fundamental to the reasonable expectations of stakeholders claiming an oppression remedy.

Here, again, we are told not only that there is a 'fair treatment' component of the fiduciary duty, but also that it is fundamental to the duty (and not merely to the oppression remedy, since the Supreme Court interprets the fiduciary duty coextensively with the oppression jurisprudence).

No sooner are we led to believe, however, that judges are to pay careful attention to the welfare of individual constituents, than this seems once again to be denied.

> The fact that the conduct of the directors is often at the centre of oppression actions might seem to suggest that directors are under a direct duty to individual stakeholders who may be affected by a corporate decision. Directors, acting in the best interests of the corporation, may be obliged to consider the impact of their decisions on corporate stakeholders, such as the debenture holders in these appeals. This is what we mean when we speak of a director being required to act in the best interests of the corporation viewed as a good corporate citizen. However, the directors owe a fiduciary duty to the corporation, and only to the corporation. People sometimes speak in terms of directors owing a duty to both the corporation and to stakeholders. Usually this is harmless, since the reasonable expectations of the stakeholder in a particular outcome often coincide with what is in the best interests of the corporation. However, cases (such as

---

[43] In a similar vein, the court stated, ibid., at para. 64:

> Determining whether a particular expectation is reasonable is complicated by the fact that the interests and expectations of different stakeholders may conflict. The oppression remedy recognizes that a corporation is an entity that encompasses and affects various individuals and groups, some of whose interests may conflict with others. Directors or other corporate actors may make corporate decisions or seek to resolve conflicts in a way that abusively or unfairly maximizes a particular group's interest at the expense of other stakeholders. The corporation and shareholders are entitled to maximize profit and share value, to be sure, but not by treating individual stakeholders unfairly. Fair treatment – the central theme running through the oppression jurisprudence – is most fundamentally what stakeholders are entitled to 'reasonably expect'.

> these appeals) may arise where these interests do not coincide. In such cases, it is important to be clear that the directors owe their duty to the corporation, not to stakeholders, and that the reasonable expectation of stakeholders is simply that the directors act in the best interests of the corporation.[44]

This returns us to the conception of the corporation as something distinct from its stakeholders. This view is further reinforced by an unorthodox move, without citation to authority, that reverses one of the most settled propositions under the oppression remedy; that a failure to observe the complainant's reasonable expectations is sufficient to ground a remedy. According to the court:[45]

> . . . to complete a claim for oppression, the claimant must show that the failure to meet this expectation involved unfair conduct and prejudicial consequences within s. 241 of the *CBCA*. Not every failure to meet a reasonable expectation will give rise to the equitable considerations that ground actions for oppression.

Thus, the complainant whose reasonable expectations are denied can no longer automatically expect a remedy. A further demonstration must be made that this amounts to conduct that is oppressive, unfairly prejudicial etc. In short, there is a 'need' to ensure that all corporate stakeholders are treated fairly, and this 'fair treatment' component of the duty is 'fundamental', but in the end, all of this counts for naught, since fairness must be submerged to the best interests of the corporation as an abstraction.

As if this uncertainty and confusion was not enough, the court also states that '[t]he corporation and shareholders are entitled to maximize profit and share value, to be sure, but not by treating individual stakeholders unfairly'.[46] This returns us to a sort of conditional shareholder primacy, in which directors are entitled to pursue shareholder wealth maximization subject to the constraint of treating other constituencies fairly. Needless to say, this is more than mildly puzzling, insofar as the court spares no pains in the balance of its judgment to reject shareholder wealth maximization.

'May' or 'must'?

Another area of confusion arises in relation to whether, in connection with the duty of loyalty, the directors 'may' consider the welfare of one or more corporate constituencies, or 'must' do so.

Initially, following *Peoples*, the court adopts the view that directors

---

44 Ibid., para. 66.
45 Ibid., para. 89.
46 Ibid., para. 64.

may, but are not required to consider various different constituencies that are or may be affected by corporate conduct:[47]

> In *Peoples Department Stores*, this Court found that although directors *must* consider the best interests of the corporation, it may also be appropriate, although *not mandatory*, to consider the impact of corporate decisions on shareholders or particular groups of stakeholders. [Emphasis added by Supreme Court]

But later on in the judgment, the court abandons this *laissez-faire* stance and firmly embraces the view that the directors *must* do so.[48] For example, in considering whether, on the facts, the directors acted in accordance with their fiduciary duties, the court states:

> It is apparent that the directors considered the interests of the debenture holders and, having done so, concluded that while the contractual terms of the debentures would be honoured, no further commitments could be made. This *fulfilled the duty of the directors to consider the debenture holders' interests.*[49] [emphasis added]

As discussed further below, the court held that the directors had a duty to consider the welfare of the debenture holders because they were able to establish a reasonable expectation to such consideration. But even though 'must' is thus delimited in scope, even this relatively modest reach is inconsistent with the idea, expressed in *Peoples* (and ostensibly adopted by the court in *BCE*) that 'it may also be appropriate, although *not mandatory*, to consider the impact of corporate decisions on shareholders or particular groups of stakeholders'.

If the focus of the inquiry is the corporation as an abstraction, then in fact *neither* 'may' nor 'must' makes sense; the welfare of individual constituencies is simply irrelevant. However, the 'must' formulation is particularly at odds with the corporation-as-abstraction view. If '[t]he interests of the corporation are not to be confused with the interests of the creditors or those of any other stakeholders', how is it that the directors must consider the welfare of various stakeholder groups?

Moreover, the foundation of a successful claim under the oppression remedy has long since been a violation of the complainant's reasonable expectations. Making reasonable expectations the pivot of the oppression remedy necessarily assumes that the corporation and its directors have

---

47 Ibid., para. 39. Accord, para. 40.
48 Ibid., para. 104. See also para. 82.
49 Ibid., para. 104. See also para. 66.

a duty that flows to each individual constituency – a duty not to violate that constituency's reasonable expectations. Prior to *Peoples* and *BCE*, the inquiry into whether reasonable expectations had been breached was never submerged to broader considerations of whether 'the corporation' had been harmed; it was always sufficient to demonstrate a breach of reasonable expectations, whereupon a remedy followed.

Perhaps mindful of this dilemma, the court stated:

> Thus far we have discussed how a claimant establishes the first element of an action for oppression – a reasonable expectation that he or she would be treated in a certain way. However, to complete a claim for oppression, the claimant must show that the failure to meet this expectation involved unfair conduct and prejudicial consequences within s. 241 of the *CBCA*. Not every failure to meet a reasonable expectation will give rise to the equitable considerations that ground actions for oppression. The court must be satisfied that the conduct falls within the concepts of 'oppression', 'unfair prejudice' or 'unfair disregard' of the claimant's interest, within the meaning of s. 241 of the *CBCA*. Viewed in this way, the reasonable expectations analysis that is the theoretical foundation of the oppression remedy, and the particular types of conduct described in s. 241, may be seen as complementary, rather than representing alternative approaches to the oppression remedy, as has sometimes been supposed. Together, they offer a complete picture of conduct that is unjust and inequitable, to return to the language of *Ebrahimi*.[50]

It may thus be that the court's solution of the dilemma of how to reconcile the corporation-as-abstraction view of the fiduciary duty and the individual-constituency-regarding nature of the oppression remedy is to say that it is no longer enough to show a breach of reasonable expectation. Now, the complainant must also show that the breach resulted in oppression, unfair prejudice, or unfair disregard. But what further evidence is necessary to surmount the second hurdle? Within the logic of the Supreme Court's judgment, the answer would seem to be 'harm to the corporation'. This, however, simply defies logic. If the gist of directors' duties is harm to the corporation, then it is irrelevant whether the reasonable expectations of one or more corporate constituencies have been flouted. There is no need for the first step of the inquiry. If, however, directors' duties are individual constituency-regarding, then the second step of the inquiry is irrelevant.

In essence, the problem is that the court would require the complainant to show that its complaint is at once personal and derivative. As Justice Laskin held in *Goldex Mines Ltd. v. Revill*,[51] the two are distinct

---

50 Ibid., para. 89. *Ebrahimi v. Westbourne Galleries* [1973] A.C. 360.
51 (1974), 7 O.R. (2d) 216 (C.A.).

and separate. The complainant must choose one or the other, and the remedy follows the choice of proceeding. If a claim must simultaneously be personal and derivative, then what remedy follows? Is the complainant entitled to an individual remedy? Or is the remedy necessarily in the corporation's favour?

Are there other meanings that can sensibly bridge the first step and the second step of the inquiry? Let us focus on the court's emphasis on the oppression remedy as one grounded in 'equitable considerations'. If so, then perhaps what the court means to say is that the violation of equitable considerations cannot be trivial in order to trigger the application of the oppression remedy. Rather, it must be such as to offend the conscience of equity. While tempting, this reading at best adds nothing to existing legal principles; at worst, it serves merely to confuse. Jurisprudence emanating from the Supreme Court itself[52] establishes that a trivial breach of law may be disregarded as *de minimis non curat lex*.[53] Alternatively, a court might choose to award merely nominal damages for a minor breach of reasonable expectations. Indeed, the pre-*BCE* oppression jurisprudence makes it clear that any remedy meted out under the oppression remedy should be commensurate – and no more than so – to any violation of expectations.[54] Thus, if eliminating *de minimis* complaints is the objective for instituting a two-step process, it is unnecessary and arguably confusing.

In short, the court's new two-step process for adjudicating whether the substantive trigger of the oppression remedy has been crossed reflects the same confusion that arises in determining whether a judge 'may' or 'must' consider particular corporate constituencies. The very fact that the court directs judges to inquire into the issue of reasonable expectations suggests an individual-constituency-regarding duty. However, the fact that a breach of reasonable expectations is insufficient by itself to give rise to a remedy is suggestive of a broader, corporation-as-abstraction approach. The two do not seem to be reconcilable.

---

[52] *Sail Labrador Ltd. v. Challenge One*, [1999] 1 S.C.R. 265.

[53] See also *Canadian Foundation for Children, Youth and the Law v. Canada (Attorney General)*, [2004] 1 S.C.R. 76 ('Absent action by Parliament, other existing common law defenses, such as the defense of necessity and the "*de minimis*" defense, will suffice to ensure that parents and teachers are not branded as criminals for their trivial use of force to restrain children when appropriate.'); Robert W. Emerson, *Barron's Business Law* (Barron's Educational Services: 2009, Hauppauge, New York), p. 658. A history of the maxim may be found in Max L. Veech and Charles R. Moon, '*De Minimis Non Curat Lex*' (1947), 45 *Mich. L. Rev*. 537.

[54] *Naneff v. Con-Crete Holdings Ltd et al.* (1995), 23 O.R. (3d) 481 (C.A.).

Confounding the duty of loyalty and the oppression remedy

The court stated:[55]

> The cases on oppression, taken as a whole, confirm that the duty of the directors to act in the best interests of the corporation comprehends a duty to treat individual stakeholders affected by corporate actions equitably and fairly.

This statement confounds the duty of loyalty with the oppression remedy. As noted above, the oppression remedy was enacted to address a perceived inadequacy in the common law protections afforded minority shareholders from the predations of majority (or controlling) shareholders. Although there are ostensibly three substantive standards under the remedy (acting in a manner that is 'oppressive' or 'unfairly prejudicial to' or that 'unfairly disregards the interests' of the complainant), the courts have indicated that the overarching standard is one of 'fairness'. Thus, bad faith need not be shown. Rather, the focus of the court's inquiry will be on whether the *result* of impugned conduct was unfair to the complainant. By contrast, the statutory duty of loyalty in virtually all of the Canadian corporate law statutes (both federal and provincial) requires directors and officers to 'act honestly and in good faith with a view to the best interests of the corporation'.[56] The nature of the inquiry, focusing as it does on subjective motivations, is thus fundamentally different.

Because of the broader standard of liability enunciated under the oppression remedy, the courts have long held that the cases on fiduciary duty are relevant to a determination of whether there has been oppression. This makes perfect sense, since conduct of directors that is not undertaken honestly, or in good faith, or with a view to the best interests of the corporation, is very likely to treat one or more corporate constituencies unfairly. A breach of fiduciary duty might thus be thought of as a sufficient, but not a necessary, condition for a finding of oppressive conduct. But the reverse is not equally true. Because of the more demanding standard of liability under the duty of loyalty, that which constitutes unfairness (and hence oppressive conduct) cannot be said to be a breach of the duty of loyalty. The Supreme Court's statement that the oppression remedy informs the standard of liability under the duty of loyalty thus confuses two quite different liabilities, and ignores the comparative statutory wording of the duty of loyalty and the oppression remedy. It serves only to further confuse the standard that a court should apply in determining whether the directors have complied with their fiduciary duty.

---

55 *BCE*, supra, note 2, para. 82.

56 See e.g. Canada Business Corporations Act, R.S.C., 1985, c. C-44, s.122.

What constitutes a 'reasonable expectation'?

The same confusion is reflected in the court's contradictory statements concerning the nature of reasonable expectations. On the one hand, the Supreme Court states that 'the reasonable expectation of stakeholders is simply that the directors act in the best interests of the corporation'.[57] This is consistent with the view that the reasonable expectations of individual constituencies are irrelevant. The inquiry is entirely in respect of the corporation-as-abstraction.

However, the court also tells us that '[f]air treatment – the central theme running through the oppression jurisprudence – is most fundamentally what stakeholders are entitled to "reasonably expect"'.[58] But expecting 'fair treatment' is not the same thing as expecting that the directors act in the best interests of the corporation.

The court also states that '[t]he [three charging] phrases ["oppressive", etc.] describe, in adjectival terms, ways in which corporate actors may fail to meet the reasonable expectations of stakeholders'.[59] This is entirely inconsistent with the court's enunciation of a two-step test for success under the oppression remedy: first, demonstrating a breach of reasonable expectations, and second, demonstrating that this breach constitutes oppression, unfair prejudice, etc. If we are to take this seriously, then the two-step test amounts to demonstrating that the complainant's reasonable expectations were violated – and that this breach of reasonable expectations was itself a breach of reasonable expectations.

In another set of passages,[60] the court rehearses the jurisprudentially conventional view that reasonable expectations consist of subjective expectations, arising in relation to individual constituents or constituencies, which must then be objectively confirmed as 'reasonable' on the basis of various factors such as the nature of the relationship and dealings between the parties, past and commercial practice, the nature of the corporation, and so on. But this view squarely rejects the previously posited view that reasonable expectations are to be determined only with regard to the corporation-as-abstraction. It is also inconsistent with the other two meanings of 'reasonable expectations' just canvassed. This hodgepodge of different and contradictory meanings supplies nothing but confusion both as to the role of reasonable expectations under the oppression remedy, and how these expectations are to be determined.

---

57 *BCE*, supra note 2, para. 66.
58 Ibid., para. 64.
59 Ibid., para. 67.
60 Ibid., paras 73 et seq.

It is also worth noting that, prior to *BCE*, it was well settled that the three charging paragraphs in the oppression remedy (i.e. 'oppressive', 'unfairly prejudicial', 'unfairly disregards the interests of') reduced in essence to the idea of 'fairness'. Moreover, fairness was to be judged in terms of whether the complainant's reasonable expectations were met. This, however, seems to be the only role for reasonable expectations that finds no place in the judgment in *BCE*.

The business judgment rule and the constituency decision: what does it protect?

The business judgment rule ('BJR') in Canadian jurisprudence is essentially a rule of deference to managerial decision-making, based on the view that judges are poorly positioned to second-guess the decisions of business people. The essence of the rule is stated by the Ontario Court of Appeal in *Pente v. Schneider*:[61]

> The law as it has evolved in Ontario and Delaware has the common requirements that the court must be satisfied that the directors have acted reasonably and fairly. The court looks to see that the directors made a *reasonable* decision *not a perfect* decision. Provided the decision taken is within a range of reasonableness, the court ought not to substitute its opinion for that of the board even though subsequent events may have cast doubt on the board's determination. As long as the directors have selected one of several reasonable alternatives, deference is accorded to the board's decision . . . This formulation of deference to the decision of the board is known as the 'business judgment rule'. [emphasis in original]

As in the United States, the BJR is fundamentally process-based. Great weight is given to the formation of an independent committee of directors. As expressed by the Ontario Court of Appeal in *Pente*:

> If a board of directors has acted on the advice of a committee composed of persons having no conflict of interest, and that committee has acted independently, in good faith, and made an informed recommendation as to the best available transaction for the shareholders in the circumstances, the business judgment rule applies.[62]

Where relevant, the courts also give great weight to the obtaining of outside advice, such as an independent valuation of the corporation in any situation in which valuation is an issue.

---

[61] *Pente Investment Management Ltd. v. Schneider Corp.* (1998), 42 O.R. (3d) 177, 44 B.L.R. (2d) 115 (O.C.A.).

[62] Ibid., para. 38.

In *BCE*, the court states:

> Courts should give appropriate deference to the business judgment of directors who take into account these ancillary interests, as reflected by the business judgment rule. The 'business judgment rule' accords deference to a business decision, so long as it lies within a range of reasonable alternatives [citations omitted]. It reflects the reality that directors, who are mandated under s. 102(1) of the *CBCA* to manage the corporation's business and affairs, are often better suited to determine what is in the best interests of the corporation. This applies to decisions on stakeholders' interests, as much as other directorial decisions.[63]

While welcome, the court's application of the BJR to the constituency decision raises as many questions as it resolves. A fundamental issue is whether the BJR applies to the selection of constituencies for consideration (the 'selection stage'), the outcome of this consideration (the 'decision stage'), or both. If the former, the proposition that directors *must* consider the welfare of one or more constituencies is considerably weakened. All the board has to do is paper the record of its board and committee meetings appropriately to show that the board deliberated upon the issue of which constituencies' interests should be taken into account. If all the procedural boxes have been ticked, then under the BJR, a court should not superimpose its own views of which constituencies' interests should have been considered.

However, on the facts of *BCE*, the court held that '[t]he evidence, objectively viewed, supports a reasonable expectation that the directors would consider the position of the debentureholders in making their decisions on the various offers under consideration'.[64] This suggests that whether a particular constituency's interests are to be taken into account in the selection stage is *not* entirely a matter to be left to the directors. Rather, it is to be determined by the court, on the basis of whether the complainant constituency had a reasonable expectation that its interests would be considered in respect of the particular decision under consideration. It is only in relation to constituencies that do not have any such expectation that the BJR comes into play at the selection stage. If that is the case, the directors may decide whose welfare they will consider. As long as they have checked the appropriate procedural boxes, their decision will be protected by the BJR.

What about the decision stage? On the facts of *BCE* itself, the court found that while the debentureholders had a reasonable expectation that

---

[63] Supra, note 2, para. 40.

[64] Ibid., para. 102 ('The evidence, objectively viewed, supports a reasonable expectation that the directors would consider the position of the debentureholders in making their decisions on the various offers under consideration.').

their interests would be considered, they failed to establish that they had any particular reasonable expectation as to the outcome.[65] It is clear from the decision, however (despite what the Supreme Court says in the abstract about the role of reasonable expectations), that if the debentureholders had been able to establish such an expectation, oppression might have been found.

Thus, directors should not be too reassured by the application of the BJR to the constituency decision. If a particular constituency is found to have had a reasonable expectation applicable either to the selection stage or the decision stage, then the BJR is essentially *functus* with respect to that constituency. If, however, the complainant constituency fails to establish a reasonable expectation that is operative at either stage, the BJR is available to protect the directors' from liability.

The structural conflict of interest in the new BJR

As noted above, in *Pente v. Schneider*,[66] the Ontario Court of Appeal (in a passage endorsed by the Supreme Court in *BCE*[67]) stated:

> If a board of directors has acted on the advice of a committee composed of persons having no conflict of interest, and that committee has acted independently, in good faith, and made an informed recommendation as to the best available transaction for the shareholders in the circumstances, the business judgment rule applies.

However, the fiduciary duty enunciated by the Supreme Court makes it impossible for any director (or committee of directors) to avoid a conflict of interest – whether at the selection stage or the decision stage. The difficulty lies in the fact that directors are elected by shareholders, and only shareholders. It is thus natural that directors will pay attention first and

---

65 Ibid., paras 105–14. The court stated (ibid., para. 113):

> Considering all the relevant factors, we conclude that the debentureholders have failed to establish a reasonable expectation that could give rise to a claim for oppression. As found by the trial judge, the alleged expectation that the investment grade of the debentures would be maintained is not supported by the evidence. A reasonable expectation that the debentureholders' interests would be considered is established, but was fulfilled. The evidence does not support a further expectation that a better arrangement could be negotiated that would meet the exigencies that the corporation was facing, while better preserving the trading value of the debentures.

66 *Pente v. Schneider*, supra, note 61.

67 Supra, note 2, paras 40, 83, 155.

foremost to shareholder interests. This structural conflict is exacerbated where directors own shares in the corporation, or receive a material portion of their remuneration in stock options or some other form of equity-based compensation, as is often the case. Inside directors, in particular, are often incentivized with one form of equity-linked compensation or another. The purpose of such compensation packages is not to benefit 'the corporation' as an abstract entity, but to align the interest of directors and officers with that of the shareholders – all in the interest of promoting shareholder wealth maximization.

Is it possible for the directors to avoid a conflict of interest and satisfy the dictates of the BJR, newly cast in light of the Supreme Court's decision as to the nature of the fiduciary duty? The only possible solution is for the board to take the advice of independent outsiders in any case in which the conflict becomes material. Even in the pre-*BCE* environment, securing independent advice was often a material factor in determining that the directors had discharged their fiduciary duty.

However, the situation is quite different where an independent committee of the board works with independent outsiders to make recommendations to the full board. For one thing, it is the independent committee that decides which outsiders should be engaged, and the scope of their mandate. If there are no independent persons within the corporation to perform this function, can we have any confidence that the appropriate outsiders will be hired, or their mandates suitably crafted? Who will determine what information is provided to the outsiders?[68] Who will evaluate the input received and mediate its communication to the full board? In the absence of independent persons to perform these functions, there is a very real question about whether the very institution of seeking outside advice has been fatally compromised.

The question of what mandate independent outsiders should be given is also very much in doubt. In the pre-*BCE* environment, outsiders tasked with jobs such as delivering a fairness opinion or a corporate valuation focused their efforts exclusively on the position of the shareholders. What now is the required scope of the mandate to independent outsiders? Must they be asked to assess the affect of a decision on each and every corporate constituency? On those constituencies that the board elects to 'consider'? On the Supreme Court's chimerical abstraction, the 'better corporation'?

---

[68] It is well understood that the ability to set an agenda, establish a mandate, and to decide what information will be provided to directors are factors that can be used by insiders to corrupt the decision-making process. See e.g. Victor Brudney, 'The Independent Director – Heavenly City or Potemkin Village?' (1982), 95 *Harv. L. Rev*. 597.

What instructions must they be given about how to trade-off the interests of the various constituencies? How far-reaching must their inquiry be?

There is also a question about what kinds of persons should be hired. Investment bankers – probably the most commonly utilized outsiders – are skilled at evaluating financial claims. But do they have the expertise to evaluate the effect of a given decision on employees? The environment? The local community? If they do not have this expertise, who does?

As discussed in the last section in this chapter, actual practice at the board level is not likely to change very much following *Peoples* and *BCE*. However, Canadian corporate counsel are well advised to consider what additional procedures are now necessary to afford their clients the benefit of the business judgment rule.

The corporate law/securities law divide

While the Supreme Court has rejected shareholder primacy, the legislative mandate of securities regulators extends only to the protection of 'investors'.[69] This embraces more than shareholders, but considerably less than the full array of corporate constituencies empowered by *BCE* to complain about directorial and/or corporate conduct. In fact, the securities regulators have mostly paid attention to shareholder interests in their travails. Thus, corporate directors must somehow attempt to stick-handle through two sets of contradictory mandates.

This difficulty is no more evident that in the case of hostile takeover bids. The securities regulators have made it abundantly clear that, when confronted by a hostile takeover bid, the directors' duty is to maximize shareholder wealth. Reflecting the rationale for the creation of the takeover bid provisions in the Securities Act,[70] National Policy 62-202 states:

> In considering the merits of a take-over bid, there is a possibility that the interests of management of the target company will differ from those of its shareholders ... The primary objective of the take-over bid provisions of Canadian securities legislation is the protection of the bona fide interests of the shareholders of the target company.[71]

This shareholder focus is reflected in administrative decisions made by regulators under the Securities Act.[72]

---

[69] Ontario Securities Act, R.S.O. 1990, c. S-5 ('OSA'), s. 1.1.

[70] Report of the Attorney General's Committee on Securities Legislation in Ontario (Toronto: Queen's Printer, 1965).

[71] NP 62-202, paras 1.1 (1), (2).

[72] See e.g. *Re Chapters Inc.* (2001), 24 OSCB 1657 (Ont. Sec. Comm.).

How, then, is counsel to advise the board of directors of a target company as to their role when confronted with a hostile bid? If the directors put their securities law duty first and direct their efforts to securing the best deal for shareholders, they likely breach their fiduciary duty in corporate law. If they prioritize their corporate law duty, they fall afoul of the principles espoused by securities regulators, in which case the corporation and its directors risk an adverse administrative order,[73] civil liability,[74] or potentially severe quasi-criminal sanctions.[75]

Short versus long term

In *BCE*, the Supreme Court stated that: 'The fiduciary duty of the directors to the corporation is a broad, contextual concept. It is not confined to short-term profit or share value. Where the corporation is an ongoing concern, it looks to the long-term interests of the corporation.'[76] This proposition is entirely without citation to relevant authority, and in fact contradicts prior law on point.[77] In the context of a hostile takeover bid, for example, the Ontario Court of Appeal has stated, following US

---

[73] OSA, s. 127.

[74] OSA, s. 128.

[75] OSA, s. 122(1)(c) states: 'Every person or company that contravenes Ontario securities law . . . is guilty of an offence and on conviction is liable to a fine of not more than $5 million or to imprisonment for a term of not more than five years less a day, or to both.'

[76] Supra, note 2, para. 38.

[77] Curiously, the Supreme Court states, ibid., para. 87:

> What is clear is that the *Revlon* line of cases [from which the Canadian jurisprudence is derived] has not displaced the fundamental rule that the duty of the directors cannot be confined to particular priority rules, but is rather a function of business judgment of what is in the best interests of the corporation, in the particular situation it faces.

The Court's authority for this proposition is not pertinent case law, but an article co-written by former Delaware Supreme Court Chief Justice E. Norman Veasey (E. Norman Veasey with Christine T. Di Guglielmo, 'What Happened in Delaware Corporate Law and Governance from 1992–2004? A Retrospective on Some Key Developments' (2005), 153 *U. Pa. L. Rev.* 1399). However, the Court misinterprets the article. The passage quoted is the following:

> [It] is important to keep in mind the precise content of this 'best interests' concept – that is, to whom this duty is owed and when. Naturally, one often thinks that directors owe this duty to both the corporation and the stockholders. That formulation is harmless in most instances because of the confluence of interests, in that what is good for the corporate entity is usually derivatively good for the stockholders. There are times, of course, when the focus is directly on the interests of the stockholders [i.e., as in *Revlon*]. But, in general, the directors owe

jurisprudence, that the board of the target company must act 'in a neutral manner to achieve the best value reasonably available to shareholders in the circumstances'.[78]

The switch to 'long-term interests' is likely to provide cover to opportunistic directors to undertake self-serving actions on the basis of a superficially plausible story about the corporation's long-term interest. In particular, it almost inexorably leads to the conclusion, as against pre-*BCE* corporate and securities law alike, that directors keen on preserving their jobs may now 'just say no' to takeover bids that, in the short term, are in the best interests not merely of shareholders, but of all corporate constituencies. At least one decision by the Ontario Securities Commission so concluded[79] – although following a storm of criticism, the Commission has now resiled from that position.[80]

The different positions in corporate and securities laws concerning the chronological focus of the directors' fiduciary duty creates yet another insuperable chasm between corporate and securities law, and yet another impossible dilemma for corporate directors and their counsel.

---

fiduciary duties to the *corporation*, not to the stockholders. [Emphasis in Veasey and Di Guglielmo article]

Ibid. para. 87, quoting (2005), *153 U. Pa. L. Rev.* 1399 at 1431. However, the Veasey article goes on to state: 'This means that, as the corporation slides toward insolvency, the benefits of maximizing the value of the corporation will shift from stockholders to creditors, but, on this view, the duties of the board remain the same.' (2005), 153 *U. Pa. L. Rev.* 1399 at 1431. From this additional sentence it is clear that so long as the corporation is solvent, Veasey and Di Guglielmo are of the view that 'the corporation' *does* in fact mean primarily (if not exclusively) the shareholders. However, it is well known that as a corporation approaches insolvency, perverse incentives arise when the corporation is run in the interests of shareholders alone. It is for this reason that the Delaware courts have embraced the notion that the directors' gaze should shift from the shareholders to the creditors. This is the point that Veasey and Di Guglielmo wish to emphasize, and when they say that the directors duty is owed at all times to 'the corporation', they mean something very different from the Supreme Court's interpretation of 'the corporation'.

Delaware case law supports the above equating of shareholders with the corporation. A statement to the contrary in *Unocal Corp. v. Mesa Petroleum Co.*, 493 A. 2d 946 (Del. S.C. 1985) was effectively abandoned in *Revlon Inc. v. MacAndrews Forbes Holdings Inc.*, 506 A. 2d 173 (De. S.C. 1985).

[78] *Pente*, para. 63.

[79] *Re Neo Materials Technologies Inc.* (2009), 32 OSCB 6941; (2009), 63 B.L.R. (4th) 123 (Ont. Sec. Comm.).

[80] *Re Baffinland Iron Mines Corp.* 2010 LNONOSC 904 (Ont. Sec. Comm.).

Implications for corporate decision-making

In most cases, it is likely that boards will continue to do what they have always done – maximize shareholder value. Boards that fail to do so will find themselves at risk of losing their jobs, whether via the instrumentality of a hostile takeover bid, a proxy contest, or other means. However, where major decisions arise – particularly those that generate winners and losers among the various corporate constituencies, and hence the possibility of litigation, particular attention needs to be paid to crafting board procedures that attract the protection of the BJR.

The historical focus of judicial attention under the BJR has been on the procedural aspects of corporate decision-making, and whether these procedures have adequately addressed board conflicts of interest. As stated in *Pente*:

> If a board of directors has acted on the advice of a committee composed of persons having no conflict of interest, and that committee has acted independently, in good faith, and made an informed recommendation as to the best available transaction for the shareholders in the circumstances, the business judgment rule applies.[81]

The requirement that the recommendation be 'informed' has been met, as in US jurisprudence, by a demonstration that the board and/or independent committee gathered all information reasonably available to it and conducted a 'reasonable investigation'.

Peoples and *BCE* complicate the situation considerably by changing the lens through which corporate decision-making procedures are examined. Board procedures must now be modified to show that all corporate constituencies were treated 'fairly'. The requirement to dispense fair treatment arises at two distinct nodes; first, the selection stage, where directors decide whose interests they will consider; and the decision stage, where they actually decide the matter at issue.

In respect of both, the record of the board's deliberations should show that the board took the time and effort to assess relevant reasonable expectations, and to appropriately address them. Even absent an identifiable reasonable expectation, the record should show that the board gave consideration to any constituency that might be a material loser as a result of the board's decision. The minutes of directors' meetings should show that the board did its best to reconcile inconsistent constituent interests in a 'fair' manner, and ultimately made a decision that the board thought was in the best interests of the corporation as a whole.

---

81 *Pente*, supra, note 61, para. 38.

The issue of how directors must now inform themselves of all information reasonably available is particularly difficult given the number of constituencies potentially involved. The breadth of the information that they should gather can only be judged in relation to both the reasonable expectations of different constituencies and the prospect that a given decision will generate material losers.

The depth of the information sought is equally uncertain – particularly the role of independent advisers. Corporate counsel will have to grapple with *who* should be engaged, and their mandate and scope of inquiry – again with a view to addressing all pertinent reasonable expectations and potential losses. It is well to keep in mind that reasonable expectations are partly determined by factors extrinsic to the relationship between the complainant and the corporation (such as commercial practice). These extrinsic factors should be taken into account in determining what manner of outside expertise to engage.

The pro-active management of reasonable expectations

BCE states that there are various intrinsic factors that may give rise to reasonable expectations, such as the 'personal relationships between the claimant and other corporate actors', 'preventive steps', and 'representations and agreements'. These lend themselves to pro-active management to reduce the probability of liability.

The board must make it clear to those who are mandated to speak for the corporation not to create constituent expectations outside any constituency's strict legal rights, whether these arise in the form of promises, assurances, or mere speculations. Even statements made in the context of closed-door meetings with various constituents raise the spectre of creating extra-contractual rights. Those who speak for the corporation in such private meetings, whether formal or informal, should be instructed to be circumspect about what they say.

Where possible, contracts should include a broadly drafted 'four corners' clause that excludes legal entitlements arising not only from representations made *prior* to the date of the contract, but *afterwards* as well. These clauses should make it clear that any communication, by any person, by whatever means, giving rise to any form of expectation (whether reasonable or otherwise) is legally ineffective unless it is reduced to a formal modification to the contract. These clauses might contain a non-exclusive list of communications that the parties agree will not augment the parties' strict contract rights as reflected in the contract, such as oral communications by any person, whether authorized or not, made publicly or privately, intentionally or accidentally, and by whatever means. Such clauses should be inserted in all major contracts, including those with bondholders, employees, suppliers, customers, and so on.

IV. CONCLUSION

The Supreme Court's decision in *BCE* re-affirms the radical re-definition of directors' duties enunciated in the *Peoples* case. The newly minted duty, based on a non-shareholder-centric definition of 'the corporation', has created confusion and uncertainty in virtually every corner of Canadian corporate law, including the substantive content of the fiduciary duty and the oppression remedy; the relationship between these two liabilities; whether directors' duties are ultimately grounded in constituency-regarding 'fairness' considerations, or owed to the corporation as an abstraction, or some combination of the two; the nature of personal and derivative actions; the evidence that must be adduced to establish a breach of fiduciary duty or the oppression remedy; the meaning of 'reasonable expectations'; the evidence that must be adduced to establish a violation of reasonable expectations; the evidence that must be adduced under the oppression remedy to clear the second hurdle for success under the oppression remedy – that the breach of reasonable expectations amounted to conduct that was oppressive, unfairly prejudicial etc.; whether directors *may* or *must* consider the interests of different corporate constituencies in their deliberations; and whether directors' attention should be focused on the short term or the long term.

Peoples and *BCE* create uncertainty not only because of their manifold contradictions, inconsistencies, and intellectual incoherencies, but because the new road charted by the Supreme Court is massively inconsistent with prior case law. Particularly in the commercial domain, predictability and certainty are virtues that reduce risk for all parties and minimize transaction costs. *Peoples* and *BCE* create vast new areas of uncertainty both for solicitors advising their clients and for barristers bringing or defending cases.

For both, the uncertainty is likely to be at its greatest in relation to hostile takeover bids. The court's rejection of prior shareholder-centric case law creates an apparently unbridgeable chasm between the director's fiduciary duty in corporate law and behaviour that is demanded of directors within the shareholder-centric universe of securities laws.

Do these developments augment or reduce the likelihood of director liability? Because of the schism just adverted to in the case of hostile takeover bids, target directors are exposed to liability no matter what they do. In other contexts, it may be that if appropriate decision-making procedures are crafted, *Peoples* and *BCE* actually *reduce* the likelihood of director liability. This is because the unfocused nature of the new duty makes it very difficult for any particular constituency to complain of mistreatment. So long as directors paper the record of their deliberations appropriately, they will almost always be able to tell a story about why they did what they did, and how it advanced the interests of the corporation *as a whole* and *in the long term*, that passes muster under the BJR, whether the story is fictitious or real. This might be a good thing for defalcating or opportunistic directors, but is not good news for shareholders, corporations (which may well see their cost of capital rise), or society as a whole.

3. Directors' duties in the UK

Andrea Lista

INTRODUCTION

Company directors are the principal management body of a corporation, and, as such, are responsible for making strategic decisions, and determining and executing corporate policy. Directors in the UK are expected to make the company a success, using their skills, experience and judgment. This overall idea of directors acting for the benefit of the company is rooted in the origins of the modern company.[1]

The actions of company directors in the UK are subject to specific legal obligations that have been traditionally identified by the jurisprudence of UK courts through a long stream of case law initiated at the end of the nineteenth century, after the introduction of the limited liability Act in 1855[2] and the first Companies Act in 1844.[3]

The most recent and current Companies Act (Companies Act 2006, hereafter CA 2006) for the first time codified UK directors' duties into statutory provisions. The aim of this chapter is to offer a critical analysis of UK directors' duties and of their conceptual evolution. The quest for the examination of directors' duties will follow their current statutory structure under CA 2006. Each relevant section will be analysed in light of the case law pertaining to it.

The incipit of this chapter is the definition of company director under UK law. The analysis will then shift onto directors' duties (fiduciary duties and duties of care, skills and diligence) as they appear in CA 2006.

Finally, the chapter will consider the consequences for breach of directors' duties.

[1] See, inter alia, *Re Smith and Fawcett Ltd* [1942] Ch 304, 306, *Punt v Symons* [1903] 2 Ch 506. *Automatic Self-Cleansing Filter Syndicate Co v Cunningham* [1906] 2 Ch 34.

[2] The Limited Liability Act 1855 (18 & 19 Vict. c.133).

[3] Joint Stock Companies Act 1844 (7 & 8 Vict. c.110).

THE DEFINITION OF COMPANY DIRECTOR UNDER UK LAW

Under section 250 of CA 2006, the definition of director comprises any person occupying the position of director, regardless of whether he is officially named as one.

The term 'director' is seen as wider than simply including a person who has been validly appointed as a director and can also encompass de facto directors and shadow directors. The rationale for this broad and somehow not circumscribed definition lies with the fact that directors in the UK are, as it will be readily appreciated, subject to a series of duties which could be easily circumvented had the concept of director been well defined and specific. An 'open' definition allows a certain amount of discretion to be exercised by courts on a case-by-case basis.[4]

A *de facto director* is a person who assumes to act as a director without having been validly appointed. He is held out as a director by the company, and claims and purports to be a director, although never actually or validly appointed as such. In *Re Hydrodam (Corby) Ltd*,[5] Millett LJ defined a de facto director as:

> a person who assumes to act as a director. He is held out as a director by the company, and claims and purports to be a director, although never actually or validly appointed as such. To establish that a person was a de facto director of a company it is necessary to plead and prove that he undertook functions in relation to the company which could properly be discharged only by a director. It is not sufficient to show that he was concerned in the management of the company's affairs or undertook tasks in relation to its business which can properly be performed by a manager below board level.

Different elements will be taken into account by courts to determine the status of a de facto director, including, inter alia, whether the individual in question was held as a director, by the company, used the title, was in possession of management information etc.[6] Going above and beyond official titles and definitions, the pivotal question in determining whether

---

4 For instance, had CA 2006 referred to company directors as the persons officially appointed as such, people effectively controlling companies could have avoided to be subject to directors duties just by virtue of the fact they were never officially appointed as directors.

5 [1994] 2 BCLC 180 at para. 183.

6 See Secretary of State for Trade and Industry *v. Kaczer* [1999] 2 BCLC 351 (CA); *Secretary of State for Trade and Industry v. Tjolle* [1998] 1 BCLC 333 and *Secretary of State for Trade and Industry v. Deverell* [2001] Ch 340 (CA).

a person is a de facto director appears to revolve around the participation of the individual concerned in the governing corporate structure and the notional boardroom.[7]

By contrast, a shadow director claims not to have been appointed and is defined by section 251(1), CA 2006 as: 'A person in accordance with whose directions or instructions the directors of the company are accustomed to act.' This definition is also followed in section 251 of the Insolvency Act 1986 (IA 1986) and section 22(5) of the Company Directors Disqualification Act 1986 (CDDA 1986). In *Ultraframe (UK) Ltd v Fielding*[8] the High Court clarified a number of matters concerning shadow directors and de facto directors:

> Firstly, in relation to the question of who must be accustomed to act, this means that a governing majority of the board must be accustomed to act in accordance with the directions or instructions of the alleged shadow director. The purpose of the legislation is to catch a person who effectively controls the running of the company by controlling the board. Therefore, a person is unlikely to be within the definition of a shadow director if only one or two directors on a board of several directors follow his instruction.
>
> On the question of how must the directors react to the instructions, the directors must do something in conformity with such instructions. It is not sufficient for the alleged shadow director simply to give instructions to the directors; his instructions must be translated into action by the board.
>
> The directors must act on the alleged shadow director's directions as a matter of regular practice; it must be a regular course of conduct of the directors over a period of time.

DIRECTORS' DUTIES: THE GENERAL PICTURE AND THE STATUTORY STATEMENT OF CA 2006

The board of directors is the management body of a company and must act for its benefit; thus, it is not a surprise that company directors are traditionally viewed as fiduciaries.

The roots of the idea of directors as fiduciaries can be traced to the origins of the modern company structure, when companies were created through a deed of settlement which generally avowed the directors to be trustees of the funds and assets of the business undertaking.[9] As a result, in the past when courts were confronted with wayward directors, they were

---

7 See B. Hannigan, *Company Law*, OUP 2009, p.141.

8 Court of Appeal, Civil Division, December 12, 2003, [2003] EWCA Civ 1805.

9 See S. Sealy, 'The director as trustee' [1967] *CLJ* 83.

able to construe the fiduciary duties of directors on the basis of a sort of predefined template in the form of trustees' obligations.

In *Re Lands Allotment Co*,[10] Lindley LJ held that:

> Although directors are not properly speaking trustees, yet they have always been considered and treated as trustees of money which comes to their hands or which is actually under their control; and ever since joint stock companies were invented directors have been held liable to make good moneys which they have misapplied upon the same footing as if they were trustees . . .

In conjunction with the concept of fiduciary duties, the common law also construed the concept of duties of care and skill of directors,[11] a sort of generic legal *vademecum* which indicates the level of diligence directors need to exercise in discharging their functions.

Both fiduciaries' duties and duties of care and skills have been crystallised and codified for the first time by CA 2006. Prior to the drafting of the new Act, the Company Law Review Group was tasked with re-working the framework of company law. Much debate surrounded the work of the steering group, which culminated into the introduction of the following statutory statements on directors 'duties:

- s. 171: Duty to act within powers
- s. 172: Duty to promote the success of the company
- s. 173: Duty to exercise independent judgment
- s. 174: Duty to exercise reasonable care, skill and diligence
- s. 175: Duty to avoid conflicts of interest
- s. 176: Duty not to accept benefits from third parties
- s. 177: Duty to declare interest in proposed transaction or arrangement

These sections will be considered in turn.

Section 170, Scope and Nature of General Duties

Section 170, CA 2006 provides:

(1) The general duties specified in sections 171 to 177 are owed by a director of a company to the company.

---

10 [1894] 1 Ch 616.

11 *Re City Equitable Fire Insurance Co* [1925] Ch 407; *Dorchester Finance Co Ltd v Stebbing* [1989] BCLC 498; *Norman v Theodore Goddard* [1991] BCLC 1028.

(2) A person who ceases to be a director continues to be subject–

(a) to the duty in section 175 (duty to avoid conflicts of interest) as regards the exploitation of any property, information or opportunity of which he became aware at a time when he was a director, and

(b) to the duty in section 176 (duty not to accept benefits from third parties) as regards things done or omitted by him before he ceased to be a director. To that extent those duties apply to a former director as to a director, subject to any necessary adaptations.

(3) The general duties are based on certain common law rules and equitable principles as they apply in relation to directors and have effect in place of those rules and principles as regards the duties owed to a company by a director.

(4) The general duties shall be interpreted and applied in the same way as common law rules or equitable principles, and regard shall be had to the corresponding common law rules and equitable principles in interpreting and applying the general duties.

(5) The general duties apply to shadow directors where, and to the extent that, the corresponding common law rules or equitable principles so apply.

The basic principle rooted in common law is that directors owe their duties to the company regarded as a separate legal entity. This principle, elaborated through the case law, has been codified for the first time by CA 2006.

Section 170 encompasses that basic principle elaborated by the case law since the outset of UK company law. In *Percival v Wright*,[12] the directors offered to purchase the shares held by the company's members without disclosing that they were negotiating the sale of the company with an outsider at a higher price. The shareholders claimed the sale of the company was unlawful as the directors were in breach of their fiduciary duty to them for non-disclosure. The claim was rejected by the court as the duty was held to be owed to the company.

Under specific circumstances, courts may consider that the relationships between directors and shareholders within a specific company may give rise to fiduciary duties owed to the members. This happened in the decision of the New Zealand court of Appeal in *Coleman v Mayers*[13] cited

---

[12] [1902] 2 Ch 421.

[13] [1977] 2 NZLR 255, cited with approval by British courts (see, inter alia, *Brunninghausen v Glavanics* [1999] 46 NCSW LR 538).

with approval by British courts.[14] In *Coleman v Mayers*, due to the family nature of the company and the personal guidance usually offered by the management to shareholders, directors were held to owe fiduciary duties to shareholders (including the duty of not misleading them on the sale of shares of the company).

In the past, another issue that arose was whether directors owe a duty to creditors. On this, south-Pacific courts have taken the lead. In *Kinsela v Russell Kinsela Pty Ltd*[15] the court stated that:

> In a solvent company the proprietary interests of the shareholders entitle them as a general body to be regarded as the company when questions of the duty of directors arise . . . But where a company is insolvent the interests of the creditors intrude. They become prospectively entitled, through the mechanism of liquidation, to displace the power of the shareholders and directors to deal with the company's assets.

This passage was cited with approval by the English Court of Appeal in *West Mercia Safetywear Ltd v Dodd.*[16] *In Re Pantone 485 Ltd*,[17] the High Court, emphasised that:

> Where the company is insolvent, the human equivalent of the company for the purposes of the directors' fiduciary duties is the company's creditors as a whole, ie its general creditors. It follows that if the directors act consistently with the interests of the general creditors but inconsistently with the interest of a creditor or section of creditors with special rights in a winding-up, they do not act in breach of duty to the company.

This line of reasoning was also followed in *Colin Gwyer and Associates Ltd v London Wharf (Limehouse) Ltd*,[18] where it was held by the court that:

> As a matter of general law, and except in special circumstances which it is admitted by the defendants do not apply in this case, a director owes his fiduciary duties to the company only and not to any shareholder. In *Re Smith & Fawcett Ltd* . . . at p.306 Lord Greene MR held that directors 'must exercise their discretion bone fide in what they consider – not what a court may consider – is in the interests of the company, and not for any collateral purpose'. As this formulation indicates, the court will not consider that the directors have

---

14 See, inter alia, *Brunninghausen v Glavanics* [1999] 46 NCSW LR 538.

15 (1986) 10 ACLR 395.

16 [1988] BCLC 250 (see also, the speech of Lord Templeman in *Winkworth v Edward Baron Development Co Ltd* [1986] 1 WLR 1512). The issue has again come to the fore in two recent decisions of the Companies Court.

17 [2002] 1 BCLC 266.

18 [2003] BCC 885.

acted in breach of duty simply because in the court's opinion the exercise of their discretion was not in the company's interests. On the other hand, the court does insist that it is the directors and not some other person who determines how the board should exercise its powers. Directors must exercise their own, independent judgment when reaching a decision.

Section 171 and Duty to Act Within Constitution and Powers

Section 171, CA 2006 provides that:

> A director of a company must–
>
> (a) act in accordance with the company's constitution, and
> (b) only exercise powers for the purposes for which they are conferred.

This section crystallises the traditional common law proper purpose rule, i.e., the obligation to act bona fide in the best interests of the company and the relative concept of exercising powers for a proper purpose, i.e., not for a collateral, personal or sectional aim.[19] Section 171 subdivides that obligation into two separate duties: (a) the duty to act in accordance with the company's constitution, and (b) the duty to only exercise powers for the purposes for which they are conferred.

Section 171(a) demands that company directors are bound to respect the allocation of powers stemming from the articles of association; this typically means that directors are 'responsible for the management of the company's business for which purpose they may exercise all the powers of the company'.[20]

Section 171(a) encompasses the idea of the relationship between the board and shareholders enshrined in the articles of association and seen as a contract defining the powers and the role of the board as management body of the corporation. This concept was eloquently established in *Automatic Self-Cleaning Filter Syndicate Co Ltd v Cuninghamm*[21] and it is clearly reflected by CA 2006. This division of powers that define directors' duties is nevertheless, not of great relevance in small private companies where very often the same individuals act as shareholders and directors.

---

[19] See Hannigan, *Company Law*, note 7 above, p.179.

[20] See the Companies (Model Articles) Regulations 2008, SI 2008/3229, reg. 2, Sch 1, art. 3 (Ltd): reg. 4, Sch. 3, art. 3 (Plc).

[21] See note 1 above. See also, *Gramophone and Typewriter Ltd v Stanley* [1908] 2 KB 89, p. 98; *Salmon v Quin & Axtens Ltd* [1909] 1 Ch 311; *Howard Smith Ltd v Ampol Petroleum Ltd* [1974] AC 821, p.837; *Breckland Group Holdings Ltd v London & Suffolk Properties Ltd* [1989] BCLC 100.

In large public companies, on the other hand, this division of powers gives rise to the never-ending debate on corporate governance.

In addition to the above, section 171(b) of CA 2006 sets out the duty to only exercise powers for the purposes for which they are conferred, the so-called proper purpose rule. The foundation of the proper purpose rule arises from the idea that any managerial action needs to be taken for the best interest of, and needs to be ultimately beneficial for, the corporation. The 'two tier' obligation system enshrined in section 171 of CA 2006 substantially means that a director is first of all required to exercise his powers within the framework established by the company constitution. Nevertheless, any action will be judged at last vis-à-vis the proper purpose rule. This begs the question: what is the relationship between this 'two-tier' obligation enshrined in section 171 CA 2006? Can a director exercise his powers in a manner not germane to the articles of association, if that action fulfils the proper purpose rule? In order to answer this question, consideration needs to be devoted to the case law at the root of the section.

In *Howard Smith Ltd v Ampol Petroleum Ltd*, a case directly relevant to the matter at issue, a company named RW Millers was embroiled in a hostile takeover bid by a large petrol corporation called Ampol. The directors of RW Millers did not want Ampol to take over their company, as another company, Howard Smith, had proposed more favourable terms for taking over their company by offering guarantee of future employment to the directors of RW Millers. In order to aid the take-over by Howard Smith, the directors of RW Millers issued $10m of new shares, allegedly to finance the completion of two tankers. The new shares were instead allocated to Howard Smith Ltd with the effect of diluting the existing majority shareholding and impairing Ampol's rival bid. Without the allotment of new shares, Howard Smith Ltd had no hope of succeeding in taking over RW Millers. But with the new issue, Ampol could not complete its acquisition.

In assessing the case, the court first considered the actions of RW Millers within the framework established by the articles of association of the company. Was the allotment of new shares legitimate under the company constitution? Directors can exercise the power of allotting new shares for the purpose of attracting new capital. In this case, Mr Street J stated that the argument of the directors that the tanker purchase was the dominant purpose for the allotment of new shares was 'unreal and unconvincing'. Lord Willberforce added that:

> The extreme argument on one side is that, for validity, what is required is bona fide exercise of the power in the interests of the company: that once it is found that the directors were not motivated by self-interest – i.e. by a desire to retain

> their control of the company or their positions on the board – the matter is concluded in their favour and that the court will not inquire into the validity of their reasons for making the issue . . .
>
> It can be accepted, as one would only expect, that the majority of cases in which issues of shares are challenged in the courts are cases in which the vitiating element is the self-interest of the directors, or at least the purpose of the directors to preserve their own control of the management.
>
> Further it is correct to say that where the self-interest of the directors is involved, they will not be permitted to assert that their action was bona fide thought to be, or was, in the interest of the company; pleas to this effect have invariably been rejected . . . just as trustees who buy trust property are not permitted to assert that they paid a good price.[22]

The deviation from the proper purpose of the actions of RW Millers' directors was the decisive factor for asserting the illegitimacy of the allotment of new shares; the real scope of that action, was indeed, the protection of the self-interest of the directors.

Howard Smith Ltd v Ampol Petroleum Ltd does qualify the issue of the proper purpose and the concept of the illegitimacy of actions deviating from that template. Nevertheless, it does not address the question of whether directors can stray from the purpose of attribution of a power enshrined in the constitution in order to act in the best interest of the company.

The question was addressed in *Teck v Millar*,[23] where, similarly to *Howard Smith Ltd v Ampol Petroleum Ltd*, an allotment of new shares favoured the takeover of a specific company over a competitor against the wishes of an existing shareholder. The British Columbia Supreme Court held that an allotment of shares designed to defeat a takeover was proper even though it was made against the wishes of the existing shareholder and deprived him of control. Contrary to what happened in *Howard Smith Ltd v Ampol Petroleum Ltd*, in this case the allotment of new shares was legitimate as it was ultimately beneficial to the target company which obtained a better deal for the exploitation of very valuable mining rights. Berger J stressed that:

> provided the directors act in good faith they are entitled to consider the reputation, experience and policies of anyone seeking to take-over the company and

---

22 *Howard Smith Ltd v Ampol Petroleum Ltd* at p.834. See also *Hogg v Cramphorn* [1967] Ch 254), and *Piercy v S Mills & Co Ltd* [1920] 1 Ch 77. In *Piercy v S Mills*, the court declared an allotment of shares illegitimate on the basis that this was done 'simply and solely for the purpose of retaining control in the hands of the existing directors'.

23 (1972), 33 DLR (3d) 288 (BCSC).

> to use their power to protect the company if they decide on reasonable grounds, that a takeover will cause substantial damage to the company.[24]

If we interpret section 171 in light of *Teck v Millar*, this case arguably establishes a hierarchy between the two obligations enshrined in that section clarifying the solution in case of conflicts: the starting point is that under section 171, directors are required to act and exercise their powers within the framework established by the company constitution. Nevertheless, an ultra vires action outside the purpose of attribution for a specific power could be still considered legitimate if ultimately beneficial to the company intended as a separate legal entity.

The legislature has also intervened to ensure that directors exercise the power to allot shares for the benefit of the company. Chapter 2 of the CA 2006 requires that the power must not be exercised unless the directors are authorised to do so by the company in general meeting or by the articles. Such authority is limited to five years but can be granted with unlimited duration.

Section 172 and the Duty to Promote the Success of the Company

According to section 172, CA 2006:

> (1) A director of a company must act in the way he considers, in good faith, would be most likely to promote the success of the company for the benefit of its members as a whole, and in doing so have regard (amongst other matters) to–
>
> (a) the likely consequences of any decision in the long term,
> (b) the interests of the company's employees,
> (c) the need to foster the company's business relationships with suppliers, customers and others,
> (d) the impact of the company's operations on the community and the environment,
> (e) the desirability of the company maintaining a reputation for high standards of business conduct, and
> (f) the need to act fairly as between members of the company.
>
> (2) Where or to the extent that the purposes of the company consist of or include purposes other than the benefit of its members, subsection (1) has effect as if the reference to promoting the success of the company for the benefit of its members were to achieving those purposes.
> (3) The duty imposed by this section has effect subject to any enactment or rule of law requiring directors, in certain circumstances, to consider or act in the interests of creditors of the company.

---

24 Ibid.

At common law, the directors were subject to the duty to act in the best interest of the company as a separate legal entity and a general body.[25] In parallel to that duty, the jurisprudence created the duty to act in the interest of creditors in case of insolvency of the company.[26]

As established in the above, the duty to act in the best interest of the company is traditionally strictly linked to the common law obligation to exercise powers for a proper purpose. We have seen how under the current status quo, the proper purpose rule finds its statutory domicile in section 171, CA 2006.

The duty to act in the best interest of the company has been altered into the duty to promote the success of the company under section 172, CA 2006.

Section 172 is one of the most articulated sections dealing with directors' duties. For the purpose of the analysis of this chapter the sub-duties enshrined in section 172 will be considered in turn in the following.

Section 172 and the duty to act in good faith

According to section 172(1), a director must act in the way he considers, in good faith, would be most likely to promote the success of the company for the benefit of its members as a whole. Section 172(1) lays down a subjective test, which was elaborated for the first time in *Re Smith & Fawcett Ltd*. In this case, the company constitution allowed directors to refuse to register share transfers. After the death of Mr Fawcett, one of the two directors and shareholders, Mr Smith co-opted another director and refused to register a transfer of shares to the late Mr Fawcett's executors. Lord Greene MR held that, in absence of mala fides, this was proper, since:

> The principles to be applied in cases where the articles of a company confer a discretion on directors . . . are, for the present purposes, free from doubt. They must exercise their discretion bona fide in what they consider – not what a court may consider – is in the interests of the company, and not for any collateral purpose.[27]

The subjective test was further elaborated by subsequent case law. *In Regentcrest plc v Cohen*,[28] prior to a petition for winding up the company initiated by a creditor, the directors waived a claw-back claim which

---

[25] See *Smith & Fawcett and Gaiman v National Association for Mental Health* [1970] 2 All ER 362.

[26] See *West Mercia Safetywater Ltd v Dodd* [1988] BCLC 250.

[27] See note 1 above, p. 306.

[28] [2001] 2 BCLC 80.

the company had with two members of the board who, in return for the waiver, agreed to work for the company without remuneration for a period of years.

The liquidators brought a claim against the directors who waived the claw-back on the basis of breach of the duty to act in good faith in the best interest of the company. It was alleged that action could have not possibly been in the best interest of the company. In the judgment, Jonathan Parker LJ, stated at paragraph 120:

> No doubt, where it is clear that the act or omission under challenge resulted in substantial detriment to the company, the director will have a harder task persuading the court that he honestly believed it to be in the company's interest; but that does not detract from the subjective nature of the test.

Nevertheless, it was further emphasised that:

> The duty imposed on directors to act bona fide in the interests of the company is a subjective one . . . The question is not whether, viewed objectively by the court, the particular act or omission which is challenged was in fact in the interests of the company; still less is the question whether the court, had it been in the position of the director at the relevant time, might have acted differently. Rather, the question is whether the director honestly believed that his act or omission was in the interests of the company. The issue is as to the director's state of mind. No doubt, where it is clear that the act or omission under challenge resulted in substantial detriment to the company, the director will have a harder task persuading the court that he honestly believed it to be in the company's interest; but that does not detract from the subjective nature test.

In *Regentcrest plc v Cohen* the court, by applying 'subjective test', ultimately found that directors acted bona fide by 'waiving the claw-back claim' had the intention of maintaining a united board instead of allowing two of the directors to be engaged in litigation by the company. The fact that the action seems unreasonable to a third party even when directors are acting in the interest of the company will therefore not make the act a breach of fiduciary duty.

This was subsequently re-affirmed in *Extrasure Travel Insurances Ltd V Scattergood*,[29] where it was held that the fact that a director's alleged belief was unreasonable may provide evidence that it was not in fact honestly held at the time. Nevertheless, if after considering all the evidence it appears that the director indeed honestly believed he was acting in the best interest of the company, then he is not in breach of his duty merely because

---

29 [2003] 1 BCLC 59.

that belief appears to the trial judge to be unreasonable, or because his actions happen to cause injury to the company.[30]

The subjective test elaborated by the case law and enshrined in section 172, CA 2006, undoubtedly confers a certain amount of leeway on company directors, and might appear prima facie somehow disconnected. Nevertheless, it is important to emphasise that its rationale is rooted in the traditional reluctance of common law courts to interfere in company business and the day-to-day management of corporations. As Lord Willberforce eloquently and elegantly stated: 'There is no appeal on merits from management decisions to courts of law: nor will courts of law assume to act as a kind of supervisory board over decisions within the powers of management honestly arrived at.'[31] The line of reasoning for good faith enshrined into section 172, CA 2006 is therefore destined to make litigation in respect of the action of company directors highly unlikely. The possibility for directors using the subjective test of good faith as defence for their actions renders the success of litigation against this action quite remote. The advantage of this approach is that company directors are given business freedom with ability to rationally think and take decisions in the best interests of the company. Nevertheless, this does not necessary mean that company directors have carte blanche in their management actions. Under specific circumstances, e.g., when bad faith is relatively evident, the test of good faith no longer represents a safe harbour. In *Neptune (Vehicle Washing Equipment) Ltd v Fitzgerald*,[32] a director making the company pay a £100,000 ex gratia payment in his favour before retiring from the board could not utilise the subjective test of good faith in his defence.

Section 172 and the duty to promote the success of the company for the benefit of the members as a whole and the pluralistic approach

The duty to promote the success of the company as a whole represents an interesting innovation introduced by section 172. Traditionally, at common law the duty was to act bona fine in the best interests of the company, with the idea of the company as a commercial entity somehow prevailing vis-à-vis against the interest of the members.

The phrasing of section 172, 'to promote the success of the company for the benefit of the members as a whole' appears prima facie to suggest that the new statutory regime weighs the interest of the members higher

30 Ibid., at p.619.
31 See *Howard Smith Ltd v Ampol Petroleum Ltd*, note 21 above, pp.106–7.
32 [1995] 1 BCLC 352.

compared to the commercial entity. The rationale beneath this development can be found in the Company Law Review:

> We believe there is value in inserting a reference to the success of the company, since what is in view is not the individual interests of members, but their interests as members of an association with the purposes and the mutual arrangements embodied in the constitution; the objective is to be achieved by the directors successfully managing the complex of relationships and resources which comprise the company's undertaking.[33]

It has been suggested that the duty to promote the success of the company for the benefit of the members as a whole does not effectively alter the balance of interests in favour of shareholders. This is due to the fact that, apart from considering the interest of the member as a whole, directors are also bound by section 172 to consider the consequences of any decision in the long term, implicitly suggesting that, far from being disregarded, the interest of the commercial entity are still very much alive.[34]

Conversely, other authors pointed out that, being mentioned first, the benefit of the members collectively appears to retain a preponderant weight under the new regime.[35] It is opinion of this author, that the new statutory provision does put a new prominence on the 'membership' interests which in the past were not greatly emphasised by the case law. Nevertheless, the commercial entity still retains its utmost importance.

Far from being confined to the sphere of 'membership' and commercial entity, the duty to promote the success of a company under section 172 is also subject to the obligation to consider the long-term consequences of the actions, the need to foster business relationships, and to take into account the interests of 'stakeholders' like 'employees', 'suppliers', 'customers', impact of company in 'community and environment', and 'the likely long-term consequences of any decision'. Promoting a long-term investment culture was a key objective of the government in introducing CA 2006.

Some companies may find themselves with share registers made up of hedge funds and active value investors who look only for short-term returns. Despite that, the relevance of the long view is something a board is required to consider.

---

[33] Company Law Review Steering Group, *Modern Company Law for a Competitive Economy: Developing the Framework* (URN 00/656), para. 3.51.

[34] See Hannigan, *Company Law*, note 7 above, p.211. See also Keay, 'Ascertaining the corporate objective: An entity maximisation and sustainability model' (2008) 71 *MLR* 663.

[35] See Hudson, A. *Charlesworth's Company Law* (18th ed.), Sweet & Maxwell, 2010, p.112.

The introduction of such an inclusive statement in section 172 is the outcome of the pluralistic debate which permeated the Company Law Review prior to the drafting of CA 2006. As will be readily appreciated, such a statement gives rise to some intricate issues.

The interpretation of the inclusive statement of section 172

Section 172(1), CA 2006 requires directors to consider the six aforementioned factors in exercising their duties. This gives rise to the conundrum of defining which interest should prevail in case of conflict of interests.

The six factors listed by section 172 are, indeed, of such a conceptual diversity as to ignite uncertainty in terms of definition of prevalence of one against the other. For instance, what is going to happen if a business decision made by directors capable of securing the employment position of workers, has severe repercussions on the environment? Which interest should prevail? The employees or the environment? Or would the need to foster business relationships overcome the customers' interest?

Should the matter become contentious, how would a director prove that he had complied with the section? It has been noted that a natural reading of the prefatory words of section 172(1) *requires* the director to consider the six factors; indeed, the incipit of this subsection is the verb 'must' and the section ends by saying that 'in doing so' regard is to be had to the six factors. Therefore, it is has been suggested that the verb 'must' 'qualifies the entire provision and so requires that the six factors are considered, even if the directors decide that they are not of overriding importance in any given context'.[36] Those factors become, arguably for the first time, issues which directors are bound to take into account.

Furthermore, it is clear by the wording of section 172 that the six elements thereby listed needs to be considered among 'other factors' which are not explicitly mentioned, and can therefore be established by the directors in view of the determination of the best course of action in order to promote the success of the company.

Above all, section 172, CA 2006 appears to encapsulate a sort of political statement of the recognition of the role played by companies within a society, and their relative social responsibility. The impact of corporate actions on the community and the environment, rather than the need to protect the interest of employees epitomises the political will to deviate from the traditional common law view of company law as a means of protecting the financial interest of corporation. Section 172 could be

---

[36] Ibid., p.115.

therefore interpreted as a statement of corporate responsibility towards a wide variety of stakeholders and the society as a whole.

Be as it may, contrary to the previous provisions of CA 2006 so far analysed in this chapter, past case law does not seem to aid the interpretation of section 172. Indeed, as previously mentioned, the case law, rather than focusing directly on the principle of promoting the success of the company, was primarily concerned with the need to ensure that directors acted in the best interest of the company. In *Howard Smith v Ampol Petroleum*, for instance, we have seen that the primary concern was the protection of the commercial interests of the company versus the personal interest of the directors.

If, in light of section 172, priority will be given to the protection of the 'members as a whole', it is possible that the short-term interest of shareholders wishing to maximise the return of their investment will clash with the long-term plans of the directors. Likewise, it is also plausible to theorise conflicts of interests between members whereby some shareholders will favour a long-term plan rather than a short-time profit. In this regard, it seems clear from past case law that directors cannot favour a specific class of shareholders by taking actions which can adversely affect the interest of a different class. The leading authority is *Mutual Life Insurance Co of New York v Rank Organisation Ltd*,[37] where an entertainment company decided to offer 20 million ordinary shares to the public, with a preference to existing shareholders based in the US and Canada.

The treatment of the American and Canadian shareholders was not considered unfair, because their shareholdings and rights had not been affected. Rank shareholders had no right to expect their share interest to remain in constant proportion to the others' in the company forever.

The last subsection of section 172 compels directors, under certain circumstances, to consider or act in the interests of creditors of the company. This subsection needs to be read in conjunction with potential liabilities arising in case of wrongful trading under section 214 of Insolvency Act 1986 (i.e., continuing trading after a point of non-return is reached and it is clear that the company will become insolvent).

The idea of directors owing duties to creditors in cases of insolvency is deep-rooted in the case law, and conceptually based on the idea of compensating for the transfer of business risk to creditors caused by the principle of limited liability. By virtue of this principle, and its underlying consequence that the liability of shareholders is confined to the amount of shares they own, the business risk is effectively translated onto the

---

[37] [1985] BCLC 11.

creditors (unless they are in the position to obtain security for their credit, of course). Nevertheless, once a company becomes insolvent, the principle of limited liability and its consequences on unsecured creditors have been mitigated by the judiciary intervention which created a duty for a director to take into account the interest of creditors. New Zealand and Australian case law lead the way in this regard,[38] and their approach has been fully endorsed by English courts.

As articulately put by the court in *Colin Gwyer & Associates Ltd v London Wharf (Limehouse) Ltd*:[39]

> As a matter of general law, and except in special circumstances which it is admitted by the defendants do not apply in this case, a director owes his fiduciary duties to the company only and not to any shareholder. In *Re Smith & Fawcett Ltd* . . . at p.306, Lord Greene MR held that directors 'must exercise their discretion bone fide in what they consider – not what a court may consider – is in the interests of the company, and not for any collateral purpose'. As this formulation indicates, the court will not consider that the directors have acted in breach of duty simply because in the court's opinion the exercise of their discretion was not in the company's interests. On the other hand, the court does insist that it is the directors and not some other person who determines how the board should exercise its powers. Directors must exercise their own, independent judgment when reaching a decision . . .
>
> Where directors fail to have regard to the separate interests of their company but act instead in the interests of what they perceive to be, for example, the interests of the group of companies of which the company is a member, the court will apply a different test. In *Charterbridge Corporation Ltd v Lloyds Bank Ltd* [1970] Ch 62 at p.74 Pennycuick J held that the proper test in the absence of actual separate consideration of the interests of the company, is whether an intelligent and honest man in the position of a director of the company concerned could, in the whole of the existing circumstances, have reasonably believed that the transaction was for the benefit of the company. The effect is therefore to substitute an objective test for the normal subjective one.

The tests referred to above apply when the company is solvent and a going concern. Where a company is insolvent or of doubtful solvency or on the verge of insolvency and it is the creditors' money which is at risk, the directors, when carrying out their duty to the company, must consider the interests of the creditors as paramount and take those into account when exercising their discretion. This principle has been recognised by the

---

[38] See *Walke v Wimborne* (1976) 50 ALJR 446 and *Nicholson v Permakraft (NZ) Ltd* [1985] 1 NZLR 242. For a detailed analysis see Dawson, 'Acting in the best interest of the company – for whom are Directors 'Trustees' (1984) 11 *NZULR* 68.

[39] See note 18, pp.72–5.

Court of Appeal in *Liquidator of West Mercia Safetywear Ltd v Dodds*,[40] applying the reasoning of Street CJ in *Kinsela v Russell Kinsela Pty Ltd*.[41] It was also applied in the Court of Appeal in *Brady v Brady*,[42] per Nourse LJ, where he stated that the interests of the company in this context are in reality the interests of the existing creditors alone.

As Lord Greene MR stated in *Re Smith & Fawcett*, directors must exercise their powers for proper purposes and not for any collateral purpose. This is another aspect of their fiduciary duties. If the directors can be shown to have exercised a power conferred by the articles for a purpose other than that for which it was given their conduct is open to challenge. It is no defence for them simply to respond by asserting that they believed in good faith that their conduct was in the interests of the company. While the court will not substitute its own view for that of the board, where on an objective review of the situation it finds that an alleged requirement was, for example, not urgent or critical it may have reason to doubt or discount the directors' assertions that they acted solely for that purpose. This principle was laid down by the Privy Council in *Howard Smith Ltd v Ampol Petroleum Ltd*.[43]

Overall, the statement enshrined in section 172, CA 2006 epitomises an attempt to change the direction of the law, although perhaps not a sturdy one. How far courts are prepared to go in enforcing the provision remains to be seen; in the meantime, it is submitted that the judicial approach to section 172 will not be stringent, as if so it could impair the day-to-day management of companies. Nevertheless, the factors listed in section 172 cannot be blatantly disregarded by company directors.

Section 173(1) and the Duty to Exercise Independent Judgement

Section 173(1), CA 2006 provides that:

> (1) A director of a company must exercise independent judgment.
> (2) This duty is not infringed by his acting
>
> (a) in accordance with an agreement duly entered into by the company that restricts the future exercise of discretion by its directors, or
> (b) in a way authorised by the company's constitution.

Section 173 compels directors to act by using independent judgement. This concept is the pinnacle of any fiduciary duty in the sense that it emphasises

---

40 (1988) 4 BCC 30 at p.33 per Dillon LJ.
41 (1986) 4 NSWLR 722 at p.730 (CA, NSW).
42 (1987) 3 BCC 535 at p.552.
43 See note 21 above.

the need for establishing individual responsibility and conversely the impossibility to circumvent duties by way of discharging them to third parties.

Yet again, this section represents the crystallisation of long-standing and consolidated case law on the obligation of directors not to fetter their discretion. Contrary to shareholders who are indeed able to contract on how they will vote in the future, directors are forbidden from doing this. This is so even in the case where there is no personal gain to the director.

In *Thorby v Goldberg*,[44] the directors agreed to allot shares in a particular way in the future within the context of a wider restructuring scheme. After they failed to do so at a later stage, an action was brought against them in order to force them to honour the agreement. The court compelled the directors to fulfil the past agreement rejecting their claim of invalid fettering of their discretion. It was held that, considering that the directors took into account the interest of the company at the time of the agreement, the agreement was valid. The directors did not invalidly fetter their discretion; rather, they had already exercised it.

In *Re County Palatine Loan & Discount Co; Cartmell's Case*,[45] it was, furthermore held that the board may not delegate its discretion to others in the absence of express authority. Such an approach was fully embraced by the Court of Appeal in *Fulham Football Club Ltd v Cabra Estates plc*,[46] where a clear distinction was made between directors fettering their discretion (which is forbidden), and directors exercising their discretion in a way that restricts their future actions, which is a permissible conduct.

Overall, according to section 173(2)(b), CA 2006, the duty to exercise independent judgement is not infringed by a director acting within the framework of the company constitution. This entails that directors may legitimately delegate their powers to the extent provided by the constitution of the corporation. The extent of the possibility for a director to delegate his powers has been subject to scrutiny in *Re Barings plc (No. 5)*,[47] where it was held that:

> (i) Directors have, both collectively and individually, a continuing duty to acquire and maintain a sufficient knowledge and understanding of the company's business to enable them properly to discharge their duties as directors. (ii) Whilst directors are entitled (subject to the articles of association of the company) to delegate particular functions to those below them in the management chain, and to trust their competence and integrity to a reasonable

44 (1964) 112 CLR 597.
45 (1874) 9 Ch App 691, 43 LJ Ch 588.
46 [1994] 1 BCLC 363.
47 [1999] 1 BCLC 433 at p.489, approved [2000] 1 BCLC 523 at pp.535–6, CA.

extent, the exercise of the power of delegation does not absolve a director from the duty to supervise the discharge of the delegated functions. (iii) No rule of universal application can be formulated as to the duty referred to in (ii) above. The extent of the duty, and the question whether it has been discharged, must depend on the facts of each particular case, including the director's role in the management of the company.

Section 174 and the Duty to Exercise Reasonable Care, Skill and Diligence

According to section 174:

(1) A director of a company must exercise reasonable care, skill and diligence.
(2) This means the care, skill and diligence that would be exercised by a reasonably diligent person with–

  (a) the general knowledge, skill and experience that may reasonably be expected of a person carrying out the functions carried out by the director in relation to the company, and
  (b) the general knowledge, skill and experience that the director has.

The concept of the duty of care, skill and diligence is deeply rooted in UK company law and has been elaborated by the case law to complement the fiduciary duties directors owe to companies. In light of section 174, in discharging their duties directors are bound to exercise reasonable care, skill and diligence. One of the most controversial issues that arose from past case law was related to the nature of the test to assess such duties.

This question was faced for the first time in *Re City Equitable Fire Insurance Co. Ltd*,[48] where Romer J held that:

> There are, in addition, one or two other general propositions that seem to be warranted by the reported cases:
>
> (1) A director need not exhibit in the performance of his duties a greater degree of skill than may reasonably be expected from a person of his knowledge and experience. A director of a life insurance company, for instance, does not guarantee that he has the skill of an actuary or of a physician.
> (2) A director is not bound to give continuous attention to the affairs of his company. His duties are of an intermittent nature to be performed at periodical board meetings, and at meetings of any committee of the board upon which he happens to be placed. He is not, however, bound to attend all such meetings, though he ought to attend whenever, in the circumstances, he is reasonably able to do so.
> (3) In respect of all duties that, having regard to the exigencies of business, and the articles of association, may properly be left to some other official,

---

48 See note 11 above.

> a director is, in the absence of grounds for suspicion, justified in trusting that official to perform such duties honestly.

The test laid down by Romer J was very much of a subjective nature, meaning that a director was to have been judged to his own, subjective standard of ability, knowledge and experience, and not vis-à-vis any objective criterion. Furthermore, directors were not expected to give continuous attention to the company management.

The subjective test was subsequently modified first in relation to the assessment of the duties of executive directors. In *Lister v Romford Ice and Cold Storage Co. Ltd*,[49] it was held that in a case when a director has a service contract with a company, there is an implied term in such a contract whereby the director will use reasonable skill in discharging the duties of the office based on what might reasonably be expected from a person occupying his position.

This objective test was further extended to all directors in *Norman v Theodore Goddard*[50] the standard of care expected of directors was that of a reasonably diligent person having the knowledge, skill and experience both of a person carrying out that director's functions and of that person. In *Norman v Goddard* the test assumed a dual basis, both subjective and objective complementing the one previously elaborated in *Equitable Fire Insurance*.

The new 'two-tier' test was fully acknowledged and applied by Hoffmann LJ in *Re D'Jan of London Ltd*,[51] where a director failed to read an insurance contract and to consequently exercise the duty of disclosure of specific information to the insurer. As a result, the insurance policy was declared void, and the duties of care and skill and diligence of the director in question were questioned. Hoffmann LJ held that:

> I do not say that a director must always read the whole of every document which he signs. If he signs an agreement running to 60 pages of turgid legal prose on the assurance of his solicitor that it accurately reflects the board's instructions, he may well be excused from reading it all himself. But this was an extremely simple document asking a few questions which Mr D'Jan was the best person to answer.

This scenario triggered the violation the duties of care and skill and diligence, and the consequent personal liability of the director concerned vis-à-vis the company.

---

49 [1957] AC 555.

50 See note 11 above.

51 [1993] BCC 646 at p.648, see also *Cohen v Selby* [2001] 1 BCLC 176, CA.

By focusing the assessment of the duty of care, skills and diligence on the general knowledge, skill and experience that may reasonably be expected of a person carrying out the functions carried out by the director in relation to the company, and, the general knowledge, skill and experience that the director has, section 174 clearly appears to crystallise the test which was first elaborated in *Norman v Goddard*, and consolidated by the subsequent case law.

As far as the element of continuity of attention to the corporate business is concerned, section 174 is silent. Nevertheless, things have evolved since *Equitable Fire Insurance*, and in *Dorchester Finance Co. Ltd v Stebbing*,[52] two non-executive directors were held in breach of duties of care, skill and diligence due to the failure of attending board meetings of a subsidiary company even though it was shown that it was not commercial practice to do so.

Section 175 and the Duty to Avoid Conflicts of Interest

The duty to avoid conflicts of interest is enshrined into section 175, which recites as follows:

> (1) A director of a company must avoid a situation in which he has, or can have, a direct or indirect interest that conflicts, or possibly may conflict, with the interests of the company.
> (2) This applies in particular to the exploitation of any property, information or opportunity (and it is immaterial whether the company could take advantage of the property, information or opportunity).
> (3) This duty does not apply to a conflict of interest arising in relation to a transaction or arrangement with the company.
> (4) This duty is not infringed–
>
> (a) if the situation cannot reasonably be regarded as likely to give rise to a conflict of interest; or
> (b) if the matter has been authorised by the directors.
>
> (5) Authorisation may be given by the directors–
>
> (a) where the company is a private company and nothing in the company's constitution invalidates such authorisation, by the matter being proposed to and authorised by the directors; or
> (b) where the company is a public company and its constitution includes provision enabling the directors to authorise the matter, by the matter being proposed to and authorised by them in accordance with the constitution.

52 See note 11 above.

(6) The authorisation is effective only if–

(a) any requirement as to the quorum at the meeting at which the matter is considered is met without counting the director in question or any other interested director, and
(b) the matter was agreed to without their voting or would have been agreed to if their votes had not been counted.

(7) Any reference in this section to a conflict of interest includes a conflict of interest and duty and a conflict of duties.

Section 175 is a very articulated statement and deals with both conceptual issues and procedures for avoiding breaches, which we shall consider in turn in the following.

The underlining idea behind the duty to avoid conflict of interests is conceptually linked with the core essence of fiduciary duties, and with the concept of duty of loyalty.[53]

Consequently, liability under section 175 is destined to arise whenever a conflict or a possible conflict of interest[54] is created between the interest of the director and the company. A director must avoid a situation in which he or she: 'has, or can have, a direct or indirect interest that conflicts, or possibly may conflict, with the interests of the company'.

This is very broad definition indeed, capable of covering both actual and potential conflicts and direct and indirect interests. It applies both to a conflict of interest and a conflict of duty, i.e., between the personal interest of the director and the duty to favour the interest of the company, or when there is a conflict between duties that a director of two companies owe to the two separate corporations.[55]

It is worth emphasising that multiple directorships are perfectly legitimate under common law.[56] Nevertheless, that scenario invariably gives rise to concerns in terms of conflicts of interests. That is the reason why in *Bristol and West Building Society v Mothew*,[57] Millett LJ held that 'a fiduciary who acts for two principals with potentially competing interests without the informed consent of both is in breach of the obligation of

---

[53] See Conaglen, 'The Nature and Function of Fiduciary Loyalty' (2005) 121 *LQR* 452.

[54] See *Boardman v Phillips* [1966] 3 All ER 721.

[55] See *Transvaal Lands Co v New Belgium (Transvaal) Land and Development Co* [1914] 2 Ch 488.

[56] See *London and Mashonaland Exploration Co Ltd v New Mashonaland Exploration Co Ltd* [1891] WN 165, where it was held that no rule of law prevented a director from taking office as a director of a competitor company.

[57] *Bristol and West Building Society v Mothew* [1998] Ch 1 18, CA.

undivided loyalty; he puts himself in a position where his duty to one principal may conflict with his duty to the other'.

Disclosure of the multiple positions occupied is, thus, the first step to be undertaken by directors in order to avoid of being caught by section 175. Nevertheless, under specific circumstances, e.g., in cases where confidentiality issues arise within the context of business transactions, that might not suffice, leaving resignation as the only possible course of action.

Apart from the peculiarities arising from scenarios of multiple directorships, the duty to avoid conflict of interests encompasses various scenarios illustrated by the case law. In *Cook v Deeks*,[58] two of the three directors of a company took a valuable contract in their names diverting it from the company and were held in breach of fiduciary duties.

In *Industrial Development Consultants Ltd v Cooley*,[59] Mr Cooley was an architect employed as managing director of Industrial Development Consultants Ltd., part of IDC Group Ltd. The Eastern Gas Board had a lucrative project pending to design a depot in Letchworth. Mr Cooley was told that the gas board did not want to contract with a firm, but directly with him. Mr Cooley then told the board of IDC Group that he was unwell and requested he be allowed to resign from his job on early notice. They acquiesced and accepted his resignation. He then undertook the Letchworth design work for the gas board on his own account. Industrial Development Consultants found out and sued him for breach of his duty of loyalty.

Roskill J held that even though there was no chance of IDC getting the contract, if they had been told they would not have released Mr Cooley, so he was held accountable for the benefits he received. Roskill J rejected the argument that because he had made it clear in his discussions with the gas board that he was speaking in a private capacity, Mr Cooley was under no fiduciary duty. He had 'one capacity and one capacity only in which he was carrying on business at that time. That capacity was as managing director of the plaintiffs'.

In *Bhullar v Bhullar*,[60] a recent authority on conflict of interest, the dispute revolved around two directors of a family-owned company who acquired an estate in proximity of the company without disclosing the opportunity for purchase to the company. Jonathan Parker LJ held that there was a clear breach of the rule that directors must avoid a conflict of interest:

---

[58] [1916] UKPC 10; [1916] 1 AC 554 (23 February 1916) (on appeal from Ontario).

[59] [1972] 1 WLR 443.

[60] [2003] EWCA Civ 424.

> Like the defendant in *Industrial Development Consultants Ltd v Cooley*, the appellants in the instant case had, at the material time, one capacity and one capacity only in which they were carrying on business, namely as directors of the Company. In that capacity, they were in a fiduciary relationship with the Company. At the material time, the Company was still trading, albeit that negotiations (ultimately unsuccessful) for a division of its assets and business were on foot. As Inderjit accepted in cross-examination, it would have been 'worthwhile' for the company to have acquired the Property. Although the reasons why it would have been 'worthwhile' were not explored in evidence, it seems obvious that the opportunity to acquire the Property would have been commercially attractive to the Company, given its proximity to Springbank Works. Whether the Company could or would have taken that opportunity, had it been made aware of it, is not to the point: the existence of the opportunity was information which it was relevant for the Company to know, and it follows that the appellants were under a duty to communicate it to the Company. The anxiety which the appellants plainly felt as to the propriety of purchasing the Property through Silvercrest without first disclosing their intentions to their co-directors – anxiety which led Inderjit to seek legal advice from the Company's solicitor – is, in my view, eloquent of the existence of a possible conflict of duty and interest.[61]

In case a director finds himself/herself in a position of conflict of interests, the immediate course of action is disclosure[62] or resignation. As established in the aforementioned *Industrial Development Consultants Ltd v Cooley* resignation per se would not represent a safe harbour as the omission of the disclosure of the conflict of interest might still trigger a retroactive liability of the former director.

In recent times, the issue of disclosure has been assessed by the Court of Appeal in *Item Software (UK) Ltd v Fassihi*[63] where a director undertook parallel negotiations for a contract both on behalf of the company and on a personal level, without disclosing his personal interest. It was held that the High Court had not erred in finding that Mr Fassihi was under a duty as a director to disclose his own misconduct. It was furthermore noted that such a duty was an integral part of a director's fundamental duty to act in what he, in good faith, considers to be the best interest of the company. The directors are responsible for the success of the company's business and this is a central part to the business' strength. In this case, Mr Fassihi was unable to fulfil that duty of loyalty except by disclosing to Item his plan to acquire the contract for himself. The appeal on the disclosure issue was dismissed.

---

[61] Ibid., para.41.

[62] See *Industrial Development Consultants Ltd v Cooley*, note 58 above; *Bhullar v Bhullar*, ibid.; *Boardman v Phipps* [1967] 2 AC 46; *Movitex Ltd v Bulfield* [1988] BCLC 104; *Paragon Finance plc v Thackerar* [1999] 1 All ER 400.

[63] [2005] 2 BCLC 91.

In addition to the requirement of avoiding conflicts of interests, section 175(2) prohibits the exploitation of any property, information or opportunity (and it is immaterial whether the company could take advantage of the property, information or opportunity). The extent of this subsection can be interpreted in light of *Quarter Master UK Ltd v Pyke*,[64] where Paul Morgan QC sitting as deputy judge held:

> It is not because he has made a profit from trust property or a profit from his fiduciary position that the director is liable under the conflict rule. Rather, it is because, being in a fiduciary position, he has entered into a transaction, inconsistent with his fiduciary duty of loyalty to the company, which has yielded the profit and he has thereby misused his position. The opportunity to make the profit may not arise from the director's fiduciary position; he might just as well as have had the opportunity if he had not been in that position but even so his liability in respect of the profit arises because of the conflict of interest. In many cases, where the conflict rule applies, the director will also have taken advantage of the property of the company or of his fiduciary position but this will not always be so.

The most renowned authority on the no-profit duty is *Regal (Hastings) Ltd v Gulliver*.[65] Here, Regal Ltd owned a cinema in Hastings. The directors took out leases on two more, through a new subsidiary, to make the whole lot an attractive sale package. However, the landlord refused to negotiate the lease unless the share capital of the new subsidiary company was raised to £5,000. Regal Ltd could only afford to contribute for £2,000. Four directors then stepped in each putting in £500. The lease was signed and the business eventually sold, and the directors made a profit of nearly £3 per share. The buyers brought an action against the directors, claiming that this profit was in breach of their fiduciary duty to the company. They had not gained fully informed consent from the shareholders.

The House of Lords found that a director is in breach of his duties if he takes advantage of an opportunity that the corporation would otherwise have been interested in, but was unable to take the advantage. However the breach could have been resolved by ratification by the shareholders, which those involved neglected to do.

This brings us to the next step of our quest for the legal definition of section 175, namely the disapplications set out by section 175(3).

---

64 [2005] 1 BCLC 245.

65 [1942] UKHL 1.

Limitations of section 175

Under specific circumstances established in section 175, the conflict of interest will not ignite any legal consequence.

First, according to section 175(3), the duty does not apply to a conflict of interest arising in relation to a transaction or arrangement with the company.

Secondly, the non-conflict duty does not find application if the situation cannot reasonably be regarded as likely to give rise to a conflict of interest.

Thirdly, section 175(4)(b) empowers independent directors with the power to authorise a conflict of interest and profiting therefrom. This represents a major change in the law, as in the past directors seeking authorisation had no other option but to seek the consent of shareholders after full disclosure.[66]

The new power of independent directors to clear directors' conflicts of interests, represents a flexible method for dealing with directors' conflicts, and a large number of public and private companies are taking advantage of it. Companies wishing to use the procedure will only be allowed to do so under the following circumstances: in the case of public companies, there will be the need to amend articles of association in order to accommodate new rules enabling authorisation by the directors. Private companies incorporated before 1 October 2008, will need to enact a shareholders' resolution allowing conflicts to be authorised at director level, whereas private companies incorporated on or after 1 October 2008 will automatically be able to use the new procedure, provided their constitutions do not contain provisions to the contrary.

According to section 175, only directors who are independent of the conflict will be entitled to ratify the conflict of interests. In deciding so, they will need to take into account the need for each director to comply with his general duties to the company in making the decision, including the duty to act in the way he considers in good faith would be most likely to promote the success of the company. Furthermore, the terms on which the authorisation should be granted will need to be carefully scrutinised in terms of possible limitation of time or scope, or other possible conditional factors.[67]

---

[66] See *Netherlands Society Oranje' Inc v Kuys* [1973] 2 All ER 1222, p. 1227; *Attorney-General for Hong Kong v Reid* [1994] 1 AC 324 is advanced, further to the speech of Lord Browne-Wilkinson in *Westdeutsche Landesbank v Islington* [1996] AC 669, *Aberdeen Railway Co v Blaikie Bros* (1854) 1 Macq 461, 471; [1843–60] All ER Rep 249, 252.

[67] See Carpanini, Mackie, McDonald and Rosen, 'Directors prepare for the new law on conflicts of interests', Onswang Publications, September 2008.

Section 176 and the Duty Not to Accept Benefits from Third Parties

Section 176 states that:

(1) A director of a company must not accept a benefit from a third party conferred by reason of–

  (a) his being a director, or
  (b) his doing (or not doing) anything as director.

(2) A 'third party' means a person other than the company, an associated body corporate or a person acting on behalf of the company or an associated body corporate.
(3) Benefits received by a director from a person by whom his services (as a director or otherwise) are provided to the company are not regarded as conferred by a third party.
(4) This duty is not infringed if the acceptance of the benefit cannot reasonably be regarded as likely to give rise to a conflict of interest.
(5) Any reference in this section to a conflict of interest includes a conflict of interest and duty and a conflict of duties.

Section 176 imposes the duty on directors not to accept a benefit from a third party conferred by reason of his being a director, or his doing (or not doing) anything as director. This section which, in light of section 170(2)(b) finds application to former directors, appears to be somehow directly linked with section 175 enhancing its scope of application.

Yet again, the duty enshrined in section 176 represents the outcome of a codification process of principles stemming from the case law. In *Attorney-General for Hong Kong v Reid*,[68] *a former* Hong Kong Deputy Crown Prosecutor and then Acting Director of Public Prosecutions took bribes to obstruct prosecution of some criminals, and used the money to buy land. Due to his fiduciary relationship with the Hong Kong government, it was held that a bribe received by a fiduciary must be held on constructive trust from the moment of its receipt and consequently that any property acquired with that bribe is also held on constructive trust.

The same line of reasoning was applied in subsequent cases,[69] and

---

[68] *Attorney-General for Hong Kong v Reid* [1993] UKPC 36.

[69] See *Ocular Sciences Ltd v Aspect Vision Care Ltd* [1997] RPC 289; *Fyffes Group Ltd v Templeman* [2000] 2 Lloyd's Rep 643 (where this case was obiter); *Dubai Aluminium Company Ltd v Alawi* [2002] EWHC 2051; *Tesco Stores Ltd v Pook* [2003] EWHC 823; *Daraydan Holdings Ltd v Solland International Ltd* [2004] EWHC 622. In relation to interlocutory relief, such as Mareva injunctions, the *Lister v Stubbs* approach has also been displaced in favour of the approach in *Attorney-General v Reid: Mercedes Benz AG v Leiduck* [1996] AC 284, 300. This

then transposed into section 176. The duty thereby established can be nevertheless mitigated by various factors listed in section 176. First, there are exceptions related to benefits from related companies or service agreements.

Second, the section will not find application in cases where the acceptance of the benefit cannot reasonably be regarded as likely to give rise to a conflict of interest. This limitation covers ordinary commercial hospitality such as meals, free transport, gifts etc.

Section 177 and the Duty to Declare an Interest in a Proposed Transaction or Arrangement Under Section 177:

(1) If a director of a company is in any way, directly or indirectly, interested in a proposed transaction or arrangement with the company, he must declare the nature and extent of that interest to the other directors.
(2) The declaration may (but need not) be made–
  (a) at a meeting of the directors, or
  (b) by notice to the directors in accordance with–
    (i) section 184 (notice in writing), or
    (ii) section 185 (general notice).
(3) If a declaration of interest under this section proves to be, or becomes, inaccurate or incomplete, a further declaration must be made.
(4) Any declaration required by this section must be made before the company enters into the transaction or arrangement.
(5) This section does not require a declaration of an interest of which the director is not aware or where the director is not aware of the transaction or arrangement in question.

For this purpose a director is treated as being aware of matters of which he ought reasonably to be aware.

(6) A director need not declare an interest–
  (a) if it cannot reasonably be regarded as likely to give rise to a conflict of interest;
  (b) if, or to the extent that, the other directors are already aware of it (and for this purpose the other directors are treated as aware of anything of which they ought reasonably to be aware); or
  (c) if, or to the extent that, it concerns terms of his service contract that have been or are to be considered–
    (i) by a meeting of the directors, or
    (ii) by a committee of the directors appointed for the purpose under the company's constitution.

---

approach has not been followed in *Attorney-General v Blake* [1997] Ch 84, 96, per Sir Richard Scott VC; *Halifax Building Society v Thomas* [1996] Ch 217, 229, preferring the approach in *Lister v Stubbs*.

This section governs the scenario whereby a director has an interest in a proposed transaction with the company. This section has been devised in order to cover scenarios such as the one which arose in *Aberdeen Railway Co v Blaikie Bros*,[70] where a company was entitled to set aside a contract for the purchase of iron chairs which was concluded with a partnership due to the presence of one of the partners on the board of the company which signed the contract. This case epitomises the scenario pictured in section 177, with a director effectively the seller and purchaser of the goods. Lord Cranworth LC held that Aberdeen was not bound by the contract. The key points were expressed as follows:

> It may sometimes happen that the terms on which a trustee has dealt or attempted to deal with the estate or interest of those for whom he is a trustee, have been as good as could have been obtained from any other person – they may even at the time have been better. But still so inflexible is the rule that no inquiry on that subject is permitted. The English authorities on this head are numerous and uniform. Mr Blaikie's personal interest would lead him to an entirely opposite direction, would induce him to fix the price as high as possible. This is the very evil against which the rule in question is directed, and here I see nothing whatever to prevent its application.

Similarly, in *Movitext Ltd v Bulfield*,[71] the directors of a company leased an estate owned by them to the company, creating an obvious conflicting scenario.[72] The disclosure obligation enshrined in section 177 entails that any direct, indirect interest needs to be disclosed regardless of the fact that the director is not a party to the transaction.

In procedural terms, the interest might be declared through a declaration at a meeting of the board of directors or by means of a notice under section 184 or section 185. The declaration may be made in other ways which are not defined in the section. It has been suggested that for a director to acquire authorisation for continuing to have that interest in the transaction, a majority of the directors who have no interest in the

---

70 (1854) 1 Macq 461.

71 [1988] BCLC 104.

72 See also *Gwembe Valley Development Co Ltd v Koshy* [2004] 1 BCLC 131; *Ferraby v Hobson* (1847) 2 Ph 255; *Burrell v Burrel's Trustee* 1915 SC 333; *Aberdeen Ry. Co. v Blaikie Bros*, see note 66 above. The right to avoid a contract for non-disclosure is not affected by the provisions of the first EC Directive: *Coöperative Rabobank 'Vecht en Plassengerbeid' BA v Minderhoud* [1998] 2 BCLC 507, ECJ; *Parker v McKenna* (1874) L.R. 10 Ch.App. 96 at p.118, per Lord Cairns LC; *Transvaal Lands Co. v New Belgium (Transvaal) Land Co*, see note 54 above; *Costa Rica Ry. v Forwood* [1901] 1 Ch. 746, CA; *Newgate Stud Company v Penfold* [2004] EWHC 2993 (Ch).

transaction must agree to the company continuing with the transaction in which one of their number has an interest.[73]

Some interests, nevertheless, fall outside the scope of application of section 177. For instance the duty does not cover interest of which the director is not aware or where the director is not aware of the transaction or arrangement in question.

Furthermore, under section 177(5), a director need not declare an interest if it cannot reasonably be regarded as likely to give rise to a conflict of interest, or in case the other directors are already aware or ought to be aware of the interest at stake. Finally the obligation of disclosure does not concern terms related to service contracts that have been or are to be considered by a meeting of the directors, or by a committee of the directors appointed for the purpose under the company's constitution.

DIRECTORS' LIABILITY FOR BREACH OF DUTY

The breach of any of the duties enshrined in sections 172–177 will ignite liabilities of directors the nature of which is subject of scrutiny in the following.

Section 178(1) states that the consequences of breach (or threatened breach) of sections 171–177 are the same as would apply if the corresponding common law rule or equitable principle applied. Furthermore, the duties in those sections (with the exception of section 174 (duty to exercise reasonable care, skill and diligence)) are, accordingly, enforceable in the same way as any other fiduciary duty owed to a company by its directors that the consequences of any breach or threatened breach of a director.

This means that there is no codification of directors' liabilities arising from breach of duty, with the consequences for any breach are left to the principles arising from the aforementioned case law considered for each section above.

On a general level, the definition of a fiduciary under common law can be found in *Bristol & West Building Society v Mothew*,[74] where Millett LJ endorsed the observations of Southin J in *Girardet v Crease & Co*[75] as follows:

> The word 'fiduciary' is flung around now as if it applied to all breaches of duty by solicitors, directors of companies and so forth . . . That a lawyer can commit

---

73 See Hudson, *Company Law*, note 35 above, p.123.

74 *Bristol and West Building Society v Mothew* [1998] Ch 1, p.16.

75 (1987) 11 BCLR (2d) 361, 362.

> a breach of the special duty [of a fiduciary] . . . by entering into a contract with the client without full disclosure . . . and so forth is clear. But to say that simple carelessness in giving advice is such a breach is a perversion of words.[76]

This definition of fiduciary can be arguably transferred to company directors as the management body and trustees of the company assets,[77] with the duties owed by them intended as fiduciary duties. The classic statement relating to the position of directors as fiduciaries was expressed by Lindley LJ in *Re Lands Allotment Co*[78] as follows:

> Although directors are not properly speaking trustees, yet they have always been considered and treated as trustees of money which comes to their hands or which is actually under their control; and ever since joint stock companies were invented directors have been liable to make good monies which they have misapplied upon the same footing as if they were trustees.

As for the nature of a claim against a director, the foundation for this can be found in *Foskett v McKeown*,[79] in which it was held that:

> A beneficiary's claim against a trustee for breach of trust is a personal claim. It does not entitle him to priority over the trustee's general creditors unless he can trace the trust property into its product and establish a proprietary interest in the proceeds. If the beneficiary is unable to trace the trust property into its proceeds, he still has a personal claim against the trustee, but his claim will be unsecured. The beneficiary's proprietary claims to the trust property or its traceable proceeds can be maintained against the wrongdoer and anyone who derives title from him except a bona fide purchaser for value without notice of the breach of trust. The same rules apply even where there have been numerous successive transactions, so long as the tracing exercise is successful and no bona fide purchaser for value without notice has intervened.

Overall, the main consequence of interpreting the position of the directors as trustees, and their duties as per CA 2006 as fiduciary is that any breach of fiduciary duty would entail the obligation on the directors' part to reinstate the trust assets, to account for any profit made and make good of the losses.[80]

From this perspective, the position of a director in breach of his fiduciary duties seems to occupy a particular position within the common law

---

[76] Ibid.
[77] See Hannigan, *Company Law*, note 7 above, p.303.
[78] See note 10 above, p.63.
[79] [2000] UKHL 29.
[80] See Hannigan, *Company Law*, note 7 abovc, p.304.

system. The case law indeed appears to testify that the director's obligation to make good the losses suffered by a company is applied in a more stringent way compared to the obligation to pay damages.[81]

[81] See *Ferraby v Hobson* (1847) 2 Ph 255; *Burrell v Burrell's Trustee* 1915 SC 333; *Aberdeen Ry. Co. v Blaikie Bros.* see note 66 above. The right to avoid a contract for non-disclosure is not affected by the provisions of the first EC Directive: *Coöperative Rabobank 'Vecht en Plassengerbeid' BA v Minderhoud*, note 72 above; *Parker v McKenna* (1874) LR 10 Ch. App. 96 at p.118, per Lord Cairns LC; *Transvaal Lands Co. v New Belgium (Transvaal) Land, Co.* [1914] 2 Ch. 488, CA; *Costa Rica Ry. v Forwood* [1901] 1 Ch. 746, CA; *Newgate Stud Company v Penfold* [2004] EWHC 2993 (Ch), [1991] BCLC 1045; [1992] BCLC 1084. See also *Re Neptune (Vehicle Washing Equipment) Ltd (No. 1)* [1995] 1 BCLC.

4. Almost codified almost 20 years on: the effect of the Companies Act 1993 on the development of directors' duties in New Zealand

Susan Watson

The New Zealand Companies Act 1993 arose out of a lengthy law reform process given its conceptual grunt by the work of the Law Commission. Despite the inevitable tinkering by parliamentarians and the ubiquitous drafts people, the final version of the Act remained broadly similar to the Law Commission draft. One of the most interesting features of the Act is that it was an early attempt to codify directors' duties; other jurisdictions have since set down common law duties into legislation so the New Zealand experience in the almost 20 years since the Act came into force provides an interesting case study of the consequences of crystallising somewhat ephemeral common law duties into statutory form.

The first objective of the Companies Act 1993, set out in its long title, is to reaffirm the value of the company as a means of achieving economic and social benefits through the aggregation of capital for productive purposes, the spreading of economic risk, and the taking of business risks. Appropriate legislative controls on the operation of companies are key to their continuing viability and key to governments around the world continuing to permit businesses to be operated in that form. With some statutorily mandated duties, the aim is to find ways to facilitate good decision-making, including mandating that those who manage a company, its directors, put the interests of the company before their own interests when the two may be in conflict and requiring that when they make decisions directors act in good faith. Broadly speaking, these duties are fiduciary in origin. Other duties imposed on directors aim to ensure that the shield of limited liability is not used by those who control companies to take unacceptable risks at the expense of creditors. In New Zealand there is a positive obligation on directors not to trade recklessly (in s 135), and an obligation not to allow the company to enter into obligations that it will not be able to perform (in s 136). There is also a statutory duty of care (in s 137) and a duty to comply with the Act and the constitution. Although explicitly not owed to creditors, these duties were included primarily to protect the interests of creditors. In this chapter, I do not discuss the application of the statutory duties relating to creditors, instead focusing on the statutory duties of honesty and loyalty.

Directors of companies have long been accepted as falling into the category of fiduciaries. Some commentators argue that far from exhorting moral behaviour, the fiduciary doctrine properly understood is 'far more cynical, functional and instrumentalist in outlook, focusing on lessening the danger that a fiduciary's undertaking will not be properly performed'.[1] Whilst there is no consensus over the range of obligations owed by fiduciaries, there can be no doubt that all fiduciaries owe fundamental obligations of loyalty to the interests of their beneficiaries.[2] Some of the duties of directors set out in ss 131–149 of the Companies Act 1993 stem from the equitable obligations of honesty and loyalty owed by directors to the company as beneficiary. With the exception of the duty to disclose interests, which in the Companies Act 1993 is a duty owed to shareholders individually; these statutory duties are expressed to be owed to the company.[3] The duty of directors to disclose share dealings, which, if it is fiduciary in nature must have been included for the benefit of shareholders, is a duty that is owed to individual shareholders.

New Zealand's Companies Act 1955 was modelled on the Companies Act 1948 (UK). In its 1989 report on the reform to the Act, the Law Commission commented that the law relating to the duties of directors was inaccessible, unclear, extremely difficult to enforce and in urgent need

---

[1] M Conaglen, 'The Nature and Function of Fiduciary Loyalty' (2005) 121 *LQR* 452, 454.

[2] For commentary suggesting that the duty of loyalty is not fiduciary, see R Flannigan, 'Reshaping the Duties of Directors', (2005) 84 *Can Bar Rev* 365 and M Conaglen, *Fiduciary Loyalty* (Hart Publishing, Oxford, 2010); but cf.: *Bristol & West Building Society v Mothew* [1998] Ch 1 and also *Aberdeen Railway Co Ltd v Blaikie Brothers* (1854) 1 Macq 461, discussed below, where the court clearly considered that Blaikie as a director was akin to a trustee. See also, T Frankel, *Fiduciary Law* (Oxford University Press, 2011).

[3] Section 169(3) confirms that the duty of good faith in s 131, the obligation to use powers for a proper purpose in s 133 and the duty relating to the use of company information are duties owed to the company and not to shareholders. However, the duty to disclose interests in s 140 and the duty to disclose share dealings in s 148 are duties owed to individual shareholders.

of reform.[4] In the Law Commission's view, the duties in the Companies Act 1993 were gleaned from a large volume of complex case law: 'it was time to distil the general principles from the cases and express them in a statute, to make them more accessible'.[5]

Opinion is divided on whether the statutory duties set out in the Companies Act 1993 attempt to, or succeed in, codifying the common law duties.[6] At the very least, the pre-existing case law remains relevant in understanding the origins of the rules and in assisting in interpreting them. Perhaps the statement of Heath J in *Benton v Priore*[7] that ss 131–138 of the Act 'should be seen as a restatement of basic duties [developed by the common law] in an endeavour to promote accessibility to the law' represents the predominant view.

DUTY OF GOOD FAITH

Section 131 states that, when exercising powers or performing duties, a director must act in good faith and what the director believes to be in the best interests of the company.[8] This duty is considered to be fundamental; indeed, the Law Commission favoured this duty prevailing over all others. The Law Commission recommendation did not survive in the final version of the Companies Act 1993, with no hierarchy of duties included. Nevertheless, as will be discussed further in this chapter, where there is a conflict between duties, the New Zealand courts have consistently held that section 131(1) prevails.

The management powers of the company are conferred on the board; that is the directors collectively in section 128. However, the statutory duty of good faith in section 131(1) is owed individually by each director to the company. Thus, when making decisions collectively as part of the board, each individual director must act in good faith and in the best interests of the company. Professor Sealy points out that the 'duty' of good faith is not

---

4 Law Commission, *Company Law: Reform and Restatement* NZLC R9, Wellington, Law Commission, 1989.

5 Ibid., para 185.

6 It was suggested in *Manukau City Council v Lawson* 21/5/99, Morris J, HC Auckland CP210/SW99 that the duties' provisions are a code. See N Campbell [2001] *CSLB* 53; P Watts [2001] *NZ Law Rev* 293; J Farrar, *Corporate Governance: Theories, Principles and Practice* (3rd ed.), Melbourne, Oxford University Press, 2008, 110.

7 *Benton v Priore* [2003] 1 NZLR 564, para 46, followed in *Sojourner v Robb* [2006] 3 NZLR 808.

8 Companies Act 1993, s 131(1).

so much a duty but rather grounds 'upon which a corporate decision may be challenged as irregular and held to be void or voidable'.[9] In determining this irregularity, the decision-making of each individual director who comprises the board and took part in the decision can be scrutinised. If the decisions of directors come under scrutiny, directors may be obliged to show not just that they acted in a way that they subjectively believed to be in the interests of the company, but that they took steps to consider all alternatives before deciding on a course of action.

The Law Commission favoured the test of what was in the best interests of the company being objective, so that the director had to hold the belief on reasonable grounds.[10] This version of section 131 would have resembled the equivalent Australian provision where directors are required to exercise their powers and discharge their duties in good faith in the best interests of the corporation and for a proper purpose.[11] In the final version of the Companies Act 1993, however, the test was expressed as being subjective, based on what the director *actually* believes, an adoption of the approach of the English Court of Appeal in *Smith v Fawcett Ltd.*[12] The requirement to exercise powers for a proper purpose is included in section 133 and arguably imposes an objective element.[13] In Professor Sealy's view, the common law duty to act bona fide in the interests of the company as a whole is best given the meaning that a decision must be 'genuine', rather than merely 'in good faith', meaning honest.[14] In addition, in the application of section 131(1) by the courts it is becoming increasingly clear that any such belief held by directors must be reasonably held.

---

9 L S Sealy, '"Bona Fides" and "Proper Purposes" in Corporate Decisions' (1989) 15 *Mon LR* 265, 268.

10 Law Commission, *Company Law*, note 4 above, para 195. Some commentators consider that the Law Commission's draft version was preferable. See Tompkins J, 'Directing the Directors: The Duties of Directors under the Companies Act 1993' (1994) 2 *Waikato L Rev* 13, 19. The Australian provision, which requires directors to exercise their powers and discharge their duties in good faith in the best interests of the corporation and for a proper purpose imposes an objective element (Corporations Act 2001 (Aus), s 181).

11 Corporations Act 2001, s 181.

12 *Re Smith v Fawcett Ltd* [1942] Ch 304, 304–5 (CA).

13 See also the discussion in R P Austin and I M Ramsay, *Ford's Principles of Corporations Law* (13th ed.), Australia, LexisNexis Butterworths, 2007, ch 8, 336–431.

14 Sealy, 'Bona Fides', note 9 above, 269. The example of the genuineness requirement Professor Sealy uses is the case *Re Halt Garage (1964) Ltd* [1982] 3 All ER 1016 where Oliver J struck down as not a genuine award of remuneration the payment of a substantial salary to a bedridden director.

For example, in *Hedley v Albany Power Centre Ltd (in liq)*[15] Wild J stated that in order to form a view about what was in the best interests of a company, the directors needed to:[16]

> (a) Identify the options available to [the company];
> (b) Assess each of those options: its present and prospective value to [the company]; its advantages and disadvantages, again both present and prospective; and
> (c) Compare each option on the basis of (b).

In *Robb v Sojourner*, the Court of Appeal, by rejecting an argument to the contrary, accepted that a defence based on section 138, which allows directors to rely on the advice of competent and reliable delegates, should be available as a defence for a breach of section 131.[17] The apparent acceptance by the court that relying on competent and reliable employees and delegates is a defence introduces a further element of objectivity into the test in section 131. Similarly, in the same case, the Court of Appeal opined that evidence of payment of fair value would have meant that the remedy of account of profits would not have been available.[18] It thus appears that the statutory formulation of section 131(1), as applied by the New Zealand Court of Appeal, requires that opinions that underpin decisions made by directors in good faith must be reasonably held. Conversely, reliance on objectively formed information will be used as evidence of good faith by directors.

A director complies with the duty in section 131 if the director's primary motivation is to act in a manner that the director genuinely believes to be in the best interests of the company. Negligence, even gross negligence, is not the same as disloyalty and is, therefore, unlikely to be considered a breach of section 131.[19] If the director has mixed motives, there is authority that says that the courts should determine what the main purpose of the directors was.[20] It is not required that directors in all cases avoid personal gain as a result of their honest and good faith supervision and

---

15 *Hedley v Albany Power Centre Ltd (in liq)* [2005] 2 NZLR 196.

16 Ibid., para 64.

17 *Robb v Sojourner* [2007] NZCA 493.

18 *Ibid.*, para 30.

19 See *Motorworld Ltd (in liq) v Turners Auctions Ltd* 17/2/10, Lang J, HC Auckland CIV-2007-404-6558 (HC) and see the discussion of the case in P Watts, 'Gross negligence and the director's duty of loyalty-two recent cases' [2010] *CSLB* 99.

20 *Mills v Mills* (1938) 60 CLR 150. See also the discussion of the proper purpose doctrine below.

management of the company, either directly through remuneration or, indirectly, through the increased value of any shares in the company that the director might hold.[21]

So long as the primary motivation of directors is to act in the best interests of the company, directors may favour other interests that they have. Directors cannot, however, take actions that favour their own interests where the directors cannot genuinely believe they are acting in the best interests of the company. In *Sojourner v Robb* in the High Court Fogarty J stated categorically that director/shareholders of a company who sold the business of an insolvent company at an undervalue to a new company they controlled were not acting in good faith.[22] The fact that the directors personally thought they were acting in the interests of the company was irrelevant.[23]

In *Sojourner* the directors approved the sale of the assets of the company to another company controlled by the directors. In assessing the value of the assets, the Court of Appeal, which affirmed the High Court decision, included the value of the goodwill in the business, including the value attached to directors as employees. The failure by the directors to include their own goodwill value when determining the price of the business was treated by the Court of Appeal as evidence of a lack of good faith. It is suggested that this is because, at the time the decision about the sale price was made, the directors must have been aware of their own intentions to continue through other entities to act as customers and to work as employees in the company purchasing the business. As such, a remedy of account of profits for the breach of the duty of good faith that took into account the value of the goodwill was justified.

Considering the fundamental importance of the provision, there has been a surprising dearth of cases where section 131(1) of the Companies Act 1993 has been invoked on its own. Often in cases where a director has usurped a business opportunity of the company, counsel prefer to frame their submissions on the basis that there has been a breach of fiduciary duty by directors, ignoring the Companies Act 1993 altogether or referring to it in only a cursory way.[24] One explanation as to why actions have not

---

[21] *Peoples Department Stores Inc (Trustee of) v Wise* [2004] 3 SCR 461; 244 DLR (4th) 564 (CanSC).

[22] *Sojourner v Robb*, note 7 above. The decision was upheld on appeal and the discussion by Fogarty J of good faith apparently accepted by the Court of Appeal: *Robb v Sojourner*, note 17 above.

[23] *Sojourner v Robb*, note 7 above, para 103.

[24] See eg *Stichbury v One4All Ltd* (2005) 9 NZCLC 263,792; *Bendall v Marshall* (2005) 5 NZCLC 263,772.

been brought on the basis that directors have breached duties set out in the Companies Act 1993 might be that there is an absence of remedies in the legislation itself. Although disaffected parties can seek leave to bring a derivative action for a breach of section 131, it is not clear what remedies are available for a breach of the statutory duty. By way of contrast, successfully establishing a breach of fiduciary duty by a director will open up a range of equitable remedies for a successful litigant.[25] It is for that reason that the 2007 decision of the Court of Appeal in *Robb v Sojourner* is significant.[26] The Court of Appeal allowed a creditor, bringing an action pursuant to section 301 of the Companies Act 1993, to obtain the equitable remedy of account of profits against directors to the company for a breach of section 131(1). It would appear that the equitable remedies are now available for breaches of the statutory duties relating to honesty and loyalty. In *Blanchett v Keshvara*[27] the court said that on the facts of a case involving payments to related parties, there was no difference between the general fiduciary duty at common law and the duty set out in section 131.[28]

WHAT ARE 'THE INTERESTS OF THE COMPANY'?

Conceptually the Law Commission's proposed hierarchy of duties was significant since the 'hierarchy makes explicit the equation of "the company" with the enterprise itself'.[29] Earlier in its report, the Law Commission highlighted the confusion about whether the 'best interests of the company' requires assessment 'of the company as the collective shareholders or as the enterprise itself'.[30] Pointing out that the notion of the company equating with the collective shareholders derived from the old joint stock company concepts from the mid-nineteenth century, the Law Commission explained that such a conceptualisation of the company does not take into account the notion of corporate personality perfected in case law. The Law Commission continued:

> Since it has been held that the collective shareholders include future shareholders, identification of the company with the enterprise may have been largely achieved in law. The uncertainty does, however, mean that there is considerable

---

[25] See C Noonan and S Watson, 'The Dog that Didn't Bark in *Kawhia Offshore Services Ltd v Rutherford*' (2004) 10(2) *NZBLQ* 103.

[26] *Robb v Sojourner*, note 16 above.

[27] *Blanchett v Keshvara* (2011) 10 NZCLC 264, 963.

[28] Ibid., at [37].

[29] Law Commission, *Company Law*, see note 4 above, para 195.

[30] Ibid., para 188.

scope for directors to rationalise decisions that are against the interests of existing shareholders.

As far as employees are concerned, the Companies Act 1993 in section 132 states that nothing in section 131 limits the power of a director to make provision for the benefit of employees when the company ceases to carry on all or part of its business. This provision specifically counters the effect of cases such as *Parke v Daily News Ltd*[31] where such considerations were not considered by the court to be in the best interests of the company.

Section 132 does not extend as far as the provision proposed in the Law Commission draft, which would have allowed a director to have regard to the interests of creditors and employees.[32] It also does not go as far as the equivalent provision in the Companies Act 2006 (UK).[33] That provision mandates that a director must act in a way that the director considers, in good faith, would be most likely to promote the success of the company for the benefit of its members as a whole.[34]

No express statutory obligation on directors to consider any interests beyond those of the company exists.[35] However, statutory directors' duties, which support an assertion that 'the company' includes other groups, have been included in the Companies Act 1993. Although in section 169(3) the duties set out in section 135 (the reckless trading provision) and section 136 (the obligation on directors not to allow the company to enter into obligations it will not be able to perform) are stated to be owed to the company, it is suggested that these duties can only have been included to protect the interests of creditors of the company.[36] The common law equivalent of the obligation in section 131 acts as a defence for directors against existing shareholders of the company if directors do, in fact, consider the interests of creditors. There can be little doubt that the statutory

---

31 *Parke v Daily News Ltd* [1962] 2 All ER 920.

32 Law Commission, *Company Law*, note 4 above, cl 103.

33 Companies Act 2006 (UK), s 172.

34 Ibid., s 172(1).

35 The Law Commission favoured the inclusion of a provision that allowed a director to have regard to the interests of creditors and employees when performing duties as a director: Law Commission, *Company Law Reform: Transition and Revision* NZLC R16, Law Commission, Wellington, 1990, 'The Draft Companies Act', cl 103.

36 The Law Commission discussed the duties. The argument that the company is a legal entity distinct from its shareholders and that the interests of creditors must be considered when there is a substantial risk to creditors of the company is supported by Miller J in *Kings Wharf Coldstore Ltd (in rec & liq) v Wilson* 24/11/05, Miller J, HC Wellington CIV-2001-485-954.

provision would operate in a similar way if existing shareholders brought an action on the basis that the directors of the company considered the interests of the creditors of the company ahead of shareholders, at least when the company was insolvent.

The extent to which directors, in order to comply with section 131(1), can consider the interests of creditors of the company was discussed in *Mountfort v Tasman Pacific Airlines of NZ Ltd*[37] with the judge concluding that:

> the 'general obligation [under the former legislation] to maintain the company's capital' recorded by Richardson J in *Nicholson v Permakraft*[[38]] has now been superseded by what may be expressed as a general, albeit imperfect, obligation not to trade while insolvent, which is to be inferred from the whole scheme of the Act. The obligation to maintain solvency could not be absolute, because that would destroy the very justification for limited liability which requires the protection of directors who, acting reasonably and in good faith, are unable to prevent the failure that is both a regular fact of business life and the justification for limited liability. The obligation is imperfect because breach does not, per se, attract legal consequences for the directors. But it is nevertheless an obligation because it is the premise on which there is unconditional entitlement to continue to trade.

In *Vercauteren v B-Guided Media Ltd*, a director who advised his co-directors to declare dividends when the company was not solvent was in breach of section 131(1). The judge considered that creditors are persons to whom the company has on-going obligations; 'the best interests of the company include the obligation to discharge those obligations before rewarding the shareholders'.[39] Directors will not breach section 131 if they consider the interests of creditors if the director has reason to doubt the solvency of the company. In *FXHT Fund Managers Ltd (in liq) v Oberholster*,[40] Venning J considered that where a director has reason to doubt the solvency of the company, the duty in section 131 may require the director to consider the position of creditors as opposed to the interests of shareholders. In that case, it was argued that a director ensured trade creditors were paid to protect his potential personal liability as guarantor, and also to ensure that the company was making a profit, which would

---

37 *Mountfort v Tasman Pacific Airlines of NZ Ltd* [2006] 1 NZLR 104, 112.

38 *Nicholson v Permakraft (NZ) Ltd* [1985] 1 NZLR 242, 255 (CA).

39 *Vercauteren v B-Guided Media Ltd* 8/2/10, White J, HC Auckland CIV-2009-404-3953, para 52 quoting Fogarty J in *Sojourner v Robb*, note 7 above, para 102.

40 *FXHT Fund Managers Ltd (in liq) v Oberholster* (2009) 10 NZCLC 264, 562.

benefit him as a shareholder. Venning J did not consider that to be a breach: 'it can hardly be said to be a breach of s 131 to ensure trade creditors are paid, and to ensure the company was making a profit'.[41]

A rationale for considering the interests of creditors when a company is insolvent is that in insolvency the creditors become the residual claimants, just as in a solvent company the shareholders are the residual claimants.[42] This rationale was set out in the judgment of Fogarty J in *Sojourner v Robb*,[43] (also discussed above), quoting from the then current edition of Gower and Davies.[44] Fogarty J somewhat acerbically commented that '[d]irectors of a company who are also the only shareholders of the company do not naturally believe that the best interests of the creditors of the company are the best interests of the company'.[45]

Fogarty J also took the opportunity to discuss the statutory duty set out in section 131(1), indicating that a belief that an action is in the best interests of the company may not be enough to satisfy the obligation set out in that section:[46]

> In this context the standard in s 131 is an amalgam of objective standards as to how people of business might be expected to act, coupled with a subjective criterion as to whether the directors have done what they honestly believe to be right. The standard does not allow a director to discharge the duty by acting with a belief that what he is doing in the best interest of the company, if that belief rests on a wholly inappropriate appreciation as to the interests of the company. If a director believes that the duty to act in the best interests of the company is a duty always to act in the best interests of the shareholders, and never in the interests of the creditors, in a situation of doubt as to the solvency of the company, the director cannot be said to be acting in good faith. Creditors are persons to whom the company has ongoing obligations. The best interests of the company include the obligation to discharge those obligations before rewarding the shareholders.

When affirming the High Court decision, the Court of Appeal rationalised the basis of the obligation owed to creditors by directors in a slightly

---

[41] Ibid., 566.

[42] See also *West Mercia Safetywear Ltd (in liq) v Dodd* [1988] BCLC 250 (CA) and the discussion in P Davies, *Gower and Davies' Principles of Modern Company Law* (7th ed.), London, Sweet & Maxwell, 2003, 372–4.

[43] *Sojourner v Robb*, note 7 above.

[44] P Davies, *Gower and Davies' Principles*, note 42 above, 371.

[45] *Sojourner v Robb*, note 7 above, para 98. See also the discussion of Clifford J in *Jordan v O'Sullivan* 138, Clifford J, HC Wellington CIV-2004-485-2611, para 69.

[46] *Sojourner v Robb*, note 7 above, para 102. The decision of Fogarty J was upheld by the Court of Appeal: *Robb v Sojourner*, note 16 above.

different way, as an obligation that arises near insolvency. The obligation to creditors cannot be overridden by shareholders but cannot be enforced by creditors.[47]

NOMINEE DIRECTORS

The legitimacy of the interests of nominating shareholders was generally not recognised at common law, with directors being obliged to act in the interests of the company as a whole rather than in the interests of their nominating shareholders. The Companies Act 1993 might be seen as providing a pragmatic balance between commercial reality and the common law by allowing directors to act in the interest of their nominating shareholders in limited circumstances. Section 131 requires directors so acting to be expressly permitted by the constitution of the company in the case of a joint venture company[48] or a wholly owned subsidiary company.[49] In the case of a partially owned subsidiary, the right must be included in the constitution and, in addition, all other shareholders must consent to the nominee director taking into account the interests of the holding company.[50]

For nominee directors with conflicting obligations, balancing those obligations in accordance with the Companies Act 1993 is proving difficult. The Companies Act 2006 (UK), in section 173, requires directors to be independent in their decision-making but there is no equivalent statutory provision in the New Zealand Companies Act. Directors can be appointed to the board for reasons that might lead to their interests conflicting with those of the company. Common examples are a shareholder who is also a director or a director who is a nominee of a large shareholder. Alternatively, situations may arise where the interests of the directors

---

[47] *Re New World Alliance Pty Ltd; Sycotex Pty Ltd v Baseler* (1994) 51 FCR 425, 445 (FCA) in *Robb v Sojourner*, note 17 above, para 25. The Court of Appeal also referred to the views expressed by Cumming Bruce and Templeman LJJ in *Re Horsely & Weight Ltd* [1982] Ch 442, 454–5 (CA), adopted by Cooke J in *Nicholson v Permakraft (NZ) Ltd* [1985] 1 NZLR 242, 250 (CA) and expressed to the same effect in *Kinsela v Russell Kinsela Pty Ltd (in liq)* (1986) 4 NSWLR 722, 730 by the New South Wales Court of Appeal, followed and applied by the English Court of Appeal in *West Mercia Safetywear Ltd (in liq) v Dodd*, note 42 above, 252.

[48] Companies Act 1993, s 131(4).

[49] Ibid., s 131(3).

[50] The section was changed from 'companies incorporated to carry out joint ventures' to 'companies carrying out joint ventures' to make it possible for shelf companies to be used for joint ventures.

are in another sphere. For example, another business enterprise that the director is involved in may conflict with the interests of the company. The UK provision may indicate recognition that, provided they are disclosed, such conflicts of interest need not necessarily affect the decision-making of the director. It is suggested that, even in the absence of an express statutory duty, when such conflicts arise the fundamental duty of the director is loyalty to the company. That loyalty requires independence of thought where the director must put any other interests aside and focus on the interests of the company. The provisos in section 131, by allowing directors, in admittedly limited circumstances, to put other interests ahead of the interests of the company in their decision-making, may well reflect the commercial reality by recognising what nominee directors do. Nevertheless, the provisos do erode the fundamental duty of loyalty. Also the survival of the equitable remedies and the propensity of litigants to bring actions outside of the Companies Act 1993 call into question the extent to which nominee directors or directors of joint venture companies can rely on the protections provided in section 131.

The problem inherent in nominee directors considering interests of others ahead of interests of the company was clearly illustrated in *Shell (Petroleum Mining) Co Ltd v Energy Infrastructure Ltd.*[51] The joint venture company in that case had not altered its constitution in accordance with the provisos in section 131. The directors appointed by one joint venture partner asserted that the directors appointed by the other joint venture partner had voted in favour of resolutions that were not in the best interests of the company. The Court of Appeal did not accept the argument that, in the absence of a constitution amended in accordance with section 131(4), the directors had a special responsibility to those who nominated them. Far more problematic, the court considered, was determining whether, in acting in the interests of their nominating shareholder, the directors were acting in the best interests of the company. Although New Zealand does not have a business judgment rule, there is a 'business judgment principle' where courts are reluctant to substitute their own views for those of the directors or to question the correctness of management decisions unless they were clearly arrived at in bad faith.

Difficulties with the provisos to section 131 were even more starkly illustrated in *Kings Wharf Coldstore Ltd (in rec & liq) v Wilson.*[52] Section 131(2) permits a director of a company that is a wholly owned subsidiary, when

---

[51] *Shell (Petroleum Mining) Co Ltd v Todd Petroleum Mining Co Ltd* 3/8/05, CA70/05.

[52] *Kings Wharf Coldstore Ltd (in rec & liq) v Wilson*, note 36 above.

authorised by the constitution, to act in the best interests of the holding company even if so acting may not be in the interests of the subsidiary company. The company was in liquidation and one of the issues was the extent to which the director could rely on section 131(2) when the company was insolvent. The director argued that the Justice and Law Reform Select Committee had considered and rejected the inclusion of the wording of the corresponding Australian provision, which does not allow a director in such a subsidiary to act in the interests of the parent company when the subsidiary is insolvent or becomes so because of the director's act.[53] It was argued that the nominee director therefore acting in the interests of the parent was legitimate. The court rejected this argument, stating that the duty not to engage in reckless trading set out in section 135 was a duty owed to the company as a legal entity separate from the shareholders. It followed that a breach could not be ratified by the shareholders alone. Therefore the power under section 131(2) was not available when section 135 was breached. The court cited with approval a statement of Baragwanath J in *Mountfort v Tasman Pacific Airlines of NZ Ltd*[54] where his Honour said that section 131(2) was an ancillary rather than a core provision that could not over-ride 'the fundamental requirement of solvency'.[55]

It is probably therefore safe to conclude that not only s 131(2) but in fact all the provisos to s 131 do not negate the fundamental requirement set out in s 131(1) that directors act in good faith and the best interests of the company as a whole. Whether or not the'company' is generally to be regarded as the enterprise or as the shareholders as residual claimants, there can be no doubt that when the company is insolvent the interests of creditors must be taken into account. The requirement to take the interests of creditors into account can be rationalised in one of two ways: either because the creditors comprise one of the interests included in the enterprise or because in insolvency the creditors have become the residual claimants. Despite New Zealand's failure to adopt the actual wording from the equivalent Australian provision, when a subsidiary or joint venture company is insolvent the directors must consider the interests of the company, which, in those circumstances at least, will include the interests of creditors. The requirement exists whether or not the company has, pursuant to ss 131(2) to 131(4), included clauses in its constitution that permit the directors to consider the interest of the nominator ahead of the interests of the company.

---

53 Ibid., para 106.
54 See note 37 above.
55 Ibid., para 82.

DUTY TO EXERCISE POWERS FOR A PROPER PURPOSE

The board – the directors acting collectively – is given statutory management powers by virtue of section 128(1) of the Companies Act 1993. The board and the directors are also given other powers such as the power to issue shares in the Act. Section 133 of the Companies Act 1993 says that a director must exercise a power for a proper purpose.[56] Unsatisfactorily, the term 'proper purpose' is not defined and it was already clear when the Act came into force that '[o]f all the enacted directors' duties, this is likely to be the most troublesome'.[57] Indeed, one commentator has remarked that the provision was among the 'most Delphic sections in the 1993 Act'.[58] In fact, the Law Commission did not favour the inclusion of the provision.

As anticipated, the common law 'proper purpose doctrine' has been used to interpret and apply the statutory provision on the rare occasions when the provision has been invoked.[59] This is most often when counsel set out a ragbag of duties which have allegedly been breached when applying for leave to bring a derivative action pursuant to section 165. A case where it was used successfully is *Blanchett v Keshvara*.[60] A director made a number of payments for the benefit of third parties at a time when the company was insolvent. That director was found to be in breach of a number of her statutory duties. In relation to section 133, the court noted that a director acting in entirely good faith may still be in breach of their duties by using their power for something other than for which it was intended.[61]

When making decisions and exercising powers, people may have mixed motives. Often directors may exercise a power for several purposes. One of the purposes may be a proper purpose and one of the purposes may be an improper purpose. The proper purpose doctrine was refined by the Privy Council, in *Howard Smith Ltd v Ampol Petroleum Ltd*,[62] clarifying that

---

56 Companies Act 1993, s 133.

57 See Tompkins J, 'Directing the Directors', note 10 above, 20.

58 P Watts, 'Statutory Formulation of Directors' Duties – Some Issues' [2003] *CSLB* 95.

59 *Re Cameron's Coalbrook Steam Coal and Swansea and Lougher Railway Co; Bennett's Case* (1854) 5 DeGM&G 284, 298; *Hogg v Cramphorn Ltd* [1967] Ch 254; *Howard Smith Ltd v Ampol Petroleum Ltd* [1974] AC 821 (PC) (followed in *Baigent v D McL Wallace Ltd* (1984) 2 NZCLC 99,122); *Whitehouse v Carlton Hotel Pty Ltd* (1987) 162 CLR 285 (HCA).

60 *Blanchett v Keshvara* (2011) 10 NZCLC 264, 963; [2011] NZCCLR 34.

61 Ibid at [63].

62 *Howard Smith Ltd v Ampol Petroleum Ltd*, note 59 above.

the courts will determine the substantial purpose of the directors when exercising the power.[63]

Howard Smith Ltd v Ampol Petroleum Ltd[64] is the leading case in New Zealand on the application of the proper purpose doctrine. It was considered by Prichard J in *Baigent v D McL Wallace Ltd.*[65] Prichard J, after discussing *Howard*, said that the purpose of powers such as the power to allot shares are well defined and restricted in scope. The use of those powers to affect the voting structure of the company would be an abuse of powers. However, Tompkins J, writing extra judicially, was not so sure:[66]

> Certainly some purposes are clearly not proper, generally because they are purposes relating to the directors' own interests rather than the interests of the company. But what if the directors refuse to approve a share transfer because they believe bona fide and for good reason, that the transferee will harm the company?

Some commentators have been troubled by the fact that the issue of shares by the directors had the effect of thwarting the wishes of the majority of the shareholders. However, the majority of shareholders are not the company. At least in a company where the powers have a statutory source, as in New Zealand by virtue of section 128 of the Companies Act 1993, the shareholders are not the source of the powers of the board.[67]

There may be an advantage in invoking the statutory duty rather than its non-statutory equivalent. Apparently, regarding the non-statutory equivalent proper purpose doctrine as involving a misuse of fiduciary power, the exercise of a power for an improper purpose could be ratified by the meeting of shareholders.[68] Section 177(4), which preserves the non-statutory rules of ratification, would appear to continue to make ratification possible. Obtaining leave pursuant to section 165 to bring a derivative action may then be problematic if ratification has taken place. No authority exists though, that would permit a breach of the statutory duty set out in section 133 to be ratified.

---

63 *Hogg v Cramphorn Ltd* was followed by the High Court of Australia in *Whitehouse v Carlton Hotel Pty Ltd*, note 59 above, with the court adding that, in the case of more than one dominant purpose, the test was whether the power would not have been exercised in the particular way *but for* the improper purpose.

64 See note 59 above.

65 *Baigent v D McL Wallace Ltd*, note 59 above, 122.

66 Tompkins J, 'Directing the Directors', note 10 above, 25.

67 See Chapter 11, this volume.

68 *Hogg v Cramphorn Ltd*, note 59 above; *Bamford v Bamford* [1970] Ch 212; *Winthrop Investments Ltd v Winns Ltd* [1975] 2 NSWLR 666 (NSWCA).

The proper purpose doctrine is almost always invoked to prevent the issue of shares in a situation where the interests of one group of shareholders may be favoured over the interests of another group of shareholders. Indeed, in *FXHT Fund Managers Ltd (in liq) v Oberholster*,[69] Venning J held that a claim that a director breached section 133 was conceptually quite different from a normal proper purpose case confirming that fact situations where the courts are willing to consider a breach of section 133 may be narrow. The case involved the exercising of a power by a director to ensure trade creditors were paid and the company was making a profit rather than protecting the interests of investors.

There are a number of cases in other jurisdictions where a court has similarly held that a board cannot issue shares for the purpose of defeating the voting powers of existing shareholders by creating a new majority.[70] However, as pointed out above, such actions in New Zealand are likely to be in breach of the Takeovers Code. Shareholders of companies (that are not Code companies) where such behaviour takes place, can apply for leave to bring a derivative action, pursuant to section 165, for a breach of section 133.

TRANSACTIONS IN WHICH DIRECTORS HAVE AN INTEREST

The strict equitable principle that will not allow a director to have a conflict of interest, like the one seen in *Aberdeen Railway Ltd v Blaikie Brothers*[71] is effectively negated by the provisions of the Companies Act 1993. For the statutory negation of the equitable rule to be effective, an interested director must disclose interests to the board and to the shareholders. If the transaction in question is in the ordinary course of business or is for fair value, it will be enforceable against the company whether or not disclosure takes place.

It may, however, be dangerous for an interested director to rely entirely on the statutory provisions. It is suggested that, if the director also acts as corporate agent and is directly involved with transactions with the third party in which the director also has an interest, then it may be more difficult for a director to prove, in accordance with section 131, that

69 See note 40 above, 562.

70 See a survey of the cases in Austin and Ramsay, *Ford's Principles*, note 13 above, paras 8.210–8.270.

71 *Aberdeen Railway Co Ltd v Blaikie Brothers* (1854) 1 Macq 461.

he or she acted in good faith and what he or she believes to be the best interests of the company. If, however, the director limits involvement in the transaction to taking part in the collective decision-making as part of the board, then disclosure of the interest by the director will, in most situations, be sufficient to ensure that the transaction is enforceable. The Court of Appeal in *Robb v Sojourner*,[72] have made it clear that disclosure by interested directors to shareholders in accordance with section 140 will not be sufficient for those directors to avoid liability when the company is insolvent or nearing insolvency and where there is evidence that the directors may not have acted in the best interests of the company.

In its report, the Law Commission commented that the case law on self-interested transactions had proved to be too strict and the modifications by articles and statute were unsatisfactory.[73] The Companies Act 1993, which strongly resembles the Law Commission draft provisions on self-interested transactions, allows a director to disclose a conflict of interest both to the board and in the interests' register of the company. That disclosure must be made in accordance with section 140. Any transaction entered into in which a director has an interest (disclosed or undisclosed) becomes voidable – the transaction can be avoided within three months of disclosure to the shareholders if it is not in the ordinary course of business and not for fair value.

The origins of fair value, meaning the value of a transaction objectively assessed as a way of immunising related party transactions from challenge, are in various strands of case law in US jurisdictions some of which derive from earlier English doctrine and others from local variations. The form of provision most commonly found in modern statutes first emerged in a significant manner in the California Corporations Code in 1929.[74] The drafting of the Californian Code was carried out by a team of lawyers led by Professor Henry Ballantine, who later wrote *Ballantine on Corporations* and was a leading corporate law scholar.[75]

The innovation in the Californian Code was the requirement that the 'contract or transaction is just and reasonable as to the corporation at the

---

[72] See note 16 above.

[73] Law Commission, *Company Law*, note 4 above. The Contractual Remedies Act 1979 arguably negated the common law principles, and waiver clauses such as the one found in cl 84 of table A of the Companies Act 1955 provided for disclosure by a director to the board.

[74] Similar provisions existed in Codes in Ohio, New York, New Jersey, Nevada and Maryland but these were not influential.

[75] Thomas W Dahlqist, 'Henry W. Ballantine' (1949) 37 *California Law Review* 171.

time it is authorized or approved'. Writing in 1931 about the drafting of the Code,[76] Ballantine commented that those running corporations found the disqualification of directors for self-dealing to be too strict.

It has been suggested that fairness in self-interested transactions was originally intended to require procedural fairness rather than substantive fairness and to have been derived from the rules relating to fair dealing.[77] But Ballantine talks about the exigencies of modern business requiring a practical working rule for self-dealing, making it clear that the rule was not derived from case law. Also, it is clear from Ballantine's own discussion of the provision that the focus was on substantive fairness.

The Companies Act 1993, in section 139, contains an elaborate definition of the term 'interested' that would capture all direct or indirect interests that directors might have in the company. There is also a catch-all clause; 'is otherwise directly or indirectly materially interested in the transaction'.[78]

It is important, nevertheless, to note that the definition of 'interested' is only given for the purposes of the Act. It may be possible for a director to be interested at common law, but not under the Act. In those circumstances, the common law disability or duty of the director will continue to apply.

Every company must keep an interests' register. Once it has been established that a director is interested, that director has a duty to make disclosure to the board and cause the interest to be entered in the interests' register.[79] If the company only has one director, the interest should immediately be noted in the interests' register.[80] The director must be aware of

---

[76] H W Ballantine, 'Questions of Policy in Drafting a Modern Corporation Law' (1931) 19 *California Law Review* 465, 476.

[77] See A Bulbulia and AR Pinto, 'Statutory Responses to Interested Directors' Transactions: A Watering Down of Fiduciary Standards?' (1977–8) 53 *Notre Dame Law Review* 201, 209:

> The drafters of the statute did not intend to affect the voidability of transactions which were unfair, but to overcome the problems created by the "involvement" of interested directors in the approval or ratification process. Thus the statute, by dealing only with the director's involvement, was aimed at curing procedural problems, not at assuring substantive fairness.

See also Law Commission: Company Law Reform and Restatement 1989, at para 525. 'The test of fairness is coupled with disclosure provisions. It may be said ultimately to derive from the rule in *Coles v Trecothick* (1804) 9 Ves Jun 234.'

[78] Companies Act 1993, s 139(1)(e).

[79] Ibid., s 140(1).

[80] Ibid. The rule at common law is the same: see *Neptune Vehicle Washing Equipment Ltd v Fitzgerald* [1996] Ch 274.

the interest – there is a defence for a director under the provision if the director did not learn of the conflict of interest until after the transaction was completed.

Significantly, and in a departure from the previous legislation,[81] unless prohibited by the constitution, a director interested in a transaction may attend a meeting where the transaction is considered and may be included among the quorum. The director may also vote on and sign documents relating to the transaction and generally act as if he or she were not interested in the transaction.[82]

The disclosure procedure may be avoided in closely held companies. If the board is able to obtain the unanimous written consent of all shareholders, and all persons on whom the constitution imposes the rights and obligations of a shareholder, it need not carry out the disclosure procedure.[83] The consent of any shareholder may be withdrawn at any time.[84] Unless the concurrence of the shareholders is for one particular transaction, details of any subsequent transaction must be sent to all shareholders (and those with the rights and obligations of shareholders).[85]

It is not clear whether formal disclosure of a director's interest to the board is required where the board is already aware of the interest. Australian and English authority suggests that disclosure in those circumstances may not be necessary.[86] However, the statutory requirement that any interest be entered in the interests' register is not negated by the knowledge of the board of the interest. The prudent path to take would be to disclose in accordance with the statutory provisions.

Generally, failure to disclose does not affect the validity of a transaction,[87] although it may render the director liable. It is possible,

---

81 This provision is however in accordance with *Hely-Hutchinson v Brayhead Ltd* [1968] 1 QB 549 (CA) where the failure by a director to disclose his interest under the equivalent provision in the English legislation did not render the contract void but voidable at the instance of the company.

82 Companies Act 1993, s 144.

83 Ibid., s 107(3). Following *Robb v Sojourner*, note 17 above, interested directors should not rely on this provision to avoid potential liability if the company is insolvent or nearing insolvency.

84 Companies Act 1993, s 107(6).

85 Ibid., s 107(7).

86 *Woolworths Ltd v Kelly* (1991) 9 ACLC 539 (NSWCA); *Lee Panavision Ltd v Lee Lighting Ltd* [1992] BCC 620; [1992] BCLC 22 (CA) cf., *Neptune (Vehicle Washing Equipment) Ltd v Fitzgerald*, note 80 above.

87 Companies Act 1993, s 140(3). This provision is however in accordance with *Hely-Hutchinson v Brayhead Ltd*, note 81 above, where the failure by a director to disclose his interest under the equivalent provision in the English legislation did not render the contract void but voidable at the instance of the company.

however, for the company to avoid transactions where a director is interested. The right to avoid expires within three months of the transaction being disclosed to shareholders. Cancellation is only possible though, if the company did not receive 'fair value' in the transaction. There is a presumption, which can be rebutted by evidence, that transactions entered into in the ordinary course of business and on usual terms and conditions are 'fair'.[88] Transactions are most likely to be avoided therefore when they are outside the ordinary course of business or not on usual terms and conditions. Whether or not fair value was paid will also affect the liability of directors. Although under equitable principles the fairness of the consideration will not be a defence against a claim for account of profits, the Court of Appeal has stated that if a contract could not be avoided pursuant to section 141 because fair value was paid, it would be anomalous to allow a related claim against interested directors for account of profits.[89] Although it is not completely clear, it is arguable that this new rule is intended to supersede the equitable rule, with the Court of Appeal indicating a preference for the North American approach.

The issue of whether a transaction can be set aside because there was no declaration of interest was considered by the Court of Appeal in *Rockyana Lodge Ltd v Stenberg*[90] (although the decision was based on the antecedent provisions in the 1955 Act). The case was part of the fallout connected with a relationship breakdown and transfer of property previously owned by the partners in the relationship. Although there had been no declaration of interest by the director, the Court of Appeal concurred with Potter J's finding that the non-disclosure was a technical breach only, since a quorum of two of the three directors knew about the interest.

The court will determine fair value on the basis of the information known to the company and the director at the time the transaction was entered into.[91] Therefore, because of possible special knowledge of the director, a transaction that may be at market value is not automatically at fair value. Other factors may be taken into account.

The term 'fair value' is not defined in the legislation meaning cautious directors will ensure any transaction in which they are 'interested' in terms of section 139 is entered into scrupulously, so that a question of fair value

---

88 Companies Act 1993, s 141(2), (4).
89 *Robb v Sojourner*, note 17 above, para 30.
90 *Rockyana Lodge Ltd v Stenberg* (2000) 8 NZCLC 262,130 (CA).
91 Companies Act 1993, s 141(3).

cannot arise. In the Court of Appeal decision *Thexton v Thexton*,[92] which related to fair value in share dealing under section 149, it was made clear that, as applied in relation to section 149 at least, disclosure of all relevant information is not enough to ensure that fair value is paid. Fair value is to be determined objectively. Following *Thexton*, it was not clear whether the test in section 141 for fair value is also viewed as objective or whether it depends on equality of information between the two parties. However, since the potential unfairness to the company will be brought about because of possible influence that a director may have over the negotiations or the decision-making in a way that may favour third parties, it is suggested that the test can only be objective. Following *Robb v Sojourner*, it seems clear that fair value will be assessed objectively and will include the value of good will, including good will associated with the interested directors.[93] Presumably the objective valuation must also be based on all information known by the directors.

In *Catley v Waipa Corporation Ltd*,[94] in the context of an application for leave to bring a derivative action, Duffy J held that the burden of proof for proving fair value was paid even in an action for account of profits, rests with those seeking to uphold the transaction.

A company can set down more extensive avoidance rights in its constitution.[95] Also, even if a director complies with the disclosure requirements, a conflicted director must still act in the best interests of the company.[96] It is crucial that directors are aware that disclosure pursuant to section 140 does not obviate the obligation of directors to comply with the duty set out in section 131(1) to act in good faith and in the best interests of the company. *Hedley v Albany Power Centre Ltd (in liq) (No 2)*[97] provides a salutary lesson about the strictness of the standard that remains in place. The judge said:[98]

> In short, I doubt that a conflicted director can discharge his s 131(1) duties. The liquidators have rightly pointed to s 140 and 144 of the Act, but equally correctly (in my view) point out that neither of those sections overrides a director's s 131(1) duty. Thus, a director cannot, by disclosing his personal or other interests or conflicts, avoid liability under s 131 if he fails faithfully to consider,

---

92 *Thexton v Thexton* [2001] 1 NZLR 237; (2001) 9 NZCLC 262,432 (HC) and *Thexton v Thexton* [2002] 1 NZLR 780; (2002) 9 NZCLC 262,777 (CA).

93 *Robb v Sojourner*, note 17 above, paras 32–47.

94 *Catley v Waipa Corporation Ltd* [2010] NZCCLR 24.

95 Companies Act 1993, s 141(6).

96 *Rusher v Owen* 9/6/99, Potter J, HC Auckland AP17-SW99.

97 *Hedley v Albany Power Centre Ltd (in liq) (No 2)* (2006) 9 NZCLC 264,095.

98 Ibid., para 16.

and act in, what is in the company's best interests (as opposed to his own, or those of another person(s)).

If a transaction is set aside, the interests of third parties are protected. If property is acquired from anyone other than the company for valuable consideration and without knowledge of the circumstances of the original transaction, the third party has the right to retain the property even if the original transaction is set aside.[99]

Finally, it is worth noting that the statutory duty of disclosure set out in section 140 covers situations where there may be a conflict of duties to the extent where an individual who is a director of a company does not deal directly with the company but is the director, trustee or partner of an entity which does. Also the extended definition of 'director' found in section 126 means that those in accordance with whose instructions a director or the board may be required or accustomed to act,[100] those delegated management powers by the board,[101] and those who are allocated board powers in the constitution of the company,[102] as well as those who occupy the position of director by whatever name called,[103] will, if interested in terms of section 139, be obliged to disclose their interest to the board pursuant to section 140. The consequence of the broad definition of 'director' in s 126 and the wide reaching definition of 'interested' in section 139 can only mean that the transactions requiring disclosure in terms of section 140 will be wider than many realise. For example, a bank may advance a new loan at a higher interest rate to a company that is an existing customer. If section 126(1)(b)(ii) is interpreted widely, the bank may be regarded by a court as 'a person in accordance with whose directions or instructions the board of the company may be required to act'. The bank will be an interested director in terms of section 139. If the bank does not disclose pursuant to section 140 the company may be able to avoid the transaction pursuant to section 141(1).[104]

---

99 Companies Act 1993, s 142.
100 Ibid., s 126(1)(b)(i), (ii). See chapter 11 for a discussion of the provision.
101 Ibid., s 126(1)(c).
102 Ibid., s 126(1)(b)(iii).
103 Ibid., s 126(1)(a).
104 The bank might argue, in terms of s 18(1)(a), that the company cannot argue that the Act has not been complied with and thus that the loan is unenforceable. However, as the deemed director, the court may not regard the bank to be a 'person dealing with the company'.

USE OF COMPANY INFORMATION

The Companies Act 1993, in section 145, prohibits the disclosure or use of confidential company information by directors or employees. Confidential information is information which would not otherwise be available to the director or employee.[105] In determining what will be deemed confidential, the Australian courts, considering the equivalent Australian provision, have said the information protected by the section is the sort of information equity would protect by way of injunction.[106]

Confidential information cannot generally be used or disclosed by employees except for the purposes of the company or as required by law.[107] Directors of the company can, however, disclose or use confidential information if they are first authorised to do so by the board and it is unlikely to prejudice the company. In those circumstances, particulars of the circumstances surrounding the disclosure must be entered in the interests' register of the company.[108] If it is later found that the disclosure did prejudice the company then, notwithstanding the director having authorisation from the board, it is probable that the director will be liable to the company. If there is any doubt, a prudent director would therefore still obtain the approval of shareholders before making disclosure.[109]

Situations can arise when a major shareholder or creditor of the company has the right to appoint a nominee director to the board to represent its interests. This representation may involve no more than keeping the shareholder informed of what is going on in the company or, in the case of a creditor's nominee, the health of the investment. Clearly, though, a potential conflict of interest exists. In those circumstances, the Act allows disclosure of information by the nominee provided the name of the person to whom the information is disclosed is entered in the interests' register. The board does, however, have the power to prohibit disclosure by the nominee director.[110]

---

105 Companies Act 1993, s 145(1).

106 *Rosetex Co Pty Ltd v Licata* (1994) 12 ACSR 779 (SC NSW); *Wright v Gasweld Pty Ltd* (1991) 22 NSWLR 317.

107 Companies Act 1993, s 145(1).

108 Ibid., s 145(3).

109 For a further discussion of the scope of the prohibition on the misuse of confidential information by directors, see B Harris, 'Fiduciary Duties of Directors under the Companies Act 1993' [1994] *NZLJ* 242, 242–3.

110 Companies Act 1993, s 145(2). In *Kings Wharf Coldstore Ltd (in rec & liq) v Wilson*, note 36 above, a director was not liable under s 145(1) because s 145(2) allowed disclosure to the person whose interest he represented.

CORPORATE OPPORTUNITIES

In the course of their activities on behalf of the company, directors may come across business opportunities and may decide to exploit those business opportunities for their own gain.

Exploiting a business opportunity of the company can be evidence of a director not acting in good faith. In *Kings Wharf Coldstore Ltd (in rec & liq) v Wilson*, a director claimed that a business opportunity could not be exploited by a company because it was insolvent ('drunk with debt')[111] Miller J did not allow the insolvency of the company to affect the obligation of the director; a receiver, if appointed, would have retained the business opportunity.

Corporate opportunity cases are not unusual in New Zealand. In *Holden v Architectural Finishes Ltd*,[112] in a discussion that has been cited and followed frequently, McGechan J stated that directors' fiduciary duties had two aspects:[113]

1. A duty of good faith; i.e. to act as the director honestly sees as being in the best interests of the company;
2. Both (i) not to profit from the company and (ii) not to place himself in a position where the company's interests and his own personal interests conflict.

McGechan J then listed relevant precepts:[114]

> (a) A director may not take, or indeed make use of, his company's property . . .
> (b) A director may not take over ('usurp') less tangible property such as an existing company distribution . . .
> (c) Likewise, a director cannot take for himself a specific 'business opportunity', e.g. a chance to obtain an agency, which the company is pursuing, or would or might pursue . . .

A good illustration of a director usurping a business opportunity of the company is seen in *Thorrington v McCann*,[115] where an executive director

---

[111] *Kings Wharf Coldstore Ltd*, note 36 above, para 51.

[112] *Holden v Architectural Finishes Ltd* (1996) 7 NZCLC 260,976, 261,025-261,028. The decision was appealed *Architectural Finishes Ltd v Holden* 7/4/97, CA272/95.

[113] Ibid.

[114] Ibid.

[115] *Thorrington v McCann* (1998) 8 NZCLC 261,564.

of a successful tavern took up a renewal of a lease of the tavern on his own behalf rather than the company's.

In some cases, judges extend the obligation to business opportunities that the company would not take up, even if it had the chance. As Allan J pointed out in *Hunter Grain Ltd v Price*,[116] the principle is policy driven; if directors were able to take up opportunities where their companies could not, they would be tempted to downplay the company's ability to take up the opportunity. Similarly, as the English Court of Appeal put it: 'If an opportunity comes to him in his capacity as fiduciary, his principal is entitled to know about it. The director cannot be left to make the decision as to whether he is allowed to help himself to its benefit.'[117]

Commentators and the courts are divided on the extent to which the corporate opportunity doctrine is encompassed in the Companies Act 1993. Usurping corporate opportunities can be viewed as the directors misusing confidential information of the company. Section 145 says that directors who have information in their capacity as a director or employee of the company must not make use of or act on that information. Following such an approach, so long as the director acquired the information leading to the opportunity in his or her capacity as a director of the company, then that director would have an obligation to make the opportunity available to the company first. A breach of such an obligation would be covered by section 145 of the Companies Act 1993 and would also probably involve a breach of section 131(1), the duty of good faith. A consequence of this approach is that the corporate opportunity doctrine is treated as a breach of confidence. This approach does, however, limit the ambit of the corporate opportunity doctrine to the misuse of information acquired by a director in his or her capacity as a director, or, sometimes, as an employee of the company.

Alternatively the corporate opportunity doctrine may not be covered by the Companies Act 1993 specifically. The doctrine may rather stem from the fiduciary obligations of directors.[118] Proponents of this view argue that it unduly stretches the meaning of the term 'information' to say that it encompasses all corporate opportunities. Often the use of confidential

---

[116] *Hunter Grain Ltd v Price* 258, Allan J, HC Tauranga CIV-2008-470-192 para 54, referring to McGechan J in *Holden v Architectural Finishes Ltd*, note 112 above, para 88.

[117] *Re Allied Business & Financial Consultants Ltd: O'Donnell v Shanahan* [2009] 2 BCLC 666, 671.

[118] For a good discussion of this view see S Scott, 'The Evolving Corporate Opportunity Doctrine: Is New Zealand Law Being Left Behind?' (2005) 11 *NZBLQ* 264.

information and the usurpation of a corporate opportunity will take place at the same time – in a sense one will lead to the other.

A strong argument in favour of regarding the usurpation of a business opportunity of the company as a breach of section 145 and, probably, section 131(1) of the Companies Act 1993 is that the directors' duties' provisions are at the very least a restatement and are perhaps even a codification of the duties in place when the Act was drafted in the early 1990s. Because the corporate opportunity doctrine existed at that time, the legislature must have intended the doctrine to be encompassed in the legislation.

The Law Commission Report provides little guidance about whether the usurpation of a business opportunity is a use of company information, merely stating that:[119]

> Directors should be under a duty to maintain company information in confidence. Directors who use such information without company approval and without paying adequate value to the company for the information should be liable for any loss suffered by the company.

A strong argument in favour of an approach that treats the corporate opportunity doctrine as a separate doctrine is the implicit recognition that the obligation of individuals who are directors not to usurp business opportunities of the company may stem as much from the other legal relationships such an individual may have with the company as from the position of director. Such an individual may also be an employee and owe the co-existent fiduciary obligations of an employee to the company; that individual may be a corporate agent and owe the co-existent obligations of a corporate agent to the company. The corporate opportunity doctrine does not just apply to directors but also to senior executives of a company;[120] the obligations may not arise because the individual occupies the office of director but rather because the individual in question is a senior employee and corporate agent. The correct view may be that expressed by Struan

---

[119] Law Commission, *Company Law*, note 4 above, cl 92. See also the discussion by Struan Scott in S Scott, 'The Evolving Corporate Opportunity Doctrine', ibid, 271. Although Scott does not consider that s 145 wholly encompasses the corporate opportunity doctrine, he considers that the Law Commission saw s 145 extending to the doctrine.

[120]

> A senior executive may owe fiduciary duties to a company and these duties are analogous to those owed by a director, see *Canadian Aero Service Ltd v O'Malley* (1973) 40 DLR (3d) 371 (CanSC); *SSC & B Lintas NZ Ltd v Murphy* (1981) 1 NZCLC 95-044. References to 'director' include these senior executives

Scott, ibid., n 1.

Scott: that whilst protection of confidential information is an important aspect of the corporate opportunity doctrine, it is not the whole of it.[121]

Cases decided since the implementation of the Companies Act 1993 do not make matters much clearer. In particular, the corporate opportunity doctrine was discussed at length by McGechan J in *Holden v Architectural Finishes Ltd*[122] without section 145 being mentioned.

Section 145 has been applied to the usurpation of a corporate opportunity. In *Stichbury v One4All* Ltd[123] the plaintiff husband alleged, among other things, that his estranged wife has misapplied assets and company information. The actions taken by the wife included incorporating a new company, One4All (2004) Ltd, which took over the lease for the premises previously occupied by the original company One4All Ltd. Section 145 was invoked on the basis that the defendant wife had 'taken advantage of her position as a director of the company and misused associated knowledge and information she gained in that role'.[124] This misuse of information included client and customer lists, company policies and procedures and also company market knowledge and future business opportunities. In the context of deciding whether or not to give leave for a derivative action, the associate judge decided that the claim in part at least appeared to have merit.

In *Tweedie and Others v Packsys Ltd*,[125] the plaintiff, who was a director of Packsys Ltd, applied for leave to bring a derivative action on the basis that the other director in the company had set up Packsys Pty Ltd in Australia without the leave of the New Zealand company. The defendant director argued that there was never any chance that the New Zealand operation could set up business in Australia. The plaintiff director alleged that there was a breach of section 145 (along with ss 131, 133, 134 and 140). The plaintiff director also argued that the defendant director breached his fiduciary duty to Packsys by setting up the Australian company and by taking for himself an opportunity available to the New Zealand company; in particular appropriating an agency that was the property of the New Zealand company. In giving leave, Williams J considered that the director should arguably be seen 'in breach of his duty as a director of Packsys because he has foreclosed that company's opportunity to expand into the Australian market'.[126] Some judges appear to consider

---

121 Ibid, 265.
122 See note 112 above.
123 See note 24 above.
124 *Ibid.*, para 33.
125 *Tweedie v Packsys Ltd* (2005) 9 NZCLC 263,845.
126 Ibid., para 47.

that the corporate opportunity doctrine exists in addition to the duties set out in the Companies Act 1993 but arising out of the fundamental duty of directors to avoid and conflict between their own interests and their duty to the company.

It is, therefore, not yet clear the extent to which the duty relating to confidential information set out in section 145 encompasses the developing corporate opportunity doctrine. The extent of the obligations of a director may depend on whether the director in question is a part-time non-commercial fiduciary such as a non-executive director, or a full-time executive commercial fiduciary, such as an executive director. It is suggested that the corporate opportunity doctrine, at least as it applies to executive directors, may be related more to their fiduciary relationship with the company as employees and corporate agents. As such, the principles of agency and employment law will operate to establish the extent of their obligations. For non-executive directors, who may not be corporate agents (and for executive directors when acting in their role as directors on the board), section 145, which does not generally permit the use of information directors acquire in that role, will establish the extent of the obligations of directors in respect of information that they acquire in that capacity.

SHARE DEALING BY DIRECTORS

Section 149 of the Companies Act 1993 establishes a statutory duty on directors to ensure that, in any share dealing the person they acquire shares from or sell shares to, receives or pays fair value. The statutory duty would make the common law duty redundant were it not for the fact that the statutory duty only applies to a director acquiring or disposing of the shares directly. The provision does not encompass situations where the director acquires or disposes of the shares through another entity the director controls, such as a company. Acquisition through a company was precisely what occurred in *Coleman v Myers*.[127] The common law cases thus remain relevant.

In an attempt to capture share dealings by others on behalf of directors of the company, the Companies Act 1993 contains a detailed definition of 'relevant interest' in section 146. The definition includes, together with a director holding shares, a director being the beneficial owner of a share either directly or indirectly by means of any trust, agreement, arrangement

[127] [1977] 2 NZLR 225.

or understanding. If any person or body with any connection with a director of a company deals in its shares, the director should ensure the dealing does not come within the definition of relevant interest in section 146 or the exceptions (which include lenders, share brokers and proxies) in section 147. If a relevant interest does exist, the director must forthwith after incorporation or after the shares are bought or sold, and in accordance with section 148, disclose to the board:

- The number and type of shares;
- The nature of the relevant interest;
- The consideration; and
- The date of the sale or purchase.

These details must be entered in the interests register.[128]

Section 149(1) states:

> If a director of a company has information in his or her capacity as a director . . . being information which would not otherwise be available to him or her but which is information material to an assessment of the value or other securities issued by the company . . . the director may acquire or dispose of those shares or securities only if in the case of an acquisition, the consideration given for the acquisition is not less than the fair value of the shares or securities; or in the case of a disposition the consideration received for the disposition is not more than the fair value of the shares or securities . . .

If sections 148 and 149 impose a fiduciary duty on directors to individual shareholders, this duty can be viewed as a major extension of the fiduciary obligations of company directors in the Companies Act 1993. An alternative view exists. Sections 148 and 149 could be regarded as an extension of the insider trading prohibitions that exist for listed companies in the Securities Markets Act 1988 into the companies' legislation. Thus, the obligation can be viewed as arising not so much because the individual selling shares is a director but because that individual, by virtue of his or her position as a director, has access to information that gives him or her an unfair advantage in the transaction.

The issue of whether fair value has been paid if both parties to a transaction have the same information was considered by both the High Court and then the Court of Appeal in *Thexton v Thexton*, which involved a share transaction between a father (who had subsequently died) and his son.[129]

---

128 Companies Act 1993, s 148(2).

129 *Thexton v Thexton* [2001] 1 NZLR 237; (2001) 9 NZCLC 262,432 (HC).

'Fair value' is to be determined 'on the basis of all information known to the director or publicly available at the time'.[130] On the facts Salmon J decided that the plaintiff did not have all the information material to an assessment of the value of the shares. (The fair value was agreed by expert witnesses to be $790,000 not the $250,000 paid.)

The judge discussed how fair value could have been determined if in fact the plaintiff had been given all the material information:[131]

> There are at least two ways in which Parliament might restrict insider trading in order to prevent the abuse of insider information. One is to require the insider to disclose the information to the other party. The other is to require the insider to trade at a price that reflects the value of the information. There are sound law and economics arguments, which suggest that the first of these two methods is the better. Nonetheless, I consider that the wording of s 149 points conclusively to the second.

To support his interpretation, Salmon J pointed to the use of the words 'only if' in section 149, which he considered suggested that the provision was only concerned with the price at which the shares were traded. In Salmon J's opinion, there was nothing from which a requirement of disclosure could be inferred. However, with respect, the key element of the subsection is that 'fair value' must be paid. The part disclosure plays hinges on the interpretation of 'fair value'. It was Salmon J's view that fair value in section 149 was not determined by whatever value two equally informed people put on the shares but instead was an objective concept. To support this interpretation, Salmon J relied on two sources of authority: other provisions of the Companies Act 1993 and the 1989 Law Commission report on the draft version of the Act.

The Law Commission report stated that a 'director who is in possession of material price-sensitive information has two options: to abstain from trading or to ensure that the person with whom he or she is dealing receives fair value'.[132] It is suggested that the statement by the Law Commission provides little guidance about what approach to interpretation of section 149 should be used; the statement merely makes it clear that the director must ensure that the person on the other side of the transaction pays or receives fair value; it does not set out whether this should be achieved by disclosure or by a valuation of the shares.

The term 'fair value' is used elsewhere in the Act: in section 141(2) in

---

130 Companies Act 1993, s 149(2).

131 *Thexton v Thexton*, note 129 above, 442.

132 Law Commission, *Company Law*, note 4 above, para 542.

relation to transactions entered into by a company where a director has an interest in both sides of the transaction. It is suggested that the test for fair value in section 141(2) can only be objective because the potential unfairness when a director is involved in two sides of a transaction is not caused by a disparity of information but rather because of the risk that the director, as a result of the conflict of interest, will not ensure fair value for the company. The approach of the Court of Appeal in *Robb v Sojourner*,[133] where the availability of account of profits as a remedy depended entirely on whether the company had received fair value, lends support to this view. It is suggested that the risk which the legislature was attempting to redress in section 149 was different. Here, the risk is that one shareholder, because of his or her position as a director of the company, will have an informational advantage over the person on the other side of the transaction. Disclosure of that information would negate the risk by removing the informational advantage of the director. The Securities Markets Act 1988 regulates share trading by directors and other insiders in listed entities. That Act does not impose a test of objective 'fair value'; instead the focus is on disclosure and on ensuring that those who are information insiders cannot exploit their informational advantage. It is suggested that section 149 should be applied in the same way for share dealing in companies not caught by the Securities Markets Act 1988.

However, the Court of Appeal agreed with Salmon J's interpretation of the provision with Richardson P concluding:[134]

> In our view there is nothing in the section to support the proposition that a director intending to deal in shares in the company has a duty to disclose to the prospective buyer or seller information material to value which the director has in his or her capacity as director and that disclosure frees the director from liability and renders the agreed price unassailable. The section does not even contemplate the passing of information from the director to the other party as a consideration relevant to liability or to quantification of the resulting liability for breach. On the contrary, on an ordinary reading of the section at each step the provisions adopt the abstain or pay fair value premise.

Clearly the section as currently interpreted by the courts imposes a requirement not of disclosure on directors who buy and sell shares in a company but a positive obligation to ensure that the party on the other side of the transaction pays or receives fair value. Factors such as

---

133 *Robb v Sojourner*, note 17 above.

134 *Thexton v Thexton*, note 129 above. For a critique of the High Court decision on this point, see S Watson and G Gunasekara, 'Shareholder Buy-Outs: New Problems for Directors of Unlisted Companies' (2001) 7 *NZBLQ* 265–75.

a discounted price because of a close family relationship (surely a factor in *Thexton*) will not be sufficient to discharge the obligation imposed on company directors by section 149. Nor will full disclosure to a party in an equal bargaining position.

The issue of whether fair value in section 149 is tied to the professional valuation standard of 'fair value' was considered by the Supreme Court in *Fong v Wong*.[135] The case involved the compulsory acquisition of shares in a family business following a falling-out between the shareholders. There was no informational asymmetry in the case, as both were directors of the company and thus had access to all information relevant to the value of the shares. When determining fair value or fair market value for valuation purposes, there is usually a discount for minority holdings of shares. The Supreme Court considered that in cases where there has been a falling-out between shareholders in a closely held quasi-partnership company, value should be determined on a pro rata basis; that is without a discount for a minority interest. 'This is because such a discount would usually not be fair as between vendor and purchaser in terms of: (a) the alternative (i.e. winding up); (b) what each gains and gives up on the transaction; and (c) the quasi-partnership nature of the underlying relationship.'[136]

The Supreme Court left the broader question open. 'There may be scope for argument as to what if any difference there is between "fair market value", "fair value" and "market value" arguments which in practice may depend on the relevant legislative or contractual context.'[137] The Court of Appeal also left the question open, stating that they were not convinced that fair market value and fair value really were different concepts, but accepting that the expert evidence that showed that they were.[138] The expert evidence, which is discussed in the High Court judgment, focuses on fair value being determined on the basis of what the vendor gave up and the purchaser obtained.[139]

Onerous on directors as section 149 may seem, its current drafting renders it a toothless tiger if it is interpreted literally. Section 149, by referring to a director acquiring or disposing of the shares, can only mean that a director must disclose the acquisition or disposal of a relevant interest and pay fair value only if that director is acquiring or disposing of the shares directly. Section 149 therefore does not capture share dealing by persons or companies related to the director; it thus negates the purpose of having

---

135 *Fong v Wong* [2010] NZSC 152.

136 Ibid, para 5.

137 Ibid, para 6.

138 *Fong v Wong* [2010] NZCA 301.

139 *Wong v Fong* (2010) 10 NZCLC 264,660, para 49.

a detailed definition of 'relevant interest' in section 146.[140] Granted, the application of the term 'director' extends beyond those appointed as directors but, in *Coleman v Myers*, it was a director who used another vehicle to trade the shares. Such a transaction would not be caught by section 149 as the entity trading the shares could not be said to be a director as defined in section 126(1)(a) or a deemed director as defined in sections 126(1)(b), (c) or (d).

If the transaction in *Coleman v Myers* was carried out under the regime imposed by the Companies Act 1993, the Myers would hold a relevant interest in the shares in the company through their holding company. They would therefore have a statutory obligation to shareholders to disclose their share acquisitions in the interest register of the company pursuant to section 148 but no statutory obligation to comply with section 149.

The argument that section 149 did not apply was advanced at a late stage in *Fong v Wong*,[141] where the shares were acquired and disposed of through trusts. The Supreme Court commented that this appeared to be a new argument and one that was unsustainable as it would allow the obvious purpose of the section to be subverted by a trust that was associated with the director.[142]

CONCLUSION

New Zealand, like Australia, was not subjected to the harshest effects of the global financial crisis. New Zealand has not, however, been immune from the resulting financial meltdown; it took place in the largely unregulated finance company sector. The fallout from that failure has been an inevitable focus on corporate governance and directors' duties. The cases, which have involved imprisonment of some finance company directors have led to calls for re-examination of directors' duties and the resulting likely criminalisation for breaches of section 131, the duty of good faith, and section 135, the reckless trading provision. On the other side, directors have argued that the inchoate nature of their duties and the increasing risk of liability justify increased fees.

How much the pioneering attempt to codify directors' duties found in the Companies Act 1993 has acted to enhance good corporate governance

---

[140] For a further discussion of this point, see S Watson, 'Coleman v Myers Under the 1993 Act' (1995) 1 *NZBLQ* 168.

[141] *Fong v Wong* [2010] NZSC 120.

[142] Ibid, para 1.

will inevitably be judged against the backdrop of the finance company failures. That may be unfair. The regulatory failure around finance companies related more to securities regulation (where reform is also taking place). The newly established regulator, the Financial Markets Authority, has been given some teeth. A robust interpretation of sections 139 to 144 when directors are called to account for related party transactions is still possible. All steps are of course ex post. Effective corporate governance depends on ex ante compliance by directors with their fundamental obligation to lead companies well. Duties, whether statutory or derived from the common law, mandate rules of conduct by directors. The content of such duties cannot set out to a full extent the ways in which members of boards should act when confronting the challenges of leading a company. At the very least directors can expect that the nature of these rules of conduct should be expressed clearly and, to that extent at least, the Companies Act 1993 is a success.

PART II

DIRECTORS' DUTIES IN OTHER JURISDICTIONS

5. Directors' duties in Italy

Carlo Amatucci

INTRODUCTION

In contrast to other jurisdictions, where the interests to be pursued by directors are clearly defined, a very distinctive feature of Italian Company Law is the lack of clarity in how directors have to discharge their fiduciary duties. Directors' duties are numerous and heavily regulated by the Civil Code, mainly through the lens of directors' liability.

The key feature is traditionally interpreted as an implicit recognition of the directors' duty to enhance the shareholder value. Notwithstanding, there is considerable debate about the idea that shareholders' interests cannot be merely reduced to the distribution of dividends. The shareholder value should be based – and this strongly influences directors' duties – on a long-term perspective and characterized by the limits set by the law in several fields including labour law, environmental protection, product liability and quality standards, trade transparency etc.

On this premise, the chapter analyses the core fiduciary duties of Italian directors in public and private companies.

1. THE NATURE OF DIRECTORS' DUTIES

According to Italian law, the management of public limited liability companies belongs exclusively to the directors. They carry out all the actions required to achieve corporate financial objectives.

The core concept of the company's management is specified by art. 2380-bis c.c., according to which 'the management of the company belongs exclusively to the directors who act for the fulfilment of the corporate purpose'. The rule does not allow the company to divide the corporate powers between directors and shareholders. It adopts the managerial model which does not bind directors to shareholders in the management of the company and satisfies the needs of rapid decisional procedures and efficiency which should characterize the management of public companies. It satisfies also the content of this management, making clear that the managing power embraces all the acts that are not expressly given by law to the general meeting of shareholders. In just a few cases the Civil Code (v. art. 2364, n 5) recognizes the power of shareholders to take resolutions on management issues. In some cases the articles of association may require a shareholders' resolution to approve specified acts.

The decisional independence of directors, reinforced by the Reform of 2003, goes in the direction of weakening shareholders' powers, but not up to the point of inducing directors to fulfil interest others than those of the shareholders.

The relationship between the company and its directors has been debated for a long time. Directors' powers are exclusive and mainly derive from company legislation. Consequently, shareholders cannot deprive them of the powers, nor can they give them directives or revoke their decisions.

This independence makes the relationship between directors and shareholders quite unique. In a very limited way it resembles the agency relationship, yet it cannot be exclusively qualified as such, nor can it be regarded as a contract of employment.

For a significant period of time some scholars believed that directors' powers derive from the special contract between them and the company,[1] others thought they derive from the same company's contract (articles of association), representing the execution of the company's contract.[2]

2. THE DUTY TO FULFIL THE COMPANY'S INTEREST AND THE ABSENCE OF A LEGAL DEFINITION IN REGARD TO OTHER INTERESTS THAT DIRECTORS MUST PURSUE

Contrary to other jurisdictions where the interests to be pursued by directors are clearly defined (see for the United Kingdom section 172 of the Companies Act), Italian company law has a very distinctive feature represented by the lack – despite a dense regulation of directors' fiduciary duties in the Civil Code – of clear objectives that directors have to achieve through their time in office. The only provision which dictates what has to inspire their activity is art. 2380-bis c.c., according to which directors have to carry out the corporate purpose. This and other rules help us to

1 G. Minervini, *Gli amministratori di società per azioni*, Milano, 1956.
2 F. Galgano, *Diritto commerciale. Le società*, Bologna, 2009, p. 309–10.

conclude that directors have to fulfil the company's interest despite the fact that the Civil Code does not define it, as we will see later.

One can infer to whom such duties are owed by looking at the liability provisions, since directors can be held liable towards the company, its creditors, minority shareholders, individual shareholders and third parties. Therefore, directors' duties and their standards are mainly seen through the lens of directors' liability. Italian Courts interpret and apply these rules – especially in case of directors' liability – to those who act as de jure or facto directors, in other words regardless of whether they have been duly appointed or not.

In theory, the lack of a clear legal definition of other interests to be pursued could open the doors for directors to pursue interests other than those of shareholders. On the contrary, this key feature is interpreted as an implicit recognition of the fact that directors have to pursue objectives which enhances the shareholder value, which happens to be equally lucrative for not only companies but also mutual funds and cooperatives. No rule authorizes directors to assess, in their decision-making process, the stakeholders' interests.

In the absence of such a rule, directors cannot equally consider shareholders and stakeholders, nor take decisions which privilege interests different from shareholders' ones. Stakeholders' interests can be pursued when this can turn out to become an advantage for the company or when failing to do so could become harmful for the company (i.e. reputational effects) or when shareholders expressly authorize directors to do so.

The only provisions in the Civil Code that explicitly force directors to take into account the interests other than those of shareholders are arts 2394 and 2395 c.c. The first makes directors liable to the company's creditors for not observing the duty to preserve the company's assets – when they prove insufficient to satisfy their claims – the second makes directors liable to individual shareholders or third parties who have been directly prejudiced as a result of intentional or negligent acts.

Less relevant is the directors' duty to disclose, in their annual report to the general meeting, information regarding the company's business affecting the environment and company employees (art. 2428 c.c.). Equally, the directors' duty (contained in art. 103, c. 3-bis of the Consolidated Act), in listed companies, to assess – in the case of takeover bids – the effects that the success of the offer will have on the company's interests, the labour force and on the logistics and production. Having discharged this duty, it is for the shareholders of the target company to evaluate the offer.

Special regulations also impose on all companies the adoption, by the directors, of adequate structures and instruments to prevent unlawful conduct and crimes (l. 231/2001), as well as compliance with special rules in the banking sector. These are special provisions which are aimed at preventing the breach of duties and the obvious consequences affecting the company, namely its reputation and financial losses; nevertheless, these sets of rules do not specifically mean that there is a legal recognition of corporate social responsibility. In the absence of a legal definition of what the interest of the company is, Italian scholars still debate it and consequently about the issues of the corporate social responsibility.

A reliable and well-accepted definition considers the company's interest as one based on what the constitutional or contractual documents of the company establish in the sense that this agreement is, thoroughly and in good faith, assessed by the majority of shareholders, and it is also executed by the company directors with diligence and loyalty.[3]

However, in the Italian legal literature the idea that the interest of shareholders cannot be reduced to the mere division of profits is gradually developing. The shareholder value should be based on a long-term perspective and take into account the limits set by employment law, environmental protection, product and quality standards, trade transparency etc.[4]

The point is that these regulations do not limit directors' duties to exclusively acting for the interest of shareholders who could request directors to consider the interest of other constituencies, namely employees, the environment etc.

Having no special rules, with the exception of art. 2639 c.c. – which for corporate and bankruptcy crimes makes no difference for those who exercise the powers without any formal appointment – it is worth mentioning, that Italian Courts apply the rules on directors' fiduciary duties and subsequent liabilities to shadow directors as well.

3. THE GENERAL DUTY OF CARE AND THE DUTY OF SKILL

Italian law requires that, in the managing of the company, directors have the same fiduciary duties and liabilities of those who manage third-parties' assets.[5] Also widely recognized is the *Business Judgement Rule*, therefore

---

[3] R. Costi, *Relazione di sintesi*, in *L'interesse sociale tra valorizzazione del capitale e protezione degli stakeholders. In ricordo di Pier Giusto Jaeger*, Milano, 2010, p. 192.

[4] P. Montalenti, *Interesse sociale e amministratori*, in *L'interesse sociale*, cit., p. 99.

[5] G. Ferri, *Le società* in *Trattato di diritto civile italiano*, fondato da F. Vassalli, vol. X. 3., Utet, 1987, p. 710.

directors' decisions cannot be challenged on the ground of failing to achieve the wanted results.

Directors' duties can be divided into two main categories: general duties and specific duties. General duties are the duty of care and the duty of loyalty. Some of the specific duties are expressly provided by the Civil Code rules, others can be inferred by various regulations (Civil Code and special provisions).

The first general duty is regulated by art. 2392 c.c. – modified by the Reform of 2004 – which states that:

> directors have to fulfil the duties imposed upon them by law and by the articles of association with the diligence required by the nature of the office and their specific capabilities. They are jointly and severally liable to the company for damages deriving from the non-observance of such duties, except for functions vested solely in the executive committee or materially vested in one or more directors.

This duty must be related to the duty of the directors to act in an informed manner, according to art. 2381, § 5°.

The 'diligence required by the nature of the office' represents the duty of care, and it has been interpreted in a way that a director will be held liable when, in making decisions – e.g. voting at board level – he has not acted with the professional standard of diligence, has acted when uninformed or has not requested the necessary information, has not given adequate consideration to the circumstances and, especially, has not prudently assessed the risks.

The reference to the 'specific capabilities' emphasizes the subjective test to which the duty of skill is subject to. Hence, this subjective standard should take into account the directors' education, professional experience and the knowledge for which he/she had been appointed and/or offered to work for the company.[6]

Therefore, to determine the standard of diligence the court will consider the company's dimension, the type of business, and the personal qualifications held by the appointed director. The standard of diligence will be higher depending upon the complexity of the business and the level of the uncertainty faced by the director and will also take into account the director's individual capabilities.[7] Clearly, this does not mean that directors

---

[6] C. Angelici, *Diligentia quam in suis e Business Judgment Rule*, in *Riv. dir. comm.*, 2006, I, 677; S. Pescatore, *Spunti sulla novellata gestione dell'impresa nella società per azioni*, in *Scritti in onore di Vincenzo Buonocore*, vol. III, t. III, Milano, 2005, 3420.

[7] P.G. Jaeger, F. Denozza, A. Toffoletto, *Appunti di diritto commerciale*, Giuffrè, 2010, p. 373–4.

have to be skilful in accounting, finance or any business sector run by the company, it just ascertains that the standard rises proportionally to the level of complexity and structure of the corporate body.

4. THE DUTY OF LOYALTY, TO ACT IN THE COMPANY'S INTEREST: DIRECTORS' INTERESTS

As previously said, directors are requested to fulfil the company's objectives, as a result of being the managers of the resources invested by shareholders. Consequently, 'in carrying out the corporate purpose, directors cannot have any other motivation than company's interest'. Nevertheless, Italian law does not necessarily consider the director's interest opposite to the company's interest.

The duty to act in the company's best interest is found in art. 2391 c.c. which imposes on the director the duty to notify other directors and the board of statutory auditors 'of any interest which he, on his own or on behalf of third parties, has in a given transaction, pointing out the nature, terms, origin and scope thereof'. This disclosure has to be appropriate and complete in order to allow the recipients to be aware of the situation and assess it. In other words, the board has to evaluate the prevalence of the company's interest comparing it with that of the external interests. If the director fails to disclose he may be held liable. Directors are not permitted to take part in meetings deliberating about potential conflicts of interest and cannot cast their votes. Consequently, managing directors will have to refrain from carrying out the transaction in which their personal interest is latent and will have to present for consideration, the so-called conflict of interest, to the board of directors. In companies with a sole director it is the general meeting of shareholders who will deal with the conflict of interest issue.

In cases where the board decides to go ahead with the transaction, the board's resolution will indicate the reasons and its convenience for the company. Directors will have to assess and evaluate the consequences of carrying out the transaction, which may be exacting, especially in finding the right balance between the company's interest and the director's. The decision has to be motivated and must prove that regardless of the potential conflict, the company's own benefit outweighs that of the director so that it is ultimately beneficial to the corporate body.

In cases of non-observance of these provisions or in cases of resolutions made either by the board or the executive committee, the board of directors and internal auditors (sindicaci) could challenge the validity of the conflicting transaction 'within ninety days from the date thereof, in the event they may harm the company' (art. 2391 c.c.) in which case the director conflicting with the interest of the company must abstain from voting in passing such resolution.

For publicly held companies only art. 2391-bis c.c. requires that directors have to adopt and disclose rules – pursuant to the general principles set forth by Consob (the Italian Securities and Exchange Commission) – to ensure the formal and substantial transparency and fairness of the transactions with related third parties and disclose such transactions in the director's report. Where there is a conflict of interest in relation to complex transactions in terms of value and indeed nature, directors have the right to be assisted by independent experts.

Whilst such principles of increased transparency have caused a positive impact on the market, some doubts arise with regard to the choice of submitting the most delicate cases to the scrutiny of independent experts, whose efficiency has been questioned following worldwide financial scandals.

5. THE DUTY TO ACT IN THE COMPANY'S INTEREST: COMPETITION AND BUSINESS OPPORTUNITIES

The duty of directors to act in the company's interest implies also that they cannot acquire the status of partners with unlimited liability in competing companies, nor carry out competing business on their own behalf or on behalf of third parties. The duty also limits the possibility of accepting directorship or general managing positions in competitor's boards, unless authorized to do so by the shareholders in general meeting. The breach of this duty implies that they may be removed from their office and are liable for damages (art. 2390 c.c.).

Acting in the company's interest means also that directors cannot use, for their own or third parties' benefit, data, information or business opportunities which they come across while exercising office (art. 2391 c.c.). In pursuing these self-dealing transactions or misappropriations – considered anticompetitive torts[8] – to the detriment of the company or which deprive the company of related advantages, directors may incur personal liability

---

[8] F. Barachini, *L'appropriazione delle* corporate opportunities *come fattispecie d infedeltà degli amministratori di S.p.a.*, in *Il nuovo diritto delle società. Liber Amicorum Gian Franco Campobasso*, vol. 2, Utet, 2006, p. 628.

and be held liable to compensate the company in damages. It is worth mentioning that alongside the available remedies in company law, competition law provides further assistance.

6. DIRECTORS' DUTIES IN GROUPS OF COMPANIES

The directors' duty to act in the company's interest faces a major challenge in cases where the company belongs to a group, as happens to the vast majority of the large Italian companies. It is not clear, and it is strongly debated, whether the general duties are the most effective ones for dealing with the typical agency problems of the groups. This is the reason why the Reform of 2003 introduced a partial regulation of the duties – and consequent liabilities – that directors of the parent company have to observe in the interest of the subsidiaries.

Although art. 2497 c.c. refers to the parent company, or to any other entity which controls the subsidiary (even an individual), it is clear that the following duties fall mainly upon the directors of the parent company. The rule – which is again a rule of liability from which we infer the nature of the duty – states that in the exercise of the controlling power the parent company has to take care of the subsidiary interest and observe the principles 'of fair company and business management'.

Should the parent company fail to act in such a way, the parent company and its directors are directly liable to the shareholders of the controlled company. Such liability encompasses damages caused to the profitability and the value of their shares, as well as to liability to the company's creditors for damages caused to the company assets. The rule specifies that no liability occurs if it appears that no damage was suffered in the light of the overall outcome of the controlling power or when the damage was fully prevented. A clear application of the so-called compensation advantages theory.

7. THE DUTY TO MONITOR AND TO ACT IN AN INFORMED WAY

Where the articles of association or the shareholders' meeting allows, the board of directors may delegate their powers to an executive committee made up of some of its members or to one or more of its members. In this case the non-executive directors have to set the contents, restrictions and terms for the exercise of the powers delegated. They may always issue guidelines to the executive directors and take over transactions falling in the scope of the delegated powers.

In other words, non-executive directors have the duty to monitor efficiently the activity of the executive directors and can always exercise their powers if needed, especially when the information shows signs of risk for the company. As we have previously seen, art. 2381 c.c. states that executive directors ensure that the organizational, administrative and accounting structure be suitable for the nature and size of the company. Therefore, they review the strategic, industrial and financial plans of the company, when they are drafted. And finally they assess the general course of business, on the basis of the report provided by the executive directors.

Executive directors, at least every six months, have to report to the non-executive and to the auditors on the general course of business and its foreseeable evolution as well as on the most significant transactions carried out by the company and its subsidiaries. However, it is thought that six months is a long period of time and that such reports should be made more frequently.

A very significant duty for non-executive directors is the requirement that they are well informed before they act, having gathered all due information (art. 2381, par. 6). Each director may request that the executive directors provide information relating to the management of the company at the board's meeting. This duty implies a power for the director, since he will not act in an informed way if he fails to ask to executives and officers for all the information he needs to evaluate every single decision. The problem is that such information is given at a board meeting, which means that the single director cannot directly inquire at the company's offices to get this information by himself. This is the reason why the provision has been widely criticized.

Let us consider the case where the information provided by the executive was not adequate, especially in situations of high risk or danger. Or the case that non-executive directors have doubts about the fair conduct of the executive directors. In these cases, the non-executive directors could not investigate by themselves but rather ask the suspicious delegates to give them, in the board meeting only, the information they need. Needless to say that this does not appear to be an efficient way of obtaining the information needed.

8. THE DUTY TO DRAW UP ACCOUNTS

Another specific duty of directors (art. 2423 c.c.) is to draw up the yearly accounts of the balance sheet, the profit and loss account and the notes on the accounts. They have to do so in a clear manner so that the accounts will give a true and fair view of the company's assets and liabilities, financial position and yearly profit or loss. This duty is crucial for the management of the company. The accounts will be accompanied by a report drawn up by the directors on the company's situation and on the progress of the company's business both as a whole and in the various fields in which it has operated, including subsidiaries, with particular regard to costs, income and investments. The report will need to comply with the information required by art. 2428 c.c.

9. DUTIES RELATED TO THE CAPITAL AND TO THE WINDING UP OF THE COMPANY

The articles of association may give directors the power to increase the capital one or more times up to a specified amount and for the maximum period of five years (from the date of the company's registration).

But it is with regards to potential losses of the capital that the role of the directors becomes significant. Art. 2446 c.c. requires that should the capital diminish by more than one-third due to losses, directors will summon the shareholders' meeting without delay to take appropriate action. In cases where the loss is less than one-third within the following financial year and the shareholder meeting should reduce the capital in proportion to the losses, directors will have to secure the court's permission to go ahead with the reduction in line with the losses shown in the accounts.

If, by reason of the loss of more than one-third, the capital falls below the minimum, which is €120.000 (for a public limited-liability company), the directors will have to summon the shareholders' meeting to decide on the reduction of capital and the simultaneous increase to an amount not lower than the said minimum, or on the transformation of the company for example into a private company (art. 2447 c.c.).

If one of these resolutions is not taken by shareholders, the winding up the company occurs (art. 2484 c.c.). In this event directors will have to ascertain the occurrence of the cause for winding up the company and will have to register such certification at the Register of Companies. Therefore, they will have to summon the shareholders' meeting which will appoint the liquidators and decide the criteria for the liquidation.

In cases of delay or omission directors will be held jointly and severally liable for damages suffered by the company, shareholders, creditors and third parties (art. 2485 c.c.).

Until the liquidators are appointed directors maintain the power to manage the company only for purposes of preserving the company's assets and their value. Again they will be held liable for damages caused to the same categories as a consequence of acts or omissions committed in violation of this rule (art. 2486 c.c.).

10. DUTIES RELATED TO THE FUNCTIONING OF THE COMPANY'S ORGANS

Directors are under a duty to call shareholders' meetings (art. 2366 c.c.) at least once a year for the approval of the accounts and when they are requested to do so by as many shareholders as representing at least 20 per cent in public companies and 10 per cent in private companies, of the capital or the lower percentage set out in the articles of association, and the agenda must indicate the point to be dealt with at the meeting. (art. 2367 c.c.). If they do not take action the court, having heard the members of the board and the statutory auditors, in case the refusal proves unjustified, may issue an order for the calling of the meeting and appoint the chairman. The call upon request by shareholders is not permitted for matters that are for the general meeting to decide or upon proposals, projects or reports submitted by the company directors.

In particular, the chairman of the board, selected by the board members (unless appointed by the shareholders' meeting) summons the board meetings, sets out the agenda, coordinates the works and verifies that all directors are provided with suitable information to be covered in the agenda (2381 c.c.).

11. DIRECTORS' LIABILITY

As previously mentioned, directors have to fulfil the duties imposed upon them by law and by the articles of association with the diligence required by the nature of the office and their specific capabilities. Therefore they are jointly and severally liable to the company for damages deriving from the breach of these duties, except for functions vested solely in the executive committee or materially vested in one or more directors (art. 2392). The provision further requests that if directors are aware of facts or circumstances – from which liability may originate – and fail to do all they can to prevent such events from occurring or to eliminate or reduce their consequences, they are still jointly and severally liable.

Liability for breach of duties does not extend to the director who, without fault opposes the resolution proposed, has his dissent recorded without delay in the minutes of meetings and resolutions of the board and immediately gives written notice to the chairman of the board of statutory auditors.

The enforcement of directors' liability is regulated by art. 2393 c.c. An action for liability is brought – within five years from the end of their office – pursuant to a resolution of the meeting of shareholders. The resolution entails their removal from office as long as it is made by the vote of at least one-fifth of the company capital. In such case, the same meeting appoints the new directors.

The company may waive its right of action and settle the dispute, provided that such waiver and settlement are approved by an express resolution of the meeting and provided that there is not an opposing vote of a number of minority shareholders representing at least one-fifth of the company capital.

The historical reasons which make it difficult for minority shareholders to enforce directors' liability forced the Italian policy makers to adopt art. 2393-bis c.c., which provides that the company actions against directors, can be brought also by shareholders representing at least one-fifth (one-twentieth in widely held companies) of the company capital or the other fraction of capital – in any case not to exceed one-third – set forth by the articles of association. They bring the action in their names yet in the company's interest. This percentage should be kept during the entire duration of the trial.

The company must be summoned in court and the writ of summons must be served on the company, also in the person of the chairman of the board of statutory auditors. Shareholders appoint one or more shareholders' representatives (lawyers).

Should the claim succeed, the company will have to reimburse the plaintiffs for the legal costs and the expenses borne during the investigation of the events. Plaintiffs may waive their right to claim legal costs for as long as it is for the company's benefit.

Directors can be liable to company creditors for the breach of their duties concerning the preservation of the company's assets should these assets prove insufficient for the satisfaction of their claims (art. 2394 c.c.). The waiver of the action by the company does not prevent creditors from suing and any settlement may be challenged by creditors only through an action for revocation (rescission) when the relevant requirements are met.

These actions against directors do not affect the right to claim damages of an individual shareholder or third party who has been directly affected as result of intentional or negligent acts by the directors (art. 2395 c.c.). This action can be brought within five years from the occurrence of the wrongful act, which is thought to have prejudiced the shareholder or third party.

In cases of bankruptcy, administrative liquidation (the insolvency procedure for banks, insurance companies and investment companies) and extraordinary administration (the insolvency procedure for large companies) the actions against directors may be exercised by the receiver, the commissioner liquidator and the special commissioner (art. 2394-bis c.c.).

The enforcement of directors' liabilities has worked efficiently in insolvency procedures, whereas great criticism questions their efficacy when companies are still in the course of business.

6. Directors' duties in China

Marcos Jaramillo

When we talk about "Chinese law", many people smile and ask, "is there Chinese law?" Surely they have heard, or suffered, the consequences of the difference between the theory and the practice of law in that country: excessive governmental meddling, the intervention of the Communist Party, local protectionism, fraud and manipulation in the markets, weak enforcement, judicial corruption at certain levels, are only some of the elements that cause there to be a great difference between the theory and the practice of law in China.

To begin with, is there a rule of law in China? Actually, the Chinese have made an immense and valiant effort to have the rule of law. It is really impressive to see the quality and quantity of its laws, institutions and studies in such a short period of time. But there still is a great distance to travel for a rule of law in China to achieve the standards of Western countries. One of my courses in the Law School of Pontificia Universidad Católica de Chile is precisely "The Rule of Law in China" and there we are seeing, with very specific research, the different areas in which there still is a great distance to travel.

But continuing with the idea that we started with, is there Chinese law? It seems a silly question, but many people ask it. The answer is that of course there is law in China. In addition, certainly, thousands of years before laws were developed in the majority of the countries of my readers: the Chinese had formidable organization, an immense bureaucracy, great emperors and terrible sanctions for people who did not comply with the laws. But if you pay attention, the "law" that emanated from the authority in China historically has been in a special form criminal law and administrative law. It is for this reason that for the Chinese, state power and public order are the main part of the law. Because of their culture, what they fundamentally see is the "collective" good and not the "individual" person with his dignity and rights. The statement of a Chinese student in the United States is impressive in this respect: after a long time of being in that country, "*I realized that before I am a Chinese, I am a human being*. And before I am a human being, I am just another one of the millions of sentient beings."[1] Before, he saw "the Chinese" and "the others," now he sees that "everybody is a human being." In this manner, private law, civil law and commercial law were not developed by the authority, but rather by the same individuals who purchased, sold and carried out commercial activities, as customs. To this we must add that Confucianism, Chinese morality, looked with disdain upon traders.

The last dynasty, the Qing, fell in 1912, giving rise to a Republic that was politically weak with many factions fighting over power. In that state, although laws were dictated, there were no great advances in the legal practice. The battles among several factions kept going until the two strongest armies met for the final time: the Kuomintang of Chiang Kai-shek and the Communist Party of Mao Tse-tung. Mao won, creating the People's Republic of China in 1949. At the beginning it was thought that it would give more liberties, but the regime quickly closed ranks. And with regard to what interests us, codes were not dictated, law schools were closed and many great law professors such as Jiang Ping were sent to work in the countryside. The Cultural Revolution (1966–76) ended with the death of Mao, and with it several changes began to appear in China. Actually and although behind the scenes, the person who was called to take the reins of the country, Deng Xiaoping, announced in December 1978 a new "Open Door" policy, the opening up to foreign countries, to start vertiginous economic development. The authorities realized that lawyers and law (Western-style) "were necessary," which is why they also reopened the Ministry of Justice, the law schools, and they returned to study this branch of knowledge. But they had to start practically from zero: that is what is impressive (to the point that they have currently reached) but, at the same time, it is one thing to have laws, law schools, but another thing as to how it is taught, how it is understood and how it is applied in practice. You can perceive that in so few years and with all of their cultural and intellectual baggage (so different from ours), it is impossible, absolutely impossible, that they understand the same or something close to what we understand.

Their laws are very new. For example, the PRC[2] Company Law dates from only 1993 and the large and significant legal changes to that law which we discuss in this chapter are only from 2005. On the other hand, the Law on Lawyers was enacted only in 1996.

Therefore, in practice, and without yet setting forth the peculiarities of

---

[1] Zilon Wang, "Confessions of a Chinese Nationalist", Huffington Post, October 26, 2012. In <http://www.huffingtonpost.com/zilong-wang/chinese-students-america_b_2025439.html> (accessed on April 17, 2013).

[2] PRC: People's Republic of China.

Chinese law and their parallel systems (which we will see below),[3] although the Chinese have the best of intentions we will probably have problems understanding their business transactions and how to carry them out, problems with understanding laws, rights and personal obligations. The attorney Randall Lewis tells us that in China, "you would be surprised how many operational people don't really understand what is contained within the key contracts or the key obligations of all players until a dispute arises".[4] Also, the same attorney tells us that "it is likely that due to educational and cultural issues, these people[5] do not fully understand the true meaning of a contract".[6]

But then why should we bother ourselves with China and why is China currently so important and why does it continue to attract investments and business people? It is because it is a gigantic country with 1.3 billion inhabitants that we cannot ignore it. It is the primary commercial partner with a large number of countries, it is already the second largest economy in the world (and is on the road to being the first very soon) and according to the 2012 poll of the US-China Business Council, 89 per cent of the companies polled are receiving profits, the highest annual rate of all of the polls taken by this organization.[7]

In China there is a hierarchy of norms. At the highest level after the Constitution are the laws. However, there are many administrative authorities that also issue their norms, as will be evidenced herein. In addition, in a peculiar manner, the Supreme Court of China issues "interpretations" of the laws, without cases being submitted to it for its decision, but rather on its own initiative through "interpretive rules", through consultations with legislative and administrative authorities of the country, assuming the role of real supplemental legislation.[8]

---

[3] Together with the legislation itself are the administrative agencies and courts that at times intervene without law and, in addition, we must add the actions of the Chinese Communist Party.

[4] Randall Lewis, Associate General Counsel, Asia Pacific at Danone (Shanghai, China), "Dealing with a Chinese partner? Keep these simple pointers in mind", China Law Blog Debates (LinkedIn), August 2012.

[5] "Most Chinese businessmen over the age of 50" (Randall Lewis Associate General Counsel, Asia Pacific at Danone (Shanghai, China), "Seek (or provide) balanced legal advice when entering into any China deal. Consider this:", China Law Blog Debates (LinkedIn), August 2012).

[6] Ibid.

[7] The US-China Business Council, "USCBC 2012 China Business Environment Survey Results: Continued Growth and Profitability; Tempered Optimism Due to Rising Costs, Competition, and Market Barriers", The US-China Business Council, Washington D.C., October 2012, p. 3.

[8] Logically, then there are also Judicial Interpretations to Chinese Company Law.

Although in the PRC Company Law together with the directors there are often supervisors and managers in top management positions, in this chapter we will limit ourselves to civil liability of the directors in companies in China, both in theory as well as in practice.

LEGAL SCOPE

The Chinese legal system by general rule follows the continental European model, although China still does not have a Civil Code.[9]

In China there is a general corporate regulation and another only for foreigners, (the so-called Foreign Invested Enterprises, FIEs), in which at least 25 per cent of its ownership has to be that of foreign investors.

A FIE company can be:

- A Wholly Foreign Owned Enterprises (WFOE),
- An Equity Joint Venture (EJV),
- A Cooperative Joint Venture (CJV),
- And, in exceptional cases, a Foreign Invested Partnership Enterprise (FIPE).

And these may take the form of a limited liability company or a corporation, to which the FIE rules apply in the first place, and in the alternative the general rules.[10] Both the limited liability company as well as the corporation has a board of directors. In practice, the majority of the FIEs in China are limited liability companies.

The FIEs are only permitted to carry out business activities in accordance with the scope of the business activities approved by the authorities of the government.

The legal scope of corporate governance[11] in China has taken form rapidly in the last two decades. The two most important norms are the PRC Company Law, originally enacted in December 1993, which entered into force in 1994, and has been subsequently amended in 1999, 2004 and 2005, and the Code on Corporate Governance for Listed Companies of 2002, issued by the China Securities Regulatory Commission (CSRC) and the State Economic and Trade Commission (SETC).

---

[9] It is thought that there will soon be a Civil Code, because the Chinese have already legislated, in different laws, all of the fundamental themes of civil law such as Property Law.

[10] Art. 218 PRC Company Law.

[11] 公司治理 (gongsi zhili) in Chinese.

If we want to divide the regulation of our study according to its hierarchy we have to distinguish between four levels: the Basic Laws, the Administrative Regulations of the first level, the Regulatory Norms of the second level and the Self-regulation Norms.

- Basic Laws, either formulated by the People's National Congress or its Standing Committee:
  - The Company Law
  - The Securities Law
  - The Law on the State-Owned Assets of Enterprises
  - The Accounting Law.
- Administrative Regulations of the first level, formulated by the State Council:
  - Opinions on Promoting the Reform
  - Opening and Steady Growth of Capital Markets
  - Circular of the State Council on its Approval of the CSRC's Opinion on Improving the Quality of Listed Companies.
- Regulatory Norms of the second level, formulated by the ministries, commissions, the People's Bank of China, and other agencies, under the jurisdiction of the State Council, among others:
  - Code of Corporate Governance of Listed Companies
  - Regulations on Information Disclosure of Listed Companies
  - Guidelines on Articles of Association of Listed Companies
  - Guiding Opinions on the Establishment of the System of Independent Directors in Listed Companies
  - Implementation Opinion on Issues relating to Application of Law for Administration of Examination and Approval and Registration of Foreign-invested Companies.
- Self-regulation Norms, by the stock exchanges, among others:
  - Rules on Listing Stocks
  - Trading Rules.

Although the binding effect of a law in China is quite clear, there are norms such as the Code of Corporate Governance of 2002 whose binding effect is not known with certainty. The CSRC can instruct companies to make corrections in accordance with the Code. The Code requires the companies that are listed on the exchange to deliver information in accordance with the current state of corporate governance in the company. But is it binding?

On the other hand, in 2006 the authority that is responsible for registering the companies, the State Administration for Industry & Commerce (SAIC), together with another three state authorities issued an "Implementation Opinion"[12] on the application of the PRC Company Law in relation with the FIEs.

The latter document indicates to us that only the board of directors is a necessary entity in an Equity Joint Venture or a Cooperative Joint Venture under the form of a limited liability company. However, for the case of Wholly Foreign Owned Enterprises the company must comply with the other provisions of the PRC Company Law. Is it binding?

This ambiguity in relation to the binding effect is also applied to the basic regulations of internal control that entered into force on July first 2009, which play the role of guidance and suggestion.[13]

It could be "soft law", that is to say rules that are issued by an authority but that do not create binding rights and duties, such as recommendations, technical visits, codes of conduct, standards, model laws etc. However, despite not creating binding rights and duties their non-compliance brings with it serious practical consequences in relation to the authority.

The administrative soft law topics are something that one must take into account in Asia where said rules are always complied with. Many studies have been made about administrative soft law in Japan.[14] However, studies of administrative soft law in China are beginning to be done. For example, Professor Nicholas Calcina Howson indicates to us that:

> China's securities regulator enforces insider trading prohibitions pursuant to non-legal and non-regulatory internal 'guidance'. Reported agency decisions indicate that enforcement against insider trading is often possible pursuant to this guidance, as the behavior identified is far outside of the scope of insider trading liability provided for in statute or regulation.[15]

---

[12] The Implementation Opinion on Issues relating to Application of Law for Administration of Examination and Approval and Registration of Foreign-invested Companies.

[13] Although the suggestions of the authority play a very strong and formal role.

[14] In Chile, for example, during the 39th National Conference of Public Law in Santiago, Professors Marcos Jaramillo and José Luis Lara presented the paper "About the so-called Administrative Soft Law. Notes regarding the Japanese and Chilean experience", which is about to be published. The Japanese section discusses "administrative guidance" in Japan.

[15] Howson, Nicholas Calcina, "Enforcement without Foundation? – Insider Trading and China's Administrative Law Crisis", *American Journal of Comparative Law*, Vol. 60, No. 4, p. 955.

LEGAL NORMS[16]

The faculties of the board of directors are listed in article 47 PRC Company Law:

1. to convene the meeting of the shareholders assembly, and to report on its work to the board;
2. to implement the resolutions adopted by the shareholders assembly;
3. to decide on the operational plans and investment plans of the company;
4. to draw up the annual financial budget plan and final accounts plan of the company;
5. to draw up plans for profit distribution and plans for making up losses of the company;
6. to draw up plans for the increase or reduction of the registered capital and the issue of corporate bonds of the company;
7. to draw up plans for the merger, division, dissolution and transformation of the company;
8. to decide on the establishment of the internal administrative bodies of the company;
9. to decide on the appointment or dismissal of the manager of the company and the matters concerning his remuneration, and upon recommendation of the manager, decide on the appointment or dismissal of the deputy manager(s) and persons in charge of the financial affairs of the company, and on the matters concerning their remuneration;
10. to formulate the basic management system of the company; and
11. to exercise other functions and powers stipulated by the company's articles of association.

In addition, the corporations that are listed on the exchange have a special legal regime indicated in articles 121 to 125 PRC Company Law.

Looking at the regulation in more detail, the PRC Company Law contains some stipulations on the qualifications and obligations of the

[16] For the translation to English of the PRC Company Law we have utilized what is indicated in: <http://www.china.org.cn/china/LegislationsForm2001-2010/2011-02/11/content_21898292.htm>, and for the translation of the PRC Securities Law we have utilized what is indicated in: <http://www.grandall-law.com/china-laws-regulations/laws-regulations-securities/securities-law-of-the-peoples-republic-of-china-revised-in-2005.html>.

directors of the corporations and the limited liability companies (arts 147–153 PRC Company Law).

The section on qualifications contains a list of persons who cannot be directors. The list in article 147, paragraph 1, indicates the following persons:

1. a person who has no or limited capacity for civil conduct;
2. a person who was sentenced to criminal punishment for embezzlement, bribery, seizure of property or misappropriation of property or for sabotage of the socialist market economic order, where less than five years have elapsed after the expiration of the period of execution; or a person who was deprived of his political rights for the commission of a crime, where less than five years have elapsed after the expiration of the period of execution;
3. a person who, being a director or the head or manager of a company or enterprise that went into bankruptcy and liquidation, was personally liable for the bankruptcy of the said company or enterprise, where less than three years have elapsed from the date liquidation of the company or enterprise is completed;
4. a person who, being the legal representative of a company or an enterprise, the business license of which was revoked for violation of law and which was ordered to close down, was personally liable for the above, where less than three years have elapsed from the date the business license of the company or enterprise is revoked; or
5. a person who fails to liquidate a relatively large amount of personal debts when they are due.

FIDUCIARY DUTIES

Both the PRC Company Law and the Code of Corporate Governance, as well as other norms, explicitly indicate the duties of loyalty and diligence of the directors. In general terms, if a director infringes the law, administrative regulations or the company's articles of association, placing in danger the interests of the shareholders, they may sue the director before the courts and request indemnification.

It was with the PRC Company Law, amended in 2005, that the "Fiduciary Duties", in their Anglo-Saxon model, took legal form. Article 148 PRC Company Law indicates to us:

> Directors (. . .) of a company shall observe laws, administrative regulations and the company's articles of association and shall assume the duties of loyalty and diligence to the company.

> Directors (. . .) of a company shall not take advantage of their functions and powers to accept bribes or collect other illicit earnings, and shall not take illegal possession of the property of the company.

DUTY OF LOYALTY

Article 149 PRC Company Law specifies a duty of loyalty, identifying a set of acts or of actions that directors may not carry out:

1. misappropriating the funds of the company;
2. opening an account in his own name or in the name of another person to deposit the funds of the company;
3. in violation of the stipulations of the company's articles of association or without the consent of the shareholders' assembly, the shareholders' general assembly or the board of directors, loaning the funds of the company to another person or using the property of the company to provide guarantee for another person;
4. in violation of the stipulations of the company's articles of association or without the consent of the shareholders' assembly or the shareholders' general assembly, entering into a contract or conducting transactions with the company;
5. without the consent of the shareholders' assembly or the shareholders' general assembly, taking advantage of his position to seek commercial opportunities, which belong to the company, for himself or for another person, or operating for himself or for another person the same kind of business as that of the company where he is holding a post;
6. taking into his own possession the commissions from transactions conducted by another person with the company;
7. disclosing secrets of the company without authorization; or
8. other acts committed in violation of the duty of loyalty to the company.

The earnings received for any action that is realized in violation of the previous list shall belong to the company.

In relation to conflicts of interest there is a general regulation in article 21 and a special regulation in article 125, both in the PRC Company Law.

Article 21 tells us that (. . .) directors (. . .) of a company shall not take advantage of their affiliated relations to damage the interests of the company. He shall be liable for compensation in case of a violation of the provisions of this paragraph that causes losses to the company.

Article 125 stipulates that where the director of a listed company is affiliated with an enterprise that is involved in the matters on which a resolution is to be made at a meeting of the board of directors, he shall not exercise his voting right on such a resolution, nor shall he exercise the voting right on behalf of another director. Such a meeting of the board of directors may be held with the attendance of more than half of the directors who are not affiliated with the enterprise, and the resolution made at the meeting of the board shall be subject to adoption by more than half of the unaffiliated directors. Where the number of unaffiliated directors present at the meeting of the board is less than three persons, the matters shall be submitted to the shareholders' general assembly of the listed company for deliberation.

On the other hand, article 97 of the Guidance for the Articles of Association of the Listed Companies also follows what is indicated with regard to the duty of loyalty of the directors in the PRC Company Law, and indicates that if a director causes damage to the company, he must assume his liability through indemnification for damages. The company may add other requirements in the Articles of Association.

Chapter 3 of the Guidance on Appointment and Activities of Directors of Listed Companies of the Shanghai Stock Exchange also specifies the duty of loyalty specified in the PRC Company Law. In the first place, the directors must not damage the interests of a company that is listed on the exchange for the interests of a third party; and if discovering that the behavior of a company that is listed on the exchange or a third party damages the interests of the company, the directors will ask them to explain and correct the damage and to make a report to the board of directors on a regular basis. In the second place, the director must disclose to a company that is listed on the exchange matters such as horizontal competition, business contacts, debtor-creditor relations, shareholding, and other business connections or conflicts of the director or his close relatives. The related directors cannot vote. In the third place, a director must keep the secrets of a company that is listed on the exchange and not release material information that a company that is listed on the exchange has not transmitted to the public in general through the established means of communication.

Article 4 of the Shenzhen Stock Exchange Small and Medium Enterprise Board Director Conduct Guidance indicates to us the basic principles of the duty of loyalty: a director must be loyal to the company, its shareholders and their interests exercising his power within the scope of his functions and authority, having the interests of the company as the starting point, and strictly avoiding conflicts between his interests and the interests of the company.

DUTY OF CARE (DILIGENCE)

Article 150 PRC Company Law indicates to us that where a director (. . .) violates laws, administrative regulations or the company's articles of association in performance of his duties for the company, and thus causes losses to the company, he shall be liable for compensation. Also, article 151 PRC Company Law stipulates that where the shareholders' assembly or the shareholders' general assembly requests directors (. . .) to be present at its meeting, they shall attend the meeting as non-voting participants and subject themselves to inquiries by the shareholders. Furthermore, directors (. . .) shall truthfully provide relevant information and data to the board of supervisors or the supervisors of a company with limited liability where there is no such board of supervisors, and shall not hinder the exercise of the functions and powers by the board of supervisors or the supervisors.

With more detail, article 98 of the Guidance for the Articles of Association of Listed Companies indicates that the director is also responsible for the duty of diligence towards the company. This includes, ensuring that the behavior of the company complies with the laws, administrative regulations and economic policies in China, that the commercial activity does not exceed the scope of business activities delimited by the business license, and that the shareholders are treated fairly. The director must also inform himself about the operational situation and the administration of the company on a regular basis, which issues written opinions regularly ensuring that the information made public by the company is truthful, correct and complete, and that the company can add more requirements to the duty of diligence in its articles of association in accordance with its specific situation.

Chapter 4 of the Guidance on Appointment and Activities of Directors of Listed Companies of the Shanghai Stock Exchange also indicates details of the duty of diligence of the director.

Article 4 of the Guidance on the Shenzhen Stock Exchange Small and Medium Enterprise Board Director Conduct Guidance indicates the basic principles of the duty of diligence of the director. The directors must be diligent and responsible, they must positively attempt to realize their duties using their knowledge, abilities and experience, help the company's compliance with the laws, regulations, stock exchange rules and the articles of association of the company and attempt to protect the rights and interests of the company and of the stockholders.

Although much progress has been made, it is most unfortunate that the reform of 2005 to the PRC Company Law missed the opportunity to introduce a "standard" for the duty of care, or some mention in relation to the business judgment rule. Its application is being requested by Chinese academics.

CORPORATE SOCIAL RESPONSIBILITY (CSR)

With the 2005 amendment of the PRC Company Law, the concept of CSR was introduced into the law. Article 5, paragraph 1, PRC Company Law states that in its operational activities, a company shall abide by laws and administrative regulations, observe social morals and commercial ethics, persist in honesty and good faith, accept supervision by the government and the public, and assume social responsibility.

The concept of CSR was later detailed in relation to state companies. For example, article 17 of the Law of the People's Republic of China on State Owned Assets in Enterprises dated October 28, 2008, and the Guiding Opinion on Fulfilling Social Responsibility by Central Enterprises dated December 29, 2007.

According to the CSRC, "instead of maximising shareholders' interest alone, companies now take a more holistic view of how their decisions and actions might affect stakeholders and make compensation or repayments accordingly,"[17] which is why directors in China must seriously take into account CSR.

ENFORCEMENT

PRC Company Law

The PRC Company Law indicates civil sanctions under the form of liability for damages against a director of the company.

In accordance with article 150 PRC Company Law where a director (. . .) violates laws, administrative regulations or the company's articles of association in performance of his duties for the company, and thus causes losses to the company, he shall be liable for compensation.

In addition, article 113 PRC Company Law indicates that directors shall be liable for the resolutions adopted by the board of directors. Where a resolution of the board violates laws, administrative regulations, or the company's articles of association, or the resolutions of the shareholders' general assembly, and thus causes serious losses to the company, the directors participating in the adoption of such a resolution shall be liable for compensation to the company. However, where a director is proved to

---

17 OECD, "Corporate Governance of Listed Companies in China – Self-Assessment by the China Securities Regulatory Commission", OECD Publishing, Paris, 2011, p. 95.

have expressed his objection to such a resolution when it was put to the vote and his objection was recorded in the minutes of the meeting, he may be exempted from such liability.

PRC Securities Law

The PRC Securities Law also contains a broad range of sanctions of private law, for example, against insider trading and market manipulation. In this law the focus is on the liability for false information and for the infraction or violation of rights during takeovers.

In relation to false information, article 69 PRC Securities Law stipulates that where the prospectus, measures for financing through issuance of corporate bonds, financial statement, listing report, annual report, midterm report, temporary report or any information as disclosed that has been announced by an issuer or a listed company has any false record, misleading statement or major omission, and thus incurs losses to investors in the process of securities trading, the issuer or the listed company shall be subject to the liabilities of compensation. Any director (. . .) or any other person of the issuer or the listed company directly responsible shall be subject to the joint and several liabilities of compensation, except for anyone who is able to prove his exemption of any fault. Where any shareholder or actual controller of an issuer or a listed company has any fault, he shall be subject to the joint and several liabilities of compensation together with the relevant issuer or listed company.

In relation to takeovers, article 214 PRC Securities Law indicates that where a purchaser or any controlling shareholder of a purchaser takes advantage of the acquisition of a listed company to injure the legitimate rights and interests of the target company as well as the shareholders thereof, it shall be ordered to correct and given a warning. Under any serious circumstances, a fine of 100000 yuan up to 600000 yuan shall be imposed. Where any loss is incurred to the target company or the shareholders thereof, it shall be subject to the liabilities of compensation according to law. The person in charge and any other person directly responsible shall be given a warning and imposed a fine of 30000 yuan up to 300000 yuan.

Direct Lawsuits

Article 153 PRC Company Law indicates to us that where a director (. . .) violates the provisions of laws, administrative regulations or the company's articles of association and thus damages the interests of the shareholders, the shareholders may bring a lawsuit to a people's court.

However, the interpretation of this norm is not clear. The first question is what the "interests of the shareholders" means. The second question is related to who is the defendant in the lawsuit: the director, only him, also others?

Derivative Lawsuits

With the 2005 amendment of the PRC Company Law, the possibility was created for derivative lawsuits against directors, supervisors and top managers who infringe the provisions of the laws, administrative regulations or the company's articles of association "in performance of his duties for the company" (art 150 PRC Company Law). Article 152 PRC Company Law was introduced, which states that where a director or senior manager causes losses to the company, as specified in Article 150 of this Law, the shareholders of a company with limited liability, or the shareholders of a company limited by shares individually or jointly holding one per cent or more of its shares for 180 or more consecutive days may request, in writing, the board of supervisors or the supervisors of the company with limited liability where there is no such board, to bring a lawsuit to a people's court; and where a supervisor causes losses to the company, as specified in Article 150 of this Law, the shareholders mentioned above may request, in writing, the board of directors or the executive director of a company with limited liability where there is no such board, to bring a lawsuit to a people's court.

Where the board of supervisors or the supervisor of a company with limited liability where there is no such board, or the board of directors, or the executive director refuses to take legal proceedings after receiving the written request from the shareholders as specified in the preceding paragraph, or fails to take legal proceedings within 30 days from the date it/he receives such a request, or under emergency situations, failure to take legal proceedings immediately results in irreparable damage to the interests of the company, the shareholders specified in the preceding paragraph shall have the right, in their own names, directly to bring a lawsuit to a people's court in the interests of the company.

Where another person infringes upon the lawful rights and interests of a company and thus causes losses to the company, the shareholders specified in the first paragraph of this Article may bring a lawsuit to a people's court in accordance with the provisions of the preceding two paragraphs.

It is not clear who "the others" are in this case. The Chinese academics are of the opinion that "the others" not only include the controlling shareholders and the persons who truly control the company, but also "others who are subject to private law" who damage the rights of the company or infringe upon the duties that they owe to the company (creditors of the company) and "persons who are subject to public law", for example, administrative authorities that damage the rights and interests of the company.

In addition to the foregoing there is another question to resolve: who must sue the shareholder in the case of an infraction of the controlling shareholder? Both authorities indicated in article 152 PRC Company Law, that is, the board of directors and the board of supervisors are under the control of the controlling shareholder and therefore it is very unlikely that they will issue a fair decision. Naturally, the directors and the supervisors have an obligation of loyalty and diligence towards the company and its interests.

With regard to the application in practice in China by the shareholders, Professors Howson and Clarke indicate to us[18] how these derivative lawsuits have been brought after they were explicitly authorized with the 2005 reform of the PRC Company Law. They found that there has been considerable use of this mechanism both by plaintiffs as well as by judges, even before its formal recognition in the law. However, we must take note that this extensive use seems to be restricted to limited liability companies, their use being absent in corporations, including State Owned Enterprises (SOEs). We will see that the answer to this is how the SOEs function in practice discussed below.

Work Report of the Board Of Directors to the Shareholders' Assembly

Articles 28 and 29 of the Rules for the General Meetings of Shareholders of Listed Companies indicate that in the annual assembly of shareholders, the directors should inform about their work. Also, they must explain and clarify the petitions made by the shareholders. These annual reports of the work of the board of directors deliver an institutional mechanism to effectively implement their duties.

Non-legal Sanctions of the Stock Exchanges

Public criticism realized by the stock exchanges of Shanghai and Shenzhen in relation to certain companies that are listed on their exchanges plays an

---

[18] Nicholas C. Howson and Donald C. Clarke, "Pathway to Minority Shareholder Protection: Derivative Actions in the People's Republic of China." In *The Derivative Action in Asia: A Comparative and Functional Approach*, edited by D. Puchniak, H. Baum, and M. Ewing-Chow, 243–95. International Corporate Law and Financial Market Regulation. Cambridge University Press, 2012.

important role as a punishment and deterrence mechanism in the Chinese capital market.[19] It is that "shame" (losing face) is very humiliating for Asians and as the Chinese are a society where the collective is crucial, avoiding being publically criticized is important.

Others

The Chinese mass media have certainly developed in recent years. *Caijing* is a prestigious economic magazine that has revealed financial scandals. However, they still do not have the same strength or scope to reveal them as they would if they were in the West.

Application in Practice by Some Courts

As we have already seen, the 2005 amendment of the PRC Company Law brought us, among other things, fiduciary duties. Article 148, which describes the duty of loyalty and the duty of care of the directors, and article 149 specifies the concept of the duty of loyalty. From what has been said it becomes apparent that these duties have entered into China together with the amendment of the law. But in reality, according to Howson,[20] this is a misinterpretation. He has been researching the Chinese state institutions and some courts have been utilizing these concepts for a long time. The legal amendment would be a *post facto* confirmation of what was already being applied by some courts.

But why have some courts applied the fiduciary duties without any reference to the law? The answer is that the commercial companies already existed, investments in shares already existed, and they needed mechanisms to effectively police the directors in the sense that they were complying with their role. There were no norms, the traditional Chinese practices did not resolve the matter and no state authority was competent or independent in those years. The courts, then, were the solution.

The concept of fiduciary duties was imported to China at the beginning of the 1990s from Hong Kong only for PRC-domiciled issuers accessing foreign capital markets, including Hong Kong. The Chinese regulating

---

[19] Liebman Milhaupt "Reputational Sanctions in China's Securities Market," *Columbia Law Review* Vol. 108 (2008), p. 929 et seq.

[20] Nicholas Calcina Howson, "The Doctrine That Dared Not Speak Its Name: Anglo-American Fiduciary Duties in China's 2005 Company Law and Case Law Intimations of Prior Convergence." In *Transforming Corporate Governance in East Asia*, edited by H. Kanda, K. Kim, and C.J. Milhaupt, 193–254. New York: Routledge, 2008.

entity at that time, the PRC Commission on the Restructuring of the Economic System (CRES), issued on July 10, 1993 a Letter of Comfort to the Stock Exchange of Hong Kong, in which it indicated that in the Standard Opinion[21] of 1992 had the same doctrinal content as the "fiduciary duties" of the laws of Hong Kong. What a tremendous statement! It said that in China the principles of "fiduciary duties" were applied, without any legal basis and in an era when there still was not even a law on companies! However, it did not mean much because the PRC Company Law of 1993 did not contain any article that was related to fiduciary duties.[22]

Despite the aforementioned, it is impressive that an administrative authority, the CSRC, tried during the rest of the 1990s through 2005 to place the notion of fiduciary duties in the specific regulation for the companies that are listed on the exchanges in China, despite there not being a law in such respect. And why? The answer has to do with the fact that many of the top officials of the CSRC had studied law, accounting or finance in common law countries where the doctrine of fiduciary duties was applied. They wanted the Chinese system to be "modern", hopefully having the confidence of the foreign investors. Also, from abroad, explicit recognition of that doctrine by Chinese authorities was wanted.

But it was a difficult battle because the vast majority of the legal academics (those who with frequency draft the laws in China) resisted the concept, indicating that China did not have in its laws an Anglo-Saxon model but rather a Continental European one.

If the aforementioned was understood with respect to a few public officials of the CSRC, well trained in foreign laws including common law, it was very surprising for Howson[23] to find that the Chinese judges, often dismissed because of their lack of formal education, just happened to be the ones who had been applying the principles of fiduciary duties since the 1990s without any legal basis![24]

However, in 2005 fiduciary duties appeared in the PRC Company Law.

---

21 During that era the only regulation on companies in the PRC.

22 Although it recovered the language through a few special rules that were put in force in August 1994 with respect to companies that were domiciled in the PRC that listed their shares abroad, including Hong Kong.

23 Nicholas Calcina Howson, "The Doctrine That Dared Not Speak Its Name: Anglo-American Fiduciary Duties in China's 2005 Company Law and Case Law Intimations of Prior Convergence". In *Transforming Corporate Governance in East Asia*, edited by H. Kanda, K. Kim, and C.J. Milhaupt, 193-254. New York: Routledge, 2008. p. 212.

24 But, I must admit that for me it was not a great surprise because a Chinese judge was among my classmates in my doctoral studies in Japan in the 1990s when

It is explained that it was a "signal of modernization", and that despite a model of state property and socialist orthodoxy and of loyalty between the Ministries and the SOEs.

And not only that but also these fiduciary duties were placed in a completely new procedural context, permitting a direct lawsuit to be filed by the shareholders against the directors; a cause of action based on the breaking of the duties of care and loyalty; a mechanism for a derivative action; implicit fiduciary duties of the controlling shareholders; and new basis for the piercing of the corporate veil through the courts.

Application in the Practice by the Party-State

As we have indicated, China is in the process of legal modernization. It still does not have a rule of law with Western standards because, among other things, the Communist Party interferes with the actions of companies, especially the SOEs. In the West little is known about the real operation of these companies. Lin and Milhaupt have written a stupendous article in the Stanford Law Review[25] in which they significantly clarify the inner workings of these companies. This article was previously on the internet as a "working paper" for the reading and commentary of specialists. And it was published in Spanish in the December 2013 issue of the Revista Chilena de Derecho of Pontificia Universidad Católica de Chile. It is an article that was especially praised by a famous professor of Chinese law, Stanley Lubman, in the blog China Real Time, of the *Wall Street Journal* in March 2012.[26]

Theory and practice, law and reality, can be very distant in China. Therefore, a truthful legal statement about this country must not be limited to a positive legal statement of the law, as we have already indicated, but also must explain what is occurring in reality.

Lin and Milhaupt tell us that the SOEs are organized in vertically integrated groups. Each group has a central holding company, the State-Owned Assets Supervision and Administration Commission (SASAC),

---

we just happened to be studying fiduciary duties and we attended seminars on the issue!

[25] Li-Wen Lin and Curtis J. Milhaupt, "We are the (National) Champions: Understanding the Mechanisms of State Capitalism in China", *Stanford Law Review*. April 2013, Vol. 65 Issue 4, pp. 697–759.

[26] Stanley Lubman, "China's State Capitalism: The Real World Implications", China Real Time Blog, The Wall Street Journal, March 1, 2012 <http://blogs.wsj.com/chinarealtime/2012/03/01/chinas-state-capitalism-the-real-world-implications/> (accessed on April 16, 2013).

which is the majority shareholder within a "core company". The "core company" has the majority of the shares in the SOEs that make up the group, which includes a finance company for its members, and a research center, for the innovation of the group. SASAC is the true controller of the transfer of shares in SOEs, in which many of them do not even have directors.

Among the groups, in turn, there is an interaction through alliances, joint ventures and holding of shares.

On the other hand, however, there is a structure of the Chinese Communist Party that is parallel to what is indicated in the laws (that is, parallel to what is indicated in the previous part of this chapter). The Party has a formidable structure with divisions and subdivisions. In the case of our study, the Organization Department of the Party is fundamental in choosing the top management of the SOEs. Some managers are also members of the government and of the Chinese Communist Party. There is an extensive and dense network of interpersonal relationships, not only between companies but also including the government and the Chinese Communist Party, collaborating in a broad range of activities.

There is a *Networked Hierarchy*, a term utilized by Lin and Milhaupt to indicate the characteristics of corporate governance from top to bottom within the business groups, united through profound links to other institutions controlled by the state. And, in addition to this, the *Institutional Bridge* for the case of the use of ties that unite separate components of the system. In this manner the networks that promote the circulation of information are created.

As the Chinese are very practical, they are more interested in the commercial results being stimulated by the government, than the legal formality. And, in this way, with that network of connections, from the government to the companies, it could be that they are realizing the work in the Chinese economy that in other countries is realized by formal legal institutions. In this way, at present, those business groups that are promoted by the government and intertwined with the leaders of the Communist Party can be fundamental for the successful development of the regime.

These networks facilitate the flow of information. They also develop the exchange of relations and the collaboration in many levels of production and in the processes of implementation of public policies. This, in turn, delivers powerful incentives to the leaders because the success in an area brings rewards in others, as the career advancement in the company or the Party.

Internally, the components of the group, logically including the directors, are much interconnected to the broadest system of the industrial organization that the group belongs to. Although the business groups are different from one another, both legally as well as functionally, as would be expected, they are linked in different ways through an intergroup joint venture, strategic alliances and the holding of shares. But even more important for the union between the groups is the existence of the party-state, acting through SASAC and the Organization Department of the Party.

The structures of the internal government of the group are specified in a legally binding document called Articles of Grouping. In practice, the parent company dictates the terms of the Articles of Grouping. If we only look at the documents, in many cases the Articles of Grouping provides administration structures to facilitate the making of group or delegated decisions but, in general, in practice the parent company actually controls the decision-making processes. In this manner, corporate governance in a Chinese business group goes from top to bottom, from the parent company to the other companies.

As would be expected, the Communist Party plays a very important role in the designation of personnel in the business groups. One-third of the employees in the national SOEs are members of the Communist Party and there are authorities of the party in each one of the levels of the hierarchy of the business group.

But why is the Party involved in the companies? It is thought that in order to advance the economic reform the support of the Party was needed. In addition, it serves to supervise the personnel of the SOEs. As McGregor says:

> the Party's control over personnel was at the heart of its ability to overhaul state companies, without losing leverage over them at the same time . . . The party body with ultimate power over personnel, the Central Organization Department, is without a doubt the largest and most powerful human resources body in the world.[27]

As we have indicated, there is a considerable distance between the theory and practice of law in China. But we have to make a difference. If we are discussing "company" law and its related institutions, there is a large breach: direct participation of the Party in the naming of the directors, the practice of SASAC to bypass the board of directors in the naming of the directors and their remuneration, among other themes, go against the essence of a "company" law according to what we understand about

---

[27] Richard McGregor, "The Party: The Secret World of China's Communist Rulers", HarperCollins Publishers, New York, 2010, p. 69.

"company" law outside China. But if we are discussing the norms that regulate the formation of business groups and their corporate governance, among others, the breach between the law and practice in the Chinese SOE sector substantially becomes smaller. It is that logically, the practice goes according to the prevailing economic system, in which the Chinese state sector in the present goes along advancing at the cost of the private sector.

Whether China will come closer to or will move away from the Anglo-Saxon model of civil liability of the directors is uncertain. According to Lin and Milhaupt:

> our narrative at least suggests the possibility that ensuing reforms will further enhance and legitimize state control over important corporate assets rather than impel a transition to dispersed ownership structures and diminished political involvement in corporate governance.[28] As we have shown in respect of the national-champion groups,[29] there are overrides of corporate law principles at key points to ensure continued party-state control.[30]

But then, is it necessary to continue struggling in China for a system that is similar to the Anglo-Saxon system? We believe the answer is yes because it is that system that has turned out to be better in practice, and although it is not utilized in a majority of the large SOEs in the present, those norms can serve as a basis so that a strong, healthy and varied private sector grows in China.

---

[28] The application of antitrust law is a different matter. If the antitrust regime were applicable to the large state companies, the structure of capitalism of the state would be practically impossible. For this same reason, it is almost unconceivable that the antitrust law would be vigorously applied to the public sector without a great change in the political system.

[29] National-champion groups: SOE groups.

[30] Li-Wen Lin y Curtis J. Milhaupt, "We are the (National) Champions: Understanding the Mechanisms of State Capitalism in China", *Stanford Law Review*. April 2013, Vol. 65 Issue 4, p. 754.

7. A brief note on directors' duties of care and loyalty in Portugal

Pedro Pais de Vanconcelos

1. GENERAL DUTIES OF DIRECTORS – ART. 64(1) OF THE COMPANIES CODE

Duties of company directors in Portuguese Law developed from a simple formulae to ever increasingly detailed statutes. For a long time, since at least 1888 (Commercial Code), duties of directors were legally based on the contract of mandate. The relationship between the director and the company was seen as contractual, and directors were bound by very broad and general duties of diligence and loyalty. Later, in 1969, the law (Decree-Law 49,381, of 15.11.1969), expressly obliged the directors to act "with the diligence of a judicious and orderly manager"[1] (diligência de um gestor criterioso e ordenado). An even more detailed formula was added more recently: "the directors of a company must act with the diligence of a skilful and careful manager, in the interest of society, taking into account interests of shareholders and employees".[2]

Finally, art. 64º(1) of the Companies Code was revised in 2006. Its wording is now:[3]

---

[1] "Diligência de um gestor criterioso e ordenado".

[2] "Os gerentes, administradores ou directores de uma sociedade devem actuar com a diligência de um gestor criterioso e ordenado, no interesse da sociedade, tendo em conta interesses dos sócios e dos trabalhadores)".

[3] "1. Os gerentes ou administradores da sociedade devem observar:

a) Deveres de cuidado, revelando a disponibilidade, a competência técnica e o conhecimento da actividade da sociedade adequados às suas funções e empregando nesse âmbito a diligência de um gestor criterioso e ordenado; e
b) Deveres de lealdade, no interesse da sociedade, atendendo aos interesses de longo prao dos sócios e ponderando os interesses dos outros sujeitos relevantes para a sustentabilidade da sociedade, tais como os seus trabalhadores, clientes e credores."

> 1. Directors of the company shall abide by:
>
> (a) Duties of care, with the availability, the technical competence and the knowledge of the company's activities adequate to their functions and with the diligence of a scrupulous and orderly manager; (b) Duties of loyalty, in the interest of company, taking into account the long-term interests of shareholders and considering the interests of other persons relevant to the sustainability of company, such as the employees, customers and creditors.

The legal relationship between the company and its directors was traditionally based on mandate, implied or express. However there was discussion whether the dominant interest to be pursued by the management should be the interest of the company or the interest of the shareholders. Now the mainframe of directors' duties is clear: directors owe their duties primarily to the company and secondarily to "long-term shareholders" and stakeholders. The law does not protect the interest of shareholders who buy and sell aiming to make profit out of market speculation (short-term shareholders). In case of controversy among shareholders, the interest of the company is defined by majority vote in the general meeting. Hence the interest ruling the directors is the interest of the company as defined by shareholders' majority vote.

2. DUTY OF CARE

Directors are obliged to be "available". This means that they should be present or, at least, ready to put in an appearance, when necessary, depending on the actual need of the company. Some companies must be managed on a permanent basis, but others may need a limited intensity of management. The board of directors of companies limited by shares (SA) should meet at least once a month unless otherwise provided in the articles (art. 410.2). The board of big public companies usually meets every week or day, but the board of lesser companies, like family companies, very seldom meet. The frequency depends on how often it is convenient or necessary.

The law also obliges the directors to be "technically competent" and to have an "adequate knowledge of the company activities". One should not agree to be appointed director of a company unless being, or at least feeling, personally, technically and professionally capable to exercise the office "with the diligence of a scrupulous and orderly manager". This rules out ignorance or incompetence, in general or specifically with relation to the trade of the company, as an excuse for bad management.

The main issue raised by the duty of care, as imposed by the Portuguese law, is the trade risk. All business is inherently risky. Profit is the return – quid pro quo – of risk, not of investment. Management without risk is bad management, sometimes as bad as reckless management. Risk involves uncertainty and hence the possibility of loss. Losing money does not evidence necessarily, just by itself, a breach of the duty of care. There is a wide room between a "risk averse" conservative management and risky speculative dealing. It is sometimes difficult to decide when management is reckless and, hence, illicit.

Directors must be able to prove that, prior to business decisions, mostly prior to risky decisions, there was a professional and careful entrepreneurial study and assessment of the risks involved, and that those risks were not taken lightly or negligently. Some directors show a tendency to excessive dependency on consultancies prior to important business decisions. Sometimes this is not a way to improve the quality of investment, but to avoid civil liability of directors in case of loss.

3. DUTY OF LOYALTY

Duty of loyalty is mainly related to the issue of conflict of interests. When taking management decisions, directors must take into consideration the interest of the company prior to their own interest, personal or professional. Therefore when attending meetings of the board, directors have the duty to disclose all situations from which a conflict of interest may arise. They should disclose the circumstances completely and in detail, and may participate in the discussion of the conflict of interest and of the decision to be taken, but cannot vote. Usually directors disclose and explain, but abstain from discussing the matter and leave the room to avoid influencing the decision. The fact is then mentioned on the minutes of the meeting. They also usually abstain from participating in any acts or deeds related to the matter.

Second to the interest of the company, the directors should have regard to the interest of long-term shareholders. Short-term shareholders are seen as speculative, and hence directors should abstain from interfering in stock exchange prices of the company's shares, unless the interest of the company or the long-term shareholders is at stake. When managing the company, the directors should aim at profits, higher dividends, and shareholder value, but on a medium- or long-term perspective.

Also the interest of stakeholders should be respected. The law refers to "persons relevant to the sustainability of the company, such as employees, clients and creditors" but this should not be read as excluding persons to whom the sustainability of the company might be important, such as the community where it is located, and other relevant interests such as environmental, social or cultural.

Two main issues related to the duty of loyalty are the appropriation or diversion of business opportunities and directors' salaries, fringe and other benefits.

4. DUTY TO ACT WITHIN THE OBJECT OF THE COMPANY

The Companies Code (art. 6.4) specifically provides that directors shall not exceed the limits of the objects clause. Directors' acts, on behalf of the company but exceeding the limits of the objects clause (ultra vires), are valid and binding on the company. However, directors are liable and must compensate (civil liability) the company for all damages incurred as a consequence of those acts. Nevertheless, all profit arising from those acts belong to the company. This regime corresponds to EU Directive 68/151/CEE.

It was traditionally controversial whether donations and guarantees were within the object of the company. Following the leading decisions of the courts, articles 6.2 and 6.3 of the Companies Code state, since 1986, that donations are acceptable, depending on circumstances and financial condition of the company; giving guaranties, personal or real, to other companies is allowed inside the same group of companies or if there is a justified interest of the company. Courts are usually strict when assessing the interest of the guarantor. Regarding donations, general practice and courts are permissive, depending on the importance of values involved and the nature of the beneficiary. It is a common practice of big companies to subsidise many kinds of non-profit organizations, such as sports, cultural, arts, social and charity.

5. DUTY TO REPORT AND TO RENDER ACCOUNTS

Every year the directors have to report and render the accounts of the company to shareholders at the annual general meeting. This obligation includes the duty to organise and keep a proper accountancy system in accordance with laws and regulations in force. This is often a serious issue, due to a tendency for misleading reporting and "creative accounting".

Besides civil and criminal liability for false accounting, directors may be removed by the general meeting. After voting the management report and company's accounts, each director is submitted to a confidence vote along with the management as a whole. Directors who fail to obtain this confidence vote cannot continue and are removed from office.

Directors have a duty to inform the shareholders and to answer their questions, either before or during the annual general meeting. The so-called right to inform shareholders is ruled by the law in detail (arts 288–292 CSC). Directors are obliged to answer the questions of shareholders truly and completely, although not without some limitations stated by the law. Whenever accumulated losses reach more than 50 per cent of the share capital of the company (art. 35 CSC), directors must call a general meeting to inform the shareholders, so that they may pass a resolution for the reduction of capital, the dissolution of the company or any other solution. Shareholders are not obliged to pass any resolution and may leave the situation as it is, but notwithstanding, directors have a specific duty to call the general meeting to provide information on the matter.

6. DUTY TO MONITOR

Directors have a duty to know what happens inside the company. It is not an acceptable excuse for a director to say that they did not know. Hence, the directors must organise and implement an efficient system of internal control of the company. This also applies to subsidiaries in a group of companies.

This is a serious issue in cases of directors' liabilities, when one defendant alleges the ignorance of some facts and other or others the ignorance of other facts, and all those facts are together the cause of damage. It would be too easy to avoid liability this way, as it is normal that people at higher levels of the company hierarchy do not have knowledge of the other facts, known by people, at lower levels of the company. Directors are bound to familiarize with the company's business activities, therefore their liability is assessed both in accordance with what they actually know and/or what they should know and not ignore.

7. DUTY TO MANAGE

Directors are appointed to manage the company. Members of partnerships may interfere in the management, but not so shareholders of companies. Shareholders of companies cannot interfere in the matter of management (art. 405 CSC); they have the power to remove directors but not to give them orders. Hence a higher discretion of management in companies than in partnerships.

In reality it is considered "normal", and it is very frequent, that the members of the board somehow reflect the *spectre* of shareholders, or of the main shareholders. Some boards of directors look like miniatures of the general assembly. Some directors, in fact, act as employees or representatives of some shareholders whose interest they protect in office. Shareholders who have a decisive influence on specific directors, because they have the capacity to cause their appointment or removal, either by provisions of the articles, or shareholders agreements, or by their voting power, are jointly liable with those directors under their influence (art. 83º CSC).

All directors must be natural persons. When companies are designated as directors, they must appoint individuals to office. Individual directors shall give some kind of guarantee, accepted by law, to cover civil liability arising from wrongful acts, unless exempt by resolution of the general meeting. Exemption is not permitted to public listed companies. The value of the guarantee may be stipulated in the articles but shall not be less than €250.000 in listed and €50.000 in non-listed companies. This guarantee is usually given as an insurance: this insurance cannot be paid by the company. Directors shall give this guarantee within 30 days or the appointment will be without effect. Directors must act personally and disclose their quality when acting on behalf of the company. They cannot be represented by someone else in office, but they may empower other persons to act on behalf of the company.

8. CIVIL LIABILITY OF DIRECTORS

Directors are responsible for their management. They may incur civil liability to the company, its shareholders, creditors and other stakeholders.

The legal system of directors' liability is controversial and prone to disagreement among specialists. As in general liability law in Portugal, it is based on separation of illicity and fault (culpa) and on the distinction between acts (or omissions) against the law (legal liability) and acts (or omissions) in breach of contract, or contractual obligations (contractual liability). The main difference is the proof of fault, which is presumed in contractual liability and must be proved by the victim in legal liability.

Liability of directors towards the company is of contractual nature. It is considered as arising from a breach of contractual duties. Therefore directors have the burden of proving that their acts (or omissions) were not their fault. They also have to prove that they acted "on an informed base, free from their personal interest and in accordance with criteria of entrepreneurial rationality" (art. 73.2 CSC). In short, they have to prove their own innocence.

Prior to filing the legal action against its own directors the company must have a general meeting so that the shareholders may debate and take a resolution on the matter by simple majority. Shareholders owning a minimum 5 per cent of share capital (2 per cent in listed companies) may file a derivative action against directors on behalf of the interest of the company if the general meeting decides not to sue. Companies usually prefer to remove the directors without suing them for damages, because a judicial action may, by itself, be damaging and detrimental. Liability actions filed by companies against directors are rare. They can cause bad publicity and disclosure of more or less confidential, sometimes embarrassing, data and facts. It is controversial whether minority shareholders may sue prior to a general meeting or should first call for a general meeting to discuss the matter and only file the derivative action after the shareholders' meeting refused or abstained from doing it.

Liability of directors towards shareholders, creditors and other stakeholders is not so severe. It is of a legal nature (the relationship between them and the directors is not of contractual nature). Hence, shareholders, creditors and other stakeholders must prove the unlawfulness of the acts (or omissions) and fault (culpa) of the directors as prerequisites of liability. Creditors are entitled to demand compensation only for breach of legal provisions aimed at the general protection of creditors, such as to avoid dissipation of the company assets by the directors. Liability of directors towards creditors depends on assets becoming insufficient for the payment of their credits as a consequence of directors acts (or omissions). Shareholders may demand compensation from directors for damages "directly" suffered as consequence acts (or omissions) in breach of the law or the articles, with fault (culpa). It is not infrequent that employees sue directors for damages caused by breach of labour laws, regulations and contracts, such as for illicit dismissal, bullying or harassment at work.

Finally, directors may be liable for unpaid tax and social security debts.

PART III

DIRECTORS' DUTIES BEYOND COMPANY LAW

8. The limits of directors' duties in fostering corporate social responsibility and the idea of a multi-stakeholder board

S.H. Goo and Désirée Klingler*

INTRODUCTION

> For in most giant corporations, no specific executive official or board member is responsible for protecting the interests of employees, consumers, the environment, or local communities. No one outside of senior management reviews the most important business decisions to assure their compliance with financial integrity, efficiency, or long-term corporate goals. Because these concerns become everybody's general interest, they become nobody's particular interest – and often go unattended.[1]

Every day numerous human rights abuses are committed by thousands of corporations around the globe. They happen in both developing and developed countries. Recent examples are the Foxconn suicides in

* I would like to thank Professor John Ruggie of Harvard University for his kind invitation to speak at the International Conference on the issue of directors' duties and human rights that inspired the author's further research and led to the preparation of this paper, and his assistant Vanessa Zimmerman for her assistance. I would also like to thank the Cambridge University Law Faculty and Harvard Law School for receiving him as a visitor to carry out the research in 2010, and Barry Rider, Sarah Worthington, Lilian Miles, Simon Goulding, Hisaei Ito, John Coffee, Curtis Milhaupt, Mark Roe, Louise Kaplow, Lucian Bebchuk, Reinier Kraakman, Nobuko Yamagishi, Sabrina Bruno, Tyler Giannini, Chris Jochnick, Suzannah Linton, Richard Breeden, Shen Wei for the stimulating discussion and thoughts, comments, suggestions and questions on the ideas discussed in this paper. I am a member of the Hong Kong Government's Standing Committee on Company Law Reform, but views expressed in this paper do not represent the SCCLR and any errors and omissions herein are my sole responsibility.

[1] Nader, R., Green, M. and Seligman, J. (1976), *Taming the Giant Corporation* (New York: Norton) 126.

Shenzhen or the BP Oil spill in the U.S.[2] The abuses that companies are involved or implicated in range from denials of freedom of expression or association, unfair trials, abductions, arbitrary detentions, violence, rape and sexual abuses, torture and ill-treatment, deaths and genocide, to all forms of discrimination, harm to the environment and health and safety issues. These abuses happen practically all over the world; in many sectors of the economy: agriculture, food, tobacco, apparel and textiles, commercial sex and pornography, finance, health, media, manufacturing, chemicals, metals, plastics and basic materials, weapons, security equipment, and technology. The global financial turmoil of 2008 triggered by the subprime mortgage crisis, which led to a series of financial institutions' failures and debts crises, has also had its impact on companies.

There is no shortage of laws and regulations to prohibit or prevent abuses. In addition to the various areas of law (criminal law, employment and labour law, health and safety law, environmental law etc.), a row of principles, codes and guidelines exists: the Universal Declaration of Human Rights; the UN Sub-Commission Norms on Business and Human Rights; the Equator Principles; the European Parliament Code of Conduct; the Extractive Industries Transparency Initiative (EITI); the Geneva Conventions on humanitarian law; the Global Reporting Initiative; the ILO Declaration on Fundamental Principles and Rights at Work; the ILO Tripartite Declaration; the Kimberley Process; the OECD Guidelines; the UN Global Compact; the UN Millennium Development Goals; the UN Principles for Responsible Investment; the Voluntary Principles on Security and Human Rights; as well as guidelines prepared by businesses, governments, judges, NGOs and others.

We also rely on environmental, social and governance (ESG) disclosure as well as reporting through rules of exchanges for listed companies (e.g. HKEx consultation paper on ESG reporting), international and regional initiatives (e.g. renewed EU strategy 2011–14 for CSR) and guidance for small- and medium-sized enterprises (SMEs) (e.g. CSR Guide for SMEs in Hong Kong).

But why are abuses still happening? It is because there are always gaps in our laws and problems with enforcing such laws. Admittedly, legislation takes time and effort and may never materialize. It often plays the catching-up game and is enacted only when there is a major crisis or disaster, which obviously comes too late for what has happened. Further, there are the difficulties with enforcement of the law with which especially developing countries are confronted due to inadequate resources, experience, training,

---

[2] For a list of over 5000 companies that are linked to some sort of abuses or alleged abuses see <http://www.business-humanrights.org/Home>.

and legal infrastructure, corruption of public officials, or lack of independent judiciary. But why are corporations so rigorously taking advantage of legal loopholes or breaking laws? It is because of the motive to maximize profit as enshrined in corporate law, in particular in Anglo-American common law, which mandates profit maximization as the sole purpose of a corporation. This has profound implications in terms of corporate respect for non-shareholder interests and abuses.[3] Whilst the corporate law in civil law jurisdictions does not mandate profit maximization in quite the same degree as Anglo-American law, the only major group of non-shareholders whose interest is looked after is the employees through co-determination law.

In November 2009, the UN Special Representative on Corporate Law and Human Rights called a meeting in Toronto to discuss the issue of corporate abuses of human rights in various countries, especially by multinational corporations, and to consider how corporations can be made more responsive to human rights concerns, e.g. workers' rights, prevent environmental pollution caused by their operation, and eliminate unsafe products. The discussion of the meeting was centered upon reforming directors' duties so that directors would cause the company to respect human rights. However, as will be explained below, there are limits to the effectiveness of this approach. Whilst the current corporate law in the U.S.[4] and the U.K.[5] does not prevent directors from making socially responsible decisions at the cost of the company's profit maximization, it does not mandate them to do so. And there is no incentive for directors to make such socially responsible decisions given that their compensations are often tied to the company's share price or profit. Thus, the existing directors' duties do not improve the current situation and it is difficult to see how these duties may be reformed in future.

---

[3] For a documentary film on how profit maximization, as part of capitalism, has destroyed American society see 'Capitalism: A Love Story' by Michael Moore (2009).

[4] Many states in the U.S. adopted constituency statutes in the 1980s to protect directors in making decisions for the benefit of non-shareholder interests and together with the business judgment rule, to shield directors who make profits sacrificing socially responsible decisions from shareholder law suits. Unfortunately these statutes were used by management to protect themselves from hostile takeovers, and were not used for the interests of non-shareholders.

[5] Whilst the UK Companies Act 2006, s 172 requires directors to take into account the interests of a list of non-shareholder interests, this is prefaced on the condition that it is for the interest of the shareholders, which means profit maximization. Some might argue that, given the judicial deference to the board decisions, it is possible for directors to always argue that their apparently socially responsible decisions are in fact in the interest of the shareholders and therefore they are unlikely to be sued or found liable.

This leads to a different approach to the problem. Since abuses occur when stakeholder interests are ignored, why not let stakeholders protect their own interests? It seems that the most direct way to achieve this goal is to give them a presence on the board where key company decisions are made. In other words, stakeholders should have directors representing them on the board of directors. This is not a revolutionary idea.

Employees have had representatives on the board in Germany for years. The U.S. has been debating for ten years about giving shareholders proxy access and in September 2010, the SEC adopted Rule 14a-11 to give shareholders who have owned 3 per cent of the voting power continuously for three years, the right to nominate directors for up to 25 per cent of the company's board seats at each election. This rule was finally implemented on October 4, 2010. Furthermore, the idea of employee representatives in the board was debated in the U.S. and the U.K. in the 1960s and 70s.

The idea was first suggested in the U.S. by Nader, Green and Seligman.[6] Mitchell recently retold the story of how Mel Eisenberg's idea of a monitoring board was welcomed but in the end hijacked by the American Bar Association (ABA), the Conference Board, and the Business Roundtable and turned into a protective shell for directors.[7] There was never any serious debate about Nader et al.'s idea of a stakeholder representative board. The endorsement of Eisenberg's monitoring board by the ABA Guidebook, the Conference Board Report and the Business Roundtable completely rejected the possibility of corporate reform along the political lines that reformers like Nader were arguing for.[8] The Business Roundtable also resoundingly rejected the idea of constituency directors or co-determination.[9]

Having faced so many recent scandals, it may be time to revisit this idea and expand it to include stakeholders other than just employees. As Mitchell points out:

> the contemporary board is a defensive institution. Such a board is not and, I argue, was not designed to serve the goal of ensuring the responsible and efficient management of the large public corporation. Building reform on this model is almost certain to fail. Reformers who truly believe in boards must

---

6 Nader, Green, and Seligman, note 1 above, 125; see also <www.tamethecorporation.org>.

7 Mitchell, L.E. (2010), The Trouble with Boards, in Kieff, F.S. and Paredes, T.A. (eds), *Perspectives on Corporate Governance* (New York: Cambridge University Press), 31–4.

8 Ibid., 35–47.

9 Business Roundtable (1978), 'The Role and Composition of the Board of Directors of the Large Publicly Owned Corporation', *Business Lawyer* 33: 2105–6.

> reconceptualize the very purpose of a board before engaging in meaningful reform. In this case, building on the past simply won't do.[10]

Whilst Mitchell does not offer any solution, he does point out the possibility of having 'some other substantive modification of the role of the board and, with it, its composition'.[11]

In order to give regard to non-shareholder interests, we need to be convinced that companies exist not just for making profit for shareholders, but also for the benefit of the whole society in which they operate.[12] Whilst opinions are divided on this issue, it is argued here that companies exist for the benefit of the whole society. The current Anglo-American shareholder supremacy approach does not allow this objective to be achieved, resulting in many human rights abuses. If we want to keep the present system, it would be important to strengthen the ethics of directors to include stakeholders' considerations, which is a separate issue discussed elsewhere,[13] and to change the law on directors' duties requiring them to also act for the interest of non-shareholders, which seems almost certain to fail. However, before ethics are cultivated, we may improve the system by having a board representing all stakeholders so that their interests will be directly considered and looked after by themselves with, of course, the inevitable compromises each director has to make on the board. This will result in longer, presumably animated discussions and a reduction of profit but arguably better corporate decisions and actions that will respect human rights and reduce abuses.

I. CORPORATE SOCIAL RESPONSIBILITY AT LARGE

1. What is a Company for?

The terms on which companies should be allowed to possess power have been well argued:[14] it is for the social good. As Henry Carter

---

[10] Mitchell, note 7 above, 59.

[11] Ibid., 61.

[12] For the school of this argument, see Parkinson, J.E. (1993), *Corporate Power and Responsibility: Issues in the Theory of Company Law* (Oxford: Clarendon Press).

[13] See Miles, L. and Goo, S.H. (2013), 'Corporate Governance in Asian Countries: Has Confucianism Anything to Offer?' *Business and Society Review* 118(1): 23–45.

[14] See Parkinson, note 12 above, 31.

Adams pointed out in his presidential address to the American Economic Association in 1896:

> Corporations originally were regarded as agencies of the state. They were created for the purpose of enabling the public to realize some social or national end without involving the necessity of direct governmental administration. They were in reality arms of the state, and in order to secure efficient management, a local or private interest was created as a privilege or property for corporation. A corporation, therefore, may be defined in the light of history as a body created by law for the purpose of attaining public ends through an appeal to private interest.[15]

This statement is based on the concession theory. But today many corporations are no longer seen as agents of the state. Nor is this supported by the contract theory. However, according to a political theory on the legitimacy of private power, the possession of social decision-making power by companies is legitimate only if the state of affairs is in the public interest. In other words, companies are given enormous power only if this serves the public interest.[16]

Corporations were therefore granted certain privileges in return for their social utility and given the ever-enlarging impact of corporations on society today, they should continue to be run for their social utility. However, often they are no longer run for this purpose. This is due to the combination of a number of factors:

(i) the competition of state chartering in the U.S., leading to the adoption of nominal corporation law to garner chartering business which raises revenue for the states involved;
(ii) there is no competition in the oligopolies sectors that are dominated by large corporations;
(iii) remedial law to compel companies to pollute less or disclose more is difficult to obtain because big corporations can yield political powers to avoid legislation and delay enforcement;
(iv) federal regulators are often captured by big corporations with people coming from or going to regulated firms;
(v) labour unions have become rather ineffective as a countervailing power to management generally;
(vi) shareholders are so diffused and divorced from corporate governance that they often 'vote with their feet' rather than being active in monitoring the management; and

---

[15] Quoted in Nader, Green, Seligman, note 1 above, 63.
[16] Parkinson, note 12 above, 31.

(vii) the board of directors has also proved to be largely dysfunctional as a monitoring board.[17]

These factors are as true today as they were in the 1970s when Nader identified them.

As Parkinson pointed out, public interest would be better served if companies were sometimes to engage in profit-sacrificing social responsibility rather than rigidly adhering to the formula of profit maximization within the law.[18] As he further argued, it would be desirable to reform the controls regulating management power in order to permit or mandate increased corporate responsiveness to the interests of non-shareholder groups and search for other measures to ensure that proper weight is given to these interests in company decision-making.[19]

2. Objections to Profit-sacrificing Social Responsibility

But why does the law not allow for profit-sacrificing social responsibility? As Parkinson analysed, there are three objections to such responsibility, namely the efficiency argument,[20] the deference argument,[21] and the

---

17 Nader, Green, and Seligman, note 1 above, 63–4.

18 Parkinson, note 12 above, 304 ff.

19 Ibid., 304 ff.

20 Friedman, M. (2001), 'The Social Responsibility of Business to Increase its Profits', in Beauchamp, T.L. and Bowie, N.E., *Ethical Theory and Business* (New Jersey: Prentice Hall); Friedman, M. (1962), *Capitalism and Freedom* (Chicago: University of Chicago Press) 133; Rostow, E.V. (1959), 'To Whom and for What Ends is Corporate Management Responsible?' in Mason, E.S. (ed.), *The Corporation in Modern Society* (Cambridge: Harvard University Press) 64; Hayek, F.A. (1982), *Law, Legislation and Liberty*, Vol 3 (Chicago: University of Chicago Press) 81–2; Levitt, T. (1970), 'The Dangers of Social Responsibility', in Marshall, H.D. (ed.), *Business and Government: The Problem of Power* (Lextington, Massachussets: D.C. Heath and Company) 35–6; Stone, C.D. (1985), 'Public Interest Representation: Economic and Social Policy Inside the Enterprise', in Hopt, K.J. and Teubner, G. (eds), *Corporate Governance and Directors' Liabilities* (Berlin: De Gruyter) 122; Easterbrook, F.H. and Fischel, D.R. (1989), 'The Corporate Contract', *Columbia Law Review* 89: 1447; Easterbrook, F.H. and Fischel, D.R. (1991), *The Economic Structure of Corporate Law* (Cambridge: Harvard University Press).

21 Friedman, M. (1962), *Capitalism and Freedom*, ibid., 133; Hayek, F.H. (1969), 'The Corporation in a Democratic Society: In Whose Interest Ought it and Will it be Run?', in Ansoff, H.I. (ed.), *Business Strategy* (London: Penguin Books) 231; Manne, H.G. (1972), in Manne, H.G. and Wallich, H.C., *The Modern Corporation and Social Responsibility* (Washington, D.C.: American Enterprise Inst. for Public Policy Research) 30–1; Posner, R.A. (1986), *Economic Analysis of*

shareholders' money argument.[22] However, he concluded that there is nevertheless a positive case for social responsibility to improve standards of corporate governance.[23] We will focus on the first objection here. There is no doubt that the policy of profit maximization has allowed many Anglo-American corporations to be run 'efficiently' (in the sense of making the most profits possible for themselves – or what may be called firm-level efficiency) and to grow exponentially, especially when the companies command some form of oligopoly or monopoly in the market. This, however, is done at huge and unquantifiable costs to the state in which the company operates in terms of extra health care, environmental pollution, social welfare and subsistence for low-income workers and unemployment benefits. These are costs that are not internalized in a company's operation but are nevertheless real costs of its operation that are born not by the company but by the state.

If these unquantifiable costs are taken into account, can we still be so sure that the profit maximization policy would result in allocative efficiency for the society as a whole (or what may be called societal-level efficiency)? 'Where producers can externalize costs there is also an efficiency issue, since they will make decisions that involve a misallocation of resources', Parkinson remarked.[24] Furthermore, he pointed out the following:

> if the signals provided by the market are systematically distorted as a result of weak competition and other forms of market failure, then following those signals will not always lead to the most efficient available outcomes. Once this is acknowledged the local and tangible benefits of social responsibility begin to look more attractive than the speculative and abstract social gains flowing from a rule of strict profit maximization.[25]

In any event, there is no perfectly efficient market as there are often information asymmetries between the parties to the transaction. Voluntary

---

Law, 3d ed, (Boston: Little, Brown) 396; Rostow, E.V. (1959), 'To Whom and for What', ibid., 68; Baumol, W.J. and Blackman, S.A. (1991), 'Social Policy: Pricing Devices to Aid the Invisible Hand,' in Baumol, W.J. and Blackman, S.A., *Perfect Markets and Easy Virtue* (Cambridge, Massachussets: Blackwell) 46.

[22] Fischel, D.R. (1982), The Corporate Governance Movement, *Vanderbilt Law Review* 35: 1273; Easterbrook, and Fischel (1989), The Corporate Contract, note 20 above, 1446–8; Barry, N. (1991), *The Morality and Business Enterprise* (New York: Macmillan) Chapter 2.

[23] For an account of these arguments, see Parkinson, note 12 above, 304 ff.

[24] Ibid., 311.

[25] Ibid., 310–11.

disclosure or sharing of information will not benefit the party who possesses the information but will increase the overall efficiency of the transaction. Exploiting the ignorance of the other party in the pursuit of profit maximization would reduce the overall efficiency of the transaction for the society. The pursuit of self-interest by a company may result in the exploitation of miscalculation or weak bargaining power of the other party and lead to breach of trust. This, in turn, may cause higher transaction costs in drafting and policing terms designed to protect their interests and a reduced level of business activity. Thus, compliance with ethical standards may contribute to the efficient functioning of the economy as a whole.[26]

The profit sacrificing social responsibility approach is particularly important in developing countries where the legal protection for workers' rights and environmental degradation are often weak, both in terms of the law and its enforcement. As the salaries are very low in these countries, companies have more room to absorb any payment increases and if workers are treated as assets rather than liability, there will be enormous gains in productivity. For example, it has been suggested that changes in workforce management could boost manufacturing productivity anything between 50 and 400 per cent.[27]

Indeed, this is done in state-owned enterprises in China where they often have to hire more people than they need in order to prevent unemployment leading to social unrest. The SASAC, the largest shareholder in the SOEs representing the state, ordered refiners to cap their prices when oil prices surged in 2008. Otherwise retail oil prices would have risen to a level unbearable to the national economy.[28] Such profit-sacrificing actions seem contrary to the allocative efficiency of the company but in the overall picture of the welfare of the community and the economy they may be an efficient thing to do. In China, these actions are taken by the largest shareholder SASAC and are rarely taken by shareholders or boards of directors who represent them in an Anglo-American company, save in extreme circumstances where failure to take these apparently 'profit-sacrificing' actions would severely eat into the profits of the company. Critics might quite legitimately argue that SASAC as a representative of the state may not have the knowledge or expertise to know what would be the right things to do in certain economic situations and may even take the wrong

---

26 Ibid., 315.

27 Holland, T. (2010), 'R wages should propel the next wave in productivity gains', SCMP, 15 September 2010, B10.

28 Cai, J. (2010), 'Reforms to make SOEs world class', SCMP, 15 September 2010, B2.

action, or they may not have the incentive to do the right things as they are the agents of the state.

Differently, stakeholder representation on the board would allow for intensive discussions among specialists to find out what is the best thing to do in each circumstance, as each stakeholder director is most knowledgeable in his field and argues for the interest of his constituency. Consequently, any decision would take into account the interest of stakeholders, shareholders and to some extent the interest of the corporate body as a whole.

3. Criticism of the Anglo-American Shareholder Supremacy

It is clear that the Anglo-American's shareholder supremacy is losing ground and credibility in defending shareholder interests. Companies cannot be allowed to operate solely for the benefit and profit maximization of the shareholders. They must operate for the benefits of those involved and affected by their operation. But not even the enlightened shareholder value approach under section 172 of the UK Companies Act 2006 fully reflects this or allows it to be achieved because taking into account the interests of non-shareholders is prefaced by the profit maximization: non-shareholder interests will only be taken into account if it would be 'for the benefit of its members as a whole' (UK Companies Act 2006, s 172).

If it would not be for the benefit of the members to consider the interest of non-shareholders, e.g. the workers, directors are perfectly entitled to ignore them. In fact, one may even go as far to say that they should ignore such interests or they risk being sued by the members for the breach of their duties. Although the imperfections in the techniques of legal control mean that managements are able, should they so desire, to make quite substantial departures from the profit goal without fearing judicial intervention, and if companies do sacrifice profits in favour of social interests, this is done almost certainly within narrow bounds.[29] The legal situation in the U.S. is similar. Even though its constituency statutes do allow directors to take into account stakeholder interests which are also protected by the business judgment rule, many directors' executive compensations are tied to the profit of the company.

4. The Multi-stakeholder Board

A different approach allowing non-shareholder interests to be properly considered is needed. One possibility is to have a governance structure that

---

[29] Parkinson, note 12 above, 304.

allows non-shareholders to participate in the decision-making process of a company. A possible solution would be to have stakeholder directors appointed by various constituencies to represent their interest on the board of directors, each owing a duty to his or her constituency to act diligently and for the interest and benefit of his constituency. Thus, one would have directors representing majority and minority shareholders, workers, consumers, community and the environment respectively.

As they would each owe a duty to their constituency, they would be able to act entirely for the interests of their constituency, and finally for the interest of the company as a whole. The interest of the company as a whole would be the combined interests of all stakeholders, and not the traditional view of the isolated interests of the members. There will be no conflict of interests for each director as would be the case under the enlightened shareholder approach, where some directors may find it difficult to balance the interests of the various stakeholders and shareholders. Each director would be able to act for the interest of the stakeholders he represents as long as it is in the interest of the company as a whole. The interest of the company as a whole would require each director to act in a co-operative spirit with other stakeholder directors whilst advocating and pursuing the interest for their constituency.

The decision would be made by all directors representing the different constituencies through the ballot box. Stakeholders would have better access to corporate information regarding major corporate decisions, would be able to take part in the debate, may raise questions about the proposed corporate decision, could influence the outcome of the decision and ultimately vote to approve or reject the proposed resolution. This would force them to make various comprises or sacrifices in order to get what their constituencies request depending on the dynamics of the board and the interests of other stakeholders. This could arguably lead to better corporate decisions in terms of serving the interests of non-shareholders. Thus, companies may have to agree to pay workers more, or pollute the environment less, or make safer and better products resulting in less profit for the shareholders in order to get their support for a particular decision. Workers may have to accept lower pay than they demand in order to keep their jobs and promise to increase efficiency and output. Environmental directors may have to accept a less stringent standard in pollutant discharge to get the support of other stakeholders or shareholder directors.

Also, stakeholders' participation enables critical issues to be discussed on the board level, and if necessary to be made public, forcing shareholder directors to make compromises in order to protect the company's reputation in the community in which it operates.

The idea of stakeholder participation in the corporate decision-making process is not new. In Germany, co-determination between shareholders and workers in the supervisory board has been practiced for years. Whilst it is true that employees rarely succeeded in vetoing a board resolution, their interest is clearly taken into account by the board. In Japan, although there is no formal co-determination by workers in the board, many directors are appointed from the rank of workers, owing allegiance to the workers and therefore looking after their interests. In Germany and Japan, banks, as creditor and shareholder of a company, are also heavily involved in the corporate decision-making process and are keen to protect their own interests.

In practice, there are the jurisdictions and companies that already have stakeholder representation on the board of supervisors. While our proposal is to have a single-tier stakeholder board, experience from the two-tier board system may nevertheless be illuminating.

II. JURISDICTIONS INTEGRATING STAKEHOLDERS

In corporate governance two main alternative board structures exist: the unitary board and the two-tier board system. While the former is common in the U.S. and U.K., the two-tier board structure is mainly present in continental Europe and Asia. Many companies with a two-tier board system include stakeholders – especially employees – in their corporate governance structure, whereas their Anglo-American counterparts are less stakeholder-orientated.

While various countries involve stakeholders in the corporate decision-making process, such as France,[30] China[31] or Japan,[32] this chapter will

---

[30] See Aste, L.J. (1999), 'Reforming French Corporate Governance: A Return to the Two-Tier Board?', *George Washington Journal of International Law and Economics* 32: 1–72; Hopt, K.J. and Leyens, P.C. (2004), 'Board Models in Europe – Recent Developments of Internal Corporate Governance Structures in Germany, the United Kingdom, France, and Italy', *European Company and Financial Law Review* 2: 135–68.

[31] See Firth, M., Fung P.M.Y. and Rui, O.M. (2007), 'Ownership, Two-tier Board Structure, and The Informativeness of Earnings – Evidence from China,' *Journal of Accounting and Public Policy* 26: 463–96.

[32] See Bonn, I., Yoshikawa, T. and Phan, Ph.H. (2004), 'Effects of Board Structure on Firm Performance: A Comparison between Japan and Australia', *Asian Business and Management* 3: 105–25; Heftel, C.L. (1983), 'Corporate Governance in Japan: The Position of Shareholders in Publicly Held Corporations', *University of Hawaii Law Review* 5: 135–206; Kim, K.A. and Limpaphayom, P.

focus on two countries which served as role models and have well-established rules: Germany and the Netherlands.

1. German Supervisory Board and Works Council

As is well-known, in the German approach, the most prominent system with a two-tier board structure, corporate governance is divided into two separate bodies: the supervisory board and the management board.[33] While the supervisory board is comprised entirely of outside directors, the management board consists wholly of executive directors.[34]

Co-determination, a process which aims to establish a close relationship between the employees and the company, takes a central role in the German approach. It operates on two organizational levels: the supervisory board and the works council.

In the supervisory board, half of its members represent the interests of the employees and are appointed by them. The remaining members and the chairman are appointed by the shareholders.[35] The supervisory board members representing the employees consist of employee delegates, one senior employee and two or three representatives of trade unions. While the employees appoint their delegates,[36] the employee delegates appoint the senior employee[37] and the representatives of the trade unions.[38]

The second level is represented by the works council. All its members are appointed by the personnel of the company. Whereas the supervisory board is a mandatory monitoring body in each company, the employees of a company have the right, but not the obligation, to establish a works council.[39]

(1998), 'A Test of the Two-tier Corporate Governance Structure: The Case of Japanese Keiretsu', *The Journal of Financial Research* 21(1): 37–51.

33 See for more details du Plessis, J. (2004), 'The German Two-Tier Board and the German Corporate Governance Code', *European Business Law Review* 15: 1139–64; Jungmann, C. (2006), 'The Effectiveness of Corporate Governance in One-Tier and Two-Tier Board Systems – Evidence from the UK and Germany', *European Company and Financial Law Review* 4: 434.

34 See Tricker, B. (2012) *Corporate Governance (Principles, Policies and Practices)*, 2d edn (Oxford University Press) 52.

35 German Co-Determination Act 2011, § 7 and 8.

36 Ibid., §§ 10 ff.

37 Ibid., § 15

38 Ibid., § 16

39 German Works Constitution Act 2009, § 1.

2. Dutch Structure Regime

The Netherlands also has a two-tier system in place, consisting of a management and a supervisory board; there are however some differences between them as pointed out below.

In Dutch law, different legal regimes exist that determine the corporate governance of a company; among those are the common regime and the structure regime. The common regime is applicable to SMEs, while the structure regime applies to corporations with a certain number of employees and amount of capital. Other than for SMEs, the formation of a supervisory board is mandatory for corporations under the structure regime.[40]

In contrast to the German approach, the Dutch supervisory board has no labour seats and is not appointed by the workers and the shareholders.[41] However, the works council, shareholders and managing directors can propose candidates to the supervisory board. In this case the works council and the shareholders both have a right to object to appointments.[42] Like the German model, the Dutch system does have a works council, which, in contrast to the German system, is mandatory for corporations with a certain number of employees.[43] As in Germany, the works council is directly appointed by the workers of the enterprise.[44]

III. COMPANIES INTEGRATING STAKEHOLDERS

Besides the legal frameworks of different jurisdictions that promote stakeholder involvement, there also exist practical examples from different

---

40 See Maassen, G.F. (2002), *An International Comparison of Corporate Governance Models – A Study on the Formal Independence and Convergence of One-tier and Two-tier Corporate Boards of Directors in the United States of America, the United Kingdom and the Netherlands* (3rd edn, Amsterdam: Spencer Stuart) 146.

41 Slagter, W.J. (1994), Institutional Investors and Corporate Governance in the Netherlands, in Baums, T., Buxbaum, R.M. and Hopt, K.J. (eds), *Institutional Investors and Corporate Governance* (Berlin: Walter de Gruyter); van Ees, H., Postma, T.J.B.M. and Sterken, E. (2003), 'Board Characteristics and Corporate Performance in the Netherlands', *Eastern Economic Journal* 29(1): 44.

42 Massen, An International Comparison of Corporate Governance Models, note 40 above, 160; Maassen, G.F. and van den Bosch, F.A.J. (1999), On the Supposed Independence of Two-tier Boards: formal structure and reality in the Netherlands, Scholarly Research and Theory Papers 7(1): 32; Slagter, in Baums, Buxbaum and Hopt, ibid., 52.

43 Maassen and van den Bosch, ibid., 33.

44 Dutch Works Council Act 1971, Art. 6.

industries that have moved far beyond the legal imperatives. In the following, two companies with a corporate democracy are shown.

1. Dutch Breman Group[45]

The Dutch Breman Group is a medium-sized construction engineering firm which designed and implemented a corporate democracy model over 30 years ago. It consists of six different institutions; among them the Employee Association, the Advisory Board, Breman Beheer (the group's management), and Brebank (the group's supervisor).

The Breman model of corporate democracy is based on twelve features that can be assembled into three groups (see Table 8.1 below). The third group encompasses the Group's democratic decision-making rules,

Table 8.1 Corporate democracy in the Breman model

Shared Residual Claims	1. Shared equity between Breman Employee Association and shareholders
	2. Profit sharing between employees and Breman Beheer
	3. Fixed interests on capital provided by shareholders
	4. Priority shares held by Brebank in Breman Beheer
Supportive Organizational Structures	5. Breman Employee Association with a board elected by employees
	6. Brebank consisting of an employee director, a shareholder director, and an independent director
	7. Breman Beheer responsible for strategic decisions
	8. Advisory board consisting of two employee and two shareholder representatives
Democratic Decision-Making Rules	9. Election procedure where the firm's works council appoints the firm's management
	10. Equal approval of key decisions by the firm's management and the firm's works council
	11. Arbitration safety net when unanimity in Brebank cannot be achieved
	12. Decision web with the shareholder, the Breman Employees Association, and the independent director as key decision-makers

[45] This paragraph is based on information from de Jong, G. and van Witteloostuijn, A. (2004), Successful Corporate Democracy: Sustainable Cooperation of Capital and Labor in the Dutch Breman Group, *Academy of Management Executive* 18(3): 54–66.

including the election procedure, the approval of key decisions, the central decision-making body consisting of the shareholders, the employees and the independent directors, and lastly an arbitration body to solve divergences of opinion. Based on these rules of corporate democracy the Breman Group has been efficiently and successfully performing for many years.

2. ATSIC in Australia[46]

In the course of the debate on stakeholder democracy, Turnbull used two companies by way of illustration of different governance modes.[47] Even though the Spanish Mondragon Cooperatives serve as a very successful example of stakeholder democracy,[48] ATSIC provides a more exceptional organizational structure. ATSIC was an Australian Government body through which indigenous people were involved in the government process. Even though it was liquidated in 2004,[49] it is worthwhile looking at its structure.

The indigenous people were represented in the Board of Commissioners, which consisted of commissioners elected by regional councils, a chairperson and two persons chosen by the Minister. Throughout Australia different regions were defined and grouped into zones. Each region (first stage) elected its own regional council, and all regional councils in a zone (second stage) elected one as a commissioner. Turnbull describes this concept as a 'two-stage electoral college system of representation'[50] which can serve as a template for the representation of the consumers and the environment in the multi-stakeholder board as will be discussed below.

IV. CRITICAL APPRAISAL OF A MULTI-STAKEHOLDER BOARD

Among scholars critical opinions were expressed regarding concepts of stakeholder integration. In the context of social responsibility, Parkinson

---

46 This paragraph mainly bases on information from Turnbull, JSE 19, 321–60.

47 Ibid., 327–31; see also Driver and Thompson, JMG 2002, 125 who suggest a four-tier structure involving the Shareholder Meeting, a Works Council, the Board of Directors, and a Corporate Senate where the interests could be brought together.

48 Information on Mondragon Corporation is available at <http://www.mondragon-corporation.com/ENG.aspx>.

49 See ANTS, available at <http://www.atns.net.au/agreement.asp?EntityID=618>.

50 Turnbull, JSE 1994, 338.

pointed out the three objections: efficiency, deference and shareholder's money arguments.[51] In line with these arguments, Hansmann and Kraakman recapped the stakeholder model's tendency to inefficient decisions, paralysis, or weak boards which create additional costs.[52] A very sceptical position regarding the efficiency of multiple constituencies is taken by Bainbridge.[53] His critics concern the loss of confidentiality,[54] the divergence of employee and shareholder interests which not only impedes consensus but also permits management to pursue its own self-interest, as well as the indifference of workers to corporate decisions.[55]

These and other concerns[56] are taken up and will be addressed in the context of a multi-stakeholder board based on concepts outlined in the preliminary section. For the analysis, the challenges are arranged into three groups: challenges relating to decision-making, organization, and implementation.

1. Challenges Relating to Decision-making

(a) Concern: inefficient decision-making

One major concern regarding stakeholder integration relates to the efficiency of the decision-making process. As argued among the critics, the integration of stakeholders into the board might lead to a delay in decision-making as the procedure becomes more complex. This, in turn, would contradict the fast-changing business environment.

But before looking for practical solutions, one needs to ask what efficiency in the corporate context means. As discussed, the main goal from the shareholders' perspective is profit maximization. However as mentioned earlier, externalizing costs to the company's stakeholders such as the employees, customers or the environment,[57] is not efficient either.

---

[51] Parkinson, note 12 above, 304 ff.

[52] Hansmann, H. and Kraakman, R. (2001), 'The End of History for Corporate Law', *Georgetown Law Journal* 89: 445.

[53] Bainbridge, S.M. (2008), The New Corporate Governance in Theory and Practice (New York: OUP); Bainbridge, S.M. (1996), Participatory Management Within a Theory of the Firm, *Journal of Corporation Law* 21.

[54] See Ottervanger, T.R. and Pais, R.M. (1981), Employee Participation in Corporate Decision Making: The Dutch Model, *International Lawyer* 15: 393–410.

[55] Bainbridge (2008), 45–9; Bainbridge (1996), 657–730, both note 53 above.

[56] See also Roe, M.J. (1999), 'Codetermination and German Securities Markets', in Blair, M.M. and Roe, M.J. (eds), *Employees and Corporate Governance* (Washington, D.C.: Brookings Institution Press) 194 ff.

[57] See Blair, M.M. (2003), 'Shareholder Value, Corporate Governance, and Corporate Performance: A Post-Enron Reassessment of the Conventional

For a company to work efficiently from a comprehensive point of view, costs must be internalized. This goal can for example be achieved through the introduction of a board representing the various stakeholders of a company. To meet this goal, trade-offs must be made.

Looking at the other side of the coin, integrating stakeholders does not only burden a company but also provides for advantages. By integrating stakeholders into the corporate process, the company can exert a higher degree of control. Suppliers for example would not only be bound by contracts but would also have to comply with the company's code of conduct, e.g. prohibiting child labour. Thus, if the practical challenges can be overcome, such a multi-stakeholder board would create a win-win situation for both the stakeholders and the company and therefore contribute to the societal efficiency as a whole.

(b) Solution: expedited decision-making

In order to overcome an allegedly inefficient decision-making process and meet the fast changes in business environment, an expedited decision-making procedure can be adopted. A conceivable approach is to let the shareholder directors decide as a rule, and require the approval of the stakeholder directors for important matters or when the interests of stakeholders are affected.

Stakeholder approval for important decisions

In the German system, the management board is responsible for the administration, while for 'certain types of business' the consent of the supervisory board is required.[58] It lies in the discretion of the supervisory board to decide which matters require its agreement.[59] According to the German Corporate Governance Code, the approval of the supervisory board is required for businesses that are of 'fundamental importance'.[60] These include 'measures that fundamentally change the financial position of the company and the results of its operations and its cash flows'.[61]

Similarly, in the Dutch structure regime the approval of the supervisory board is required for major decisions. The Dutch Civil Code lists financial

---

Wisdom', in Cornelius, P.K. and Kogut, B. (eds), *Corporate Governance and Capital Flows in a Global Economy* (New York: Oxford University Press) 57 f.

58 German Stock Corporation Act 2011, § 111 s 4.

59 Hempel, J.M. and Wiemken, F. (2006), Managerhaftung im Wandel: Sarbanes-Oxley und Corporate Governance in Deutschland (Bremen: Salzwasser-Verlag) 26.

60 German Corporate Governance Code 2010, § 3.3.

61 Ibid.

matters such as the issuance of shares, major investments, or the filing for bankruptcy but does also request for the assent in personnel matters such as the termination of the employment of a substantial number of employees or a drastic change in employment conditions.[62]

In line with these two approaches, one could give the shareholder directors a general power to decide on ordinary matters, and ask for the approval by stakeholder directors for fundamentally important matters that have a major impact on the finances of the company. Like the German approach, it would lie in the discretion of the stakeholder directors to decide which matters require their approval.

Approval when stakeholders are affected

Another scenario requiring the approval of stakeholder directors is when the interests of the stakeholders are affected. Matters that are of a purely commercial or administrative nature would only require the approval of the shareholder directors. Environmental or labour-related issues, however, would also entail the consent of the respective stakeholder directors. Here, the critical question is where to draw the line.

With regard to the German works council this problem is solved by providing the latter with three different rights of co-determination in social, commercial and personnel matters. In *social matters*, the works council has a genuine right of co-determination, which means that measures only become effective with its approval. It affects employment conditions such as working hours, extra work, holiday regulations and safety measures.[63] With regard to *commercial matters*, the works council has an enforceable right of co-determination when there is a serious change in business such as the closure, transfer or consolidation of the business.[64] When it comes to *personnel matters* such as recruitments or relocations, the works council can only refuse its approval according to a certain catalogue of reasons, e.g. when measures infringe the law or disadvantage other employees.[65]

Similarly, the Dutch works council can disapprove changes of certain *employment conditions*,[66] can render advice on decisions with regard to *significant changes in business*,[67] and has the right to receive information on *corporate decisions*.[68]

---

62 Dutch Civil Code, Art. 2: 274, § 1.
63 German Works Constitution Act 2009, § 87 s 1.
64 Ibid., § 111 ff.
65 Ibid., § 99 s 1 and 2.
66 Dutch Works Council Act 1971, Art. 27.
67 Ibid., Art. 25.
68 Ibid., Art. 31.

In line with these schemes, for each constituency different degrees of co-determination rights for distinct areas may be defined which directly affect stakeholder interests, relate to big changes in business, or only indirectly affect stakeholder interests. For compliance and entrenchment purposes, these rights of co-determination may be enshrined in the by-laws of the company.

Mechanism if stakeholders refuse approval

In order to avoid a stalemate in case stakeholders refuse their approval of a corporate decision, an appropriate mechanism to overcome the situation needs to be in place.

If in the German system the supervisory board refuses its consent, the management board can ask for the approval of the shareholders' meeting.[69] With regard to the works council, three possibilities according to the rights of co-determination in social, commercial and personnel matters exist. If, in *social matters*, the employer and the works council cannot reach an agreement, the company's arbitration committee decides the matter.[70] In terms of *commercial matters*, a two-stage procedure exists. If no settlement between the employer and the works council can be achieved, the parties can ask for mediation conducted by the Federal Employment Agency. In case this attempt remains unsuccessful, the company's arbitration committee can be invoked.[71] If the works council refuses its consent on *personnel matters*, the employer can request for the approval of the regional labour court.[72] In the Dutch structure regime, the works council may lodge an appeal with the Enterprise Section of the Amsterdam Court of Appeal against a decision by an entrepreneur which has been taken against the advice of the works council.[73] If in the Breman model unanimity in the Brebank, the group's supervisor, cannot be achieved, an arbitration safety net is activated.

In our view, alternative dispute resolution (ADR) procedures are to be preferred over court proceedings. They are confidential and decisions are reached more quickly. In the corporate context different forms of ADR may be applied.[74] In order to facilitate the communications, a facilitator may be invited to a board meeting. Another alternative constitutes

---

[69] German Stock Corporation Act 2011, § 111 s 4.

[70] German Works Constitution Act 2009, § 87 s 2.

[71] Ibid., § 112.

[72] Ibid., § 99 s 4.

[73] Dutch Works Council Act 1971, Art. 26, § 1.

[74] See for the different forms of ADR Nolan-Haley, C. (2001), *Alternative Dispute Resolution in a Nutshell* (2nd edn, St. Paul: West Group).

mediation where the mediator can help generate options.[75] In arbitration the arbitration panel can render binding decisions and therefore exert the most power. Arbitration has proved to be very successful in the German approach and also in the Breman Model, and may therefore serve as a good solution for the multi-stakeholder board.

2. Challenges Relating to Organization

(a) Adequate board representation

Another difficulty concerns the allocation of decision-making power in the multi-stakeholder board. If one relies on majority voting instead of a consensus-based process,[76] the composition of the board is key. Since conventional unitary boards consist entirely of shareholder representatives, reducing their power to one fraction of the constituencies would be a harsh incursion. From a practical point of view, one should allow the shareholder directors to represent at least one-half of the multi-stakeholder board. The question, however, is whether to allocate the percentage of the board representation equally among shareholder and stakeholder directors or whether one group should have a preponderant say. This is mainly a political question.

In the German system, one-half of the supervisory board consists of employee representatives and the other half of shareholder representatives including the chairman. Since the chairman has a casting vote when there is a voting tie, shareholders have more weight in the decision-making process.

By granting the directors equal voting rights, one would acknowledge the same importance to the company's social responsibility as to its profit maximization. A proposed solution to achieve this goal is to appoint an independent chairman with the power to break a voting tie. The independent director could be jointly appointed by shareholder and stakeholder directors. However, the inclusion of independent directors on the board is highly controversial.[77] In practice, the management often appoints

---

[75] Lampe, M. (2001), 'Mediation as an Ethical Adjunct of Stakeholder Theory', *Journal of Business Ethics* 31: 165–73.

[76] See Arrow, K.J. (1974), *The Limits of Organization* (New York: Norton) 63–79 who suggest a consensus-based decision-making body at the top of an authority-based structure.

[77] See Cohen, L., Frazzini, A. and Malloy, Ch.J. (2012), 'Hiring Cheerleaders: Board Appointments of 'Independent' Directors', *Management Science* 58(11): 1–20; Sturms, D.V. (1999), 'Enhancing the Effectiveness of Independent Directors: Is the System Broken, Creaking, or Working?' *Villanova Journal of Law and*

people sympathetic to its policy. In the case of a voting tie, the preferred solution would be to refer the case to an arbitrator and let him decide on the matter, as outlined above.

(b) Critical constituency representation

Another challenge relates to the representation of the stakeholder constituencies. In order that the representatives may be appointed, the constituencies must first be defined. There are at least six stakeholder groups which may have interests in the company's conduct. While some constituencies are limited in their number and can therefore be demarcated easily, others are more challenging. Among the first group are the employees, suppliers, creditors and shareholders. More difficulties arise with the consumers and the environment.

There are several options to define what the environment constituency is. One idea is to define the constituency based on the local community where the company is operating. The constituency could include, according to the worst-case scenario, the areas and people that would be directly affected by an environmental accident and would eventually claim for damages.[78] Another possibility is to let a national environmental protection organization appoint the representative. This option faces a two-fold problem. First, what if there is no national organization where the company is incorporated? Second, a national organization might be unsuitable to represent the environment when it comes to multinational corporations. An option, more apt for multinationals, would be to let an international environmental organization appoint the respective representative. As NGOs are not related to a specific state and form part of the private sector, a company might favour an NGO such as Greenpeace[79] appointing the representative instead of a governmental organization.

Looking at the consumer constituency, similar options exist. For the definition of the constituency, one could base on the end consumers of a company. Since this, in the case of large companies, would represent a

Investment Management 1(2): 103–41; Higgs, D. (2003), *Review of the Role and Effectiveness of Non-executive Directors*, available at <www.dti.gov.uk/cld/non_exec_review>; Hong Kong Institute of Chartered Secretaries (2006), The Duties and Responsibilities of Independent Non-Executive Directors of Hong Kong Main Board Listed Companies, January 2006, available at <http://www.hkics.org.hk/media/publication/ attachment/1725_INED.pdf>.

78 See BP Oil Spill Class Action Claim Settlement from March 2012, Economic Zone Maps and Real Property Settlement Maps, available at <http://www.bfw-lawyers.com/bp-oil-spill-settlement-claims/>.

79 Greenpeace, available at <http://www.greenpeace.org/international/en/>.

huge number, it seems less practical. One could again let a national consumer protection organization appoint the representative. As the consumers of multinationals are not limited to a country but are spread all over the world, the most favourable option is to let an international consumer protection organization such as the non-profit organization Consumer International[80] appoint the director.

3. Challenges Relating to Implementation

(a) Appropriate target companies

A fundamental and practical question is how and where the concept of a multi-stakeholder board should be implemented. As a first step of implementation, it is examined which companies constitute optimal targets for the adoption of a multi-stakeholder board.

While the idea of such a concept is not limited to any type or size of company, it is practically most sensible to implement the concept first in large companies acting at the international level. Multinational enterprises (MNEs) may be more susceptible to such a concept since many of them have been in the media or involved in court proceedings because of human rights' violations or environmental pollution, and therefore have an interest in setting a positive example.[81] Another reason is that MNEs have a more significant impact on society due to their substantial transaction volume and may therefore serve as role models for smaller local companies.

In our view, there is a significant incentive for MNEs operating in developing countries or having a history of abuse to adopt such a representative board. Therewith, they may prevent or face the critics and make the first step to internalize costs instead of outsourcing externalities to other, weaker countries.

(b) Level and degree of implementation

Since MNEs have business activities all over the world, the implementation of a multi-stakeholder board should be introduced at the international rather than the national level. Even though one could link MNEs to the place where they are incorporated and enact national rules for the adoption of such a multi-stakeholder board, adoption at the international

---

80 Consumer International, available at <http://www.consumersinternational.org/>.

81 See BP, Shell, Nike, or Apple; see for further examples Werther, W. and Chandler, D. *Strategic Corporate Social Responsibility, Stakeholders in a Global Environment*, 2d edn (Los Angeles: Sage Publications) 281 ff.

level provides for more advantages: guidelines on an international level ensure a certain degree of harmonization and further allow supervising the activities of a company in its entirety not merely limited to the parent company incorporated at a certain place. Moreover, the countries would not forfeit their attractiveness as a business location by adopting stricter rules than other jurisdictions.

As mentioned, in our view the implementation of the suggested stakeholder board should take place on a voluntary basis. This idea goes in line with the current practice in CSR that provides for a voluntary compliance on the part of the companies. Even though many authors plead for mandatory rules in CSR and some countries have already taken legislative actions,[82] it seems difficult to introduce such a stakeholder board on a mandatory basis *ab initio*.

As a first step, we therefore suggest placing the adoption of stakeholder boards at the disposal of the companies. As experience has shown, many ideas which were first adopted internationally and on a voluntary basis, have later been implemented into national laws after having proven successful or an increase in pressure has taken place.[83]

(c) Competent body for implementation

Proceeding on the premise that the concept of a multi-stakeholder board should be first adopted at the international level on a voluntary basis, the question arises as to which organization would be the competent body for its implementation.

---

[82] Bendall, J. (2004), 'Barricades and Boardrooms: A Contemporary History of the Corporate Accountability Movement', *Technology Business and Society Programme Paper* 13: 14–18; Gayo, S. (2012), 'Mandatory and Voluntary Corporate Social Responsibility Policy Debates in Indonesia' (Chiang Mai: International Conference on International Relations and Development), available at <http://www.icird.org/ 2012/files/papers/Sabela%20Gayo.pdf>; Kerr, M., Janda, R. and Pitts, Ch. (2009), *Corporate Social Responsibility: A Legal Analysis* (Canada: LexisNexis) 30 ff; Perrault Crawford, E. and Clark Williams, C. (2010), 'Should corporate social reporting be voluntary or mandatory? Evidence from the banking sector in France and the United States', *Corporate Governance* 10(4): 512–26; Price, T. (2010), 'Corporate Social Responsibility: Is Good Citizenship Good for the Bottom Line?' in *Issues for Debate in Corporate Social Responsibility: Selections from CQ Researcher* (Thousand Oaks: Sage Publications) 19 f; Ward, H., *Legal Issues in Corporate Citizenship* (London: International Institute for Environment and Development), available at <http://www.iiedorg/pubs/pdfs/16000IIED.pdf>; Wettstein, F. and Waddock, S. (2005), 'Voluntary or Mandatory: That is (Not) the Question, Linking Corporate Citizenship to Human Rights Obligations for Business', *Zeitschrift für Wirtschafts-und Unternehmensethik* 6(3): 304–20.

[83] See for example the Basel Accords.

As the adoption should take place at the international level, an international organization seems to be the most suitable. While several organizations are active in the field of business and human rights,[84] the UN and the OECD seem to be most appropriate for the implementation of the proposed stakeholder board as they have a large number of members.

As the concept of a multi-stakeholder board should target MNEs first, the OECD, which developed the 'OECD Guidelines for Multinational Enterprises',[85] might be an appropriate body for its implementation. Similarly, the UN has been very active in the area of CSR. The High Commissioner for Human Rights was not only responsible for the establishment of the UN Global Compact[86] but also developed the Guiding Principles on Business and Human Rights.[87] As the UN already possesses the necessary expertise, authority and for later purposes also the enforcement power, it appears to be the most suitable body to establish guidelines for the implementation of a multi-stakeholder board for multinational corporations.

V. CONCLUSION

Whilst market is arguably the best way to allocate resources efficiently, and corporations exist to reduce transaction costs, the Anglo-American corporate law has allowed many costs of a corporate action to be externalized. This leads to inefficient results for the society as a whole. It also leads to poor consideration of social justice by corporations and human rights abuses. The corporate law should support the market economy but at the same time enable social justice to be achieved. In order to meet the growing demand of the international community asking companies to take social responsibility for their business activities and perceive their role and impact on environment and society as whole, new concepts that allow internalizing of the companies' costs need to be developed.

---

84 The International Labor Organization (ILO), the World Trade Organization (WTO), the Global Reporting Initiative or Ceres, both non-profit organizations that promote economic sustainability, available at <https://www.globalreporting.org/ > and <http://www.ceres.org/>.

85 OECD Guidelines for Multinational Enterprises 2011, available at <http://www.oecd.org/ investment/guidelinesformultinationalenterprises/1922428.pdf>.

86 UN Global Compact, available at <http://www.unglobalcompact.org/>.

87 Guiding Principles on Business and Human Rights: Implementing the United Nations 'Protect, Respect, Remedy' Framework, available at <http://www.ohchr.org/Documents/Publications/GuidingPrinciplesBusinessHR_EN.pdf>.

A stakeholder representative board is one way towards achieving this goal. There are indisputably difficult issues about the composition of the board and power sharing among the different stakeholders to be resolved but it is a step in the right direction. As many issues relating to the effectiveness or practicalities of its implementation remain, this chapter suggests as a first step the implementation of a multi-stakeholder board for multinational corporations at the international level on a voluntary basis, partly due to their history of abuse, and to their reputation and impact in the international community. With the proposed board integrating multiple stakeholders, further discussion and research on stakeholder democracy may be encouraged and stir the creation of new ideas that can find their way into practice.

9. In loco parentis: directorial duties to consumers

Theresa A. Gabaldon

INTRODUCTION

This just in – not all decisions made by economic actors are completely rational. Social psychologists have long taught, and legal analysts now often concede, that human beings have cognitive limits that may be routinely exploited in a variety of ways, including the method in which an issue is framed. Unsurprisingly, corporate America has been paying psychologists and other social scientists for years and has handily plumbed their insights in devising products and marketing campaigns. The result is a marketplace in which ads for fast food and diet aids compete for position before the eyes of a progressively overweight population, and billions of dollars are spent on products for children that, by and large, their parents may not really want them to have.

The traditional view of corporate law asserts that the corporation serves society via the satisfaction of consumers' revealed preferences, which dictate the ultimate allocation of resources contributed by corporate investors, workers, and managers. The recognition that there are easily manipulable "bounds" on rationality, self-interest and free will severely weaken this theory's underpinnings. If corporations in fact create the preferences they then satisfy, it is corporate managers and their social science advisors who are deciding that a tsunami of wealth should go into the production and consumption of junk food and violent video games.

Nowhere is the problem of consumer exploitation more starkly illustrated than in the case of marketing to children – children who are, very literally, being shaped by corporate America.[1] This chapter seeks, first,

[1] As this may suggest, however, there are other contexts in which the bounded rationality of consumers suggests the need to alter the duties of corporate decision-makers. The author has called for such an alteration *vis à vis* financial consumers. Gabaldon, T. "*Half-a-Cup Better than None: A Pragmatic Approach to Preventing the Abuse of Financial Consumers*", (2013) G.W.U. L. Rev. 81, 929.

to provide facts and figures in support of this assertion. It then proposes a solution involving a change in the functioning of corporate boards and assesses that solution from the theoretical perspectives of a number of schools of legal thought. It concludes with an appendix providing additional detail for those considering the practicalities of implementation.

THE OXYMORON OF CHILDREN'S PURCHASING POWER

Children between the ages of four and 12 engage in over $24 billion of direct consumer purchasing each year.[2] Their preferences are said to affect an additional $300 billion of annual consumer transactions.[3] When the influence of older children also is taken into account, the "purchasing power" of the childish market is nothing short of monstrous.[4]

It seems obvious that "purchasing power" is, in the context of childish consumption, an oxymoron. Few people could contend that children are strictly rational. As a general matter, they are more prone to take risks and value short-term over long-term consequences than any other age group.[5] More specifically, they demand and acquire the products that are marketed to them, rather than those which might be deemed "best" for them from an adult point of view. Even if this were not otherwise demonstrated by both experience and the scientific studies alluded to below, it is clear that advertisers believe it to be the case: they attempt to establish brand loyalty in young children,[6] and spend billions each year on youth marketing.[7] In fact, fast food companies dedicate most of their promotional budgets to targeting children.[8] This is, of course, for good reason.

---

2 McNeal, J. "*Tapping the Three Kids' Markets, American Demographics*", (1998) http://www.demographics.com/Publications/AD/98<uscore>ad/ad980429.htm, accessed 25 October 2011.

3 Hymel, M. "*Consumerism, Advertising, and the Role of Tax Policy*", (2000) Va. Tax Rev. 20, 347, at p. 405.

4 Ibid. One 1992 study estimated that year's spending by teenagers at $93 billion.

5 Atwood, B. "*The Child's Voice in Custody Litigation: An Empirical Survey and Suggestions for Reform*", Ariz. L. Rev. (2003) 45 629, at p. 657.

6 Nestle, M. *Food Politics: How the Food Industry Influences Nutrition and Health*, Berkeley, US: University of California Press. (2000) p. 25.

7 Woodhouse, B. "*Reframing the Debate about the Socialization of Children: An Environmentalist Paradigm*", U. Chi. Legal F. (2004) 85, at p. 102.

8 Nicholson, M. "*McLibel: A Case Study in British Defamation Law*", Wis. Int'l L. J. (2000) 18, 1, at p 139.

As Professor Angela Campbell[9] has documented, children are more trusting than adults, tending to view advertisements as advice from a friend. Children under five generally cannot distinguish between commercials and programming (including news programming); children under eight generally cannot understand that commercials are designed to persuade them to make purchases. The average American child views more than 40 000 commercials a year[10] and spends 28 hours a week watching television (many of them in his or her own bedroom);[11] "mass-mediated story tellers," most of them commercially sponsored, speak to these children on an average of at least seven hours a day.[12]

Television and other electronic forms of entertainment have hazards in addition to exposure to commercials. Television viewing, video gaming, and computer gaming are correlated with weight gain.[13] Moreover, experts believe that television viewing is a prime explanation for increasing attention deficit disorders[14] and has a negative correlation with school performance.[15] They also suggest that playing video games involves "stimulus addiction," leading players to crave increasing levels of stimulation, which can be satisfied through increasing violence.[16] Some studies show that violent video games increase short- and long-term aggressive tendencies.[17] As will be discussed below, one's inclination to accept the validity of studies of this sort, or, for that matter, the assessment of any so-called expert in any field, is subject to cultural predetermination and fit with world view. What is important for purposes of analysis, however, is

---

9 Campbell, A. "*Ads2Kids.com: Should Government Regulate Advertising to Children on the World Wide Web?*", Gonz. L. Rev. (1998) 33, 311, at p. 320.

10 Woodhouse op cit., at p. 102.

11 Walsh, D. et al *Physician Guide to Media Violence*, Chicago, US: American Medical Association, (1996) p. 8.

12 Fox, R.F. *Harvesting Minds: How TV Commercials Control Kids*, Westport, US: Greenwood Publishing Group, (1996) p. 12.

13 Ebberling, C. et al, "*Childhood Obesity: Public-Health Crisis, Common Sense Cure*", The Lancet (2002) 360, 473, p. 475; Gortmaker, S. et al, "*Television Viewing as a Cause of Increasing Obesity Among Children in the United States*, (1996) 1986–1990", Archives Pediatrics & Adolescent Med. 150, 356, at p. 356.

14 Christakis, D. et al, "*Early Television Exposure and Subsequent Attentional Problems in Children*", Pediatrics (2004) 113, 708, at p. 710.

15 Woodhouse, op cit., at p. 107.

16 Campbell, T. "*Did Video Games Train the School Shooters to Kill? Determing Whether Wisconsin Courts Should Impose Negligence or Strict Liability in a Lawsuit Against the Video Game Manufacturers*", Marq. L. Rev. (2001) 84, 811, pp. 819–22.

17 Anderson, C. and Dill, K. "*Video Games and Aggressive Thoughts, Feelings, and Behavior in Laboratory and in Life*", J. Personality & Soc. Psych. (2002) 78, 772, at p. 778.

that the facts demonstrated and/or risks suggested resonate with at least some proportion of the adult population that is responsible for the rearing of children.

This chapter uses the term "childish preference" to describe those desires of children that are subject to commercial exploitation – that is, subject to stimulation by profit-seeking manipulation, whether by advertisement, celebrity endorsement, product placement or deliberate addiction. For instance, advertising sugar-laden breakfast cereal on television shows watched by children is an attempt to exploit childish preference, as is placing that cereal at child eye-level on grocery store shelves. Paying a sports figure to wear clothing of a type marketed to children is an attempt to exploit childish preference. Deliberately increasing the violence of video games marketed to children to stimulate the appetites jaded by the last escalation is an attempt to exploit childish preference. And, as experience and social science tell us, many of these attempts succeed.

THE ROLE OF PARENTAL PREFERENCE

In the past, there has been no attempt whatsoever to integrate concern for the welfare for childish or other vulnerable consumers into the laws structuring internal corporate governance. Moreover, laws requiring rating and/or censoring and/or limiting advertising to children have not been particularly successful in the United States.[18] As a practical matter, this almost certainly is because the market provided by childish preference is so vast that corporations have strong incentives both to oppose regulations of this sort and to seek to subvert them.[19] As a formal matter, though, proposed regulations have tended to founder on the shoals of arguments about what parents should be permitted and expected to do on behalf of their children.[20] In fact, framing the issue of regulating children's consumption in terms of prospective interference with existing parental

---

[18] Munger, L. "*Comment: Is Ronald McDonald the Next Joe Camel? Regulating Fast Food Advertisements Targeting Children in Light of the American Overweight and Obesity Campaign*", Conn. Pub. Int. L.J. (2004) 3, 456, pp. 475–6; Beales, H. III "*Advertising to Kids and the FTC: A Regulatory Retrospective that Advises the Present*", Geo. Mason L. Rev. (2004) 12, 873.

[19] When successful, this is referred to as the problem of "deep capture" Yosifon, D, "*The Consumer Interest in Corporate Law*", U.C. Davis L. Rev. (2009) 253, at p. 269.

[20] In describing a Federal Trade Commission rulemaking, later negated by Congress, that limited advertising to children, a *Washington Post* editorial said "[t]he proposal, in reality, is designed to protect children from the weaknesses of

rights apparently endows the antiregulatory argument with sufficient psychological freight as to make it irresistible to most lawmakers.

On the other hand, it seems quite clear (both on the basis of common sense and empiric study) that many of the objects of childish preference are not what parents, left to their own devices, would choose for their children.[21] At the same time, they are not objects that parents successfully deny. There are real-world explanations for what otherwise might appear to be moral abdication. First, overworked and time-pressed parents may not be able to fully research the attributes of the objects in question before they are purchased. Second, they may not feel they have time or energy to seek alternatives. Third, they may feel trapped by the problem of the commons.[22] Thus, they may reason that if they invest in rigorous monitoring of their own children's consumption, but other parents do not, the "spillover" effects on the monitored children are unavoidable.[23] Moreover, the psychological insights referred to in the Introduction help explain just why parental intercession cannot impede the flow of arguably undesirable acquisitions into the hands of children. Parents may not be as irrational as their children, but neither are they themselves immune from manipulation.

DECISIONS, DECISIONS

Professor Gregory Mitchell[24] has invoked the term "legal decision theorists" to refer to the scholars who advocate the behavioral analysis of law. These theorists have applied the insights of social psychology and related fields toward the goal of developing an account of how decisions are made in contexts relevant to law and law-making. In evaluating the operation of financial markets and profit-making entities, they frequently have challenged assumptions about the rationality of the relevant actors. They have questioned the ability of many such actors to act in accordance with procedural norms of rationality (such as consistency and assimilation

---

their parents – and the parents from the wailing insistence of their children". "The FTC as National Nanny", *Washington Post* A22, 1 March 1978.

21 Hymel, op cit., at p. 388.

22 The "problem of the commons" problem arises when the benefits of an activity do not accrue solely to the actor Samuelson, P. "*Pitfalls in the Analysis of Public Goods*", J.L. & Econ. (1967) 10, 199.

23 Woodhouse, op cit., at p. 106.

24 Mitchell, G. "*Why Law and Economics' Perfect Rationality Should Not be Traded for Behavioral Law and Economics' Equal Incompetence*", Geo. (2002) L.J. 91, 67 ("Incompetence"), at pp. 78–9.

of new information), focusing on the cognitive heuristics that predictably permit humans to make decisions and/or identify their own preferences in light of limits on time, information, and cognitive ability. Legal decision theorists thus have concluded that "human decision-making processes are prone to non-rational, yet systematic, tendencies," resulting in "bounds" on rationality and free will.[25]

Although decisionmaking may be systematically nonrational, it seems clear that lack of rationality does not occur uniformly across all populations and in all situations. There may be educational, cultural, and many other types of variance; there is, for instance, documented variance dependent on the decisionmaker's accountability.[26] This recognition may be reassuring insofar as it does contemplate that responsible social planners can act rationally – or, at any rate, better than the rest of us. The prospect of intersubject variation does not, however, undercut the insight that, in some situations, many individuals make nonrational decisions in predictable ways. One of these has to do with the tendency to eschew strictly self-interested courses of action, engaging instead in some amount of altruistic decisionmaking (leading to identification of bounds on self-interest as a type of bounded rationality). A second has to do with willingness to respond to role assignment by engaging in conduct that is expected rather than responsive to individual taste. In this regard, studies described below have assessed and demonstrated participants' willingness to administer electric shocks to other participants and to act as abusive prison guards when they perceive it is their "job" to do so in furtherance of science.

Another phenomenon identified by legal decision theorists that is critical to analysis has to do with the tendency to respond to the framing of a decision in predictable ways. It has, for instance, been fairly well established that decisionmaking is affected by whether an outcome is described in terms of achieving a gain or of avoiding a loss (with decisionmakers generally considering the latter to be more important).[27] Similarly, there is a clearly revealed bias in favor of remaining with the status quo. This means, for instance, that if a retirement plan is designed as one into which employees must opt, there will be significantly less participation than if it is a plan in which participation is the default.

Legal decision theorists also have made the claim that many individuals

---

25 Hanson, J. and Kysar, D. "*Taking Behavioralism Seriously: The Problem of Market Manipulation*", N.Y.U. L. Rev. (1999) 74, 632, at p. 633.

26 Mitchell, (Incompetence) op cit., at p. 110.

27 Korobkin, R. "*Libertarian Welfarism*", Cal. L. Rev. (2009) 97, 1651 at p. 1658.

do not test hypotheses in logical fashion, instead preferring to solicit confirming evidence and failing to perceive disconfirming evidence.[28] Relatedly, they have identified a confirmation bias "in accordance with which exposure to a competing position will not dislodge and may even strengthen the antecedently held position."[29] It is fairly easy to see how corporate advertisers could shape the so-called decisions of both children and parents by appeal to this particular heuristic. Basically, if celebrity endorsement or other presentation in an ad, or product placement in a movie, successfully creates the hypothesis that ownership of an item is correlated with success, glamor, or the like, many consumers will not subject that hypothesis to anything like rigorous logical questioning.

There are many other examples of heuristics that may be, and almost certainly are, exploited by advertisers. Professors Hanson and Kysar[30] have done a particularly thorough job of describing them as part of their call for changes in prevailing schemes for product liability. Interestingly, other researchers examining heuristic reaction to product presentations have documented the relative resistance of senior citizens to manipulation, as compared to populations of younger adults.[31] Research into the use of heuristics by children is not as well developed as adult research, but children's perception of advertisements as "advice from a friend" does little to suggest that they would in any way be more resistant to manipulation than the relatively young adults who are likely to parent them.

LET'S GET CRITICAL

Legal decision theory sometimes is viewed as the product of a group of scholars fairly recently self-identifying as practitioners of "law and behavioral economics."[32] This group has both noted the importance of the various phenomena identified above and written broadly on various corporate law subjects; its possible views on the subject of exploitation of childish consumers are discussed in more detail in a subsequent part of this

---

[28] Hanson and Kysar, op cit., at p. 650.

[29] Sunstein, C. "*Deliberative Trouble? Why Groups Go to Extremes*", Yale L. J. (2000) 110, 71, at p. 155.

[30] Hanson and Kysar, op cit.

[31] Tentori, K. et al, "*Wisdom and Aging: Irrational Preferences in College Students but not Older Adults*", Cognition (2001) 81, B87, at pp. B87–8.

[32] Mitchell, G. "*Taking Behavioralism Too Seriously? The Unwarranted Pessimism of the New Behavioral Analysis of Law*", Wm. & Mary L. Rev. (2002) 43, 1907 ("Pessimism"), at pp. 1913–16 and n. 12.

chapter. There is, however, another recent school that is making significant contributions to legal decision theory. "Critical realists" have helpfully identified shortcomings in law and behavioral economics, and have advanced the proposition that conversation about rationality, bounded or otherwise, underestimates the importance of situational influence on behavior.[33] This systematic failure to reckon with situation is said to be part and parcel of the promotion of "dispositionist discourse" in which (faulty) intuition and so-called common sense lead us to attribute behavior to individual "disposition," or choice, and to be blind to such realities as biologic response to manipulated products and environments. They do not neglect the possibility of manipulation of "frames" and other information: critical realists even note the possibility that scientific discourse may be captured by economic actors in such a way as to create appeals to world views that would otherwise lack support. By way of illustrating their contentions, critical realists have made a convincing case that it is situational manipulation, rather than bad personal choices, that has led to the obesity epidemic afflicting America's children and adults.[34]

THE CASE FOR CONCERN

Quite Shocking

As noted above, there are studies demonstrating willingness to administer increasingly painful electric shocks as part of a "teaching" experiment; fairly consistently, the willingness to follow the directions of the experimenter, notwithstanding cries of pain from the putative subjects, hovers at 61–66 percent.[35] Relatedly, in the famous "Stanford prison" experiment, randomly assigned "prison guards" rapidly became abusive (while the randomly assigned "prisoners" just as quickly became dysfunctionally depressed).[36] The implications of these phenomena as an analogy for corporate law are sobering. If the majority of individuals are willing to cause

---

[33] Hanson, J. and Yosifon, D. "*The Situation: An Introduction to the Situational Character, Critical Realism, Power Economics, and Deep Capture*", U. Pa. L. Rev. (2003) 152, 129, at p. 136.

[34] Benforado, A. et al, "*Broken Scales: Obesity and Justice in America*", Emory L. J. (2004) 53, 1645, at p. 1797.

[35] Burger, J. "*Replicating Milgram: Would People Still Obey Today?*", Am. Psychologist (2009) 64, 1.

[36] Haney, C. et al, "*Interpersonal Dynamics in a Simulated Prison*", Int'l J. Criminology & Psychology (1973) 1, 69, at pp. 69–73.

pain either in accordance with the ideal of scientific service or in accordance with the perceived demands of a role they have voluntarily assumed, might they not be just as willing to inflict pain on non-shareholders in accordance with the perceived demands of the role of corporate director? And what if it were precisely the individuals who were most willing to repeatedly and consistently administer the "shocks" to non-shareholders prompted by their roles as members of the board of directors who were most willing to assume – and continue – in those positions?

Accountability

One would generally anticipate that accountability would tend to improve the quality of decisionmaking, insofar as the decisionmaker might be expected to take more care (engage in less shirking) and eschew self-interest more thoroughly than otherwise would be the case. Accountability researchers have suggested, however, that "self-critical and effortful thinking" is most likely where a decisionmaker feels he or she will be accountable to an audience with an interest in process rather than specific outcomes.[37] Where the views of the audience on outcomes are known, it may well be the case that decisionmaking processes will be truncated and existing biases will be exaggerated. This is not particularly good news in the case of corporate directors. It is an open secret that the combination of the business judgment rule and statutes and provisions in articles of incorporation holding directors financially harmless means there is no real legal accountability for the outcome of directorial actions (or, within reason, for the shoddiness of the procedures through which those actions are taken).[38] Instead, directors are accountable to markets, with their accountability outcome "scores" flashing on the scoreboard of stock price. It is no surprise that they consistently conduct themselves so as to see that score increase.

A WHOLE LOT OF SOMETHING GOING ON

Social scientists aptly caution legal scholars against employing tools they have not been trained to use. No doubt the neophyte's invocation of

---

[37] Lerner, J. and Tetlock, P. "*Accounting for the Effects of Accountability*", Psychol. Bull. (1999) 125, 255, at p. 258.

[38] Hammermesh, L. "*Why I Do Not Teach Van Gorkum*", Ga. L. Rev. (2000) 34, 477, at pp. 345–9.

studies about role identification, framing or the like, will sometimes lead to overstatement, as well as oversight. It has been suggested that many legal decision theorists have not carefully distinguished experimental and survey empiricism and have failed to reckon with the latter. Survey empiricism has demonstrated, for instance, that in at least the field of consumer lending, the model of law and behavioral economics has no more predictive power than a stricter law and economics model (discussed below) premised on classic rationality.[39] At the same time, social scientists appear to believe that their insights should be taken seriously, and have acknowledged that at least some suggestions based on legal decision theory "risk no harm."[40]

This chapter takes the position that it does no harm to acknowledge the reality that corporations at least sometimes attempt to manipulate childish preferences in ways parents are helpless to prevent. It does no harm to acknowledge that corporate decisionmakers have been encouraged to believe it is their duty to engage in such manipulation. It is the task of the remainder of the chapter to persuade that it would do no harm to counter this belief.

DE-BIASING

In the past, authors expressing concern for the plight of consumers have made a number of suggestions. These include regulation of advertising, criminalizing exploitation, giving shareholders a voice on exploitation, and making directors directly accountable to consumers.[41] Suggestions falling in the last category – director accountability to consumers – have been forthcoming for decades and have taken a variety of forms, including imposing a new fiduciary duty and/or permitting consumers to vote in directorial elections. These suggestions have been both extensively criticized and to no real avail.

The proposal of this chapter is more modest. Professor Gregory Mitchell has written of "de-biasing reforms" to be employed in behavior research. His suggestions include "asking or directing experimental

---

39 Wright, J. "*Behavioral Law and Economics, Paternalism, and Consumer Contracts: An Empirical Perspective*", NYU J.L. & Liberty (2007) 2, 470, at pp. 474–5.

40 Mitchell, op cit., (Incompetence), pp. 132–5.

41 Gabaldon, T. "*Joe Camel Explains It to the Board: Corporate Law, Women in the Workplace, and the Exploitation of Children*", Duke J.L. & Policy (2006) 13, 203, at pp. 230–31.

subjects to consider alternative or opposing arguments," and "asking experimental subjects to explain their choices."[42] This chapter proposes that these reforms be employed in the case of corporate directors making decisions relevant to the exploitation of childish consumers.

Doubtless, objections could be raised. Discussed at length below are the speculated theoretical reactions of a number of schools of legal analysis. More practically, would-be critics might say "Why just consumer exploitation? Why not the environment? Why not global warming?"[43] They might also warn of the can of worms opened when trying to identify the appropriate level of detail at which the de-biasing reforms might be triggered.

These practical criticisms are apt, but there are practical responses. First, mindfulness with respect to a variety of social issues would not be a bad thing. Although there might be a point at which the task of considering all, or even a large number of, possible social issues might become daunting, continuing to allow directors to hide from them in a black box marked "business judgment" simply means there will be little progress on any such issue. Moreover, the point of overload is, at the moment, quite distant.

The second practical objection is well taken, but not fatal. A requirement that members of the board specifically consider the exploitation of childish consumers does not dictate how deeply the board must inquire. Must they consider every product and read every ad? Consult decision-making and other behavioral experts? Almost certainly, the members of a corporate board accustomed to doing little more than monitoring management would need some help; some sort of up-the-line contemplation and reporting on the issue of prospective exploitation would be required. Reports from those in the bowels of the corporation who themselves deal

---

42 Mitchell, op cit., (Incompetence), at p. 134.

43 Interestingly, the Securities and Exchange Commission has moved toward requiring disclosure about how global warming is expected to affect the businesses of reporting companies (Douglass (2009), p. 1119). This might be expected to prompt internal reflection about the extent to which such companies are contributing to the problem and the possibility that they might be forced to change their practices. For those concerned with global warming, this is a step in the right direction. Of a piece with this approach are the requirements of the Sarbanes-Oxley Act of 2002 that publicly traded companies disclose whether they have financial experts on their audit committees and whether they have codes of ethics. Public Company Accounting Reform and Corporate Responsibility Act (Sarbanes-Oxley) 15 U.S.C. §7264 (2011); 15 U.S.C. §7265 (2011). These disclosures presumably have required boards of directors at least briefly to grapple with the underlying issues and have not-so-surprisingly correlated with increases both in financial experts and ethics codes.

with the experts consulting on product and ad design presumably would be particularly helpful. The appendix to this chapter provides questions a board might be prompted to answer and procedures that might be imposed.

BACK TO SCHOOL

It is sometimes said that all thinking people agree that the purpose of the corporation is to benefit society. Many corporate law scholars contend that the mechanism through which this is to occur is shareholder primacy, sometimes alternately formulated as the corporate goal of profit maximization. Over the last 40 years or so a staggering amount has been said about this subject. It nonetheless is important to examine the relation that this guiding myth of American corporate law bears to the exploitation of vulnerable consumers, and thus to the proposed method of beginning to address this exploitation. This examination commences with a consideration of the contractarian approach to corporate law, which may be credited with the deification, if not the invention, of shareholder primacy.

THE CONTRACTARIAN APPROACH

The Nexus of Contracts and Shareholder Primacy

The law and economics school of legal analysis describes the corporation as a "nexus of contracts" among capital providers, managers, employees, and others (including consumers), all of whom conduct themselves in a manner that is rationally self-interested.[44] Adherents of this school, sometimes known as "contractarians," characterize the "best," or "most efficient," corporate law as providing the set of default contract rules most likely to minimize transaction costs. These rules generally reflect the assumption that corporate managers – generally the board of directors – act as fiduciaries for the shareholders. Limiting the duties of the board of directors to serving shareholder interests is thought to be the single best method of limiting managerial opportunism and shirking, owing to the relative efficiency of monitoring by a single class of beneficiaries. The

---

[44] Jensen, M. and Meckling, W. "*The Theory of the Firm: Managerial Behavior, Agency Costs, and Ownership Structure*", J. Fin. Econ. (1976) 3, 305, at pp. 306–7.

board therefore is regarded as responsible for maximizing the residual value of the firm remaining after non-shareholder claimants are satisfied. This easily translates to a sweater set of assertions that the goal of the corporation is to make money for its shareholders and that the interests of shareholders must be preferred over those of all others with interests in the firm.[45] The resulting template for corporate law is known as the "shareholder primacy" model. Under this view, even a modest proposal to encourage the board of directors to be purposely mindful of interests other than those of shareholders is controversial.

Contractarians necessarily do acknowledge the existence of externalities and other market imperfections that they believe should be regulated, if at all, by laws preserving the efficiency of the corporate form – in other words, external laws telling corporations what they must do.[46] In their view, then, if consumer irrationality is a problem, it should be addressed by regulation of advertising content or the like. The duty of the board of directors would be no more than to monitor corporate compliance with applicable law.

Does Shareholder Primacy Truly Demand Consumer Exploitation?

If one were to accept the contractarian goal of shareholder primacy as a given, but still were concerned about consumer exploitation, a moment or two of thought might be given to the question of whether shareholder primacy indeed demands such exploitation, provided only that it is legal. The first step is to acknowledge that most jurisdictions do have statutes authorizing corporate philanthropy or statutes that provide that the board of directors may take interests of nonshareholders into account – often both. Exploitation of consumers, then, is not legally compelled. Statutes aside, the well-known common law business judgment rule limits judicial second-guessing of directorial decisionmaking, leaving at least a modicum of unreviewable room for considering nonshareholder interests.

Notwithstanding the legal latitude to consider nonshareholder interests without fear of personal liability, there is an impressive array of extralegal forces prompting corporate boards to observe a shareholder primacy norm. These include perceived susceptibility to hostile takeover, fear of relative disadvantage in raising capital, and psychological acculturation. It is psychological acculturation that this chapter seeks to address.

---

[45] Easterbrook, F.H. and Fischel, D.R. *The Economic Structure of Corporate Law*, Cambridge, US: Harvard University Press, (1991), at pp. 35–9 and 90–94.

[46] Fischel, D. "*The Corporate Governance Movement*", Vand. L. Rev. (1982) 35, 1259, at p. 1271.

The argument of the contractarians against the proposal and in favor of psychological acculturation toward shareholder primacy manifest through profit maximization is one of normative desirability: social utility is maximized when corporate profits are maximized, so directors should act accordingly (and be acculturated to so act) even where not subject to legal compulsion. This means, as a policy matter, that consumer preferences indeed should be manipulated if that will contribute to the corporate bottom line. Only if public recognition of the practice were to be likely, and were apt to lead to enough public outcry to result in boycotts, legal prohibition, or something of the sort should manipulation be limited. Market experience to date presumably reflects that corporate decisionmakers do not generally expect such a rebound.

Without doing the heavy lifting to establish that consumer manipulation is immoral, it nevertheless is worth a moment to ask whether the goal of shareholder primacy logically compels morally questionable but legal acts. One response is definitional: if an act is legal and profitable, its corporate pursuit is morally correct, leading, as law and economics assume, to a more profitable society.[47] In this view, other moral determinations should be left to external regulation, and not be made part of the corporate calculus. Thus, if child pornography or assassins for hire were the most profitable possible lines of business, and not illegal, it would be best if the members of the board of directors felt that it were their duty to enter those lines.[48] This means that the normative desirability of a

---

[47] This should not be read as suggesting that the proponents of law and economics any longer make claims that wealth maximization is a moral principle or that, without constraint, it is not normatively objectionable. *See* http://linguafranca.mirror.theinfo.org/0005/posner.html, accessed 25 October 2011 (discussing renunciation).

[48] This argument, if made, soon would founder on the shoals of practicality. First, there obviously is no way to determine what the single most profitable business is, and, second, if all corporations entered it, it would no longer be the most profitable. Human judgments must be made as to what lines of business, among a great variety, generally will produce profits. These judgments provide ample opportunity for the incorporation of moral taste. It may be that some lines will repel both some managers and some investors but it is somewhat unlikely that the choice not to pursue those lines will be articulated in very many cases. The same may not be true, however, once a general line of business has been selected, and the question becomes how best to achieve profitability within that line. It would seem that here choices may be more limited and thus somewhat clearer. Suppose, for instance, that the managers of a particular company learn that an inexpensive, reliable machine can replace half its workforce. Due to the economy, it is unlikely that displaced workers will find new jobs anytime soon. Is it nonetheless the duty of the directors to substitute the machine? A clear question will elicit a clear answer

strictly profit-centered approach to corporate decisionmaking depends on a critical assumption about the effectiveness of external regulations in reflecting shared moral judgments (such as those about child pornography and murder). Once it is conceded that the assumption is false, the claim of normative desirability is impaired.[49]

To further illustrate this argument, assume that a corporation manufactures men's clothing. It determines that it can sell more clothing, and be much more profitable, if the fabric weave incorporates subliminal computer-generated images, exposure to which arouses interest in sex acts with children. Assume that such imagery is not presently illegal as deceptive advertising or otherwise[50] and that the corporation does not expect any sort of meaningful consumer backlash, primarily because it believes discovery is unlikely. It foresees that illegalization eventually will occur, but believes the practice could be quickly abandoned at little out-of-pocket cost. Should it really be the duty of the board of directors to order use of the weave?

This hypothetical is meant to confirm, of course, what most already recognize: legality and shared morality cannot be conflated. Surely there are areas where the two differ, if for no reason other than timing, lack of discernment, or regulatory capture. Manipulation of consumer preference well may be such a case.

OTHER APPROACHES

Although more-or-less dominant for decades, the contractarian approach faces competition. Brief descriptions are provided below, along with speculation as to the possible responses of each school to the proposal that corporate directors be prompted toward mindfulness of the exploitation of children.

---

from some quarters. If the duty of the directors simply is profit maximization, it is out with the workers and in with the machine. The normative desirability of the economic solution might once have meant that there was no moral issue, as far as hardest-core practitioners of law and economics were concerned. Of course, the relative clarity of that response suggested to others a different conclusion.

49 In fact, it might even be argued that the economic approach is tolerable only to the extent that external regulation succeeds in reflecting the dictates of common morality.

50 Arguably, the standards currently in existence are broad enough to prohibit subliminal advertising of at least some products. 15 U.S.C. §52(a)(1) and (2) provide: "It shall be unlawful for any . . . corporation to disseminate . . . any false advertisement . . . for the purpose of inducing, or which is likely to induce, directly or indirectly the purchase of food, drugs, devices, services, or cosmetics. . . ."

Behavioral Economics

As noted above, the contractarian approach is the product of strict law and economics analysis. One of its more vigorous recent challengers is a close relative known as behavioral economics (a branch of the legal decision theory described above). Behavioral economics accepts the insights of social science and utilizes empirical studies of human behavior in order to reassess some of the assumptions of the traditional law and economics movement.[51] Its proponents have established to their own satisfaction that not all economic actors act in their own-self interest – in some instances because of predictable cognitive heuristics, in some because of altruism, and in some because of garden variety stupidity.

In accepting that shareholders' self-interest is bounded to the extent that their views of normative desirability can contemplate altruistic benefits to others, behavioral economics might be used to formulate a different version of shareholder primacy. In this version, shareholder welfare might be examined in terms of what shareholders affirmatively desire other than profit maximization. Taking this a bit further, one might reason that individual shareholders are consumers, and often the parents of consumers, and so would prefer less manipulation, at least of children, even if it led to less profitability. This possibility, however, presents at least three difficulties. The first is that a number of shareholders are not individuals but institutions. This problem may be assumed away, perhaps, by positing that after all institutional stacking, or "nesting" is considered, individual shareholders will be revealed. The second is the perceived problem of the commons. If the shareholders of Corporation A understand that Corporation A will limit manipulation but believe that Corporation B will continue the practice, they are apt to regard their sacrifice as pointless. The third is that not all shareholders are parents and not all shareholders would believe that manipulation is possible. Presumably, it is this type of diversity of viewpoints that explains why mainstream corporate America does not, by and large, attempt to accommodate the possible non-monetary preferences of shareholders as to a number of matters in addition to consumer manipulation.

Nonetheless, in considering both predictable cognitive heuristics and the possibility that sometimes people are stupid, behavioral economics provides additional fodder for the analysis of consumer exploitation. It has given rise to at least two interesting approaches intended to address

---

51 Jolls, C. et al, "*A Behavioral Approach to Law and Economics*", Stanford L. Rev. (1998) 50, 1471.

problems created by the "bounding" of rationality and free will. These are libertarian paternalism and asymmetric paternalism.

One of the heuristic phenomena noted by behavioral economics has to do with the importance of how a decision is framed. This recognition has led some of the school's adherents to propose the approach known as "libertarian paternalism," pursuant to which policymakers would determine which resolution of an issue generally is preferable, and frame decisionmaking contexts accordingly. Although individuals thus are psychologically encouraged to make decisions in the manner selected by the policymakers, deviation – or "opting out" – is permitted. A simple example involves placing fruit before sugary desserts in school cafeteria lines.[52] The idea is that children will then find themselves with apples on their plates and less room for other desserts, but those who are "rational" enough to see through the ploy also are free to bypass the fruit and go straight for the Twinkies. Given this example, the model does seem somewhat questionable, since it seems to call on actors to self-prove rationality by veering away from the choice urged by presumably well-informed social planners. In fact, this observation tends to suggest that although elements of choice may be preserved in a scheme for reasons of political philosophy, that preservation has little to do with a purported dichotomy between rational and irrational.

Libertarian paternalism has been criticized for failing to grapple with the situational constraints on individuals' ability to opt away from a prompted decision – in other words, the "libertarian" part of the claim becomes meaningless.[53] It also has been noted that libertarian paternalism simply does not deal with the many instances in which those who frame issues are market rather than government actors.[54] In fact, Professors Sunstein and Thaler, the fathers of libertarian paternalism, do not attempt to extend their approach to entities the goal of which is profit-maximization, perhaps in the belief that free market competition ultimately will reveal collective "real" preference.[55] This overlooks, of course, the possibility of market failure based on manipulation.

---

[52] Sunstein, C. and Thaler, R. "*Libertarian Paternalism is not an Oxymoron*", U. Chi. L. Rev. (2003) 70, 1159, at pp. 1165–6.

[53] Mitchell, G. "*Libertarian Paternalism is an Oxymoron*", Nw. U. L. Rev. (2005) 99, 1245, at p. 1254.

[54] Yosifon, D. "*Legal Theoretic Inadequacy and Obesity Epidemic Analysis*", Geo. Mason L. Rev. (2008) 15, 681, at pp. 707–8.

[55] Similarly but more obviously, mandating, or even strongly recommending, frames for corporate actors to use in their own decisions about products and promotion is not apt to be a proposal that Professors Sunstein and Thaler would

Behavioral economic analysis has spurred the growth of another approach recognizing that humans do not always act in the ways that conventional law and economics would forecast. The "asymmetric paternalism" school calls for paternalistic action where the benefits to irrational individuals significantly outweigh the cost to rational individuals of losing the right of choice.[56] This easily would go so far as to permit the government to directly dictate the frames pursuant to which particular products are marketed, thus protecting the irrational while still leaving the rational – capable of avoiding the framing effect – freedom to choose. It also would permit governmental placement of at least some limits on product lines. Take, for example, the current system for rating video games, ostensibly prohibiting "M" rated games from being sold to children. Children thus are deemed legally irrational and are purportedly protected from the games unless adults choose to provide them. Adults (17-year olds) are deemed legally rational, and have the ability to buy the games for themselves and those who are younger. Unfortunately, while this system seems to be a masterstroke from the standpoint of asymmetric paternalism, it has been a practical failure: most M-rated games actually are marketed to those under 17.[57] This is not to say, by any means, that the theory has nothing to commend it, but it suggests that what looks good on paper may lose traction when the rubber hits the road.

Asymmetric paternalism does appear to assume that individuals can be neatly sorted by rationality, whereas it is unlikely that there are very many individuals who are wholly rational or irrational at all times, even in a focused context such as making consumption choices. The possibility of mixed rationality does not seem to be a fatal flaw – as is the case with libertarian paternalism, people may (perversely) self-prove rationality with respect to any particular decision by opting away from the prompted choice. More tellingly, asymmetric paternalism also has been subjected to the criticism that the ability to choose is always situationally constrained by elements that even high-minded social planners may not, for any number of reasons, be able to predict or accommodate.

---

be prepared to endorse. Most notably, libertarian paternalism is an attempt to respond to perceived lack of rationality. Hijacking the theory to counter a motive of profit-maximization would identify that motive as something other than rational – a position that Professors Sunstein and Thaler clearly have not taken.

[56] Camerer, C. et al, "*Regulation for Conservatives: Behavioral Economics and the Case for 'Asymmetric Paternalism'*", U. Pa. L. Rev. (2003) 151, 1211, at p. 2112.

[57] Garry, P. "*Defining Speech in an Entertainment Age: The Case of First Amendment Protection for Video Games*", SMU L. Rev. (2004) 57, 139, at p. 143.

In any event, separate from direct limits on production or marketing is the question of whether asymmetric paternalism might provide a justification for either mandating or encouraging framing in corporate decision-making about production or marketing. If one does accept – as adherents of asymmetric paternalism do – that less than completely rational consumers can be affected by framing and other cognitive biases, a problem clearly exists. Is addressing that problem by trying to rewire the decisions of corporate directors sufficiently protective of the choices of assumed rational consumers to pass muster? One would rather doubt this would be the case insofar as production considerations are concerned: since the point of the exercise is to reduce the development of products to exploit the market of vulnerable consumers, the products available to fully rational consumers also would be reduced. On the other hand, prompting directors to be more benevolently mindful of the cognitive biases of vulnerable consumers in approving marketing campaigns would seem to be quite unproblematic.

THE PROGRESSIVE APPROACH

During the 1990s, a group of vaguely-to-expressly self-identifying communitarian corporate law scholars also self-identified as "progressive" and proceeded to express their rejection of shareholder primacy.[58] Corporate progressives generally endorse an expansion of the goals of the corporation and the duties of management to include responsibility to other constituents, frequently arguing for the recognition of enforceable fiduciary duties running from directors to groups such as creditors and employees. As an alternative or supplemental approach, progressives also have proposed methods of increasing the board's discretion to recognize nonshareholder interests. These methods include extending the terms for which members of the board are elected and adopting statutory safe harbors for consideration of the interests of nonshareholder constituencies. It has also been suggested that board members be given additional fiduciary duties owed to, and enforceable by, other stakeholders. Although corporate progressives have not devoted much attention to the issue of consumer exploitation, their general concern with corporate social responsibility and the interests of nonshareholders suggests that consumer protection initiatives would receive strong support.

---

[58] Millon, D. "*Communitarianism in Corporate Law: Foundations and Law Reform Strategies*", Mitchell, Lawrence ed., Progressive Corporate Law 1, Boulder, US: Westview Press. (1995), pp. 16–22.

The Team Production Model

The "team production" approach speaks the language of neoclassical economics, but makes somewhat different starting assumptions.[59] The consequence is a set of conclusions that often resonate with corporate progressives.[60] Team production scholars characterize the board of directors as an independent "hierarch" mediating among all those with "team specific" inputs to the corporation. In this view, the proper function of the board is to employ the inputs of financiers, workers, communities, and others in order to maximize the value of the firm. Not incidentally, this requires the board to allocate corporate profits among all inputting groups in a manner all participants will accept. Although the proponents of the model have not characterized consumers as having team-specific inputs, they have acknowledged the board of directors' ability to engage in corporate philanthropy and presumably would find aversion to exploitation an acceptable motivation for directorial decisionmaking. Moreover, the writing of Professor Einer Elhuage,[61] a proponent of the approach, generally endows the team production model with sufficient latitude to permit the board to engage in moral decisionmaking extensive enough to roughly emulate the non-self-interested conduct of entrepreneurs.

Feminism

The multiple concerns of feminists share a common overlay of focus on the position of women in a patriarchal society, and a common goal of expunging the perceived inequalities of that position.[62] As part of the feminist undertaking, the experience of women is examined, the values of women are explored, and existing legal and social structures are assessed in terms of their arguable congruence with that experience and those values. This type of analysis does not necessarily presuppose that the experiences and values of all or most women are different from those of all or most men, but the possibility that a difference exists dictates the approach. The probability that values and experience may vary woman to woman is an

---

[59] Blair, M. and Stout, L. "A Team Production Theory of Corporate Law", *Va. L. Rev*. (1999) 85, 249, at p. 249.

[60] Note, however, that the adherents of this model specifically disavow identification as progressives.

[61] Elhauge, E. "*Sacrificing Corporate Profits In The Public Interest*", N.Y.U. L. Rev. (2005) 80, 733.

[62] Littleton, C. "*Feminist Jurisprudence: The Difference Method Makes*", Stan. L. Rev. (1989) 41, 751, at p. 753.

analytic challenge with which feminists constantly grapple. Nonetheless, if the values of even some women identifiably and predictably diverge from those underlying a legal regime, it is a matter with which to be reckoned.

As an integral part of their analytical process, feminist scholars make use of the concept of "gender" which is defined as the socially constructed (as opposed to biological) differences between being male and female.[63] The term "gendered" sometimes is used to describe structures, analyses, etc., that are the outcome of gender. It may, for example, be said that corporate law is gendered because it predominantly is the product of men, constructed in (perhaps unknowing) reliance on their own experience of being male in society. As the discussion above inherently reveals, the landscape of mainstream corporate law analysis indeed has been characterized by such socially ascribed male features as competitiveness, formal rationality, and paternalism.

Feminist analysis willingly exposes corporate law's formal, but flawed, underlying assumptions about rationality in the marketplace. Feminist invocation of experience tells us of harried working women facing "second shifts" at home. It also tells of increasingly plump children clamoring for, and obsessed with, technology, sex, and violence. Experiential accounts do not establish scientific cause and effect, but do remind many parents of how we feel. In fact, when experience is invoked, assuming effective parental supervision of children's purchases seems very much like, in the old joke, assuming a can opener.[64] Thus, feminist support for a proposal to mitigate the exploitation of childish preferences would not be surprising.

---

63 As an example, for a time between the Industrial Revolution and the advent of the women's liberation movement, the popularly ascribed gender role of women was to remain at home, raising children (although, most certainly, some women, either as a matter of aspiration or necessity, did deviate). That gender role now, of course, has been questioned and, for some segment of society, has shifted. Case, M. "*Disaggregating Gender from Sex and Sexual Orientation: The Effeminate Man and Feminist Legal Theory*", Yale L.J. (1995) 105, 1.

64 Relational feminism, one of many feminist approaches, reflects an effort to identify and apply to legal analysis a set of values based on the shared experiences of those women ascribing to the approach. West, R. "Jurisprudence and Gender", *U. Chi. L. Rev.* (1988) 55, 1, at pp. 13–42. These values, notably including compassion and caring, may or may not be the product of centuries of male oppression. Relational feminists nonetheless accept them as socially beneficial, as well as intuitively comfortable, and generally subscribe to analytic methods believed to embody the values to be advanced. Primary among these is the grounding in women's experience referred to above. This grounding leads to examination of the actual context in which a particular issue is presented. Contextualization is regarded as vital both because it evokes empathy and because it reveals situational nuances permitting case-specific accommodations. Relational feminists, like corporate progressives,

Critical Race Theory

"A central claim of [critical race theory] is that antiracist politics and legal theory should be informed by the voices of people 'on the bottom' of discrimination."[65] In part, this is because, on issues of race,[66] voices on the bottom simply are seen as more credible than the voices of those on the top. Eliciting those voices thus promises improvement in substantive results. Moreover, inviting speech from the formerly silent has benefits of its own. This spare description of a rich new literature presents two central questions. First, how broadly is the concept of "antiracist politics and legal theory" to be defined? Second, how is one to identify those "on the bottom" with respect to any particular issue?

For purposes of corporate law, the second question is far simpler than the first because it is so very easy to identify both a "bottom" and a "top." Economically privileged white males have shaped corporations, corporate law, and corporate law commentary;[67] calling forth the voices of those "outsiders" not sharing all three of those characteristics would, from a critical race perspective, have intrinsic value in addressing relevant issues. This suggests a fairly clear answer to the first question as well. In any situation in which "top" and "bottom" are so easily identified in terms of race, gender and economic class, issues within the purview of critical race analysis clearly are implicated.

Outsiders clearly have, of course, increased their participation in financial markets in recent years; stock market participation in particular has been said to be democratizing. Still, racial minorities are less likely than whites to participate in equity markets.[68] In addition, the experience of

---

tend to reject the shareholder primacy model. The proposal made in this chapter would be well-aligned with relational feminism, both insofar as it would tempt the board of directors to contextualize their decisions, contemplating the effects of corporate action on actual children, and would represent an at least symbolic reorientation toward interests beyond those of shareholders.

[65] Carbado, D. "*Critical Race Studies: Race to the Bottom*", UCLA L. Rev. (2002) 49, 1283, at p. 1284

[66] It should be noted that, as race has come to be regarded as a matter of social construct rather than genetic immutability, the inclusion of other social categories of inequity in critical race theorization has become quite natural. Hutchinson, D. "*Critical Race Studies: Progressive Race Blindness?: Individual Identity, Group Politics and Reform*", UCLA L. Rev. (2002) 49, 1455, at p. 1459.

[67] Gabaldon, T. "*Corporate Conscience and the White Man's Burden*", Geo Wash. L. Rev. (2002) 70, 944, at p. 945.

[68] Brown, D. "*Pensions, Risk, and Race*", Wash. & Lee L. Rev. (2004) 61, 1501, at pp. 1536–8.

racial minorities as consumers can be radically different than those of white males. It is well known, for instance, that lending practices have been known to discriminate on the basis of race[69] and that minorities (and women) pay higher car prices than do white males.[70] Positing the precise views of those "on the bottom" of corporate America may be a bit risky, but it is unlikely that a chorus in favor of shareholder primacy and correlative exploitation of children would be heard. Although asking directors – a group of predominantly white males and white male wannabes – to overtly consider the welfare of childish consumers – a group that this chapter has sought to show to be on the bottom – may seem to be less than inspiring and not likely to bring about much real change, it might well fall into the category of "do no harm" reform.[71]

Contractarians Redux

Contractarians generally do not bother to respond to feminist or critical race theorists, but have produced rebuttals of the views of other schools. Some portion of these rebuttals merely have involved reiterating some of law and economics' basic assumptions in the context of an evaluation of the precise claims of the newer schools, resulting in statements along the lines of the following (specifically in response to the team production model): "By vesting shareholders with an exclusive right to a corporation's residual, then, the principal-agent model facilitates adoption of the sort of mechanisms that can reduce the risk of opportunism and thus minimize the transaction costs associated with inducing team-specific investment."[72] This is no more than a reassertion of the norm of shareholder primacy in a slightly louder voice for those who were not listening the first time, probably indicating that the debate is as much cultural as it is logical. If this is the case, it is unlikely that consensus ever will be achieved if exchanges continue along previous lines. As discussed immediately below, sufficiently divergent world views are unlikely to prevail on one another by means of public reason.

---

[69] James, F. J. et al, *Discrimination, Segregation and Minority Housing Conditions in Sunbelt Cities: A Study of Denver, Houston & Phoenix*, Denver, US: Center for Public-Private Sector Cooperation, (1983), at p. 96.

[70] Ayres, I. "*Fair Driving: Gender and Race Discrimination in Retail Car Negotiations*", Harv. L. Rev. (1991) 104, 817, at pp. 825–41.

[71] There is, however, the possibility of criticism that the appearance of progress sometimes can distract from its genuine achievement.

[72] Meese, A. "*The Team Production Theory of Corporate Law: A Critical Assessment*", Wm. & Mary L. Rev. (2002) 43, 1629, at p. 1671.

Cultural Cognition

Libertarian and asymmetric paternalism might be hailed by some for their theoretic ability to slip the paternalistic (or interventionist) camel's nose under the libertarian (or free market) tent on matters including, but not limited to, the framing of various issues. Neither approach is likely to be satisfying, however, to those who would rename the camel "communitarian" "feminist" or "critical" and invite it directly into the parlor. The theory of cultural cognition may engender the same reaction, but nonetheless may be quite compelling from a practical standpoint.

Cultural cognition theory recognizes the priority of culture in an individual's assessment of such matters as the validity of facts and the perception of risk.[73] According to the theory, "culture" or "world view" may be usefully classified by "group" and "grid." "Group" is a question of whether one is oriented toward individualism or communitarianism. "Grid" refers to whether one is inclined toward hierarchical or egalitarian values. The theory rejects public reasoning as a method of resolving intensely polarizing issues and suggests substituting a process of "expressive overdeterminism" to minimize social discord. Expressive overdeterminism calls for designing solutions that permit validation of divergent world views. Its proponents suggest, for instance, resolving the gun control debate through a system that pays bounties to gun owners who register their guns. This validates both the safety concerns of those who would prefer gun control and the autonomy of those who fear loss of the "right" to bear arms of their choosing.[74]

Even though corporate exploitation of consumers may not be sufficiently high profile to qualify as an intensely polarizing issue, perhaps it should be. It is, however, certainly one as to which divergent world views can come into play. One well can imagine that individualists and communitarians might selectively and differentially perceive the validity of scientific studies on purported links between video games and violence or between advertising and overeating. Moreover, individualists might postulate the rationality of (at least) adult consumers and oppose government intervention on either their behalf or the behalf of their children. It is precisely these values, in fact, that seem to have defeated in America attempts to adopt the same types of restrictions on advertising that have been adopted in other parts of the world.[75] Communitarians, on the other

---

[73] Kahan, D. and Braman, D. "*Cultural Cognition and Public Policy*", Yale L & Pol'y Rev. (2006) 24, 149, at pp. 150–57.

[74] Kahan and Braman, op cit., at p. 170.

[75] According to Ramsey, foreign countries afford far more stringent regulations when dealing with children, demonstrated by Sweden's ban of advertising

hand, predictably might go so far as to prefer outright governmental limitations on consumer choice if such limitations would reduce societal violence, waste of resources, ill health etc. A solution palatable to all necessarily will disappoint some.

All that said, cultural cognition does seem to teach that without cultural agreement, some problems simply will not be resolved; in fact, there will not even be a consensus that they exist. It may well be that commercial exploitation of children falls in this latter category. Thus, any attempt by those who do see a problem to resolve it must be realistically circumscribed. As to this, however, cultural cognition still might have a lesson to convey. For instance, it probably is helpful to characterize remedial proposals as simple attempts to redress market malfunction. In this guise, attempts to manipulate consumer preference should be portrayed as a close relative to fraud and thus a type of market failure. Moreover, showcasing proposed limits on, or requirements for, corporate action not as any form of paternalism but as a type of parental empowerment seems promising.

CONCLUSION

It is the contention of this chapter that anyone who believes that consumers rationally dictate the allocation of social resources is deluding him – or her – self. This can be most vividly illustrated in the case of easily exploitable children. The shareholder primacy model that might be invoked to justify consumer exploitation is neither legally compelled nor, from the standpoint of many commentators, normatively desirable. These points have relatively little to do with the way in which corporate America actually functions. Although, as cultural cognition suggests, strongly held but divergent world views will prevent either or any of the sides on this matter from prevailing as a matter of reason, progress may be made on the basis of multiple appeals. Expressions of intent to correct market failure and/or preserve parental prerogatives may be effective.

As it happens, these expressions of intent are not merely instrumental. Markets have failed our children. Parental rights, while technically observed, have been deprived of meaning. The mechanism for

directed at children under 12, Norway and Finland's ban of corporate sponsorship for children television shows, and England's move in the same direction. Ramsey, W "*Rethinking Regulation of Advertising Aimed at Children*" Fed. Comm. L.J (2006) 58, 367, at pp. 370 and 397.

these developments has been a type of corporate-launched psychological warfare. It seems not inappropriate to return fire with some of the same weapons. This chapter thus proposes a requirement that corporate directors be more mindful of at least some of the problems they cause. This requirement could take the form of a list of questions that directors would individually and collectively address before certain actions were taken. These questions, and their triggers, are detailed in the appendix below.

APPENDIX

Line of inquiry one:

As an initial matter, directors should inquire into whether the corporation they direct markets to children. The inquiry will be answered in the affirmative if: (a) in excess of one percent of gross revenue in the most recent fiscal year derived from the sale of products primarily used by or consumed by individuals between the ages of two and 18; and (b) any part of the corporation's public advertising budget relates to such products. (For instance, the cost of advertising medications to members of the medical profession would not be taken into account.)

Line of inquiry two:

If the first line of inquiry is answered in the affirmative, each member of the board of directors should be required to answer the following questions. The answers should be made public on an easily located page on the company's website denominated "Practices toward Children as Consumers."

1. Are you familiar with each product marketed by your corporation or its subsidiaries and primarily used or consumed by individuals between the ages of two and 18? If not, why not?
2. Are you familiar with your corporation's marketing strategy for each of its products primarily used or consumed by individuals between the ages of two and 18? If not, why not?
3. Insofar as you are familiar with your corporation's marketing strategy for products primarily used or consumed by individuals between the ages of two and 18, do you personally believe that the attributes of such products are fairly portrayed?
4. Insofar as you are familiar with any product or line of products marketed by your corporation and primarily used or consumed by individuals between the ages of two and 18, do you believe that any reasonable objection(s) to unregulated use or consumption could be raised by such an individual's parent or guardian? (Assume that such use or consumption would occur in a manner that is readily foreseeable, although not necessarily in accordance with the manufacturer's instructions.) If so, describe the objection(s).
5. Insofar as you are familiar with any product or line of products marketed by your corporation and primarily used or consumed by

individuals between the ages of two and 18, would you personally recommend such use or consumption?

Line of inquiry three:

If the first line of inquiry is answered in the affirmative, the board of directors should vote, after discussion, on the following resolution:

RESOLVED: We, the directors of [Corporate Name], hereby certify that the corporation has in effect reasonable measures and reporting requirements designed to assure the familiarity of the members of the board with the products of [Corporate Name] marketed to individuals between the ages of two and 18, as well as with the methods employed for such marketing. We further agree that those products and marketing methods pose no significant risk to the physical or psychological well-being of users or to the practical ability of parents to prevent access to those products.

The vote, and a 50 or more word supporting statement, of each director should be recorded and posted on the webpage described under "Line of inquiry two."

10. Connections between ethics and directors' duties in Australia

*Vivienne Brand**

I. INTRODUCTION

The history of the development of directors' duties in Australia has been one of increasing obligation. Nineteenth-century notions of director competence set a lower standard, and gave more credence to business pressures, than later formulations of the relevant duties. In 1959 Sir Douglas Menzies, a Justice of the High Court of Australia, made the extra-curial comment that '[i]t is a generalization not far from the truth, up to the present, that what the law demands from a director of a company is a high standard not so much of ability, care and diligence as of honesty'.[1] However, by the latter part of the twentieth century Australian courts were prepared to use a more objective test when assessing directors' actions,[2] and the *AWA* case[3] clarified the objective elements of the critical duty of care. It is now an accepted observation that 'the standard of care expected of company directors, both by the common law (including equity. . .) and under statutory provisions, has been raised over the last century or so'.[4] Further clarification of the standard of care and diligence expected of directors occurred more recently

* The author is grateful for the comments of Sulette Lombard and Jeff Fitzpatrick on this chapter. Errors and omissions remain of course the author's own.

[1] Sir Douglas Menzies, 'Company Directors', (1959) 33 *Australian Law Journal* 156, at 156.

[2] See, for instance, *Statewide Tobacco Services Ltd v Morley* (1990) 2 ACSR 405, affirmed [1993] 1 VR 423; *Commonwealth Bank of Australia v Friedrich* (1991) 5 ACSR 115.

[3] *Daniels & Ors (formerly practising as Deloitte Haskins & Sells) v Anderson* (the '*AWA*' case) (1995) 37 NSWLR 438 represented a 'quantum shift in expectations': Golding, G, 'Tightening the Screws on Directors: Care, Delegation and Reliance', (2012) 18(1) *UNSWLJ Forum* 14, at 14. See also Boros, E and Duns, J, *Corporate Law*, 3ed, Oxford University Press, South Melbourne, 2013, [10.4.3].

[4] *Australian Securities and Investments Commission v Rich* (2003) 21 ACLC 450 per Austin J at [71].

with the High Court decisions in the *James Hardie* litigation, and the *Centro* case,[5] the latter reflecting 'the upward trajectory of the duty of care and diligence' over the last two decades.[6]

This chapter argues that as legal analysis of Australian directors' duties has continued to develop in recent years, increased attention has been given to a diverse range of factors with the potential to make ethical issues more relevant. Developments in the critical duty of care suggest an avenue by which ethics materials such as codes of conduct and ethics policies, as well as industry standards in relation to ethics, may be incorporated in assessments of the required standard of care. Similarly, the key duty to act in the company's best interests is potentially capable, in its modern guise, of incorporating ethics considerations. At the same time increased disclosure patterns, both mandated and involuntary (including via social media and whistleblowing), as well as existing obligations in relation to corporate culture, impact on the way directors' duties are understood in ways that may facilitate incorporation of ethics factors. In addition, shifting enforcement trends in relation to Australian directors' duties in recent decades have the potential to increase the level of scrutiny applied to directors' actions generally, with implications for all matters relevant to an assessment of a director's discharge of their duties.

This chapter begins with a brief consideration of the definition of ethics, and acknowledges the overlap of ethics considerations with corporate governance and corporate social responsibility issues. It then identifies the bases of directors' duties liability of key significance for the purposes of this chapter, before considering the range of factors that may impact on a developing relationship between ethical considerations and directors' duties in Australia.

II. ISSUES OF DEFINITION

As a preparatory step to any consideration of the potential connections between directors' duties and ethics, it is useful to outline what is meant by the term 'ethics' in this chapter. 'Ethics' is used in a variety of contexts in contemporary Australian corporate literature, particularly within

---

5 *Australian Securities & Investments Commission v Healey* (2011) 278 ALR 618 ('*Centro*' case); *Australian Securities and Investments Commission v Hellicar & Ors* [2012] HCA 17; *Shafron v Australian Securities and Investments Commission* [2012] HCA 18 ('*James Hardie*' case).

6 Hill, J, 'Centro and the Monitoring Board – Legal Duties Versus Aspirational Ideals in Corporate Governance', (2012) 18(1) *UNSWLJ Forum* 60, at 63.

corporate governance and corporate social responsibility (CSR) materials. Texts on corporate governance contain entries variously on 'ethics' and business ethics, directors and ethics, and the ethical obligations of corporations.[7] Farrar has asserted the relevance of business ethics to an analysis of corporate governance, within 'an increasingly complex amalgam of law and self-regulation'.[8] An eminent general text describes the enhancement of the ethical standards of directors as forming a sub-stream of the wider corporate governance debate.[9] Corporate governance questions relating to the purpose of the corporation, and particularly to the rival merits of stakeholder and shareholder value theories, raise many issues that are characterisable as 'ethics' within Australian corporate law contexts and elsewhere. This is particularly so in relation to the question of in whose interests the directors are required to act. In the context of stakeholder analyses, for instance, communitarians have been described as eschewing economics in favour of a 'focus solely on ethics and fairness',[10] and it has been suggested that 'entrenchment of ethical standards' will ensure companies act for more than just shareholders.[11] References to ethics pervade the international CSR literature. Branco and Rodrigues have described CSR as 'ethical and moral issues surrounding corporate decision making and behaviour',[12] and in an Australian context Marshall and Ramsay argue that '[a]t its most sophisticated level of practice, CSR is integrated with governance: ethics guide corporate decision-making'.[13]

---

[7] Farrar, J, *Corporate Governance: Theories, Principles and Practice*, 3ed, 2008, Oxford University Press, Melbourne, Chapter 33 and Chapter 27; du Plessis, J, Hargovan, A and Bargaric, M, *Principles of Contemporary Corporate Governance*, 2ed, Cambridge University Press, Cambridge 2011.

[8] Farrar, ibid., at 4.

[9] Austin, R, and Ramsay, I, *Ford's Principles of Corporations Law*, 15ed, LexisNexis Butterworths, Australia, 2013, at [7.610].

[10] Keay, A, 'Tackling the Issue of the Corporate Objective: An Analysis of the United Kingdom's "Enlightened Shareholder Value Approach"', (2007) 29 *Sydney Law Review* 577, at 588.

[11] Grossman, H, 'Refining the Role of the Corporation: The Impact of Corporate Social Responsibility on Shareholder Primacy Theory', (2005) 10 *Deakin Law Review* 572, at 592; see also Corcoran, S, 'The Corporation as Citizen and as Government: Social Responsibility and Corporate Morality', (1997) 2 *Flinders Journal of Law Reform*, 53, at 54.

[12] Branco, M, and Rodrigues, L, 'Positioning Stakeholder Theory Within the Debate on Corporate Social Responsibility' (2007) 12 *Electronic Journal of Business Ethics and Organization Studies* 5, at 5; also cited by Marshall, S, and Ramsay, I, 'Stakeholders and Directors' Duties: Law, Theory and Evidence', (2012) 18(1) *UNSWLJ Forum* 29, at 30.

[13] Marshall and Ramsay, ibid., at 31.

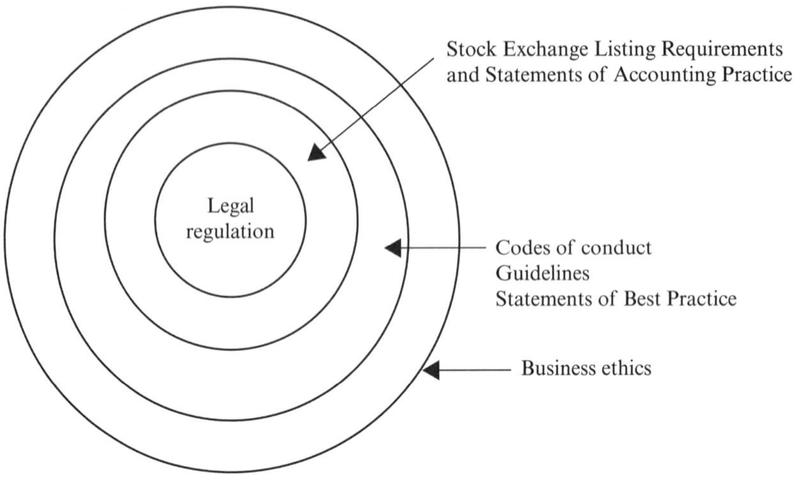

Figure 10.1 Farrar's intersection between Australian corporate law, corporate governance and ethics

Farrar offers a diagrammatic conceptualisation of the intersection between Australian corporate law, corporate governance and ethics.[14] At the centre of Farrar's series of concentric circles (shown below as Figure 10.1) is legal regulation (ie 'black-letter law'); surrounding this is a set of principles that have normative force but are not direct products of the courts or parliament (eg Securities Exchange Listing Requirements and Statements of Accounting Practice). Beyond this are located Codes of Conduct and Statements of Best Practice, and encircling these, in the 'outer penumbra' are concepts of business ethics. Similarly, the ethical obligations of business have been defined by Carroll as 'additional behaviors and activities that are not necessarily codified into law but nevertheless are expected of business by society's members'.[15]

However, despite the wide use of 'ethics' in a range of contexts in Australian corporate literature, and a very significant increase in use of the term over the last decade,[16] little formal attention has been given to

---

[14] Farrar, note 7 above, Figure 1.1, at 4.

[15] Carroll, A, 'A Three-dimensional Conceptual Model of Corporate Performance', *Academy of Management Review* 4, 497, at 500; and cited by Parker, C, 'Meta-regulation: legal accountability for corporate social responsibility', in McBarnet, D, Voiculescu, A and Campbell, T, 'The New Corporate Accountability', *Cambridge University Press*, Cambridge, 2007, at 207.

[16] A search for the key words 'directors duties' and 'ethics' in the leading Australian legal search directories for the period 1970–2012 returns 60 entries:

defining the term closely.[17] Reference to ethical principles within standard textbook discussions of directors' duties in Australia does not elucidate the issue: Austin and Ramsay's *Ford's Principles of Corporations Law*,[18] the eminent general Australian corporate law text, has no entry for 'ethics' in its index. Clarification of the sense in which the term is used in this chapter would therefore be helpful. At its most general, 'ethics' can be understood as dealing 'with values, with good and bad, with right and wrong'.[19] Many of the concerns of corporate governance and CSR also relate to values, and questions of right and wrong. However, while there are very clear overlaps between CSR concerns, corporate governance objectives and ethics issues, 'ethics' remains something different from these concepts. Corporate governance's predominantly internal focus, on appropriate structures and processes, arguably contrasts with CSR's frequent attention to the company's responsibilities in relation to external stakeholders. Ethics can be seen as being concerned with a looser conception of 'right and wrong' applying both within the corporation and in relation to its external relationships. That is, in the sense the term is used in this chapter, 'ethics' relates to the conduct of the corporation in its entirety. A company's code of ethics may be as significant for the entity's internal operations as it is for external parties, and may contribute as much to the way in which the corporation deals with its existing members as it does to the company's relationships with employees, the environment, or society more generally. Further, ethical considerations of right and wrong are capable of operating at a very general level, going beyond compliance with specific governance processes, or consideration of social obligations to

---

AGIS Informit Database, 28 March 2012. Over 80% of these entries relate to the immediately preceding ten years, while only 20% of entries are attributable to the previous 30-year period. A similar earlier paucity of literature dealing with 'the explicit ethical obligations of directors' has been described in an international context: Schwartz, M, Dunfee, T, and Kline, M, (2005) 58 *Journal of Business Ethics* 79, at 81.

17 Dang, M, and Mescher, B, 'Directors and the Ethics Components of their Duties', (2010) 7 *Macquarie Journal of Business Law* 1, at 3. The Australian Securities Exchange Corporate Governance Council's in its most recent 2014 revision of its *Corporate Governance Principles and Recommendations*, 3ed, uses 'unethical' as well as the phrase 'ethically and responsibly'; while these terms are not defined it is made clear that '[a]cting ethically and responsibly goes well beyond mere compliance with legal obligations and involves acting with honesty, integrity and in a manner that is consistent with the reasonable expectations of investors and the broader community', at 19.

18 Austin and Ramsay, note 9 above.

19 Singer, P, *A Companion to Ethics*, 1991, Blackwell, Oxford, at v, and adopted by du Plessis, et al., note 7 above, at 419.

external stakeholders. That is, ethical analysis offers a wide frame of reference, enabling assessment of a company's internal and external behaviours and activities in the light of broad concepts of 'right and wrong'. It is this sense of the term 'ethics' that informs its use in this chapter.[20]

The following section identifies the key directors' duties of relevance to this chapter, before considering factors that may influence the evolving connections between directors' duties and ethics in Australia.

III. DIRECTORS' DUTIES AND ETHICS IN AUSTRALIA

A Directors' Duties in Australia, and the Key Duties of Care and Diligence and Acting in the Company's Best Interests

Duties of directors in Australia exist as an amalgam of statutory principles (enshrined in the *Corporations Act, 2001* (Cth)) and general law (itself a combination of common law, equity, and contractual principles).[21] The subject of frequent calls for simplification and clarification,[22] the law dictates a range of often duplicatory obligations arising from one or more of these sources. Unlike the codification of directors' duties by the *Companies Act, 2006* (UK),[23] Australian directors' duties statements in the *Corporations Act* do not displace general law obligations.[24] The two key heads of liability are grouped around the concepts of due care[25]

[20] This definition represents a modification and combination of the definitions offered by Carroll, note 15 above, at 500, and Singer, note 19 above, v; it is consistent with the Australian Securities Exchange Corporate Governance Council's emphasis on the significance of an internal culture 'that promotes ethical and responsible behaviour', where such behaviour goes 'well beyond mere compliance with legal obligations' and involves 'honesty' and 'integrity': *Corporate Governance Principles and Recommendations*, 3ed, note 17 above, at 19.

[21] See for instance Boros and Duns, note 3 above, [10.3] on the duty of care.

[22] Australian Institute of Company Directors, 'Growing Complexity an Increasing Legal Minefield for Directors', 3 May 2012, at http://www.companydirectors.com.au/General/Header/Media/Media-Releases/2012/Growing-complexity-an-increasing-legal-minefield-for-directors; see also: Australian Institute of Company Directors, 2012 Director Sentiment Index summary, 3 April 2012, http://www.companydirectors.com.au/General/Header/Media/Media-Releases/2012/Federal-budget-surplus-not-vital-say-Australian-directors.

[23] Arden, M, the Right Hon Justice, 'The Companies Act 2006 (UK): A New Approach to Directors' Duties', (2007) 8 *The Judicial Review* 145, at 147.

[24] *Corporations Act, 2001* (Cth), s. 185, and see also s. 179(1).

[25] *Corporations Act, 2001* (Cth), s. 180; The *AWA* case, note 3 above;

and of acting in good faith in the company's best interests.[26] Aspects of these and related duties address conflicts of interest, fettering of discretions, use of information or position, and acting for proper purposes.[27] Relevant statutory principles include s. 182 (misuse of position) and s. 183 (misuse of information) as well as prohibitions on non-disclosure of material personal interests (s191). Additional controls apply to public companies.[28]

Despite the breadth of potentially relevant duties, it is the duties of care and diligence and of acting in good faith in the company's best interests that are key to the discussion in this chapter. This is so for the duty of care by virtue of its connection to current standards of practice, and their reflection of evolving community expectations in relation to ethics, through reference particularly to encouragement for voluntary codes of conduct. The duty to act in good faith in the best interests of the company is of critical relevance because of the significant ongoing attention given to the question of what (or who) constitutes the company's best interests, and the implications for what is the right thing for directors to do when fulfilling that duty. A focus on these two duties is also consistent with the gravitational weight of current academic and judicial consideration of directors' duties in Australia. A 2012 publication reviewing the current issues in directors' duties in Australia, with contributions by leading corporate law academics, contained three articles respectively dealing with the duty of care and diligence and on the duty to act in good faith in the best interests of the company, and only one article considering a wider list of duties. The position would have been very different several decades ago, when it would likely have been reversed.[29] This trend in turn reflects the issues of significance coming before the courts.[30] For these reasons the

---

Australian Securities and Investments Commission v Vines [2005] NSWSC 738; *Australian Securities & Investments Commission v Rich*, note 4 above; the *Centro* case, note 5 above; *Australian Securities and Investments Commission v Hellicar & Ors*, note 5 above; and the *James Hardie* case, note 5 above.

26 *Corporations Act, 2001* (Cth), s. 181; *Re Smith and Fawcett Ltd* [1942] Ch 304; *The Bell Group Ltd (in liq) v Westpac Banking Corporation (No 9)* [2008] WASC 239.

27 For a full, authoritative discussion of directors' duties in Australia see Austin and Ramsay, note 9 above, Chs 8 and 9.

28 Including limitations on the ability of interested directors to vote in meetings and restrictions on related party transactions (see s. 195, and Ch. 2E *Corporations Act, 2001* (Cth)).

29 Austin, R, Foreword, *Directors' Duties Revisited*, (2012) 18(1) *UNSWLJ Forum* 3, at 3–4.

30 More recent high profile corporate law decisions that have elucidated

discussion of directors' duties in this chapter focuses on the duty of care and the duty to act in good faith in the company's best interests.

As indicated earlier, a diverse range of factors is now identifiable in relation to Australian directors' duties which create potential links between those duties and ethics considerations. The remainder of this chapter addresses those factors.

B Existing Directors' Duties and Connections with Ethics

1. Codes of Ethics/Ethics Policies

There has been an increase in recent years in the number of companies in developed countries such as Australia choosing to adopt an ethics code or a code of conduct.[31] The Australian Securities Exchange's (ASX's) Corporate Governance Council's *Corporate Governance Principles and Recommendations* ('ASX Principles')[32] recommend that companies have a code of conduct, and stipulate that the code 'must be, and be seen to be, a meaningful statement of [the company's] core values'.[33] The ASX Principles also explicitly make the point that '[a]cting ethically and responsibly goes well beyond mere compliance with legal obligations and involves acting with honesty, integrity and in a manner that is consistent with the reasonable expectations of investors and the broader community'.[34] The ASX Principles do not constitute compulsory standards,[35] and are directly relevant only to listed public companies. However, as the standards represented by the ASX Principles become accepted over time, they have the

---

the duty of care and diligence in particular include: *Australian Securities and Investments Commission v Hellicar & Ors*, note 5 above; the *James Hardie* case, note 5 above; the *Centro* case, note 5 above, at 625 [14]; see also the *AWA* case, note 3 above.

[31] Redmond, P, 'Directors' Duties and Corporate Social Responsiveness', (2012) 18(1) *UNSWL Forum* 45, at 47; Rodriguez-Dominguez, L, Gallego-Alvarez, I, and Garcia-Sanchez, I, 'Corporate Governance and Codes of Ethics', (2009) *Journal of Business Ethics* 187, at 188, and the references cited there.

[32] ASX Corporate Governance Council, *Corporate Governance Principles and Recommendations, 3ed, March 2014.*

[33] Ibid., *Principle 3: Act ethically and responsibly*, at 19.

[34] Ibid.

[35] The ASX Corporate Governance Council notes in the *Corporate Governance Principles and Recommendations* that while listed entities are required to compare their practices with the Council's recommendations, and to disclose reasons for departures from them, listed entities are not forced to adopt the recommendations, consistent with an 'if not why not' regulatory approach: *Corporate Governance Principles and Recommendations*, 3ed, at 5.

potential to increase the likelihood of companies adopting codes of ethics, for the reasons discussed below.

1.1 Codes and the duty of care and diligence

The most probable link between directors' duties and the work done by codes, ethics policies and related materials is the duty of care and diligence. Directors of Australian companies owe a duty to act with care and diligence, and the duty is likely to have at least four bases: the employment contract (if any – this component is however particularly relevant for company officers and executive directors), equity, the common law (via the law of negligence), and statute (s. 180(1) *Corporations Act, 2001* (Cth)).[36] Over time a higher, more objective, standard of care has been established as the appropriate benchmark for the general law duty of care and diligence.[37] Similarly, the statutory provisions reflect objective requirements. However, an individual director's expertise and experience is a factor in considering liability under section 180(1).

Section 180(1) provides that directors and officers 'must exercise their powers and discharge their duties with the degree of care and diligence that a reasonable person would exercise if they 'were a director or officer of a corporation in the corporation's circumstances; and occupied the office held by, and had the same responsibilities within the corporation as, the director or officer'.

In addition, the general law of torts provides 'guiding principles for the content of the statutory standard of care'.[38] The statutory duty is accompanied by a business judgment rule defence contained in section 180(2). In *ASIC v Rich* Austin J emphasised that a director's responsibilities under section 180(1) will be assessed having regard: 'to the experience or skills that the director held himself out to have in support of his appointment to the office, on the basis that the director's actual responsibilities within the company would be affected by what was represented at the time of appointment'.[39]

---

36 On the dual equitable/negligence nature of the duty of care see particularly *Permanent Building Society (in liq) v Wheeler* (1994) 11 WAR 187 and the *AWA* case. On the duties generally, see Austin and Ramsay, note 9 above, Chapter 8, especially [8.320]. For a convenient and very lucid formulation of the bases of the current duty of care and diligence, see Boros and Duns, note 3 above, [10.3].

37 The *AWA* case.

38 *Australian Securities and Investments Commission v Vines*, note 25 above, at [1070], per Austin J.

39 *Australian Securities & Investments Commission v Rich*, note 4 above, at [48].

1.2 Recent authority on the duty of care and diligence

The responsibilities encompassed by the duty of care and diligence have received attention in Australia in two more recent, significant decisions: the rulings in *Centro*,[40] and in the *James Hardie* litigation.[41] In both cases directors of large, publicly listed corporations were found to have breached their duty of care and diligence. The former case centred on the accuracy of financial statements approved by the board, and the second decision considered the implications of an inaccurate press release made with the board's approval. The duty of care and diligence underpinned the court's decision in each case, and to this extent the legal principles in question were not novel. The decisions have, however, drawn expressions of concern from the director community as to the level of expectation placed on an Australian director.[42] Both rulings highlight the demanding practical implications of the duty of care and diligence within large, complex organisations. Middleton J made it clear, in *Centro*, that a current Australian director is expected to be inquiring in relation to those matters brought before the board, and that the essential characteristics of a critical approach and attention to detail cannot be delegated. In the context of the need to approve financial statements, the issue in question in *Centro*, Middleton J said:

> [e]ach director armed with the information available to him was expected to focus on matters brought before him and to seriously consider such matters and take appropriate action . . . [The approval of the financial statements] demands critical and detailed attention, and not just 'going through the motions' or sole reliance on others, no matter how competent or trustworthy they may appear to be.[43]

That is, within the statutory formulation of the duty of care in section 180(1), directors must exercise their powers and discharge their duties with the degree of care and diligence that a reasonable person would exercise if they were a director of a corporation in that corporation's circumstances, and had the same office and responsibilities within that corporation.[44] An essentially identical requirement arises under the general law (which is in turn supplemented by contractual and fiduciary obligations).

---

40 *Australian Securities and Investments Commission v Healey*, note 5 above.

41 *Australian Securities and Investments Commission v Hellicar & Ors*, note 5 above; *Shafron v Australian Securities and Investments Commission*, note 5 above.

42 Durie, J, 'Regulate Thyself or Else', June 2012, *The Deal*, in *The Australian*, 50.

43 The *Centro* case, note 5 above, per Middleton J, at [174].

44 *Corporations Act, 2001* (Cth), s. 180(1)(a) and (b).

1.3 The modern duty of care and diligence and the presence of ethics policies

These standards have the potential to increase the relevance of ethics issues for Australian directors as industry practice in relation to ethics policies evolves. To the extent, for instance, that a company should, from the point of view of industry standards, have an ethics policy and does not (or has one but has not complied with it), general principles of negligence and statutory formulations of the duty of care are clearly in issue. Existing conceptions of a director's duty of care in Australia ground an obligation on all directors to be aware of a company's policies, which would necessarily include any ethics codes. The majority in the *AWA* case made it clear that a director must be familiar with the company's affairs and generally monitor corporate policies.[45] The obligation to monitor the company's affairs and not over-delegate has been reinforced by the decision in *Centro*, with its emphasis on the need for the board to bring 'critical and detailed attention' to the tasks before them, and not to rely on others, 'no matter how competent or trustworthy'.[46] Austin has argued that in the hands of ASIC the legislative duty of care and diligence now amounts to 'a kind of universal tort', available when the regulator sees the need to draw attention to, or establish, standards of care in particular circumstances.[47] This is not to say that a director would be answerable for an unethical act (however defined) but rather that a director could be liable for failure to exercise an appropriate standard of care in relation to, for example, compliance with the company's own promulgated code of ethics. The court in *Centro* was prepared to identify a strong obligation on the part of directors to pay 'critical and detailed attention'[48] to the approval of financial statements; while the same high standard may not be asked of directors (yet, at least) in regard to ethics policies, the potential exists for the law to evolve in that direction. Growing concern as to the extent to which a director can reasonably be expected to stay abreast of the 'formidable' range of information flowing in to a modern boardroom[49] may be an inhibiting factor in

---

45 The *AWA* case, note 3 above.

46 The *Centro* case, note 5 above, per Middleton J, at 658 [174].

47 Austin, note 29 above, at 5. Horrigan has argued similarly, in the UK context of the extended reference points within the directors' duty in s. 172 of the *Companies Act, 2006* (UK), that '[a] less obvious and yet far more dangerous potential stalking horse for directors lurks in the shadows of the statutory duty of care': Horrigan, B, *Corporate Social Responsibility in the 21st Century: Debates, Models and Practices Across Government, Law and Business*, Edward Elgar, 2010, at 254.

48 The *Centro* case, note 5 above, per Middleton J, at 658 [174].

49 Austin note 29 above, at 5.

this respect. Nonetheless, the creation of policies sets a standard the board are thereafter presumably under an obligation to attempt to meet, and '[b]oard adoption of a code surely creates an expectation . . . that individual directors themselves will at a minimum meet relevant ethical obligations'.[50]

Further, section 180(1) imposes a 'sliding standard of care and diligence'[51] that emphasises what could be expected of a reasonable person *in the office held by*, and *having the same responsibilities as*, the director under scrutiny. Where the director in question has particular responsibilities in relation to codes of conduct or ethical matters, the potential for a breach of the duty of care and diligence is greater. In particular, where an executive director has line management responsibility for the internal audit or compliance functions of the corporation, or where (as some international evidence suggest is occurring) a board has appointed a 'social responsibility officer',[52] the subjective duty of care in relation to compliance with ethics policies would be particularly high.

An interesting question also arises as to the extent a corporation's code of ethics might constitute contractual obligations of the company owed to shareholders, indicating the potential for ethics issues to influence relationships between the company and internal stakeholders. Further, if a company's code of ethics is widely available (via the internet, for instance), potential exists for a board to face action from external (or internal) parties for breach of those codes via non-directors' duties mechanisms. These could include, for example, claiming misleading and deceptive practice in trade and commerce, under consumer protection laws, or via other statutory avenues. Such actions could in turn expose directors to potential liability for breach of directors' duties, via breach of the critical duty of care and diligence.[53]

---

[50] Schwartz et al., note 16 above, at 88.

[51] Young, N, 'Has Directors' Liability Gone Too Far or Not Far Enough? A Review of the Standard of Conduct Required of Directors under Sections 180–184 of the Corporations Act', (2008) 26 *Companies & Securities Law Journal* 216, at 220.

[52] Rose, J, 'Corporate Directors and Social Responsibility: Ethics versus Shareholder Value', (2007) 73 *Journal of Business Ethics* 319, at 329.

[53] See for instance the discussion on the extended effect of soft regulation via actions for misleading and deceptive conduct in Kingsford Smith, D, 'Governing the Corporation: the Role of "Soft Regulation"', (2012) 18(1) *UNSWLJ Forum* 82, at 90.

2. Contemporary Business Expectations and the Standard of Care

Even where a company has not specifically adopted a code of ethics, directors may be judged by industry standards that incorporate similar obligations by virtue of general industry practice. Current corporate materials in Australia frequently include references to ethics and exhortations to ethical conduct by those who manage and direct corporations. Corporate governance texts suggest that 'ethics, morals and values' will become increasingly important factors for companies,[54] and such texts may incorporate ethics concepts as part of a diagrammatic representation of current Australian corporate governance (as discussed above).[55] Feature articles in the Australian Institute of Company Directors (AICD) journal review questions such as senior directors' attitudes to how 'directors ensure the companies they oversee are behaving ethically'.[56] The AICD's widely-distributed introductory text on directors' duties specifically raises the questions of whether or not directors owe a duty to employees, and whether directors owe a 'duty to society'.[57] A search of the term 'ethics' on the AICD's homepage returns 175 entries,[58] and the peak professional body for company secretaries, the Governance Institute of Australia, requires its members to adhere to a code of ethics.[59]

This evidence of the extent to which industry has integrated ethics considerations into their materials has the potential to influence a court's assessment of the extent to which ethical conduct is required of a director. Obligations that begin as ethical responsibilities may evolve into legal requirements,[60] and as Hansmann and Kraakman have argued, corporate governance practices can be expected to precede reform in corporate law.[61] Thus current Australian corporate governance policies in relation to ethics may well provide an indicator of future legal developments, since judicial authority exists to suggest that similar forms of industry standards or 'soft regulation' are already beginning to operate as an influential factor in the

---

54 du Plessis et al., note 7 above, at 126.

55 Farrar, note 7 above.

56 Efrat, Z, 'Doing the Right Thing', Aug 2011, *Company Director* 36, at 36.

57 Baxt, R, Duties and Responsibilities of Directors and Officers, 2009, 19ed, Australian Institute of Company Directors, Sydney, at 47.

58 http://www.companydirectors.com.au/, August 2014 (an increase of over 30% on the result of the same search in 2012).

59 http://www.governanceinstitute.com.au/about-us/governance-institute-governance/ethics-and-standards/.

60 Carroll, note 15 above, at 500; and cited by Parker, note 15 above, at 207.

61 Hansmann, H, & Kraakman, R, 'The End of History for Corporate Law' (2001) 89 *Georgetown Law Journal* 439, at 455.

judicial development of directors' duties in Australia.[62] 'Soft regulation' is a descriptor applied to the range of standards, codes, listing rules of securities exchanges and similar guidelines that form part of the regulatory spectrum between statute at one end and corporate ethics at the other end.[63] This form of regulation is described by the outer shells of Farrar's corporate governance diagram (Figure 10.1, above), and potentially includes ethical concerns.

In *Australian Securities and Investments Commission v Rich*, Austin J had the opportunity to express a view on the relevance of industry standards to the assessment of the legal duty of care owed by (in that case) the chair of a listed public company.[64] In accepting the evidentiary value of expert opinion, academic writing and other commentary on the role of a public company chairman, Austin J commented that it might seem harsh to apply a standard of care to a director by reference to current usual practices, when those practices might not previously have been judicially commented on. However, Austin J drew attention to the court's obligation 'to articulate and apply a standard of care that reflects contemporary community expectations'.[65] Austin J acknowledged the limitations of much of the literature on corporate governance which 'is in the form of exhortations and voluntary codes of conduct, not suitable to constitute legal duties [and is] sometimes vague and less than compelling',[66] but opined that:

> [t]he Court must perform the difficult task of articulating a standard of care by reference to community expectations . . . [i]t seems to me preferable for the Court to embark upon this task with a measure of assistance from the kind of evidence [advanced] . . ., than to choose the only other alternative, namely to rely on unassisted armchair reflection.[67]

This approach received strong support in the *Centro* decision, where Middleton J cited Austin J's comments with approval, stating that 'the published materials on matters of corporate governance, in particular those referring to the role of directors in the review of financial statements, are of some assistance in determining the obligations to be imposed on directors'.[68] Middleton J went on to review an AICD publication offering guidance to boards on how to review a company's financial reports,

---

62 Kingsford Smith, note 53 above, at 82.
63 Ibid.
64 *Australian Securities and Investments Commission v Rich*, note 4 above.
65 Ibid., at [71], per Austin J.
66 Ibid., at [70], per Austin J.
67 Ibid., at [72], per Austin J.
68 The *Centro* case, at [192].

and noted that the guidelines were consistent with his own view of the requirements the directors should have complied with, and those placed upon directors by the *Corporations Act* and the relevant case law.[69] Interestingly, the defendant directors in *Centro* also sought to establish the usual practices expected of directors at the time, and led expert evidence to this effect. Middleton J gave his view that:

> [w]hile the usual practices of non-executive directors in 2007 do not, of themselves, determine the content of statutory norms of conduct, the extent to which the actions of a non-executive director accorded with the practice accepted in the relevant field is relevant in assessing the extent to which a particular director's actions may have fallen short of the mark.[70]

Kingsford Smith has argued that Owen J was influenced by corporate governance materials (such as the ASX Principles) in his judgment in *Bell Group Ltd (in liq) v Westpac Banking Corporation (No 9)*,[71] and further Australian judicial authority supporting reference to industry standards is available in an analogous domain. In *Dean-Willcocks v Companies Auditors & Liquidators' Disciplinary Board*, Tamberlin J had to consider whether or not the Australian Companies Auditors and Liquidators Disciplinary Board (CALDB), in carrying out its disciplinary duties, had power to have regard to professional standards and codes, including the codes of conduct promulgated by the Institute of Chartered Accountants in Australia and the Insolvency Professionals Association of Australia.[72] Tamberlin J rejected the contention that, as no legislative requirement exists for liquidators to comply with professional codes of conduct, it was inappropriate for CALDB to have regard to such standards in imposing sanctions on a liquidator for misconduct. Tamberlin J reviewed the relevant legislative provision in the *Corporations Act*[73] and noted that CALDB was empowered to cancel or suspend a liquidator's registration

---

69 Ibid., at [196].

70 Ibid., at [208]. It also seems likely that in the liability decision in *Centro* Middleton J was positively influenced by the board's corporate governance structures being consistent with the ASX Principles: Kingsford Smith, note 53 above, at 89.

71 Kingsford Smith, ibid., at 89; *The Bell Group Ltd (in liq) v Westpac Banking Corporation (No 9)*, note 26 above.

72 *Dean-Willcocks v Companies Auditors & Liquidators' Disciplinary Board*, [2006] FCA 1438. The relevant codes were the Institute of Chartered Accountants in Australia Code of Professional Conduct and the Insolvency Professionals Association of Australia Code of Professional Conduct.

73 Section 1292(2)(d)(ii) *Corporations Act, 2001* (Cth).

where the liquidator had failed to 'carry out or perform adequately or properly . . . the duties of a liquidator'. Tamberlin J found that:

> [t]here is nothing in the language of [the section] which excludes regard to professional standards and codes when deciding whether the performance is a proper and adequate exercise of the office. The reference to 'proper' and 'adequate' invites the testing of performance against a relevant standard or benchmark of performance . . . [t]he level of performance called for is that of 'adequacy'. The standard is that the duty must be performed 'properly'. The provision is designed to enable a Board representative of the commercial and accounting communities to consider whether the function has been adequately and properly carried out. To assess this, it is permissible, in my view, to have regard to the standards operative in the relevant sphere of activity.[74]

As indicated above, while this approach represents 'soft law' rather than mandatory provisions, it may still shape actions and lead to changes in approach by boards. Hill has noted, in the context of the evolution of directors' duties in Australia, the truth of the adage coined by a former judge of the High Court of Australia that 'what is in general expected of directors will tend to become the measure of what is required of them'.[75] Dominant notions in the regulatory theory literature suggest that soft law and self-regulation can be effective, and 'ethical' corporations may in fact be best achieved by self-regulation.[76] In effect this is a form of 'meta-regulation', with traditional law authorising or co-opting 'the regulatory influence of industry, professional or civil society bodies to set and enforce standards'.[77]

Such an approach represents a version of the argument made by some communitarian commentators that since concern for external stakeholders is in the ultimate best interests of the company, no change to substantive law settings is required to incorporate this perspective; the work is done by the duty of directors to act in good faith in the best interests of the corporation.[78] The duty to act in the company's best interests is the concern of the next section of this chapter.

---

[74] *Dean-Willcocks v Companies Auditors & Liquidators' Disciplinary Board*, note 72 above, at [26].

[75] Hill, note 6 above, at 64, citing Sir Douglas Menzies, note 1 above, at 164.

[76] Albeit supported by a pro-active regulator as back up: see Pascoe, J, 'Corporate Sector Whistleblowing in Australia: Ethics and Corporate Culture', (2009) 27 *Companies & Securities Law Journal* 524, at 526, and citing Parker, C, *The Open Corporation: Effective Self-regulation and Democracy*, Cambridge University Press, 2002.

[77] Parker, note 15 above, at 237. Parker was writing in the context of CSR, but the ethics position can be seen as analogous.

[78] Anderson, H, and Gumley, W, 'Corporate Social Responsibility: Legislative Options for Protecting Employees and the Environment', (2008) 29 *Adelaide*

3. Evolving Understanding of Best Interests of the Corporation

In addition to the potential for evolving industry standards to influence the interpretation of the standard of care owed by directors, the duty to act in good faith in the company's best interests has, it seems, been affected by changing expectations –and in ways that increase the relevance of ethical factors. The duty to act in good faith in the best interests of the corporation appears in section 181 of the *Corporations Act* and also arises (similarly formulated) under general law. The good faith aspect of the duty contains subjective and objective elements, so that it requires both an honest intention and a proper purpose when exercising a directorial power.[79] A fundamental concern with the duty is the appropriate definition of the 'interests of the company', and the extent to which the interests of external or semi-external stakeholders should be considered. Debate on the degree to which directors are permitted to have regard to non-shareholder interests has continued for many years in Australia as elsewhere in the common law world.[80] The issue has direct relevance for the place of ethics in directors' duties, affecting as it does the ability (or obligation) of directors to consider issues of 'right and wrong' in a wider context than shareholder wealth maximisation alone.

3.1 The accepted view of a company's best interests

The accepted view in Australia of the duty to act in good faith in the company's best interests has traditionally equated 'best interests of the company' with the best interests of the shareholders.[81] Thus while Australian directors have been permitted to consider the long-term interests of the company, and to do so with some discretion as to the factors they take into account,[82] the courts have not specifically endorsed the ability of directors to pay

---

Law Review 29, at 35. This approach also appears consistent with the direction favoured by the Australian Corporations and Markets Advisory Committee in its 2006 report on *The Social Responsibility of Corporations*. That is, the courts 'can assist in aligning corporate behaviour with changing community expectations', through their interpretation of the law, including the s. 181 requirements: Australian Government, Corporations & Markets Advisory Committee, *The Social Responsibility of Corporations*, 2006, at 111.

[79] *Howard Smith Ltd v Ampol Petroleum Ltd* [1974] AC 821; s. 181 *Corporations Act, 2001* (Cth); s. 181(1) *Corporations Act, 2001* (Cth).

[80] See for instance Marshall and Ramsay, note 12 above, at 29.

[81] *Ngurli v McCann* (1953) 90 CLR 425, at 438–9, per Williams ACJ, Fullagar & Kitto JJ; *Greenhalgh v Aderne Cinemas Ltd* [1951] Ch 286, at 291 (per Evershed MR).

[82] Keay, note 10 above, at 581. See for instance *Harlowe's Nominees Pty Ltd v Woodside (Lakes Entrance) Oil NL* (1968) 121 CLR 483, at 493 (Barwick CJ,

regard to external stakeholders' interests.[83] *Ford's Principles of Corporations Law* states clearly that there is no scope for directors to 'be generous with company resources when there is no prospect of commercial advantage to the company'.[84] There is also evidence that this was the interpretation of the powers of directors that was contained in advice informing the board's decision-making in the controversial *James Hardie* restructure, discussed further below.[85] The *Corporations Act, 2001* contains no equivalent of the UK's statement of the objective of companies,[86] with its adoption of an enlightened shareholder value approach.[87] The 2006 Corporations and Markets Advisory Committee's investigation into the social responsibility of Australian corporations considered directly the possibility of extending the factors to which directors should have regard to include external stakeholder interests, and rejected this approach.[88] Similarly, the Federal Parliamentary Joint Committee on Corporations and Financial Service's (PJC's) 2006 report on *Corporate Responsibility: Managing Risk and Creating Value* expressed concern that adopting an enlightened shareholder value approach could introduce uncertainty. The Committee gave its view that any law which imposes duties should provide clarity in relation to whom is owed the duty, and how the duty is to be discharged. The Committee used the example of the UK's (then proposed) provision requiring directors to 'have regard to a menu of non-shareholder interests' and noted that it offered 'no guidance as to what form this "regard" should take' and thus did not offer directors any guidance on what they would need to do to comply.[89]

McTiernan and Kitto JJ), and more recently, *The Bell Group Ltd (in liq) v Westpac Banking Corporation (No 9)*, note 26 above.

[83] With the exception of the interests of creditors in insolvency or near-insolvency situations: *The Bell Group Ltd* ibid., at [4418]. See also the review of the law on this point in Marshall and Ramsay, note 12 above, at 32.

[84] Austin and Ramsay, note 9 above, at [8.130]; *Hutton v West Cork Railway Co* (1883) 23 ChD 654; *Re George Newman & Co* [1895] 1 Ch 674.

[85] Redmond, note 31 above, at 45–6. This aspect of the accepted view might be thought to be consistent with Hansmann and Kraakman's well-known (and 'hotly contested': Horrigan, note 47 above, at 97) assertion over a decade ago that there is no longer any genuine rebuttal to the argument that 'corporate law should principally strive to increase long-term shareholder value': Hansmann and Kraakman, note 61 above, at 439.

[86] Keay uses this description for the statement set out in s. 172(1) of the Companies Act, 2006 (UK): Keay, note 10 above.

[87] Arden, note 23 above.

[88] Australian Government, Corporations & Markets Advisory Committee, note 78 above, at 111.

[89] Parliament of Australia, Parliamentary Joint Committee on Corporations and Financial Services, *Corporate Responsibility: Managing Risk and Creating*

3.2 The evolving 'unconfirmed regulatory consensus' in relation to a company's best interests

Notwithstanding this background, there is now evidence of an 'unconfirmed regulatory consensus'[90] in Australia that a level of director regard for non-shareholder interests is allowable. Redmond suggests that despite 'very modest doctrinal foundation', the consensus view is that directors may have regard to the interests of non-shareholders, within unclear limits, and subject to some level of resulting corporate benefit.[91] This is consistent with the conclusion of the PJC in its 2006 inquiry, which stated that '[p]rogressive, innovative directors' engage with the interests of a broader range of stakeholders than just shareholders.[92] Keay has asserted similarly that 'far-sighted' Australian directors do consider the interests of non-shareholder stakeholders where this is consistent with fostering corporate profits.[93] Further, Marshall and Ramsay have argued that although there is no judicial pronouncement or academic literature to cite for the proposition that there has been 'a shift' in the ability of Australian directors to take into account non-shareholder interests, nonetheless this has occurred.[94] Marshall and Ramsay suggest directors now have the ability to take into account non-shareholder interests where this is done with a view to overall shareholder interests, and further, that directors can at times act in the interests of other stakeholders even where there is no

---

Value, 2006, at 55–6. It is worth noting, however, that directors in Australia are under mandated obligations to have regard to the interests of stakeholders other than shareholders in specific situations by virtue of legislative provisions dealing with, for instance, employment, occupational health and safety, insolvency, consumer and competition issues, and environmental concerns, and also from a fiduciary perspective in the case of creditors where a company approaches insolvency: Anderson and Gumley, note 78 above, at 30; on the insolvency obligation to creditors see *Walker v Wimborne* (1976) 137 CLR 1, 7, per Mason J; *The Bell Group Ltd (in liq) v Westpac Banking Corporation (No 9)*, note 26 above, at [4418]. In addition, international treaty obligations import a range of obligations into Australian law that reinforce corporate obligations to external stakeholders: Anderson, H, 'Corporate Social Responsibility: Some critical questions for Australia', (2005) 24 *University of Tasmania Law Review* 143, at 157–8. An example of an international treaty obligation with particular relevance to directors and their ethics obligations is the Organisation for Economic Cooperation and Development's Convention on Combating Bribery of Foreign Public Officials in International Business Transactions, discussed below in this chapter.

[90] The phrase is Horrigan's, from Horrigan, note 47 above, at 203, cited by Redmond, note 31 above, at 48.

[91] Redmond, ibid., at 48.

[92] Parliament of Australia, note 89 above, at 59.

[93] Keay, note 10 above, at 600.

[94] Marshall and Ramsay, note 12 above, at 31.

derivative shareholder benefit, but only in very limited circumstances.[95] Interestingly, Marshall and Ramsay are able to refer to quantitative research on Australian directors' attitudes to show that the vast majority of directors believe they already have power under the law to allow for the interests of non-shareholder stakeholders.[96] Consistently perhaps with this prevailing view, Middleton J in *Centro* emphasised the significance of the role of a director, given that 'their actions may have a profound effect on the community, and not just shareholders, employees and creditors'.[97]

As with the evolution of the Australian duty of care and diligence, developments in relation to the duty to act in the company's best interests are significant for the place of ethics in directors' duties. An 'unconfirmed regulatory consensus' that recognises the place of wider stakeholder interests in directors' decision-making has significant potential to increase the extent to which directors will be permitted (and even expected) to make broader ethical assessments of 'right and wrong' in reaching decisions in the best interests of the company.

4. Disclosure (Mandatory, Recommended and Involuntary)

A trend to increase the level of disclosure expected of corporations, together with heightened risk of involuntary disclosure, also has the potential to influence the extent to which directors need to have regard to ethical concerns.

4.1 Existing obligations

Under the existing corporations regime in Australia all companies are subject to a range of disclosure obligations, including the requirement for all public and all large proprietary companies to issue annual directors' reports dealing with a review of the company's operations, details of matters likely to significantly affect operations, and performance in relation to environmental regulation.[98] Where an entity is listed, it needs to comply with additional disclosure requirements, including provision of 'information that members of the listed entity would reasonably require

---

[95] The only instance of the latter clearly identifiable at present, Marshall and Ramsay argue, is the interests of creditors on insolvency or near-insolvency: Marshall and Ramsay, ibid., at 32.

[96] 94.3% of respondents to Marshall and Ramsay's survey held this view: Marshall and Ramsay, ibid., at 40.

[97] *Australian Securities & Investments Commission v Healey*, note 5 above, at 625 [14], per Middleton J.

[98] *Corporations Act, 2001* (Cth) s. 299.

to make an informed assessment of . . . [the entity's] business strategies'.[99] The exact detail required to comply with these obligations is not mandated, but there is a clear need for directors to at least turn their mind to a relatively broad range of social issues with potential to impact on the corporation.[100] Further, ASX listed companies have an obligation to report annually on their compliance with the ASX Principles.[101] As discussed above, the ASX Principles recommend that companies 'act ethically and responsibly'.[102] The Principles also state that companies should have a code of conduct for directors, senior executives and employees, and that companies disclose that code or a summary of it.[103] Where a company has not followed the ethics recommendations, areas of discrepancy need to be identified and reasons for departures from the recommendations given.[104] A further relatively new Listing Rule obligation enlarges the category of ethics-related information required to be disclosed. An applicant for ASX listing needs to satisfy the Exchange that its directors are of 'good fame and character'. To comply with this requirement, applicants need to answer specific questions in relation to criminal records, enforcement action by an exchange or securities regulator, and bankruptcy. In addition, the ASX specifically reserves its right to have regard to any other information it has in relation to the directors.[105]

While the ASX Principles themselves are not mandatory, the requirement for listed companies to disclose their compliance (or otherwise) with the ASX Principles forms part of the Listing Rules,[106] with which all companies listed on the ASX are required to comply by virtue of their listing contract. Further, the *Corporations Act* provides legislative support for the Listing Rules, giving the court power to make orders in respect of any contravention,[107] and action may be instigated by the ASX, the Australian Securities and Investments Commission (ASIC) or a 'person

---

[99] Ibid., s. 299A(1).

[100] Anderson and Gumley, note 78 above, at 60.

[101] Australian Securities Exchange Listing Rule 4.10.3.

[102] ASX Corporate Governance Council, note 32 above, *Principle 3: Act ethically and responsibly*.

[103] Ibid.

[104] The so-called 'if not, why not' disclosure-based approach: Austin and Ramsay, note 9 above, at [7.660].

[105] Australian Securities Exchange Listing Rule 1.1 and Appendix 1A; amendments introduced with effect from 1 January 2012.

[106] As noted above, ASX Listing Rule 4.10.3 requires listed companies to disclose in their annual reports the extent to which they have followed the ASX Principles, and to explain deviations (the 'if not, why not' approach).

[107] *Corporations Act, 2001* (Cth) ss 793C, 1101B.

aggrieved' (eg a shareholder).[108] To the extent that directors fail to comply with mandated disclosure obligations there is potential for action to be taken to enforce a range of directors' duties, particularly the duty of care and diligence. Thus the disclosure requirements of the *Corporations Act*, when read in conjunction with the disclosure obligations imposed by the ASX's Listing Rules, suggest a mechanism by which consideration and disclosure of ethical concerns might become part of the discharge of larger (listed) companies' directors' duties.

The disclosure of ethics practices does not by itself guarantee a higher standard of conduct by directors, and the impact on the substantive duty of care might be slight. However, the existence of a direct nexus between potentially ethics-related disclosure obligations and directors' duties is significant. This mechanism may contribute to the creation of a culture of corporate responsibility,[109] as boards react to potential negative publicity arising from compelled disclosure of inadequate practices. Parker has suggested that one way CSR has begun to interact with legal standards is through non-binding rules that help create and shape 'corporate conscience'.[110] The 'progressive' thread of the CSR conversation includes commentators who consider enhanced corporate disclosure a mechanism by which improved social outcomes can be achieved,[111] and this argument is applicable, by analogy, to ethics concerns. If transparency via disclosure is a key determinant of directors' actions,[112] then increased disclosure obligations in relation to ethics-related matters has the potential to focus director attention accordingly, and link such issues more closely to director obligations.

4.2 Social media, whistleblowing and the impact of increased publicity

In addition to the potential for mandated disclosure to bring poor ethical practice to light, the existence of fast-evolving social media techniques increases the possibility of negative publicity for companies engaged in

---

108 Ibid., ss 1101B(1),(2).

109 Greenberg, D, 'Making Corporate Social Responsibility an Everyday Part of the Business of Business: Offering Realistic Options for Regulatory Reform', (2007) 19 *Bond Law Review* 41, at 56.

110 Parker, note 15 above, at 208; for a discussion of this concept in legal philosophy rather than corporate literature, see: Amao, O, 'Corporate Social Responsibility, Social Contract, Corporate Personhood and Human Rights Law: Understanding the Emerging Responsibilities of Modern Corporations', (2008) 33 *Australian Journal of Legal Philosophy* 100, at 104.

111 Anderson and Gumley, note 78 above, at 35; Parker, note 76 above, at 216.

112 Williams, C, 'Corporate Social Responsibility in an Era of Economic Globalization', (2002) 35 *UC Davis Law Review* 705, at 711–17.

unethical activity. The inexorable rise of social media may make it more likely indiscretions will be made public, and certainly increases the rapidity with which this can occur.[113] Requirements for, or encouragement of, whistleblower policies (which can be seen as a component of the legal meta-regulation framework),[114] form part of this involuntary disclosure trend. Increased attention to statutory protections for whistleblowers in Australia, and 'bounty' incentives (introduced in the US but with relevance to Australians interacting with US companies) may lead to higher levels of whistleblowing activity.[115] High-profile examples of whistleblowing via mediums such as Wikileaks may also popularise this kind of involuntary disclosure. In this context it is worth considering the very real possibility that the greater the level of publicity in relation to a corporation's practices, including the ethics of its actions, the greater the level of regulatory scrutiny of those activities.

4.3 The James Hardie case study

The potential for exposure of corporate practices to lead to directors' actions being challenged is well illustrated by the high-profile Australian corporate restructure of the James Hardie group. This incident also makes the point that even where directors' central duties appear not to have been breached, significant negative publicity has the potential to draw attention to other, lesser, transgressions by the corporation or its directors, with potentially dramatic consequences for the directors involved. James Hardie (through subsidiaries) had a long history of involvement in manufacture of building materials containing asbestos. The key aim of the James Hardie restructure was to isolate the group's Australian liabilities (arising from asbestos-related disease claims) from the organisation's on-going operations. For this purpose a special fund

---

113 Efrat, note 56 above, at 36.

114 Parker, note 15 above, at 220–21.

115 Whistleblowers in Australia have some existing statutory protection under *Corporations Act, 2001* (Cth), Part 9.4AAA in relation to disclosures related to breaches of the *Corporations Act*, but a 2014 Commonwealth Parliamentary inquiry made a number of specific recommendations for wide-ranging reform and improvement of the corporate whistleblowing regime in Australia: The Senate Economics References Committee, *Performance of the Australian Securities and Investments Commission*, Commonwealth of Australia, 2014, Recommendations 12–16; Mavrakis, N, and Legg, M, 'The Dodd-Frank Act whistleblower reforms put bounty on corporate non-compliance: Ramifications and lessons for Australia' (2012) 40 *Australian Business Law Review* 26; Brand, V, Lombard, S, and Fitzpatrick, J, 'Bounty hunters, whistleblowers and a new regulatory paradigm' (2013) 41 *Australian Business Law Review* 292.

was created, with the intention that it be resourced by James Hardie with sufficient assets to meet all likely future claims. Within a relatively short time of its creation it became apparent the fund was grossly inadequate for this purpose. Community concern that James Hardie's attention to shareholder profits had inappropriately displaced proper respect for employee and tort victim protection (in respect of long-tail asbestosis liability) was enormous. Media coverage highlighted the care needs of terminally ill asbestosis victims that would not be met as a result of the corporate re-organisation. Attention focused particularly on the fact that the restructuring actions of the James Hardie board did not appear to breach legal restrictions. Spender illustrates the media's reflection of this outrage with the following headline from the front page of a major daily newspaper at the time: 'The verdict: James Hardie knew it had shortchanged asbestos victims. It was deceitful and devious. And it is not legally obliged to pay up'.[116]

Ultimately public dismay at the outcome of James Hardie's actions led to an inquiry,[117] and subsequently to successful actions against key company officials and directors for breach of directors' duties. However, the action brought against the directors was based not on the merits of the decision to restructure but rather the accuracy of relevant board minutes and a related public disclosure.[118] ASIC pursued an action based on a misleading statement made to the ASX to the effect that the compensation fund was 'fully funded' to meet the claims of asbestos victims, when it clearly was not.

The board in James Hardie was constituted of a group of well-respected, high-profile individuals,[119] and legal advice on the issues in question was provided to the board by one of Australia's leading corporate law firms.[120] At the time of the relevant restructuring decisions there was presumably a degree of confidence that the direction taken was in the best interests of the company (understood as the shareholders). In assessing the events leading up to the board's approval of the relevant announcement, Heydon J paid

---

[116] Spender, P, 'Weapons of Mass Dissipation', (2005) 14 *Griffith Law Review* 280, at 287, citing Sexton, E, 2004 *Sydney Morning Herald*, 22 September 2004, 1.

[117] Jackson, D, QC, 'Report of the Special Commission of Inquiry into the Medical Research and Compensation Foundation', September 2004.

[118] *Australian Securities and Investments Commission v Hellicar & Ors*, note 5 above; *Shafron v Australian Securities and Investments Commission*, note 5 above.

[119] Similarly, in the *Centro* litigation the Court made a point of noting the directors were 'intelligent, experienced and conscientious people': *Australian Securities and Investments Commission v Healey (No 2)* (2011) 196 FCR 430, at 434, per Middleton J.

[120] A 'first-tier' firm: Redmond, note 31 above, at 46.

particular attention to the high level of public interest in compensation of asbestos victims, and noted that:

> [w]ithin the board and senior management there was a keen awareness that the success of the separation proposal depended upon the reaction of 'stakeholders'. The expression 'stakeholders' was not limited to existing or prospective shareholders. It included asbestos victims groups, unions, plaintiff's law firms, the Government and the media. The board and senior management saw the media as important in moulding reaction to what was done to remove asbestos liability from the group.[121]

The potential for strong negative public sentiment clearly influenced the High Court's assessment of the level of care and diligence with which the board should have considered the relevant public announcement and the minutes of the meeting relating to it. Publicity surrounding the restructure presumably also had the effect of making it more likely that each aspect of the transaction would attract the full investigatory powers of the regulator. A commentator in the business press immediately following the High Court's decision in James Hardie suggested that:

> [t]he first lesson . . . from the James Hardie case is that if you outrage the public you can expect to be put under the microscope by the media and others; . . . [the] second is that, once under the microscope, the blemishes we do not notice on a day-to-day basis become very apparent.[122]

As indicated above, there has been an increase in recent years in the number of Australian companies choosing to adopt codes of conduct or codes of ethics. To the extent that mandated, voluntary and involuntary disclosure all enable external (and internal) parties to be more aware of such ethics policies and activities there is increased opportunity for scrutiny to be brought to bear. Any deviation by a company from its published policies has the potential to attract negative publicity and unwanted regulatory scrutiny. This in itself is likely to reinforce the nexus between directors and ethics concerns, via an assessment of the extent to which directors have complied with both their standard of care obligations and their duty to act in the company's best interests when making those decisions that prove to be inconsistent with the company's own published standards.

---

121 *Australian Securities and Investments Commission v Hellicar & Ors*, note 5 above, per Heydon J, at para [186].

122 Hyde, T, 'Under the Microscope', *Lawyer's Weekly*, June 2012, at 23.

5. Criminal Statutory Liability Arising from Corporate Culture

One further existing link between directors' duties in Australia and ethics considerations arises by virtue of 'corporate culture' liability provisions. Australian companies are subject to an innovative criminal liability regime that applies generically to all Commonwealth offences. Relevant fault elements under the Commonwealth Criminal Code[123] are capable of being satisfied by evidence that a corporation's culture either 'directed, encouraged, tolerated or led to non-compliance' or that a corporation 'failed to create and maintain a corporate culture that required compliance'.[124] 'Corporate culture' is defined as an 'attitude, policy, rule, course of conduct or practice existing within the body corporate generally or in the part of the body corporate in which the relevant activities takes place'.[125] These liability provisions were groundbreaking at the time of their creation, and continue to represent an innovative mechanism for imposing corporate liability.[126] Significantly for the focus of this chapter, they have the potential to import into directors' general duties an obligation to provide for a positive ethical climate within a corporation. If a culpable culture is found to exist within a corporation, directors risk being implicated in possible malfeasance, creating a nexus between poor corporate culture and an argument that the directors have breached their duty of care and due diligence. Research is available to suggest that inaction by a corporation's leaders in respect of unethical conduct will impact on the behaviour of other agents within the corporation,[127] adding to the pressure on directors to ensure an ethical climate is preserved.

One area of application for the Criminal Code's novel 'corporate culture' liability provisions is the federal prohibition on bribery of foreign public officials. Amendments to the Commonwealth Criminal Code were introduced in 1999 in accordance with Australia's obligations under the Organisation for Economic Co-operation and Development's Convention on Combating Bribery of Foreign Public Officials in

---

[123] *Criminal Code Act, 1995* (Cth), Part 2.5.

[124] Ibid., s. 12.3(2)(c) and (d).

[125] Ibid, s. 12.3(6).

[126] Voiculescu, A, 'Human Rights and the New Corporate Accountability: Learning from Recent Developments in Corporate Criminal Liability', (2009) 87 *Journal of Business Ethics* 419, at 427–8; Brand, V, 'Legislating for Moral Propriety in Corporations? The Criminal Code Amendment (Bribery of Foreign Public Officials) Act, 1999', (2000) 18 *Companies & Securities Law Journal* 476.

[127] Schwartz et al., note 16 above, at 88, and see the references cited there.

International Business Transactions.[128] Although in place for over a decade the first prosecution occurred only relatively recently,[129] increasing corporate attention to the risk of contravention. The 1999 amendments shifted bribery of foreign officials from an ethics issue for Australian companies to a legal compliance concern, and the need to ensure an appropriate corporate culture for the purposes of those provisions has potential flow-on effects. As companies identify risk factors associated with bribery and misconduct it becomes more likely that codes of conduct addressing relevant factors will be generated. The Australian Institute of Company Directors now recommends that directors ensure they undertake adequate initial and ongoing due diligence in respect of businesses they partner with, to manage the potential risks of contravening bribery legislation around the world,[130] neatly illustrating the feed-back loop between raised obligations and evolving industry practice.

6. Increased Public and Private Enforcement of Directors' Duties

The final factor in this review of circumstances influencing the nexus between ethics and directors' duties in Australia is changing patterns of public and private enforcement of directors' duties. Early Australian case law in relation to breaches of directors' duties is relatively sparse, due to the power to institute proceedings against malfeasant directors lying almost exclusively with the board, rather than disgruntled shareholders.[131] However, increased involvement from the public regulator over time ensured that public as well as private consequences flowed from director misconduct, and the introduction in the early 1990s of civil consequences for breaches of directors' duties was particularly

---

[128] *Criminal Code Act, 1995* (Cth), Chapter 4 'The integrity and Security of the international community and foreign governments'; see generally, Brand, note 126 above.

[129] The so-called Securency prosecution: McDonnell, J, 'Corruption and Enforcement III: Is Australia Anti-Bribery Compliant?', available at the website for the University of New South Wales Centre for Law and Markets Regulation, http://www.clmr.unsw.edu.au/. In handing down judgment in the case of one of the executives engaged in a related offence, Justice Hollingworth referred to the fact that '[s]ecrecy, and a denial of responsibility for wrongdoing, also seem to have been part of the corporate culture at Securency at [the] time': *R v Ellery* [2012] VSC 349, at para [28].

[130] Australian Institute of Company Directors, 'The Boardroom Report' (2012) 10 *Company Director* 3.

[131] Austin, note 29 above, at 4–5; Boros and Duns, note 3 above, at [10.2].

significant in this respect.[132] At the same time private ability to take action against directors for malfeasance has increased significantly over recent decades, including through a statutory derivative action and liberalised statutory oppression proceedings.[133] Further, a burgeoning class action industry (encouraged by a fast-developing and lucrative litigation-funding market)[134] has contributed to the creation in Australia in recent years of an active shareholder litigation environment that draws ever-increasing attention to directors' liability.[135] These factors increase the potential for a breach of directors' duties in relation to ethical concerns, based on any of the potential nexus points discussed in this chapter, to be the subject of an action by an aggrieved shareholder or class of shareholders.

There are of course limitations on the circumstances in which shareholder actions can be brought. Any derivative action by shareholders needs to get past the threshold requirements present in the statutory regime, including the need to satisfy the court that the applicant is acting in good faith and that the bringing of the action is in the best interests of the company.[136] These hurdles do not, however, seem insurmountable in the context (for instance) of a group of shareholders asserting a breach by directors of obligations relating to disclosure of ethical practices within the company. The power of the ASX Principles to establish a footing for action has been observed, and is particularly significant in this context. It has been suggested the risk exists of the flood-gates being opened for 'all manner of proceedings by disgruntled stakeholders' by virtue of the

---

[132] The Australian Securities and Investments Commission's ability to institute civil actions under Part 9.4B of the *Corporations Act, 2001* became effective from February 1993; see generally Boros and Duns, ibid.; also Austin, ibid, at 252.

[133] The Chapter 2F.1A statutory derivative action was introduced by the *Corporate Law Economic Reform Program Act, 1999* (Cth); the statutory oppression action is found in *Corporations Act, 2001* (Cth), Chapter 2F.1, and was substantially liberalised in the 1980s; Boros and Duns, ibid.

[134] See Morabito, V, 'An Empirical Study of Australia's Class Action Regimes – First Report: Class Action Facts and Figures', Department of Business Law & Taxation, Monash University, December 2009, 3; Lombard, S, Brand, V, and Fitzpatrick, J, 'Private Enforcement of Liquidator Obligations' (2011) 26 *Australian Journal of Corporate Law* 256; Lim notes that litigation funder IMF (Australia) Ltd reportedly achieved a 114% return on invested capital for the financial year ended 30 June 2009: Lim, S, 'Do Litigation Funders Add Value to Corporate Governance in Australia?' (2011) 29 *Companies & Securities Law Journal* 135, at 136; see also Featherstone, T, 'Prepare for Action', June 2012 *Company Director* 30–31.

[135] Young, note 51 above, at 217, and see also the references cited there.

[136] *Corporations Act, 2001* (Cth), s, 237(2)(b) and (c).

ASX Principles' so-called comply or explain system.[137] Kingsford Smith has directed attention to the potential power of the ASX Principles as a corporate governance mechanism, but noted the hurdle represented by the cost to investors of identifying and pursuing a breach.[138] However, litigation-funded class actions offer a mechanism for overcoming information and cost asymmetries of this kind. Further, evidence that the litigation funding industry in Australia is maturing, and that participants may now be looking to work with companies as clients (perhaps, for instance, in actions against competitors) suggests an entirely new basis for increased activity in this field.[139]

Mechanisms of these kinds, that facilitate review of directors' actions, increase the possibility of a broad spectrum of directors' activities being the subject of litigation. As this trend develops, and ethics considerations for directors simultaneously gain greater prominence (as seems likely), the possibility exists of ethics becoming a mainstream issue for Australian directors.

IV CONCLUSION

Existing intersections between Australian directors' duties and ethics are identifiable, and a range of factors appear likely to increase the nexus as those duties continue to evolve. The standard of care owed by directors is responsive to changing business community expectations. Since industry standards in Australia now often include references to ethics principles, and many corporations voluntarily adopt ethics codes, ethics concerns, with associated generic concepts of right and wrong, may influence those expectations, perhaps in unforeseen ways. Contemporary understandings of the company's best interests also have the potential to incorporate ethics considerations, as an 'unconfirmed regulatory consensus' evolves that recognises the place of wider interests in corporate decision-making. At the same time mandated disclosure obligations, greater emphasis on voluntary disclosure and heightened involuntary disclosure risk (including through enhanced protection for whistleblowers and the rise of social media), all increase the likelihood of unethical corporate practices being

137 Zadkovich, J, 'Mandatory Requirements, Voluntary Rules and "Please Explain": a Corporate Governance Quagmire', (2007) 12 *Deakin Law Review* 23, at 38, and see also Baxt B, 'Corporate Governance – Is This the Answer to Corporate Failures?', (2003) 29 *Monash University Law Review* 234, at 259.

138 Kingsford Smith, note 53 above, at 91.

139 Merritt, C, 'Class Warrior', June 2012, *The Deal (The Australian)*, 18.

exposed to public review and commentary. Australian directors also need to take account of innovative corporate liability provisions that enable culpable corporate cultures to ground breaches of criminal provisions (such as foreign bribery offences). Each of these factors needs to be considered against a background trend of increased enforcement by the public regulator, and greater shareholder activism in relation to malfeasant directors, supported by fast-developing trends in litigation funding for class actions.[140]

Taken together, these factors have real potential to operate as a powerful engine for the accelerated evolution of directors' duties in Australia, and for the inclusion of ethical considerations as part of that development. Current formulations of directors' duties, and clarification of the onerous practical implications of those duties in cases such as *Centro*,[141] make it clear that the law has evolved significantly in recent decades. In time, it is possible that an obligation to give consideration to ethical concerns might represent not so much an extension of directors' duties, as a recognition of existing obligations as they play out in a modern Australian company. The need to be ethically aware, to be cognisant of the ethics codes and related practices of a corporation, and to comply with industry-mandated ethics standards, may be a '*Centro* moment' in waiting for Australian directors.

---

140 For an alert on this issue aimed at Australian company directors, see Featherstone, note 134 above, at 30–1.

141 *Australian Securities & Investments Commission v Healey*, see note 5 above.

PART IV

DIRECTORS' DUTIES IN TIMES OF FINANCIAL TURMOIL

11. Navigating financial turbulence: directors' duties in the face of insolvency

Michelle M. Harner

INTRODUCTION

In the United States, parties can elect to do business in a variety of legal entity forms. Parties – particularly those wanting to tap the public markets for financing – frequently organize their businesses in the corporate form.[1] To an increasing extent, parties also are using unincorporated entity forms such as limited partnerships and limited liability companies.[2] Regardless of the entity choice, the business's affairs are managed by individuals: typically, directors of a corporation and general partners or managers of unincorporated entities. These individuals are responsible for charting the business' course in good times and in bad, and it often is the latter scenario that proves most challenging.

---

[1] For example, parties can incorporate their business and operate it as a corporation. Laws of the state in which the business is incorporated largely regulate corporations. Alternatively, parties can forego the formal incorporation process and operate the business in an unincorporated form such as a general partnership, limited partnership, or limited liability company. Unincorporated entities generally are governed by the parties' contract, subject to certain mandatory and default rules under state law. *See, e.g.*, LARRY E. RIBSTEIN, THE RISE OF THE UNCORPORATION (2009) explaining unincorporated entity choice options.

[2] *See* Rodney D. Chrisman, *LLCs Are the New King of the Hill: An Empirical Study of the Number of New LLCs, Corporations, and LPs Formed in the United States Between 2004–2007 and How LLCs Were Taxed for Tax Years 2002–2006*, 15 FORDHAM J. CORP. & FIN. L. 459, 459–60 (2010) presenting empirical data to support statement that: "[t]he limited liability company (LLC) is now undeniably the most popular form of new business entity in the United States"; Susan Pace Hamill, *The Story of the Limited Liability Company: Combining the Best Features of a Flawed Business Structure, in* BUSINESS TAX STORIES 295, 310 (Steven A. Bank & Kirk J. Stark ed., 2005); Larry E. Ribstein & Bruce H. Kobayashi, *Choice of Form and Network Externalities*, 43 WM. & MARY L. REV. 79 (2001).

This chapter focuses on the duties of corporate directors when the corporation experiences financial distress. The general fiduciary duties of corporate directors and the beneficiaries of those duties are fairly well defined when the corporation is solvent. What those duties are and to whom they are owed become murky once the corporation experiences a liquidity issue, significant contingent liability, or other financial distress. This chapter explores these issues for directors of solvent, insolvent, and nearly insolvent corporations. It also highlights how these issues might impact general partners or managers of unincorporated entities and offers a brief comparison to the laws of other countries.

WHAT ARE U.S. DIRECTORS' FIDUCIARY DUTIES?

The internal affairs of a U.S. corporation are governed by the laws of the state in which it is incorporated. A large number of corporations are incorporated in Delaware, but corporations generally can choose their state of incorporation.[3] Accordingly, there is no uniform law that governs the internal affairs of U.S. corporations. For purposes of illustration, this chapter uses Delaware law and the Model Business Corporation Act ("MBCA") as statutory references.[4] It invokes case law from various state and federal jurisdictions as relevant to the discussion. In all cases, however, parties should understand the statutory and case law applicable in their state of incorporation or organization.

Delaware law provides that "[t]he business and affairs of every corporation organized under this chapter shall be managed by or under the direction of a board of directors . . ."[5] Likewise, the MBCA provides that "all corporate powers shall be exercised by or under the authority of the board of directors of the corporation, and the business and affairs of the corporation shall be managed by or under the direction [of the board of directors]."[6] Under both statutory schemes, the board of directors may delegate day-to-day oversight of the business to the corporation's

---

[3] *See, e.g.*, Deborah A. DeMott, *Perspectives on Choice of Law for Corporate Internal Affairs*, LAW & CONTEMP. PROBS, Summer 1985, at 161; Frederick Tung, *Before Competition: Origins of the Internal Affairs Doctrine*, 32 J. CORP. L. 33, 44 (2006).

[4] For an explanation of the MBCA, see William H. Clark, Jr., *The Relationship of the Model Business Corporations Act to Other Entity Laws*, LAW & CONTEMP. PROBS, Winter 2011, at 57.

[5] DEL. CODE ANN. tit. 8, § 141(a) (2011).

[6] MODEL BUS. CORP. ACT § 8.01(b) (2011).

officers.[7] Nevertheless, management of the corporation remains in the first instance within the exclusive purview of the board.

Although the law provides a seemingly straightforward management approach, directors and officers rarely hold a significant ownership stake in the corporation. As a result, the corporation's management is separate and largely distinct from its ownership. A schism thus exists between management and ownership, arguably creating opportunities for mismanagement at the expense of shareholders (i.e., owners). A rich literature exists exploring this phenomenon and the related agency costs.[8]

Directors have broad authority over corporate affairs but, in turn, they are accountable to the corporation and its shareholders. Directors are held accountable in various ways, most of which are grounded in state law establishing and governing fiduciary duties. Directors owe two primary fiduciary duties: the duties of care, and of loyalty. In addition,

---

[7] *See, e.g.*, MODEL BUS. CORP. ACT § 8.01(b) According to the official comments to MBCA § 8.01:

> [t]he phrase 'by or under the direction, and subject to the oversight, of,' encompasses the varying functions of boards of directors of different corporations . . . [I]n many other corporations, the business and affairs are managed 'under the direction, and subject to the oversight, of' the board of directors, since operational management is delegated to executive officers and other professional managers.

Olson Bros., Inc. v. Englehart, 211 A.2d 610, 615 (Del. Ch. 1965): "Section 141 of Title 8 provides that the business of every corporation 'shall be managed by a board of directors.' . . . [T]he corporation requires management, that is, a board of directors and such officers as may be necessary to accomplish its purpose or purposes."

[8] *See, e.g.*, ADOLF A. BERLE, JR. & GARDINER C. MEANS, THE MODERN CORPORATION AND PRIVATE PROPERTY 121–5 (1932); William W. Bratton, *Berle and Means Reconsidered at the Century's Turn*, 26 J. CORP. L. 737 (2001); Michael C. Jensen & William H. Meckling, *Theory of the Firm: Managerial Behavior, Agency Costs and Ownership Structure*, 3 J. FIN. ECON. 305 (1976), *reprinted in* MICHAEL C. JENSEN, A THEORY OF THE FIRM: GOVERNANCE, RESIDUAL CLAIMS, AND ORGANIZATINAL FORMS 83 (2003); *see also* Lawrence E. Mitchell, *The Fairness Rights of Corporate Bondholders*, 65 N.Y.U. L. REV. 1165, 1186–7 (1990):

> The principal distinction between these contributors of capital that has led to limiting bondholders' rights to those specified in their contract (in contrast to treating stockholders as beneficiaries of fiduciary duties) is that bondholders are creditors outside the statutory structure of the corporation, whose contract is specific, written, and negotiated; by contrast, stockholders are the owners of the corporation (after satisfaction of its liabilities), whose 'contract' consists of a generalized corporate charter and by-laws and is otherwise largely indeterminate.

some states impose a third primary duty through an independent duty of good faith. Delaware and some other states view the duty of good faith not as a separate duty but as an obligation subsumed under the duty of loyalty.[9] Regardless whether it is framed as an independent duty, good faith underlies the duties of care and loyalty and the business judgment rule, as explained in further detail below. Moreover, directors owe a variety of other duties, including duties of disclosure and accounting.[10]

To satisfy the duty of care:

> [a] director shall discharge the duties of a director, including the duties as a member of a committee, in good faith, with the care an ordinarily prudent person in a like position would exercise under similar circumstances and in a manner the director reasonably believes to be in the best interests of the corporation.[11]

In many states, including Delaware, the duty of care is a matter of common law developed by the courts. Although it appears akin to a negligence standard, courts generally are reluctant to impose hindsight judgment on business decisions of boards of directors.[12] Accordingly, courts generally use an evidentiary presumption called the business judgment rule in cases alleging breaches of the duty of care.

The business judgment rule presumes that, in making decisions, directors act on an informed basis, in good faith, and in the best interests of

---

[9] *See, e.g.*, Stone v. Ritter, 911 A.2d 362, 369–70 (Del. 2006): "The failure to act in good faith may result in liability because the requirement to act in good faith 'is a subsidiary element[,]' i.e., a condition, 'of the fundamental duty of loyalty.'" (quoting Guttman v. Huang, 823 A.2d 492, 506 n.34 (Del. Ch. 2003)).

[10] *See* Tamar Frankel, Fiduciary Law 7–13 (2010) describing general duties of fiduciaries.

[11] Or. Rev. Stat. § 60.357(1) (2011). *See also* Graham v. Allis-Chalmers Mfg. Co., 188 A.2d 125, 130 (Del. 1963):

> [I]t appears that directors of a corporation in managing the corporate affairs are bound to use that amount of care which ordinarily careful and prudent men would use in similar circumstances. Their duties are those of control, and whether or not by neglect they have made themselves liable for failure to exercise proper control depends on the circumstances and facts of the particular case.

[12] *See, e.g.*, William T. Allen et al., *Function over Form: A Reassessment of Standards of Review in Delaware Corporation Law*, 56 Bus. Law. 1287 (2001); Stephen M. Bainbridge, *The Business Judgment Rule as Abstention Doctrine*, 57 Vand. L. Rev. 83 (2004); Lyman Johnson, *The Modest Business Judgment Rule*, 55 Bus. Law. 625 (2000).

the corporation.[13] Plaintiffs can rebut the evidentiary presumption of the business judgment rule by showing that, among other things, the directors' conduct involved bad faith, illegality, self-dealing, or gross negligence. If the plaintiff establishes such conduct as part of its *prima facie* case, the burden generally shifts back to the director defendants to show that the decision in question nevertheless was entirely fair to the corporation. This "entire fairness" standard considers the general fairness of the decision in terms of timing, dealings among the parties, pricing, and industry standards.[14]

Notably, the business judgment rule applies only to decisions of the board of directors. To garner the protection of the presumption, directors' decisions must be grounded in a thoughtful process, free from conflicts of interest and self-dealing, and made in good faith.[15] The presumption does not arise where, for example, the directors make no decision, which is different than a decision not to take action (the latter being covered at least initially by the presumption).[16] The business judgment rule also does

---

13 *See, e.g.*, Brehm v. Eisner, 746 A.2d 244, 264 n.66 (Del. 2000):

> The business judgment rule has been well formulated by *Aronson* and other cases that '[i]t is a presumption that in making a business decision the directors . . . acted on an informed basis, in good faith and in the honest belief that the action taken was in the best interests of the corporation.' Thus, directors' decisions will be respected by courts unless the directors are interested or lack independence relative to the decision, do not act in good faith, act in a manner that cannot be attributed to a rational business purpose or reach their decision by a grossly negligent process that includes the failure to consider all material facts reasonably available (citation omitted)

See also Joy v. North, 692 F.2d 880, 885 (2d Cir. 1982): "Whatever the terminology, the fact is that liability is rarely imposed upon corporate directors or officers simply for bad judgment and this reluctance to impose liability for unsuccessful business decisions has been doctrinally labelled [sic] the business judgment rule."

14 *See, e.g.*, Cede & Co. v. Technicolor, Inc., 634 A.2d 345, 361 (Del. 1993): "Under the entire fairness standard of judicial review, the defendant directors must establish to the *court's* satisfaction that the transaction was the product of both fair dealing *and* fair price"; Sinclair Oil Corp. v. Levien, 280 A.2d 717, 719–20 (Del. 1971): "The standard of intrinsic fairness involves both a high degree of fairness and a shift in the burden of proof. Under this standard the burden is on [the controlling shareholder] to prove, subject to careful judicial scrutiny, that its transactions with [the corporation] were objectively fair."

15 *See, e.g.*, Melvin Aron Eisenberg, *The Divergence of Standards of Conduct and Standards of Review in Corporate Law*, 62 Fordham L. Rev. 437, 441 (1993).

16 *See, e.g.*, Stone v. Ritter, 911 A.2d 362, 364–5 (Del. 2006) holding that *Caremark*, which predicates liability on a "sustained or systematic failure of the board to exercise oversight", "articulates the necessary conditions for assessing

not apply in cases involving alleged breaches of the duty of loyalty and the obligation to act in good faith.

The duty of loyalty commonly demands that directors "act on behalf of the corporation and its shareholders, and [that] they . . . refrain from self-dealing, usurpation of corporate opportunities, and any acts that would permit them to receive an improper personal benefit or injure their constituencies."[17] Asserted breaches of the duty of loyalty frequently involve, among other things, allegations of conflicts of interest, personal appropriation of corporate opportunities, self-dealing, and bad faith. The Delaware Supreme Court has explained that the obligation of good faith "does not establish an independent fiduciary duty that stands on the same footing as the duties of care and loyalty."[18] Instead, "the obligation to act in good faith is subsumed within the duty of loyalty."[19] If the plaintiff pleads a *prima facie* case of breach of the duty of loyalty, the director defendants bear the burden of proving that the decision was entirely fair to the corporation.

The MBCA sets forth directors' duties in its statutory framework, articulating both standards of conduct and then, separately, liability for breaches of those standards.[20] These provisions generally track the duties described above, including the application of the business judgment rule. In fact, the standards of conduct provisions of the MBCA often are described as "aspirational" in nature, with liability attaching only to

---

director oversight liability"; Francis v. United Jersey Bank, 432 A.2d 814, 822 (N.J. 1981): "Directors are under a continuing obligation to keep informed about the activities of the corporation . . . Directors may not shut their eyes to corporate misconduct and then claim that because they did not see the misconduct, they did not have a duty to look."; Model Bus. Corp. Act § 8.31(a)(2)(iv) (2011).

[17] Lori A. McMillan, *Honest Services Update: Directors' Liability Concerns After* Skilling *and* Black, 18 Tex. Wesleyan L. Rev. 149, 172 (2011) (citing Guth v. Loft, Inc., 5 A.2d 503, 510 (Del. 1939)).

[18] *Stone*, 911 A.2d at 370:

> [T]he fiduciary duty of loyalty is not limited to cases involving a financial or other cognizable fiduciary conflict of interest. It also encompasses cases where the fiduciary fails to act in good faith . . . '[a] director cannot act loyally towards the corporation unless she acts in the good faith belief that her actions are in the corporation's best interest' (quoting Guttman v. Huang, 823 A.2d 492, 506 n. 34 (Del. Ch. 2003)).

[19] Stephen Bainbridge et al., *The Convergence of Good Faith and Oversight*, 55 UCLA L. Rev. 559, 584 (2008); *see also* Leo E. Strine, Jr. et al., *Loyalty's Core Demand: The Defining Role of Good Faith in Corporation Law*, 98 Geo. L.J. 629 (2010).

[20] Model Bus. Corp. Act §§ 8.30, 8.31 (2011).

the types of sub-standard conduct specifically identified in the liability provision.[21]

Corporate officers also are treated as fiduciaries of the corporation and are generally subject to the same standards governing the conduct of directors.[22] Individuals serving as officers thus owe duties of care and loyalty, with the corresponding obligation of good faith and the protection of the business judgment rule. The officers commonly subject to these standards include the Chief Executive Officer, President, Chief Financial Officer, Treasurer, and other individuals holding senior or executive officer positions.[23] Given the similarities in treatment, references to directors in this chapter also include corporate officers.[24]

Although the discussion above focuses solely on corporate directors,

---

[21] *See, e.g.*, Brehm v. Eisner, 746 A.2d 244, 256 (Del. 2000): "Aspirational ideals of good corporate governance practices for boards of directors that go beyond the minimal legal requirements of the corporation law are highly desirable, often tend to benefit stockholders, sometimes reduce litigation and can usually help directors avoid liability. But they are not required by the corporation law . . ." (citing E. Norman Veasey, *An Economic Rationale for Judicial Decisionmaking in Corporate Law*, 53 Bus. Law. 681, 688–99 (1998) listing "aspirational norms" after citing changes to the MBCA "separately codifying standards of conduct for directors and standards of liability . . . [that are] very well drafted and cogent").

[22] *See* Gantler v. Stephens, 965 A.2d 695, 708–09 (Del. 2009) "In the past, we have implied that officers of Delaware corporations, like directors, owe fiduciary duties of care and loyalty, and that the fiduciary duties of officers are the same as those of directors. We now explicitly so hold." (footnote omitted).

[23] *See, e.g.*, Lyman P.Q. Johnson & Mark A. Sides, *The Sarbanes-Oxley Act and Fiduciary Duties*, 30 Wm. Mitchell. L. Rev. 1149, 1205–06 (2004):

> Although often overlooked, corporate officers, including senior officers such as the Chief Executive Officer, the Chief Financial Officer, Chief Technology Officer, General Counsel, Executive Vice Presidents, the Treasurer, the Secretary, and others are 'agents' of the corporation. Agency is a fiduciary relationship. Even though senior officers of corporations typically have employment agreements, they still occupy a fiduciary status in relation to the corporate principal. (footnotes omitted).

[24] In addition, under the law of most states, controlling shareholders of a corporation owe certain fiduciary duties to the corporation and the other shareholders. *See, e.g.*, Bangor Punta Operations, Inc. v. Bangor & Aroostook R.R. Co., 417 U.S. 703, 716 n.13 (1974): "It is settled law that the fiduciary duty owed by a controlling shareholder extends primarily to those who have a tangible interest in the corporation."; Superintendent of Ins. of N.Y. v. Bankers Life & Casualty Co., 404 U.S. 6, 12 (1971): "The controlling stockholder owes the corporation a fiduciary obligation – one 'designed for the protection of the entire community of interests in the corporation – creditors as well as stockholders.'" (quoting Pepper v. Litton, 308 U.S. 295, 307 (1939)).

general partners and managers of unincorporated entities also commonly are considered to owe duties of care and loyalty under either statute or common law. For example, the Uniform Partnership Act of 1997 and the Uniform Limited Liability Company Act of 1996 provide for limited duties of loyalty and care, which may in many instances be modified by the parties' governance contracts.[25] The Uniform Limited Liability Company Act of 2006 takes a slightly different or "uncabined" approach to fiduciary duties, which may impose broader duties on managers, again subject in certain instances to the parties' governance contracts.[26] The scope of general partners' and managers' fiduciary duties is heavily dependent on the laws of the state of the entity's organization.

In sum, courts and policymakers have decided to bridge at least part of the gap in management and ownership through fiduciary duties. The business laws of the U.S. generally expect directors, general partners, and managers to be good stewards of the business entrusted to them, and they enforce this expectation through the prism of fiduciary duties. This mechanism is imperfect, and state laws often permit corporations to exculpate directors for breaches of the duty of care and to indemnify directors and officers for certain other types of alleged misconduct.[27] The utility of the mechanism also varies depending on the identity of the party seeking to enforce the fiduciary duties.

---

25 *See* UNIF. P'SHIP ACT § 103 (1997) allowing certain modifications to fiduciary duties; UNIF. LTD. LIAB. CO. ACT § 409(a), (h) (1996) providing that "[t]he only fiduciary duties a member [or manager] owes to a member-managed company and its other members are the duty of loyalty and the duty of care imposed by subsections (b) and (c)"; *see also* UNIF. LTD. P'SHIP ACT § 110(b) (2001) allowing partnership agreement to modify duties under section 408 but not eliminate the duty of loyalty.

26 *See* REVISED UNIF. LTD. LIAB. CO. ACT §§ 110, 409 (2006); *see also* Larry E. Ribstein, *An Analysis of the Revised Uniform Limited Liability Company Act*, 3 VA. L. & BUS. REV. 35, 62–77 (2008).

27 *See, e.g.*, DEL. CODE ANN. tit. 8, § 102(b)(7) (2011): "[T]he certificate of incorporation may also contain . . . [a] provision eliminating or limiting the personal liability of a director to the corporation or its stockholders for monetary damages for breach of fiduciary duty as a director . . ."; ibid., § 145(a): "A corporation shall have power to indemnify any person who was or is a party or is threatened to be made a party to any threatened, pending or completed action, suit or proceeding . . ."; ibid., § 145(g): "A corporation shall have power to purchase and maintain insurance on behalf of any person who is or was a director, officer, employee or agent of the corporation . . ."

WHO MAY ENFORCE FIDUCIARY DUTIES AGAINST U.S. DIRECTORS?

The type and scope of directors' fiduciary duties guide the legal evaluation of directors' deliberations and decisions. Nevertheless, another key factor is equally important in evaluating a director's decision and whether it might give rise to potential liability; namely, the identity of the beneficiaries of the directors' fiduciary duties. Most authorities and commentators agree that directors' fiduciary duties flow first to the corporation.[28] Whether those duties also flow to the corporation's shareholders or creditors, however, is a separate, more nuanced issue that is discussed below.

The Solvent U.S. Corporation

The overarching duty of U.S. directors frequently is shorthanded as "maximizing the wealth of shareholders."[29] This objective underlies (or should,

---

[28] *See* U.S. v. Byrum, 408 U.S. 125, 138 (1972): "[T]he directors . . . have a fiduciary duty to promote the interests of the corporation."; N. Am. Catholic Educ. Programming Found., Inc. v. Gheewalla, 930 A.2d 92, 99 (Del. 2007): "It is well established that the directors owe their fiduciary obligations to the corporation and its shareholders."; Revlon, Inc. v. MacAndrews & Forbes Holdings, Inc., 506 A.2d 173, 179 (Del. 1986): "[T]he directors owe fiduciary duties of care and loyalty to the corporation and its shareholders."; Woodward v. Andersen, 627 N.W.2d 742, 751 (Neb. 2001): "An officer or director of a corporation . . . occupies a fiduciary relation toward the corporation and its stockholders, and is treated by the courts as a trustee."

[29] *See, e.g.*, Gheewalla, 930 A.2d at 101:

> When a solvent corporation is navigating in the zone of insolvency, the focus for Delaware directors does not change: directors must continue to discharge their fiduciary duties to the corporation and its shareholders by exercising their business judgment in the best interests of the corporation for the benefit of its shareholder owners.

Dodge v. Ford Motor Co., 170 N.W. 668, 684 (Mich. 1919):

> A business corporation is organized and carried on primarily for the profit of the stockholders. The powers of the directors are to be employed for that end. The discretion of directors is to be exercised in the choice of means to attain that end, and does not extend to a change in the end itself, to the reduction of profits, or to the nondistribution of profits among stockholders in order to devote them to other purposes.

See also Jeffrey N. Gordon, *Corporations, Markets, and Courts*, 91 COLUM. L. REV. 1931, 1977 (1991): shareholder wealth maximization is "the bedrock of corporate law". *But see* Margaret M. Blair & Lynn A. Stout, *Specific Investment: Explaining Anomalies in Corporate Law*, 31 J. CORP. L. 719, 731 (2006); "There is very little

according to case law, underlie) all decisions made by directors of for-profit corporations. Consequently, directors' fiduciary duties generally are said to flow to the corporation and its shareholders.[30] Throughout this chapter, the corporation is treated as the primary beneficiary of directors' fiduciary duties with other parties being identified as additional beneficiaries of those duties where appropriate.

Identifying shareholders as additional beneficiaries of directors' fiduciary duties is important for at least two reasons. First, it suggests that directors who are weighing competing options should consider shareholders' interests in making that decision and pursue the option that is in the best interests of the corporation and shareholders.[31] Some commentators suggest that, at a minimum, the option selected by directors should maintain or at least do no harm to shareholders' interests.[32] In either case, whether directors have satisfied their fiduciary duties is evaluated, at least in part, based on the impact of their decisions on shareholders.[33]

---

in corporate law that supports [shareholder wealth maximization] and much that cuts against it."

[30] *See, e.g.*, James Gadsden, *Enforcement of Directors' Fiduciary Duties in the Vicinity of Insolvency*, AM. BANKR. INST. J., Feb. 2005, at 16: "The corporation laws of all states agree that directors owe fiduciary duties to the corporation."; Bruce A. Markell, *The Folly of Representing Insolvent Corporations: Examining Lawyer Liability and Ethical Issues Involved in Extending Fiduciary Duties to Creditors*, 6 J. BANKR. L. & PRAC. 403, 404 (1997); "Indeed, [when a company is solvent], most states impose fiduciary duties of loyalty and care on the directors and officers in favor of shareholders."

[31] *See Byrum, supra* note 28; Berg & Berg Enters., LLC v. Boyle, 100 Cal. Rptr. 3d 875, 890 (Cal. Ct. App. 2009): "It is without dispute that in California, corporate directors owe a fiduciary duty to the corporation and its shareholders . . . 'in a manner such director believes to be in the best interests of the corporation and its shareholders.'" (quoting CAL. CORP. CODE § 309(a)); Becker v. Knoll, 239 P.3d 830, 834 (Kan. 2010): "Kansas . . . imposes a very strict fiduciary duty on officers and directors of a corporation to act in the best interests of the corporation and its stockholders."

[32] *See, e.g.*, Arthur B. Laby, *Resolving Conflicts of Duty in Fiduciary Relationships*, 54 AM. U. L. REV. 75, 149 (2004): "The principal's first claim is that the fiduciary must refrain from causing harm; a claim to the performance of positive acts is secondary. At its core, the approach is self-evident. 'Do no harm' is the clarion call of every fiduciary."

[33] *See, e.g.*, Newton v. Hornblower, Inc., 582 P.2d 1136, 1146 (Kan. 1978):

> Officers and directors of a corporation occupy a strict fiduciary relationship with respect to both the corporation and its stockholders . . . Any unfair transaction induced by a fiduciary relationship between the parties gives rise to a liability with respect to unjust enrichment of the fiduciary. Where such transaction is attacked, the burden of proof is on the fiduciary to establish the fairness of the

Second, beneficiaries of fiduciary duties typically have standing to enforce those duties.[34] Accordingly, if shareholders are beneficiaries of directors' fiduciary duties, they may commence litigation against directors for alleged breaches of those duties. Whether that litigation is direct and may be brought in the shareholders' names, or is derivative and must be brought on behalf of the corporation is a separate but related issue. Many courts considering this issue find that the resolution "must turn *solely* on the following questions: (1) who suffered the alleged harm (the corporation or the suing stockholders, individually); and (2) who would receive the benefit of any recovery or other remedy (the corporation or the stockholders, individually)?"[35] This test largely affects shareholder lawsuits, as courts willing to recognize directors' fiduciary duties to creditors generally do so only in the derivative lawsuit context.

The primary argument supporting the position that shareholders are beneficiaries of directors' fiduciary duties stems from shareholders' position in the corporation's capital structure. When the company is solvent, shareholders are the corporation's residual owners.[36] After and as creditors are paid in full, they stand to gain from the corporation's success, but also bear the risk of the corporation's failure.[37]

The general mandate that directors act in the best interests of the corporation for the benefit of shareholders can pose challenges. The extreme view of this mandate suggests that directors cannot consider the interests of other corporate constituencies in making their decisions. Many states have adopted constituency statutes to mitigate this concern.[38] For example, in Connecticut, the governing statute provides

---

transaction, and to this end he must fully disclose the facts and circumstances, and affirmatively show his good faith.

[34] *See* Robert J. Stearn, Jr. & Cory D. Kandestin, *Delaware's Solvency Test: What Is It and Does It Make Sense? A Comparison of Solvency Tests Under the Bankruptcy Code and Delaware Law*, 36 DEL. J. CORP. L. 165, 170 (2011) explaining that the concept of solvency matters because "[insolvency] is the point at which creditors of a corporation gain standing to assert fiduciary duty claim."

[35] Tooley v. Donaldson, Lufkin, & Jenrette, Inc., 845 A.2d 1031, 1033 (Del. 2004).

[36] *See* Production Res. Grp., L.L.C. v. NCT Grp., Inc., 863 A.2d 772, 787 (Del. Ch. 2004): "[O]ur corporate law . . . expects that the directors of a solvent firm will cause the firm to undertake economic activities that maximize the value of the firm's cash flows primarily for the benefit of the residual risk-bearers, the owners of the firm's equity capital."

[37] *See* ibid.

[38] *See* Anthony Bisconti, Comment, *The Double Bottom Line: Can Constituency Statutes Protect Socially Responsible Corporations Stuck in* Revlon

that "in addition to complying with the [General standards of directors'] provisions of subsection (a) to (c)," the director may determine "what he reasonably believes to be in the best interests of the corporation, [and] . . . the interests of the corporations' employees, customers, creditors, and suppliers . . ."[39] In Vermont, a similar statutory provision states that "[a] director shall discharge his or her duties as a director . . . in a manner the director reasonably believes to be in the best interests of the corporation" including "corporation's employees, suppliers, creditors and customers."[40] Notably, Delaware does not have a similar constituency statute.[41]

The mandate also creates tension when a corporation is experiencing financial distress and, accordingly, the conflict between the interests of shareholders and creditors is most apparent.[42] Shareholders may benefit from high-risk, high-reward decisions because they have less to lose when the corporation is insolvent or nearly insolvent.[43] Creditors, on the other hand, may prefer more risk-neutral or low-risk decisions that increase the likelihood of some recovery. Directors typically must weigh these competing interests under extreme pressures from a variety of constituencies,

---

Land?, 42 Loy. L.A. L. Rev. 765, 768 n.13 (2009) explaining that as of 2009, 32 states have adopted some version of constituency statutes, including New York, Virginia, and Illinois.

39 Conn. Gen. Stat. Ann. § 33-756(d) (West Supp. 2012).

40 Vt. Stat. Ann. tit. 11A, § 8.30(a)(3) (2010).

41 *See, e.g.*, Frank J. Cavico & Bahaudin G. Mujtaba, *Social Responsibility, Corporate Constituency Statutes and the Social Benefit Corporation*, Int'l J. Mgmt & Admin. Sci., Apr. 2012, at 21, 25; *see generally* Mark E. Van Der Veide, *Against Fiduciary Duties to Corporate Stakeholders*, 21 Del. J. Corp. L. 27 (1996).

42 *See, e.g.*, Katz v. Oak Indus., Inc., 508 A.2d 873, 879 (Del. Ch. 1986): "Under our law – and the law generally – the relationship between a corporation and the holders of its debt securities, even convertible debt securities, is contractual in nature."; Frederick Tung, *The New Death of Contract: Creeping Corporate Fiduciary Duties for Creditors*, 57 Emory L.J. 809 (2008) explaining boards' fiduciary duties to shareholders versus creditors; Henry T.C. Hu & Jay Lawrence Westbrook, *Abolition of the Corporate Duty to Creditors*, 107 Colum. L. Rev. 1321 (2007) explaining courts' treatment of same.

43 *See, e.g.*, Paul Davies, *Directors' Creditor-Regarding Duties in Respect of Trading Decisions Taken in the Vicinity of Insolvency*, 7 Eur. Bus. Org. L. Rev. 301, 306 (2006):

> However, once the shareholders' equity has been dissipated, or has been reduced to a very low level, and there is no prospect of its being rebuilt through the company's established business model, the incentive for company controllers (if acting in the shareholder interest) is to take on excessively risky projects, for their attention can focus exclusively on the potential upside of decisions (footnote omitted).

including "employees, customers, creditors, and suppliers."[44] They need clear direction to strike an appropriate balance. As discussed below, directors have some guidance for complying with their fiduciary duties to a financially-distressed corporation but the process remains uncertain and turbulent.

The Insolvent U.S. Corporation

What really changes when a company becomes insolvent? Some commentators would say little, if anything, changes, observing that creditors still have the protections of their contracts with the corporation and shareholders still bear the greatest risk of the corporation's failure.[45] Other commentators posit that insolvency moves the role of residual owner away from shareholders and to creditors.[46] Under the latter perspective, insolvency also changes the identity of any additional beneficiaries of directors' fiduciary duties.

Many courts agree that a corporation's insolvency triggers some change in the roles of shareholders and creditors vis-à-vis the corporation. In these jurisdictions, the directors' fiduciary duties still flow first to the corporation.[47] The exercise of those duties, however, now is for the benefit

---

[44] CONN. GEN. STAT. ANN. § 33-756(d) (2010).

[45] Frank H. Easterbrook & Daniel R. Fischel, *Contract and Fiduciary Duty*, 36 J.L. & ECON. 425, 437 (1993); "Managers owe fiduciary duties to equity investors, but not debt investors or employees, because these claimants can contract at low cost, while the costs of specification are prohibitively high for the residual claimants.". *See also* Victor Brudney, *Contract and Fiduciary Duty in Corporate Law*, 38 B.C. L. REV. 595, 645 n.128 (1997):

> [D]irectors' fiduciary obligations should not shift from stockholders to creditors until the latter are unequivocally 'owners,' as presumptively evidenced by the initiation of bankruptcy or insolvency proceedings . . . Until then, if the creditors' contract does not entitle them to displace stockholders in control, it is hard to see why directors should become [the creditors'] fiduciaries . . . (citations omitted).

[46] *See, e.g.*, Royce de R. Barondes, *Fiduciary Duties of Officers and Directors of Distressed Corporations,* 7 GEO. MASON L. REV. 45, 63 (1998) explaining that when the corporation reaches insolvency, "[t]he majority rule, and the law in Delaware, is that . . . a board's duties are owed to the creditors of the enterprise"; Ramesh K.S. Rao et al., *Fiduciary Duty a la* Lyonnais*: An Economic Perspective on Corporate Governance in a Financially-Distressed Firm*, 22 J. CORP. L. 53, 64 (1996) explaining that "[a]s the firm slides into insolvency," fiduciary responsibilities are "extended to creditors in order to ensure adequate protection of their interests."

[47] *See, e.g.*, Production Res. Grp., L.L.C. v. NCT Grp., Inc., 863 A.2d 772, 790–91 (Del. Ch. 2004) stating that under Delaware law, even though the directors

of creditors – i.e., the residual owners of the insolvent corporation.[48] Accordingly, once a corporation is insolvent, its directors owe fiduciary duties to the insolvent corporation for the benefit of its creditors, while continuing to bear the burden of attempting to maximize the economic value of the firm for any potential residual benefit to the shareholders.[49]

Other courts find a change in directors' duties upon the corporation's insolvency, but that change does not necessarily equate to a complete shift in beneficiaries. For example, courts have interpreted California law as using the "trust fund" doctrine to define directors' duties to creditors in the context of insolvency.[50] Under this approach, directors' duties to creditors are limited "to the avoidance of actions that divert, dissipate, or unduly risk corporate assets that might otherwise be used to pay creditors claims. This would include acts that involve self-dealing or the preferential treatment of creditors."[51]

Although the notion of some change in the beneficiary of fiduciary duties upon insolvency is fairly well-settled, exactly when a corporation becomes insolvent and when any shift in beneficiary occurs are difficult to determine. Courts commonly define insolvency for these purposes as either "'a deficiency of assets below liabilities with no reasonable prospect

---

owe fiduciary duties to the creditors when the firm has "reached the point of insolvency," the "directors continue to have the task of attempting to maximize the economic value of the firm"; *In re* Bear Stearns Litig., 23 Misc. 3d 447, 475 (N.Y. Sup. Ct. 2008): "The directors still have the 'duty to maximize the value of the insolvent corporation for the benefit of those having an interest in it' and are required to 'engage in vigorous, good faith negotiations with individual creditors for the benefit of the corporation.'" (citing N. Am. Catholic Educ. Programming Found., Inc. v. Gheewalla, 930 A.2d 92, 103 (Del. 2007)); Finch v. Southside Lincoln-Mercury, Inc., 685 N.W.2d 154, 166–7 (Wis. Ct. App. 2004); "[T]here can be little dispute that Wisconsin courts recognize a fiduciary duty owed by the officers and directors of a corporation to maximize the value of the corporation's remaining assets for the benefit of its unsecured creditors once the corporation is both (1) insolvent and (2) no longer 'a going concern.'"

[48] *Production Res. Grp.*, 863 A.2d at 791: "[T]he fact of insolvency places the creditors in the shoes normally occupied by the shareholders – that of residual risk-bearers.".

[49] *See Gheewalla*, 930 A.2d at 103.

[50] *See, e.g.*, Berg & Berg Enters., LLC v. Boyle, 100 Cal. Rptr. 3d 875, 893 (Cal. Ct. App. 2009) holding that, under the trust fund theory, "'all of the assets of a corporation, immediately upon becoming insolvent, become a trust fund for the benefit of all creditors' in order to satisfy their claims" (citation omitted); *In re* JTS Corp., 305 B.R. 529, 535 (Bankr. N.D. Cal. 2003): "The trust fund doctrine provides that, upon insolvency, a corporation's assets become subject to a trust for the benefit of creditors."

[51] *Berg & Berg Enters.*, 100 Cal. Rptr. 3d at 893–4 (emphasis omitted).

that the business can be successfully continued in the face thereof,' or 'an inability to meet recurring obligations as they fall due in the usual course of business.'"[52] Unfortunately, defining insolvency helps but does not answer the question completely. A corporation's financial condition is rarely constant; it can vacillate daily and the evaluation often depends on accounting and other metrics.[53] As often stated, valuation is more art than science.[54]

The Nearly Insolvent U.S. Corporation

The difficulty in determining a corporation's solvency often leads to one or more periods in the corporation's financial life when the corporation is teetering on the edge of insolvency, a state often referred to as the "vicinity" or the "zone of insolvency."[55] The question then becomes to whom directors owe their fiduciary duties when operating the corporation in the

---

52 Rutheford B. Campbell, Jr. & Christopher W. Frost, *Managers' Fiduciary Duties in Financially Distressed Corporations: Chaos in Delaware (and Elsewhere)*, 32 J. Corp. L. 491, 500 (2007) quoting Delaware cases.

53 *See, e.g.*, Claire A. Hill, *Why Financial Appearances Might Matter: An Explanation for "Dirty Pooling" and Some Other Types of Financial Cosmetics*, 22 Del. J. Corp. L. 141, 163 (1997): "Another way for a company to manage its earnings is to change its accounting method [from LIFO to FIFO]."; Terry Lloyd, *Introduction to Financial Statements*, 856 PLI/Corp. 11, 13 (1994): "[A] balance sheet is always prepared for one date . . . By the time most companies have prepared and issued their balance sheet, their situations and – as a result – the account balances will have changed"; Stearn & Kandestin, *supra* note 34, at 183 explaining various tests and methodologies to define insolvency but asserting that the Balance Sheet Test and the Cash Flow test "are not as clear". *See also* Trenwick Am. Litig. Trust v. Ernst & Young, L.L.P., 906 A.2d 168, 195 n.74 (Del. Ch. 2006) defining the traditional balance sheet test by claiming that the company is insolvent when it "has liabilities in excess of a reasonable market value of assets held" (citation omitted), *aff'd sub nom* Trenwick Am. Litig. Trust v. Billett, 931 A.2d 438 (Del. 2007); *In re* Teleglobe Commc'ns Corp., 392 B.R. 561, 602 (Bankr. D. Del. 2008): "[The cash flow test] evaluates whether an entity is actually able to pay its debts as they mature in the normal course of business."

54 *See* Neuger v. Casgar (*In re* Randall Constr., Inc.), 20 B.R. 179, 184 (Bankr. N.D. Ohio 1981); "The determination of the 'fair valuation' of the debtor's assets at a specified time is, at best, an inexact science, and may often be impossible." *See also In re* Shell Oil Co., 607 A.2d 1213, 1221 (Del. 1992) referring to an expert's testimony who stated that "'[v]aluation is an art rather than a science.'"

55 *See, e.g.*, Berg & Berg Enters., LLC v. Boyle, 100 Cal. Rptr. 3d 875, 894 (Cal. Ct. App. 2009): "[W]e hold that there is no fiduciary duty prescribed under California law that is owed to creditors by directors of a corporation solely by virtue of its operating in the 'zone' or 'vicinity' of insolvency"; N. Am. Catholic Educ. Programming Found., Inc. v. Gheewalla, 930 A.2d 92, 101 (Del. 2007).

zone of insolvency. Although directors during this period still owe duties to the corporation generally, it is less clear whether the additional beneficiaries of those duties are the shareholders, creditors, or some combination of the two.

Courts approach fiduciary duties in the zone of insolvency in different ways. One approach posits that, once in the zone of insolvency, "a board of directors is not merely the agent of the residue risk bearers, but owes its duty to the corporate enterprise."[56] This approach requires directors to consider not only the interests of shareholders but also "the community of interest that sustained the corporation, to exercise judgment in an informed, good faith effort to maximize the corporation's long-term wealth creating capacity."[57] Directors thus may consider the interests of both shareholders and creditors in deciding the best way forward for the corporation.

The Delaware Supreme Court has rejected the "community of interests" approach and stated:

> When a solvent corporation is navigating in the zone of insolvency, the focus for Delaware directors does not change: directors must continue to discharge their fiduciary duties to the corporation and its shareholders by exercising their business judgment in the best interests of the corporation for the benefit of its shareholder owners.[58]

In *Gheewalla*, the plaintiff-creditor, NACEPF, sued Gheewalla and two other directors of Clearwire Holdings for breach of fiduciary duty. The three directors were employees of Goldman Sachs. NACEPF alleged that the defendants used the power obtained from the contract to "favor Goldman Sachs' agenda in derogation of their fiduciary duties as directors of Clearwire."[59] Clearwire Holdings was allegedly "either insolvent or in the 'zone of insolvency'" when NACEPF entered into an agreement with Clearwire Holdings.[60] The issue was whether a creditor can sue a debtor directly, rather than through derivative action, when the debtor is either insolvent or in a zone of insolvency. The Delaware Supreme Court provided clear guidance and held that "the creditors of a Delaware corporation that is either insolvent or in the zone of insolvency have no right, as a

---

56 Credit Lyonnais Bank Nederland, N.V. v. Pathe Commc'ns Corp., Civ. A. No. 12150, 1991 WL 277613, at *34 (Del. Ch. Dec. 30, 1991), *reprinted in* 17 DEL. J. CORP. L. 1099 (1991).

57 Ibid.

58 *Gheewalla*, 930 A.2d at 101.

59 Ibid., at 93.

60 Ibid., at 94.

matter of law, to assert direct claims for breach of fiduciary duty against the corporation's directors."[61]

Although commentators debate the full implications of the *Gheewalla* decision for creditors, most agree that it firmly establishes guidance for directors of Delaware corporations operating in the zone of insolvency.[62] Such directors should continue to manage the business in the best interests of the corporation for the benefit of shareholders. Directors in other states need to determine whether the community of interests, *Gheewalla*, or another approach governs their conduct.[63] Under either the community of interests or *Gheewalla* approach, the substance of the directors' duty (e.g., duties of care and loyalty and an obligation of good faith) and the application of the business judgment rule remain the same.[64]

Directors of insolvent or nearly insolvent corporations also should be aware that creditors and shareholders might assert claims against them

---

[61] *Ibid.*

[62] *See* E. Norman Veasey, *Counseling the Board of Directors of a Delaware Corporation in Distress*, AM. BANKR. INST. J., June 2008, at 1: Creditors do not have "direct fiduciary duty claims against directors of an insolvent corporation . . . or [when] it is in the 'zone of insolvency." *See also* Bryan Anderson, Comment, Gheewalla *and Insolvency: Creating Greater Certainty for Directors of Distressed Companies*, 11 U. PA. J. BUS. L. 1031, 1040–41 (2009) explaining that directors can "ignore the complications of the 'zone of insolvency' doctrine" and focus "their attentions exclusively on maximizing corporate value for the benefit of its shareholders," but because the *Gheewalla* court "does not provide directors or creditors with a clear method for determining when actual insolvency occurs," the directors are left with uncertainty and "unwittingly beholden to creditors because of the difficulty in determining the timing of corporate insolvency."

[63] *See, e.g., Berg & Berg Enters.*, using the trust fund doctrine to determine the directors' fiduciary duties. *But see* Geiger & Peters, Inc. v. Berghoff, 854 N.E.2d 842, 850 (Ind. Ct. App. 2006): "Indiana does not adhere to the 'trust fund' theory . . . ."; St. James Capital Corp. v. Pallet Recycling Assocs. of N. Am., Inc., 589 N.W.2d 511, 516 (Minn. Ct. App. 1999):

> "Corporate property is not held in trust" . . . [C]reditors have the right to be repaid, [but] it is equally true that they do not have the right, absent an agreement to the contrary, to dictate what course of action the directors and officers of a corporation shall take in managing the company . . . (citation omitted).

[64] *See In re* USDigital, Inc., 443 B.R. 22, 44–45 (Bankr. D. Del. 2011):

> The exculpatory provision in [Defendant's] bylaws releases the Director Defendants from claims alleging a breach of the duty of care . . . The exculpatory provisions do not, however, insulate directors from claims for breach of the duty of loyalty or for failure to act in good faith. [W]hen [the company] was navigating in the 'zone of insolvency,' the Director Defendants owed their fiduciary duties to the corporation and its shareholders, not its creditors.

that are not necessarily grounded in the traditional fiduciary duties of care and loyalty.[65] For example, creditors may assert a "deepening insolvency" claim alleging directors prolonged the corporation's life by incurring more debt to the detriment of creditors.[66] The theory argues that a more timely liquidation of the corporation – without the strain of the additional debt – would have produced greater recoveries for existing creditors. Many courts have rejected deepening insolvency claims asserted against directors as being duplicative of existing causes of action and even, in some respects, contrary to the business judgment rule.[67] Nevertheless, some courts have recognized a limited version of deepening insolvency claims based on fraud and defined as "an injury to . . . corporate property from the fraudulent expansion of corporate debt and prolongation of corporate life."[68] Moreover, in certain circumstances, directors may face liability for fraudulent conveyance claims.[69]

Gheewalla, 930 A.2d at 101; Credit Lyonnais Bank Nederland, N.V. v. Pathe Commc'ns Corp., Civ. A. No. 12150, 1991 WL 277613, at *34 (Del. Ch. Dec. 30, 1991).

65 Directors of U.S. corporations are subject at all times to laws generally applicable to non-fiduciaries, including tort law. Accordingly, parties may sue directors for claims such as negligent misrepresentation and fraud.

66 *See, e.g.*, Official Comm. of Unsecured Creditors v. R.F. Lafferty & Co., 267 F.3d 340, 347 (3d Cir. 2001).

67 *See, e.g., In re* Greater Se. Cmty. Hosp. Corp., 353 B.R. 324, 339–40 (Bankr. D.C. 2006) discussing how the deepening insolvency harm flowed from the directors' duty of care and, in particular, their failure to exercise good faith and due care in the decision-making process; *In re* Verestar, Inc., 343 B.R. 444, 477 (Bankr. S.D.N.Y. 2006) describing how a board's decision to "deepen insolvency" is subject to the duties of care and loyalty; *In re* Global Serv. Grp., LLC, 316 B.R. 451, 459 (Bankr. S.D.N.Y. 2004) holding bank directors not liable under the deepening insolvency theory for extending credit to an unworthy borrower; Trenwick Am. Litig. Trust v. Ernst & Young, L.L.P., 906 A.2d 168, 205 (Del. Ch. 2006): "That [a business] strategy results in continued insolvency and an even more insolvent entity does not in itself give rise to a cause of action. Rather, in such a scenario the directors are protected by the business judgment rule. To conclude otherwise would fundamentally transform Delaware law."

68 *In re* CitX Corp., Inc., 448 F.3d 672, 681 (3d Cir. 2006) holding that fraudulent conduct, but not negligence will sustain a deepening insolvency claim; Official Comm. of Unsecured Creditors v. R.F. Lafferty & Co., 267 F.3d 340, 347 (3d Cir. 2001); *see also In re* Lemington Home for the Aged, 659 F.3d 282, 293–5 (3d Cir. 2011).

69 *See, e.g.*, Cal Civ. Code § 3439.04(a) (Supp. 2012):

> A transfer made or obligation incurred by a debtor is fraudulent as to a creditor, whether the creditor's claim arose before or after the transfer was made or the obligation was incurred, if the debtor made the transfer or incurred the obligation . . . (2) [w]ithout receiving a reasonably equivalent value in exchange

The U.S. Debtor in Possession in Bankruptcy

Under the U.S. Bankruptcy Code, a corporation can file a Chapter 11 reorganization case to address its financial distress without proving its insolvency.[70] A Chapter 11 corporate debtor typically can remain in possession of its property and continue to operate its business while formulating its plan of reorganization.[71] The corporate debtor in these cases is called a "debtor in possession," and it has many of the same obligations and rights as a bankruptcy trustee.[72]

Although directors of a Chapter 11 debtor in possession continue to owe fiduciary duties to the corporation, federal bankruptcy law generally determines any additional beneficiaries of those duties.[73] "Debtors in possession and those who control them owe fiduciary duties to the bankruptcy estate . . . The fiduciary obligation consists of two duties: the duty of care and the duty of loyalty."[74] The bankruptcy estate consists of, among other things, all of the debtor's legal and beneficial interests in property wherever located; the beneficiaries of the estate primarily are the debtor's creditors and shareholders, with shareholders being permitted to participate in distributions from the estate only if sufficient value exists.[75]

> for the transfer or obligation, and the debtor . . . (B)[i]ntended to incur, or believed or reasonably should have believed that he or she would incur, debts beyond his or her ability to pay as they became due.

See also N. Am. Catholic Educ. Programming Found., Inc. v. Gheewalla, 930 A.2d 92, 99 (Del. 2007).

[70] *In re* SGL Carbon Corp., 200 F.3d 154, 163 (3d Cir. 1999): "It is well established that a debtor need not be insolvent before filing for bankruptcy protection."

[71] 11 U.S.C. § 1108 (2006): "Unless the court, on request of a party in interest and after notice and a hearing, orders otherwise, the trustee may operate the debtor's business."

[72] 11 U.S.C. § 1107(a) (2006) explaining rights and duties of debtor in possession.

[73] *See In re* V. Savino Oil & Heating Co., Inc., 99 B.R. 518, 524–5 (Bankr. E.D.N.Y. 1989). *See also Gheewalla*, 930 A.2d at 99: "While shareholders rely on directors acting as fiduciaries to protect their interests, creditors are afforded protection through contractual agreements, fraud and fraudulent conveyance law, implied covenants of good faith and fair dealing, bankruptcy law, general commercial law and other sources of creditor rights."

[74] *In re* Brook Valley VII, Joint Venture, 496 F.3d 892, 900 (8th Cir. 2007); *see also* CFTC v. Weintraub, 471 U.S. 343, 355 (1985): "[T]he willingness of courts to leave debtors in possession 'is premised upon an assurance that the officers and managing employees can be depended upon to carry out the fiduciary responsibilities of a trustee.'" (quoting Wolf v. Weinstein, 372 U.S. 633, 651 (1963)).

[75] 11 U.S.C. § 541 (2006 & Supp. IV 2011) (explaining scope of debtor's bankruptcy estate). *See also What Every Investor Should Know*, U.S. SEC. & EXCH.

Again, the substance of directors' fiduciary duties remains the same, and courts generally apply the presumption of the business judgment rule – as it would be applied under applicable state law – to decisions of directors during the Chapter 11 case.[76] Accordingly, the key distinction in evaluating directors' fiduciary duties at any point in a corporation's life cycle is the financial condition of the corporation. The identity of additional beneficiaries of the directors' duties may change depending on the corporation's solvency and the state law governing the internal affairs of the corporation.

Beneficiaries of Duties in Unincorporated Entities

In contrast to the large volume of case law and commentary regarding directors' duties when a corporation is experiencing financial distress, relatively little authority exists regarding general partners' and managers' duties to creditors in the contexts of insolvency and the zone of insolvency.[77] An argument exists – to the extent owners of unincorporated entities are subject to limited liability and constitute the residual owners of the business entity – that the duties of general partners and managers should resemble those

---

COMM., http://www.sec.gov/investor/pubs/bankrupt.htm (last modified Feb. 3, 2009): "In most instances, the company's plan of reorganization will cancel the existing equity shares. This happens in bankruptcy cases because secured and unsecured creditors are paid from the company's assets before common stockholders." (emphasis omitted).

[76] *In re* Pomona Valley Med. Grp., Inc., 476 F.3d 665, 670 (9th Cir. 2007) holding that business judgment rule applies in the bankruptcy context; Lubrizol Enters. v. Richmond Metal Finishers, 756 F.2d 1043, 1047 (4th Cir. 1985) applying business judgment rule "to the bankruptcy context"; *In re* Farmland Indus., Inc., 335 B.R. 398, 410–12 (Bankr. W.D. Mo. 2005) stating that debtor's former officers and directors are protected under the business judgment rule even when the corporation has filed for Chapter 11 bankruptcy; *In re* Global Crossing Ltd., 295 B.R. 726, 746 (Bankr. S.D.N.Y.2003): "[T]he Board's business judgment plainly passes [the business judgment] test as well."; *In re* Integrated Res., Inc., 147 B.R. 650, 656 (S.D.N.Y. 1992) affirming lower court decision and explaining that business judgment rule applied to the debtor while in bankruptcy.

[77] *See, e.g.*, CML V, LLC v. Bax, 6 A.3d 238, 242 (Del. Ch. 2010), *aff'd*, 28 A.3d 1037 (Del. 2011):

> Despite the ostensibly obvious implications of the statute [Section 18-1002 of the Delaware LLC Act], virtually no one has construed the derivative standing provisions as barring creditors of an insolvent LLC from filing suit. . . . Moreover, two decisions of this Court have assumed, implicitly, that a creditor of an insolvent alternative entity can sue derivatively for breach of fiduciary duty. (internal citations omitted).

of corporate directors.[78] This would require general partners and managers to consider the interests of creditors in the operation of the insolvent (and perhaps nearly insolvent) business and arguably allow creditors to pursue derivative litigation on behalf of the insolvent, unincorporated entity.[79]

At least one court has, however, held that creditors of an insolvent limited liability company do not have derivative standing to file litigation on behalf of the entity.[80] In *Bax*, plaintiff-creditor, CML, brought a derivative suit against debtor JetDirect and its corporate directors including John Bax.[81] Among other things, CML asserted that the directors breached the fiduciary duties of care and loyalty and acted in bad faith.[82] The defendants responded that the Delaware Limited Liability Company Act precluded creditor standing.[83] The court agreed with the defendants, finding that the statute was "clear and unambiguous on its face" and that a creditor was not a proper plaintiff in a derivative suit against an LLC under the statute.[84]

---

78 *See In re* McCook Metals, L.L.C., 319 B.R. 570, 594–9 (Bankr. N.D. Ill. 2005) addressing a limited liability company, the court held that "when a corporation becomes insolvent, the duties of the corporation's fiduciaries extend to its creditors . . . [moreover] corporate law principles [regarding fiduciary duties] are fully applicable to managers of insolvent limited liability companies" (internal citation omitted).

79 For example, the language of many state LLC statutes on derivative claims track corporate statutes and identify members (shareholders in the corporate context) as potential plaintiffs in derivative suits but in not in an exclusive manner. *Compare* 805 ILL. COMP. STAT. 180/40-1 (West 2010):

> No action shall be brought by a member, or transferee who is entitled to exercise the rights of a member to bring an action, in the right of a limited liability company to recover a judgment in its favor unless members or managers with authority to do so have refused to bring the action or unless an effort to cause those members or managers to bring the action is not likely to succeed,

with DEL. CODE ANN. tit. 8, § 327 (2011):

> In any derivative suit instituted by a stockholder of a corporation, it shall be averred in the complaint that the plaintiff was a stockholder of the corporation at the time of the transaction of which such stockholder complains or that such stockholder's stock thereafter devolved upon such stockholder by operation of law.

See also In re Liebl, 434 B.R. 529, 536 (Bankr. N.D. Ill. 2010) holding that a plaintiff-creditor may file a derivative action on behalf of a limited liability company.

80 *See Bax, supra* note 77.

81 *See ibid.*, at 240.

82 *Ibid.*

83 *Ibid.*, at 241.

84 *Ibid.*, at 241–2: "Under the plain language of Section 18-1002, standing to bring a derivative action is limited to 'a member or an assignee.' Read

In addition, some commentators have questioned the impact of contractual modifications to general partners' and managers' fiduciary duties on the rights of third parties, including creditors.[85] Many state statutes allow parties to limit (and in some cases eliminate) the fiduciary duties owed by general partners and managers to limited partners and members, respectively.[86] Although creditors typically are not signatories to or beneficiaries of a partnership agreement or limited liability company operating agreement, parties may contractually try to limit their liability exposure to creditors.[87] The enforcement of any such provisions likely will depend on the applicable statutory and common law. Following the lead of the *Bax* decision, courts may narrowly construe any rights of creditors in these circumstances.

---

literally, Section 18-1002 denies derivative standing to creditors of an insolvent LLC.".

[85] J. William Callison, *Why a Fiduciary Duty Shift to Creditors of Insolvent Business Entities Is Incorrect as a Matter of Theory and Practice*, 1 J. Bus. & Tech. L. 431, 452 (2007).

[86] *See, e.g.*, Cal. Corp. Code § 16103 (West 2006) allowing partnership agreement to modify duties but not "unreasonably reduce the duty of care"; 805 Ill. Comp. Stat. 180/15-5 (West 2010) stating that operating agreement cannot "eliminate or reduce a member's fiduciary duties" but providing that agreement may identify specific "categories of activities that do not violate these duties, if not manifestly unreasonable" after full disclosure and ratification; Nev. Rev. Stat. Ann. § 86.286(5) (LexisNexis Supp. 2011):

> To the extent that a member or manager or other person has duties to a limited-liability company, to another member or manager, or to another person that is a party to or is otherwise bound by the operating agreement, the member, manager or other person's duties may be expanded, restricted or eliminated by provisions in the operating agreement, except that an operating agreement may not eliminate the implied covenant of good faith and fair dealing.

[87] *See, e.g.*, Michelle M. Harner & Jamie Marincic, *The Naked Fiduciary*, 54 Ariz. L. Rev. ___ (forthcoming 2012) providing examples of liability waivers included in limited liability company operating agreements. *Cf.* McConnell v. Hunt Sports Enters., 725 N.E.2d 1193, 1214 (Ohio Ct. App. 1999):

> In the case at bar, a limited liability company is involved which, like a partnership, involves a fiduciary relationship . . . [However,] the question we are presented with is whether an operating agreement of a limited liability company may, in essence, limit or define the scope of the fiduciary duties imposed upon its members. We answer this question in the affirmative

Lola Cars Int'l Ltd. v. Krohn Racing, LLC, C.A. Nos. 4479-VCN, 4886-VCN, 2009 WL 4052681, at *8 (Del. Ch. Nov. 12, 2009): The court may not "substitute its own notions of fairness" and impose good faith obligation when the agreement was reached by parties.

WHAT ARE THE IMPLICATIONS OF A CHANGE IN ADDITIONAL BENEFICIARIES?

In general, directors need to be making decisions in good faith, on an informed basis, free from conflict, and in the best interests of the corporation.[88] This course of conduct is also at the core of the business judgment rule. A corporation's financial distress does change these basic duties. Accordingly, even though such conduct will not necessarily preclude shareholders or creditors from filing derivative lawsuits, it likely will provide directors with strong defenses in any such litigation.

Consequently, one of the primary implications of a corporation's insolvency or near insolvency is who can file any derivative litigation. As discussed above, shareholders generally have standing to file derivative litigation when the corporation is solvent and most likely when it is nearly insolvent. Creditors' ability to bring derivative litigation largely is limited to the insolvency context. Moreover, a bankruptcy trustee (or other authorized representative of the debtor's estate) cedes to that standing in any federal bankruptcy case.

The other primary potential implication is whether directors can or should be considering the interests of creditors either on par with or ahead of the interests of shareholders.[89] This often is the more challenging aspect of governing a distressed corporation. In jurisdictions following *Gheewalla*, the general guidance to directors appears to be to govern in accordance with the shareholder wealth maximization principle until actual insolvency.[90] Nevertheless, as discussed above, that guidance may

---

88 *See supra* note 13 and accompanying text.

89 *See, e.g.*, *In re* USDigital, Inc., 443 B.R. 22, 42 (Bankr. D. Del. 2011); "In Delaware, when a corporation has become insolvent . . . fiduciary duties inure to the benefit of creditors. Once a company has become insolvent its creditors become the risk bearers of the corporate director's decisions." (footnote omitted); Production Res. Grp., L.L.C. v. NCT Grp., Inc., 863 A.2d 772, 790–91 (Del. Ch. 2004):

> When a firm has reached the point of insolvency, it is settled that under Delaware law, the firm's directors are said to owe fiduciary duties to the company's creditors. This is an uncontroversial proposition and does not completely turn on its head the equitable obligations of the directors to the firm itself. The directors continue to have the task of attempting to maximize the economic value of the firm (footnotes omitted).

90 *See, e.g.*, Master-Halco, Inc. v. Scillia, Dowling & Natarelli, LLC, 739 F. Supp. 2d 100, 103 (D. Conn. 2010) discussing "New York law limiting directors'

be unsatisfactory depending on, among other things, the definition of insolvency, the investment horizons and interests of shareholders, and the corporation's restructuring alternatives. Directors in distressed situations thus are likely best served by seeking professional guidance and continuing to make thoughtful decisions based upon supporting evidence and after due deliberation.

HOW DO U.S. FIDUCIARY DUTIES COMPARE TO OTHER GOVERNANCE STRUCTURES?

Countries differ in their approaches to governance standards for directors of distressed companies. A multi-country survey is beyond the scope of this chapter. Nevertheless, this part highlights certain similarities and differences in governance schemes to further analyze the U.S. approach described above.

Many countries impose a duty of care on corporate directors either by statutory or common law.[91] This duty often is similar to the U.S. duty of care and flows to the company and shareholders. For example, the Australian Corporations Act of 2001 provides:

> A director or other officer of a corporation must exercise their powers and discharge their duties with the degree of care and diligence that a reasonable person would exercise if they: were a director or officer of a corporation in the corporation's circumstances; and occupied the office held by, and had the same responsibilities within the corporation as, the director or officer.[92]

---

fiduciary duties to creditors to only the period of actual insolvency" and *Gheewalla* and holding that "the cause of action for [breach of fiduciary duties to a creditor while a company was in the zone of insolvency] does not exist under Connecticut law."

[91] *See* Adam Plainer & Sally Willcock, Weil, Gotshal & Manges, Comparative Guide to Restructuring Procedures (2012), *available at* http://www.weil.com/files/upload/comparative_study.pdf (providing an overview of fiduciary duties under the laws of the U.S., the U.K., France, and Germany).

[92] Corporations Act, 2001, s 180(1) (Austl.). *See also* Business Corporations Act, R.S.C., c. C-44, s. 122(1) (1985) (Can.): "Every director and officer of a corporation in exercising their powers and discharging their duties shall act honestly and in good faith with a view to the best interests of the corporation; and exercise the care, diligence and skill that a reasonably prudent person would exercise in comparable circumstances."; Companies Act, 2006, c. 46, § 174 (U.K.): "Duty to exercise reasonable care, skill and diligence."

Countries imposing a duty of care also generally recognize some form of a business judgment rule.[93]

As in the U.S., the laws of many countries find significance in a company's financial distress. Some countries address alleged mismanagement in the distressed context under the auspices of the duty of care. For example, under the duty of care in the U.K., "[when] a company is clearly solvent there is no duty to consider creditors' interests [but] when a company is clearly insolvent, directors must consider creditors' interests before those of shareholders."[94] Likewise, in Canada, the Supreme Court of Canada has held that directors of distressed companies owe their duties to the corporation and not creditors under the common law duty of care but may owe duties to creditors under the statutory duty of care, which does not identify the beneficiary of the duty.[95] These approaches resemble the U.S. approach in staying focused on the company as the primary beneficiary of directors' fiduciary duties and trying to find an appropriate balance in rights for potential additional beneficiaries when the company experiences financial distress.

Some countries also tackle the issue more directly by statute, including through insolvent (or wrongful) trading laws or a duty to file an insolvency proceeding upon a company's actual insolvency. Statutory prohibitions on insolvent (or wrongful) trading generally impose liability on directors if they "knew or ought to have concluded that there was no reasonable prospect that the company would avoid going into insolvent liquidation" and then failed to take "every step with a view to minimising the potential loss to the company's creditors."[96] Directors violating insolvent trading

---

[93] *See, e.g.*, Corporations Act, 2001, s 180(2) (Austl.); "A director or other officer of a corporation who makes a business judgment . . . meet[s] the requirements of subsection (1) . . . if they make the judgment in good faith . . . do not have a material personal interest . . . inform themselves about the subject matter . . . and rationally believe that the judgment is in the best interests of the corporation."

[94] GLOBAL LEGAL GRP., THE INTERNATIONAL COMPARATIVE LEGAL GUIDE TO: CORPORATE RECOVERY & INSOLVENCY 2009, at 64 (2009), *available at* http://www.scribd.com/doc/77282203/Intl-Legal-Guide-to-Corp-Recovery-Insolvency.

[95] Peoples Dep't Stores Inc. v. Wise, [2004] 3 S.C.R. 461 (Can.). *See also* Pamela L.J. Huff & Russell C. Silberglied, *From* Production Resources *to* Peoples Department Stores: *A Similar Response by Delaware and Canadian Courts on the Fiduciary Duties of Directors to Creditors of Insolvent Companies*, 1 J. BUS. & TECH. L. 455 (2007).

[96] Insolvency Act, 1986, c. 45, § 214 (U.K.); *see also* PLAINER & WILLCOCK, *supra* note 91, at 20–21, 48–49 discussing laws of the U.K. and France. In a report requested by the European Parliament's Committee on Legal Affairs on insolvency laws of Member States in the European Union, the report notes as background that:

laws may be liable for the company's monetary losses and may be disqualified for serving as a company's director for a period of time, depending on the laws of the particular country.[97] Statutory laws imposing an affirmative duty on directors to file generally require directors to commence the appropriate insolvency proceeding for the company within a certain time period (e.g., 45 or 60 days) of when the director knew or should have known of the company's actual insolvency.[98] Directors breaching this duty may face monetary damages, criminal sanctions, or disqualification, depending on the laws of the particular country.[99]

> [i]nsolvency law . . . aims at protecting creditors' rights, while safeguarding the interests of shareholders and customers on the one hand and at avoiding liquidation of potentially viable companies on the other hand . . . The way insolvency law protects the different stakeholders may differ widely from one Member State to another . . . [I]t is important to establish the extent to which harmonization of the insolvency law within the different EU Member States is required.

Eur. Parliament, Harmonisation of Insolvency Law at EU Level 5–6 (2010). For instance,

> under Italian law liability for the acts or omissions of directors does not extend to a director who, being without fault, had expressed dissent in the resolutions of the board of directors and has immediately given written notice of this dissent to the chairman of the board of directors . . . [On the other hand, [u]nder Swedish law shareholders may under certain circumstances be liable for the continuation of the business of a company if it has lost more than half of its share capital . . . There exist no general rules as to when a director is civilly and criminally liable in the matters. Ibid., at 22.

The report concludes that: "[t]he laws of EU Member States contain significantly different rules on the liability of directors . . . and other parties involved with the debtor, increasing forum shopping and reducing good corporate governance." Ibid.

[97] *See supra* note 96 and accompanying text.

[98] *See, e.g.*, Plainer & Willcock, *supra* note 91, at 48, 74. In France: "[d]irectors are under an obligation to file for a judicial administration or a judicial liquidation within 45 days of a debtor reaching the point of *cessation des paiements*. A debtor is deemed to be in *cessation des paiements* when it is unable to face its due and payable debts with its available assets . . ." Ibid., at 48. In Germany, the duty to file "is to be fulfilled without undue delay and in any event within three weeks from the occurrence of insolvency . . . If the debtor's management has resigned or vacated office the requirement to file for insolvency extends to shareholders and, in the case of a stock corporation ('*Aktiengesellschaft*'), members of a supervisory board ('*Aufsichtsrat*')." Ibid., at 74.

[99] *See*, e.g., ibid., at 48, 74. In France: "[i]f directors fail to meet this filing requirement, this may be held to amount to mismanagement and breach of duty and the directors may be made personally liable for all or part of the debtor's shortfall of assets . . . A failure to file . . . can also result in a director being disqualified from acting as a director of an entity other than the debtor." Ibid., at

The laws of the U.S. do not prohibit insolvent trading or impose a duty on directors to file an insolvency proceeding for a federal bankruptcy case. Indeed, a company's insolvency is not a prerequisite to, or a trigger for, a federal bankruptcy case.[100] That being said, directors of U.S. companies should understand the scope and beneficiaries of their duties of care and loyalty (including their obligation of good faith).[101] In addition, they should recognize the potential for liability under non-fiduciary claims, including deepening insolvency and fraudulent conveyance claims.[102]

CONCLUSION

The law governing fiduciary duties of directors of U.S. corporations is fairly well-settled. Directors owe duties of care and loyalty, and these duties require directors to make decisions in good faith, free from conflicts of interest, and in the best interests of the corporation at all times. Potential complications arise, however, when a corporation experiences financial distress and the beneficiaries of the directors' duties become less certain. Although creditors generally assume the role of beneficiary upon actual insolvency, when that change occurs and its full implications depend largely on applicable law. Accordingly, directors should be mindful of the potential obstacles as they navigate distressed situations.

---

48. In Germany, "[n]on-compliance with the mandatory filing duty may expose the obligors of such duty to civil liability vis-à-vis the debtor and its creditors, as well as to criminal sanctions." Ibid., at 74; *see also* EUR. PARLIAMENT, *supra* note 96, at 22.

100 *See supra* note 70 and accompanying text.

101 *See supra* notes 73–6 and accompanying text.

102 *See supra* notes 65–9 and accompanying text.

12. Non-executive directors in financial institutions: a demanding standard of care

Adolfo Paolini

INTRODUCTION

Worldwide economies are experiencing difficult times due to financial inability to meet national debt payments for the foreseeable future. Countries work hard to cut costs, at the expense of certain social needs, therefore reducing budgets in areas that may impact the past, current, or future workforce. The financial turmoil caused by some of the most representative banks between 2007 and 2009 is still bearing poisoned fruits so the 2011, 2012, 2013 and possibly the 2014 vintages have been affected by this unwanted fungus.

It is no longer a mystery what happened in the recent past to precipitate the financial crisis: unscrupulous bankers[1] tried to maximise profits at any cost, while investors underestimated the risk behind certain financial operations, and regulators failed to implement either suitable rules or apply the ones already in place and some credit rating agencies masked the reality by failing to provide good intermediary services, rightly assessing the creditworthiness of financial instruments or acting as efficient gatekeepers for issuers of debt instruments.[2] It would be unfeasible to cover in this chapter all the causes of the present financial troubles so it will instead concentrate and assess only one of the neuralgic causes of this worrying time.

The point at issue is 'banking corporate governance', and, more specifically, the composition of the board of directors of banks, which may differ from the board of a company which is not a financial institution. The reality is that banks are different, as highlighted by Larisa Dragomir in her

[1] With several honourable exceptions.

[2] Veil R and Teigelack L, *European Capital Markets Law*, Hart Publishing, UK, 2013 at 414.

work *European Prudential Banking Regulation and Supervision*,[3] so their boards should be both assessed and regulated differently. The following features may explain the point:

1. Banks are opaque in the sense that they have valuable information unavailable to the markets[4] because of the secrecy rule.
2. Banks act as performers of deposit taking and lending. They are special because they are the only liquidity providers.[5] They transform liquid short-term liabilities into illiquid long-term assets. The market for financial instruments to some extent wanted to change this last feature by transferring the credit risk off-balance to other financial institutions, which in some cases allowed banks to abuse and manipulate their balance sheets.
3. Banks incur special risks,[6] since it is related to the specific character of deposits, the vulnerability of banks to exposure to contagion channels and the propensity of taking larger risks, with the reassurance that the regulator may offer financial protection.[7]

It is quite clear that the division of powers in companies is a matter to be resolved privately by the members of the corporate body and not by legislation.[8] In this sense, 'power is derived from shareholders through a process of delegation via the articles and not from a separate free-standing grant of authority from the state. This helps to underline the shareholder-centred nature of British company law'.[9] Consequently, in this 'shareholder primacy model' directors are given very wide powers to run the company,[10] which in turn gives rise to the need for an efficient checks and breaks system, in which non-executive directors (NEDs) are called to play a very important role.

---

[3] Dragomir L, *European Prudential Banking Regulation and Supervision, The Legal Dimension*, Routledge, 2010.

[4] Ibid at 27.

[5] Ibid at 28.

[6] Ibid at 27–9.

[7] Ibid at 29.

[8] Davies PL, *Principles of Modern Company Law*, Sweet & Maxwell, 2008 at 366. This is reflected in the origins of companies. In fact they develop, in the UK from partnerships where the control and power are privately exercised. Additionally, contrary to what happen in other jurisdictions – Germany being an example – in the UK there is not separate legislation for large and small companies.

[9] Ibid.

[10] MacNeil I, *An Introduction to The Law on Financial Investment*, Second Edition, Hart Publishing, UK, 2012 at 336.

THE ROLE OF NON-EXECUTIVE DIRECTORS

Undoubtedly, one of the main failures which significantly contributed to the global meltdown was the role of NEDs, who should have acted as counter-weight to executive directors.[11] For example, the Treasury Committee, in the UK, blamed, among others, NEDs who failed to act as restraining force on the executive members of the Northern Rock.[12]

Consequently, as correctly emphasised by Iain MacNeil,[13] the board of directors in public listed companies should be structured in a way that permits shareholders to control and monitor directors' decisions. Separation between management and decision control, as part of the decision-making process in large companies, is therefore paramount to maximise efficiency in managing the corporate body while controlling directors from acting in a way that places their personal interest before that of the company.[14] It is at precisely this stage that NEDs must step in, appreciate what is required and find the proper balance; failure to do so may result in the lack of internal control and monitoring, as recently decided in *Newcastle International Airport Ltd v Eversheds LLP*.[15]

But the foundation stone for finding a proper separation of power, yet maintaining the right managerial balance, is a system based on independence. This can only be achieved, as stated in the Cadbury Report in 1992, where the NEDs exercise independent judgement in dealing with strategy development, appointments and risk assessment. This report went on to emphasise that such independence is only guaranteed when it is exercised free from any business or other relationship which could materially interfere with it.[16] This aspect has been wisely illustrated in the following terms: 'having an account in the normal way with the bank of which you are a director is unlikely to affect your judgement, but if your fortunes were dependent on the bank, it would'.[17]

Despite the fact that the Companies Act 2006 does not define or

---

[11] Arora A, 'The Corporate Governance Failings in Financial Institutions and Directors' Legal Liability' (2011) *Comp Law*, 32(1), 3 at 5.

[12] Ibid at 5. See also House of Commons Treasury Committee, The Run of the Rock, 2008, at http://www.parliament. The-stationery-office.com/pa/cm200708/cmselect/cmtreasy/56/56i.pdf.

[13] MacNeil, op cit., at 338.

[14] Ibid., at 338.

[15] [2012] All ER (D) 20.

[16] The Financial Aspects of Corporate Governance, the Cadbury Report 1992, Recommendation 2.1 and 2.2 pp 57.

[17] Harvey N, 'Corporate Governance: The British Experience' (1995) *Int'l Bus L J* 947–55 at 950.

distinguish between executive and non-executive directors, nevertheless they have been defined as 'the custodians of the governance process' by the January 2003 Review of the Role and Effectiveness of Non-Executive Directors ('the Higgs Report'). It is, therefore, clear that NEDs do not have direct managerial functions since they are not involved in the day-to-day running of the business, so their main role is centred around ensuring transparency and accountability in the board's decisions, contributing to the leadership of the company,[18] acting as members of remuneration committees, contributing to the passing of resolutions where the board experiences deadlock situations, assessing the risk behind complex financial operations and keeping them informed as to the financial health of the company.[19] In order to achieve these goals and to compel them to some extent to do so, NEDs should be independent and be exposed to the same level of duties and liabilities as any other director of the company.[20]

Similarly, the OECD Principles of Corporate Governance 2004 not only focused on the issue of appointing sufficient NEDs, but also their capability of 'exercising *independent judgement* to tasks where there is a potential for conflict of interest'[21] (emphasis added). Therefore, independence seems to be paramount.

THE ROAD TO THE CORPORATE GOVERNANCE CODE 2010 AND THE UK STEWARDSHIP CODE 2010

As early as March 2009, the then Financial Services Authority (FSA),[22] intended to give a quick response to the possible causes of the crisis and identified possible solutions.

---

18 Arora, op cit., at 5.

19 A review of corporate governance in UK banks and other financial industry entities, (The Walker Review) Recommendations. July 2009,

20 *Equitable Life Assurance Society v Bowley and Others* [2003] EWCA 2263 at 41:

> the extent to which a non-executive director may reasonably rely on the executive directors and other professionals to perform their duties is one in which the law can fairly be said to be developing and is plainly 'fact sensitive'. It is plainly arguable, I think, that a company may reasonably at least look to non-executive directors for independence of judgment and supervision of the executive management.

21 OECD Principles of Corporate Governance 2004, at 25.

22 As from April 2013 the Financial Conduct Authority (FCA) has replaced the FSA.

The Turner Review, a regulatory response to the global banking crisis in March 2009, gave a clear indication that improving the effectiveness of internal risk management and firm governance was essential to identify and constrain excessive risk taking.[23] It went on to say:

> In broad terms, the role of the NED, under the leadership of the chairman, is: to ensure that there is an effective executive team in place; to participate actively in the decision-taking process of the board; and to exercise appropriate oversight over execution of the agreed strategy by the executive team.[24]

In other words, what this report suggested was that the days when NEDs could discharge their duties in a very convenient and relaxing way were evidently over. Therefore, the review unsurprisingly recommended improvements in the skill level and time commitment of NEDs.[25]

The government's response, following the collapse of some of the most representative financial institutions in the UK, was given by the Walker Review published in November 2009, which made two important suggestions as to the way financial institutions should be run. The first, was the introduction of a risk committee as an independent board that would monitor and assess the risk behind the decisions made by the board of directors and the new role that NEDs in financial institutions should play. Secondly, this new role would require putting an effective executive team in place, active participation in the decision-making process and exercising appropriate oversight over execution of the agreed strategy.[26]

This thorough analysis of corporate governance issues demonstrated that the crisis was the result of over-reliance on an inappropriate business model; management and control processes were insufficiently rigorous

---

23 Turner Review: A regulatory response to the global banking crisis, March 2009, 2.8 Risk management and governance: firm skills, processes and structures, at http://www.fsa.gov.uk/pubs/other/turner_review.pdf, at 92.

24 Walker Review, op cit., at 35, para 2.8

25

> The crisis has revealed the extreme complexity of large banking groups and the difficulties which nonexecutive directors (NEDs) face in understanding all dimensions of the risks being taken, within the time commitments typically required of NEDs. It has also raised questions about the degree of technical skill and experience required to perform risk committee functions, and whether existing bank boards have sufficient people with these technical skills. In addition it has demonstrated the vital importance of non-executive challenge to dominant chief executives pursuing aggressive growth strategies.

Turner Review, op cit., at 93.

26 Walker Review, op cit., Recommendation 23.

and there was defective diligence and judgement on acquisitions shortly before or during the crisis phase.[27] It also capitalised on the need to identify and ascertain not only the role but also the standard of the duties that NEDs need to comply with in order to control and effectively supervise the executive board.[28] For example, the review emphasised the need for banks, and other financial institutions' boards, to move from what it called 'accepted conventions' into a 'clearer expectation of behaviour involving greater readiness to test and challenge'.[29]

The most eloquent assessment of what needed to be done, is reproduced in the view by quoting the House of Lords Economic Affairs Committee in the following terms: 'Non-executive directors need experience at high level in business, public affairs and other relevant fields, the personal qualities to obtain clear and full answers from management, and the ability to understand the bank's businesses and the risks being undertaken.'[30]

Consequently the Walker Review contained several recommendations, of which Recommendation 6 seems to be of crucial importance:

> As part of their role as members of the unitary board of a BOFI, NEDs should be ready, able and encouraged to challenge and test proposals on strategy put forward by the executive. They should satisfy themselves that board discussion and decision-taking on risk matters is based on accurate and appropriately comprehensive information and draws, as far as they believe it to be relevant or necessary, on external analysis and input.[31]

After identifying the causes of the 2007 and 2008 financial crisis, which included lack of supervision and monitoring on the part of NEDs, the

---

27 Ibid.

28 The Walker Review quoted the former Combined Code in the following terms: 4.10 The role of the NED is described in the Combined Code in the following terms:

> As part of their role as members of a unitary board, non-executive directors should constructively challenge and help develop proposals on strategy. Non-executive directors should scrutinise the performance of management in meeting agreed goals and objectives and monitor the reporting of performance. They should satisfy themselves on the integrity of financial information and that financial controls and systems of risk management are robust and defensible. They are responsible for determining appropriate levels of remuneration of executive directors and have a prime role in appointing, and where necessary removing, executive directors, and in succession planning at 55.

29 Ibid., at 55–6.

30 Ibid.

31 Ibid.

Financial Reporting Council introduced two new codes, the Corporate Governance Code (CGC) 2010 and the Stewardship Code 2010. In line with the purpose of this chapter, let us concentrate on how these two pieces of legislation have impacted the role of NEDs.

The CGC correctly identified that: 'As part of their role as members of a unitary board, non-executive directors should constructively challenge and help develop proposals on strategy.'[32] The new NEDs' role will go beyond being mere spectators, so they will have to engage with the company in a way that guarantees the wellbeing of the corporate body. By reflection, the interest of shareholders, stakeholders and society at large will also be, to some extent, protected. One could suggest that including society at large among the protected parties is an exaggeration in the sense that NEDs do not owe specific duties to the outside world. In fact, in the UK both executive and non-executive directors owe their duties to the company itself and not to outsiders.[33] Nevertheless, the prominent role that banks play in society forces NEDs to exercise their role as custodians of consumers' rights. Consequently, the CGC emphasises that the role of NEDs encompasses, amongst other duties, the following:

- To guarantee the integrity of financial information;
- To guarantee that both the financial controls and systems of risk management are robust and defensible;
- To determine appropriate levels of remuneration of executive directors;
- A prime role in appointing and removing executive directors;
- A role in succession planning.[34]

Another important contribution of the CGC is to reinforce that NEDs must exercise independent judgement. This has been highlighted on several occasions in the CGC in the sense that that independence would help them to take objective decisions which ultimately benefit the corporate body. Independence is therefore guaranteed where NEDs completely detach from the executive directors and do not have anything to be grateful to them for. This point has already been identified as fact sensitive by Langley J in *Equitable Life Assurance Society v Bowley and others*:

> the extent to which a non-executive director may reasonable rely on the executive directors and other professionals to perform their duties is one in

32 Corporate Governance Code 2010. The Main Principles of the Code, at 6.

33 CA 2006, s. 170; *Percival v Wright* [1902] 2 Ch. 421 Ch D.

34 Corporate Governance Code 2010. A.4 Non-Executive Directors, Supporting Principle at p. 11.

> which the law can fairly be said to be developing and is plainly fact sensitive. It is plainly arguable, I think, that a company may reasonably at least look to non-executive directors for independence of judgment and supervision of the executive management.[35]

Three factors could adversely affect NEDs' independence, namely: appointment, personal interest and insurance. In regard to the appointment of NEDs, it is crystal clear that the executive board is largely involved with this, thus shareholders somehow play a secondary role. The risk is that 'owing their appointment to their friends and their cosy relationship with the executives, they are unlikely to rock the boat or even ask challenging questions'.[36]

Personal interests in corporate affairs is to some extent detrimental as well. A recent case in the UK can illustrate the point. In *Bonham Carter v Situ Ventures Ltd*[37] a share agreement was entered into by existing shareholders and a third party. The agreement provided that the sellers, former shareholders of the company, would be entitled to remain as non-executive directors of the company for as long as the balance was paid in full by the third party. Although the balance was paid and the non-executive directors resigned before the conclusion of the trial, the Court of Appeal was required, for defence costs purpose, to interpret the agreement in relation to the power of the buyer to remove from office the non-executive directors. The outcome was, that in construing the real meaning of the contractual clause, the buyer had the right to remove the non-executive directors, the appeal was, therefore, allowed.

The facts of the case show that both parties had a clear interest in keeping former shareholders as non-executives. The seller will hope to keep them in power somehow until the balance is paid and the buyer would benefit from the now NEDs' expertise in running the business. The question to ask is: was the independence of the NEDs guaranteed? Were NEDs more interested in recovering the balance of the share purchase agreement than in the wellbeing of the company? Or both?

Arguably, NEDs will put (and cannot be blamed for doing it) their personal interest first, consequently the objectivity expected of them is questionable.

The third factor is professional insurance, and more specifically Directors' and Officers' Liability insurance (D&O). The Companies Act

---

[35] [2003] EWCA 2263 at 41.

[36] Kiarie S, 'Non-Executive Directors in UK Listed Companies: are they effective?' (2007) *I.C.C.L.R* 18(1) 17, 23 at 19.

[37] [2013] EWCA Civ 47.

2006, section 233 establishes: 'Section 232(2) does not prevent a company from purchasing and maintaining for a director of the company, or of an associated company, insurance against any such liability as is mentioned in that subsection.' It has, therefore, become common practice to arrange for D&O cover to protect not only company directors but the company itself.

Some EU countries have a two-tier board structure, namely executive and supervisory, Germany and France are two clear examples.[38] This means that the duties and liabilities of both the executive and supervisory board are well defined, D&O carriers should consider this and bear in mind that the independence of the members of the supervisory board is only guaranteed when they are insured separately, and not with either the company or executive directors. Nevertheless, the London market does not operate in this way so it is common practice to provide cover for the executive, and for non-executive directors and the company itself.

The duty of skill, care and diligence[39] owed by directors to the company, imposes a double test, based on the fact NEDs do not manage the company on a day-to-day basis, nevertheless, it has been raised in relation to risk management, supervision and control. In attempting an early conclusion, insuring NEDs, executives and the company under the same policy, would affect independence of judgement that NEDs should have and would also create the burden to prove, in order to establish liability, a standard of care which does not identically apply to executive directors. In other words, it is believed that NEDs would be more likely to overlook certain decisions or even to relax their supervisory role, if the company arranges and pays for insurance cover.[40]

The Stewardship Code 2010, on the other hand, albeit being designed for the institutional investor in listed companies, has further developed the shareholders' duty to cooperate with the chairman as part of their ongoing monitoring of company's affairs. Principle 3: Monitoring of Companies requires shareholders to meet with the chairman on a periodical basis and not only when they have concerns and attend the general meeting as often as possible. Most importantly, institutional investors have the right

---

[38] This is a choice that EU members may have under art 38 of the EC Council Regulation No 21/572001 which came into force in August 2004. The one-tier board would be called the 'administrative organ' and the second-tier board the 'supervisory and management organ'.

[39] See below Non-Executive Directors Duty of Skill, Care and Diligence.

[40] For better analysis of the need of independent D&O cover see: Hendricks M & Fassbach B, *The German Two-Tier Corporate Board Structure and its Impact on D&O Insurance Cover*, May 2013, in www.dandodiary.com.

to consider and assess the company's explanations for departure from the CGC[41] and advise where they do not accept its position. It seems now that shareholders share with NED's the supervisory role. NEDs are therefore obliged, as part of their monitoring role, to liaise with institutional shareholders as part of their new role: 'Custodians of the Corporate Body Wellbeing'.

NON-EXECUTIVE DIRECTORS' DUTY OF SKILL, CARE AND DILIGENCE

The 2007 and 2008 financial crisis certainly forced the reshaping of the standard of care, skill and diligence required from those who accept the supervisory role of being NEDs. Despite the fact that NEDs owe to the company the same duties as executive ones, this motivated early suggestions that their liability should be capped and provide them with further protection against liabilities that may arise in discharging their board responsibilities. However, this proposition has been rejected.[42]

As suggested earlier, the duty owed by directors to the company imposes a double test, based on the fact NEDs do not manage the company on a day-to-day basis, hence it cannot and should not be the same test applied to executive directors. In fact, without being so demanding, the standard of NEDs' duty has been raised in relation to risk management, supervision and control.

---

[41] The Corporate Governance Code 2010 is not of mandatory implementation. However, companies that opt out of it must explain their reasons for not following its guidance rules.

[42] Walker Review, Mitigation of NEDs Liability:

> 2.21 This question and associated concern is based in particular on the view that the personal liability faced by directors is not dependably mitigated by directors and officers (D&O) insurance policies and that, where legal proceedings taken against an individual director are successful, the ultimate financial liability of the individual can be wholly disproportionate to the fees paid for the board role. Such concern has led to a proposition that the liability of the individual director should be capped . . .
> 2.22 . . . Such concerns may deter the interest of some talented candidates for BOFI board positions. But alongside the prospectively enhanced rewards for BOFI board membership, NEDs have major duties to discharge and it does not in this environment seem appropriate that they should enjoy further protection against challenge beyond the mitigation provided through normal D&O insurance policies. The conclusion of this Review is against the capping proposition at 40–41.

In 2004 the OECD expressed the view that the key responsibilities of non-executive directors were:

1. Ensuring the integrity of financial and non-financial reporting.
2. Review of related party transactions.
3. Nomination of board members and key executives.
4. Board Remuneration.[43]

Arguably, as highlighted by the OECD report, NEDs' knowledge and expertise can reassure that the interest of 'market participants' is duly preserved,[44] since they should act as the catalyst between the decisions of the executive committee and the impact that these decisions could make on shareholders, stakeholders and to some extent, society at large. It is also suggested that shareholders should have a direct role to play in nominating and appointing NEDs who are expected to perform specific activities such as detecting potential conflicts of interest[45] at board level or between boards where the corporate structure is so complex as to involve a number of corporate bodies within a group. Consequently, NEDs should have access to crucial information and have the opportunity to interact with relevant managers, company secretaries, auditors and even request and seek independent external advice, at the expense of the company, to understand and discharge their duties to the company effectively.[46]

In line with the OECD principles of corporate governance, the Basel Committee on Banking Supervision in October 2010 published the Principles for Enhancing Corporate Governance, which purpose it to build on what OECD proposed in 2004.

The overview of bank corporate governance has been correctly identified in the following terms:

> Effective corporate governance practices are essential to achieving and maintaining public trust and confidence in the banking system, which are critical to the proper functioning of the banking sector and economy as a whole. Poor corporate governance can contribute to bank failures, which can in turn pose significant public costs and consequences due to their potential impact on any applicable deposit insurance system and the possibility of broader macroeconomic implications, such as contagion risk and impact on payment systems.[47]

---

43 OECD, Principles of Corporate Governance, 2004, at 65.

44 Ibid.

45 Ibid.

46 Ibid., at 66.

47 Basel Committee on Banking Supervision, *Principles for Enhancing Corporate Governance*, October 2010, at 6.

The Basel Committee Principles on Banking Supervision, in line with its long-standing commitment to promote sound corporate governance practices, published in October 2010 guidelines regarding the way in which the board, including NEDs, of financial institutions should be structured, controlled and managed. The Basel Committee recognises that the only real possibility for the board of directors in financial institutions to succeed is by being supported by 'competent, robust and independent risk and control functions for which the board provides effective oversight'.[48]

It also recognizes that countries have adopted either the two-tier or one-tier structures in regard to board composition and supervision. However, it does not encourage the adoption of a specific model but the implementation of an efficient system of control and balance.[49]

Alongside reiterating that trust and confidence are essential to the functioning of the banking sector, it is the author's view that the committee has formulated crucial guidelines as to the role, duties and liabilities which NEDs should have to undertake. For example, bearing in mind the complexity of harmonising the principles underpinning extra-contractual liability,[50] the committee has suggested that the duty of care and loyalty, owed by members of the board to the company, must be governed under national laws. The point is very important indeed and has had consequences in the way in which directors' liabilities are established. Let us visualise for a moment a company with subsidiaries in countries which recognise that directors owe duties to the company, but assess the liability on different grounds, or indeed in a way not recognised by the law applicable to the parent company. This lack of harmonisation does more harm than good if the idea is to achieve a sound and effective system of banking corporate governance.

More specifically, and in respect of the role that NEDs should play, the committee requires boards to have adequate compositions in which the independence of NEDs is guaranteed. In fact, according to the report, a significant number of banks appoint NEDs as chairman of the executive committee. Ultimately, NEDs' help in achieving the optimum blend of

48 Ibid., at 2.

49 Ibid., at 5.

50 Harmonising for example, principles of extra-contractual liability or *delict*, proper of civil law legal systems with the law of torts mainly recognised in common law legal systems. Additionally, concepts like fiduciary duties from which the duty not to conflict with the interest of the company and the conflict of interest rule, stem from the fact that directors stand in a fiduciary position in regard to the company. However, fiduciary duties as a concept is not recognised in civil law legal systems.

and experience, proper of a successful financial institution, is crucial. In the same way, the committee also proposes that the audit committee should have sufficient NEDs and the latter should meet regularly with the chief risk officer of the company.

The position in the UK, which has adopted a one-tier system in which the board of the company is divided between executive and non-executive directors, is to some extent complicated. The fact that the Companies Act 2006 does not distinguish between executive and non-executive imposes upon them the same duties and liabilities, making it a difficult task to identify what is the standard of care required from NEDs in performing their duties.

Additionally, according to section 170, directors' duties are owed to the company and not to outsiders including shareholders, which limits the possibility of a director incurring liability, for breach of duty, to a third party. In *Williams v Natural Life Health Food Ltd*,[51] the House of Lords made it clear that directors owe duties to the company, and in order for a third party to make them accountable, the third party must prove that the directors have assumed certain personal responsibility to the third party. In other words, proving the assumption of responsibility creates the duty, which, once breached, could lead to a personal claim against directors. The issue is important in the sense that if it is unlikely for an executive director to incur personal liability to an outsider, the likelihood of a non-executive director incurring that liability is more than remote. However, courts have found it easier to find directors criminally liable when the director himself has been the architect of the fraud.[52]

More crucially still, the UK corporate law system does not allow for shareholders to claim against directors for reflective loss[53] on the grounds that directors' duties are owed to the company and not to shareholders individually. Consequently, it is impossible to sue as member of a class or class action. This does not mean that shareholders' interest is, or should be, totally disregarded; on the contrary section 172 of the UK Companies Act 2006 establishes:

> (1) A director of a company must act in the way he considers, in good faith, would be most likely to promote the success of the company for the benefit of its members as a whole . . .
>
> . . .
>
> (f) the need to act fairly as between members of the company.

---

[51] [1998] 2 All ER 577.

[52] *Standard Chartered Bank v Pakistan National Shipping Corporation* (No 2) [2003] 1 AC 959 (HL) and *Stone & Rolls (In Liquidation) v Moore Stephens* [2009] 2 BCLC 563 (HL0).

[53] *Prudential Assurance v Newman Industries* [2003] 3 WLR 543.

(2) Where or to the extent that the purposes of the company consist of or include purposes other than the benefit of its members, subsection (1) has effect as if the reference to promoting the success of the company for the benefit of its members were to achieving those purposes.[54]

To some extent the Companies Act 2006 seems to work in line with what has been recommended by the Basel Committee on Banking Supervision when it stated that: 'In discharging these responsibilities, the board, *as a whole*, should take into account the legitimate interest of shareholders, depositors and other relevant stakeholders'[55] (emphasis added); and also recommended by the OECD by suggesting that the directors' duty of loyalty embraces the duty 'to act in the interest of the company and shareholders'.[56]

NON-EXECUTIVE DIRECTORS' STANDARD OF CARE

The relationship that exists between NEDs and the company, even though it is fundamental for the wellbeing of the corporate body, is not close enough to give NEDs sufficient knowledge of the internal operation as to plans and/or get involved in self-dealing with the company. Consequently, claims against NEDs are more likely to find their roots in allegations concerning the breach of the duty of skill, care and diligence rather than

---

[54] CA 2006, s 172

and in doing so have regard (amongst other matters) to–
- (a) the likely consequences of any decision in the long term,
- (b) the interests of the company's employees,
- (c) the need to foster the company's business relationships with suppliers, customers and others,
- (d) the impact of the company's operations on the community and the environment,
- (e) the desirability of the company maintaining a reputation for high standards of business conduct, and . . .

(3) The duty imposed by this section has effect subject to any enactment or rule of law requiring directors, in certain circumstances, to consider or act in the interests of creditors of the company.

[55] BCBS see also Financial Reporting Council, *Guidance on Board Effectiveness*, March 2011, para 1.23. 'Non-executive directors should take into account the views of shareholders and other stakeholders, because these views may provide different perspectives on the company and its performance.' The whole report could be access at http://frc.org.uk/Our-Work/Publications/Corporate-Governance/Guidance-on-Board-Effectiveness.pdf.

[56] OECD op cit., at 24.

breaches of the fiduciary duties[57] of good faith and loyalty.[58] Additionally, liabilities following the breach of financial regulation rules, namely, disclosure, prospectuses, listing particulars and the like, are well beyond the role that NEDs play in the public companies so the possibility of incurring liability on these grounds is also very unlikely.[59] This last argument forces legislators to concentrate on the area in which liabilities may arise: negligence.

The UK Companies Act 2006, section 174 establishes:

> Duty to exercise reasonable care, skill and diligence
>
> (1) a director of a company must exercise reasonable care, skill and diligence.
> (2) This means the care, skill and diligence that would be exercised by a reasonably diligent person with–
> (a) the general knowledge, skill and experience that may reasonably be expected of a person carrying out the functions carried out by the director in relation to the company, and
> (b) the general knowledge, skill and experience that the director has.

Clearly the Companies Act 2006 distinguishes between two different limbs, namely one objective measure to assess the duty of care (what a reasonable person would do in that position); and one subjective to assess the duty of skill to which the standard is that of what a reasonable person with that level of skills, knowledge, salary and social responsibility (in the banking sector) would do.[60] The duty of care and skill has therefore moved from the less demanding test set out in *Re City Equitable Fire Insurance*[61] to a more demanding one whose origins could be said to be found in the *Barings (5)*[62] and is now the basis of section 174 of the Companies Act 2006.

---

[57] *Burns v Financial Conduct Authority* 2013 WL 2628769.

[58] Black B, Cheffins B, Klausner M and Witney S, 'In the Line of Fire', [2006] *I.C.C.L.R.* 17(4) 117–19.

[59] Ibid.

[60] Paolini A, '*Lending Sub-Prime and Advising on Financial Investments from a D & O Insurance Perspective*', [2012] *J.B.L* 432–48 at 435.

[61] [1925] Ch. 407 CA.

[62] [2000] 1 BCLC 523 . . . at 535:

> (i) Directors have, both collectively and individually, a continuing duty to acquire and maintain a sufficient knowledge and understanding of the company's business to enable them properly to discharge their duties as directors.
> (ii) Whilst directors are entitled (subject to the articles of association of the company) to delegate particular functions to those below them in the management chain, and to trust their competence and integrity to a reasonable extent,

Earlier decisions like the one in *Dorchester Finance Co Ltd v Stebbing*[63] had already confirmed that NEDs could be liable on the same grounds as executive directors are. Let us focus on a body of decisions which in one way or another have tested NEDs' duties and liabilities.

In *Lexi Holdings Plc (In Administration) v Luqman*[64] the Court of Appeal correctly decided that breaching the duty of care, on the part of NEDs, could be the causative link between the breach and the loss sustained by the company. Failing to properly supervise the board of directors is a negligent act, the occurrence of which may have precluded the company from taking early measures to prevent the misappropriation or reduction of the company's money. Furthermore, it is not a defence for NEDs to claim their lack of direct involvement with the day-to-day management of the company. On the contrary, their supervisory role entails the duty to be familiar with the business activities of the company so as to discover flaws that need immediate action.[65] In other words, as correctly pointed out by the Financial Reporting Council in March 2009, NEDs have 'a responsibility to uphold high standards of integrity and probity. They should support the chairman and executive directors in instilling the appropriate culture, values, and behaviours in the boardroom and beyond'.[66]

In *Equitable Life Assurance Society v Bowley*[67] it was decided that non-executive directors cannot even count on the fact that they have delegated

---

the exercise of the power of delegation does not absolve a director from the duty to supervise the discharge of the delegated functions.
(iii) No rule of universal application can be formulated as to the duty referred to in (ii) above. The extent of the duty, and the question whether it has been discharged, must depend on the facts of each particular case, including the director's role in the management of the company.

63 [1989] B.C.L.C 498.

64 [2009] EWCA Civ 117.

65 Ji Lian Yap, 'Hear no evil, see no evil, speak no evil: the total inactivity of non-executive directors', (2009) *I.C.C.L.R.* 20(11), 412–14 at 413:

> It is thus clear that non-executive directors must not allow themselves to be fooled by other directors of the company, as that in itself would constitute a breach of duty. Directors cannot turn a blind eye to the wrongdoings of the other directors of the company. They must be neither credulous nor gullible, and must instead be vigilant in examining the company's affairs. This is in line with the monitoring role envisaged for non-executive directors.

66 Financial Reporting Council, op cit., para 1.21. The whole report could be access at http://frc.org.uk/Our-Work/Publications/Corporate-Governance/Guidance-on-Board-Effectiveness.pdf.

67 [2003] EWHC 2263 (Comm).

and relied on executive directors to perform their duties in the most efficient way since the role of NEDs is actually to monitor and supervise the executive board.

In *Australian Securities and Investment Commission v Healey*,[68] arguably, the standard of care and skill expected from NEDs was very high and the author endorses this view. In this case, the NEDs fell below the standard of care and skill by not spotting the inaccuracy of the financial statements of the company. The court emphasised that NEDs should be able to understand, regardless how complex it is, the reports which by statute they are supposed to approve. In other words, being a NED entails the continuous duty to familiarise and understand the nature of the business of the company so he/she will be able to discover easily and /or find obvious financial inaccuracies in the company's accounts.

In *Secretary of State for Trade and Industry v Swan and others*[69] the High Court correctly assessed the level of skills and care expected of a NED who was a very experienced accountant and had held several board positions including as a non-executive for a number of companies. The case relates to the malpractice of using 'cheque kiting' to generate fictitious funds to cover for short-term cash flow problems.[70] Cheque kiting 'is the utilisation by the kiter of the period taken by the bank to clear a cheque so as to obtain a fictional increase in the balance of the payee's account before the cheque is cleared and its amount is deduced from the payer's account'.[71]

The NED knew about the cheque kiting policy, following a serious whistle-blowing incident, and failed to launch a proper investigation as to stop and/or prevent the company's fictitious financial health. As result, Mr Justice Etherton was of the view that the NED did not meet the standard of conduct which is expected from somebody in that position and with the level of experience that he had and ordered his disqualification for unfitness,[72] at the lowest of the categories established in *Re Sevenoaks Stationers Ltd*.[73]

Disqualification was also imposed on directors in the landmark Australian case of *Australian Securities and Investments Commission v Meredith Hellicar and Others*[74] where the High Court of Australia,

---

68 [2011] FCA 717.
69 [2005] EWHC 603 (Ch).
70 Ibid., at para 14.
71 Ibid., at para 13.
72 Company Directors Disqualification Act 1986, s 6.
73 [1991] Ch 164.
74 [2012] HCA 17.

overruling the decision of the Court of Appeal and confirming the decision reached by the Supreme Court of New South Wales, (the trial court), decided that seven NEDs were found in breach of the duty of care and diligence under section 180(1) of the Corporations Act 2001, by failing to reasonably, carefully and diligently approve a document, which happened to be misleading and contained inaccurate information as to the adequacy of a fund set up to meet asbestos claims. In fact, a company was created within the corporate group to meet demands arising out of asbestos claims and a fund was established to meet these demands. In reality, the so-called fund was insufficient to meet the claims, falling short by several millions. NEDs were negligent in approving the disclosure of misleading information regarding the compensation fund. Consequently, NEDs were fined and disqualified. This decision, the most important for the purpose of this chapter, confirms once more, that the days when NEDs could discharge their duties in a very relaxed way are over. The role embraces the utmost vigilance and supervision and goes as far as guaranteeing employees within a corporate group, that all measures have been taken, including the setting up of corporate funds, to alleviate and or compensate employees' potential claims. Consequently, NEDs role could go beyond the well-being of the corporate body as to include responsibility for social welfare.

Should we in principle agree that NEDs could play a significant part in guaranteeing social welfare, it is paramount to discuss if the standard of the duty of skill and care is raised proportionally to the nature, size and complexity of the corporate body. Additionally, we must discuss if that standard should be even higher when the company's main business is the provision of financial services, whose collapse would dramatically impact upon society at large.

Banks provide the liquidity needed to fuel economic growth and should act as custodians of clients' money. It is not a mystery that banks make money with customers' money so they need to guarantee some consumer protection. Banks are not charities and work for profit and it is for directors to maximise profits and materialise them into dividends for the benefit of shareholders. However, banks play a prominent role in society, in the sense that banks' insolvency or inability to provide liquidity to the market will cause a damaging effect going well beyond corporate investors and creditors. NEDs in financial institutions are therefore commissioned to help,[75] control, and supervise the executive board whose acts or omissions could lead to social financial catastrophes. Consequently, the law

[75] Financial Reporting Council, op cit., para 1.21: 'Non-executive directors have a responsibility to uphold high standards of integrity and probity. They

has been gradually developing in a way that imposes upon NEDs very high standards of care, skill and diligence.[76] This standard could only be achieved by implementing a very rigorous system whereby NEDs are trained and devote enough time to discharging their duties in accordance with a high professional standard of care.

Consequently, NEDs need to understand the corporate body and how it is organised, and should be provided with appropriate training.[77] NEDs should also collectively have the experience and competence required to properly monitor and supervise the company's business.[78] In order to successfully discharge their duties, NEDs should directly participate in the process of approval of new financial products;[79] processes which banks should already have.[80] The boards, including NEDs, should know and understand the operational structure and the risks behind financial ventures,[81] the duty could go as far as to understand the structure of a Special Purpose Vehicle (SPV) formed with the objective of achieving specific financial goals, yet this can only be achieved if NEDs act on an informed and prudent basis[82] and approach the affairs

---

should support the chairman and executive directors in instilling the appropriate culture, values and behaviours in the boardroom and beyond.'

76 As highlighted in the cases mentioned above.

77 Financial Reporting Council, op cit., para 1.18:

> A non-executive director should, on appointment, devote time to a comprehensive, formal and tailored induction which should extend beyond the boardroom. Initiatives such as partnering a non-executive director with an executive board member may speed up the process of him or her acquiring an understanding of the main areas of business activity, especially areas involving significant risk. The director should expect to visit, and talk with, senior and middle managers in these areas.

78 Ellery D, 'Supporting Non-Executive Directors', (2012) 36 *CSR* 18,137.

79 Financial Reporting Council, op cit., para 1.19:

> Non-executive directors should devote time to developing and refreshing their knowledge and skills, including those of communication, to ensure that they continue to make a positive contribution to the board. Being well-informed about the company, and having a strong command of the issues relevant to the business, will generate the respect of the other directors.

80 Basel Committee on Banking Supervision, op cit., at 21, para 88.

81 Ibid., Principle 12.

82 Financial Reporting Council, op cit., para 1.22:

> Non-executive directors should insist on receiving high-quality information sufficiently in advance so that there can be thorough consideration of the issues prior to, and informed debate and challenge at, board meetings. High-quality

of the company in the same way a prudent man would approach their own affairs.[83]

It will not be a defence for NEDs to suggest that they relied on the executive board and have no grounds to question its integrity and competence. On the contrary, NEDs should be efficient,[84] suspicious and more than vigilant to guarantee the soundness of the financial institution. A quotation from *Australian Securities and Investment Commission v Healey* may illustrate the point:

> Directors cannot substitute reliance upon the advice of management for their own attention and examination of an important matter that falls specifically within the board's responsibilities as with the reporting obligations. The Act places upon the board and each director the specific task of approving the financial statements. Consequently, each member of the board was charged with the responsibility of attending to and focusing on these accounts and, under these circumstances, could not delegate or 'abdicate' that responsibility to others.[85]

The standard is so high that early suggestions[86] that the business judgement rule[87] may mitigate this standard of duty have recently been challenged. The point at issue is whether the business judgement rule applies to NEDs in banks or is it the case that that NEDs are subject to a different and higher standard or care. This last point has recently been considered

---

information is that which is appropriate for making decisions on the issue at hand – it should be accurate, clear, comprehensive, up-to-date and timely; contain a summary of the contents of any paper; and inform the director of what is expected of him or her on that issue.

[83] OECD op cit., at 59.
[84] Financial Reporting Council, op cit., para 1.20:

> Non-executive directors need to make sufficient time available to discharge their responsibilities effectively. The letter of appointment should state the minimum time that the non-executive director will be required to spend on the company's business, and seek the individual's confirmation that he or she can devote that amount of time to the role, consistent with other commitments. The letter should also indicate the possibility of additional time commitment when the company is undergoing a period of particularly increased activity, such as an acquisition or takeover, or as a result of some major difficulty with one or more of its operations.

[85] *Asic v Healey* [2011] FCA 717 at 175.
[86] OECD op cit., at p. 59.
[87] Ibid., 'The duty of care does not extend to errors of business judgement so long as board members are not grossly negligent and a decision is made with due diligence . . .'

in the American case *FDIC v R Charles Loudermilk*,[88] where Judge Thrash cleverly concluded that bank directors and officers are different than those of ordinary business, therefore being subject to a different high standard in which the business judgement rule cannot be invoked to escape liability. He went on to suggest that there is every reason to treat bank officers and directors differently from general corporate officers and directors,[89] and this is closely connected with the fact it is society at large which suffers the consequences of bank failures, forcing government and central banks to come to the rescue, so it is ultimately the tax payer who bears the risk. On the contrary, in other business activities not associated with the business of banking, it is the shareholders who bear the risk so the impact is not on the society at large.[90] Even it has been suggested that . . .

> The very long judgement in Healey[91]. . . gives further testimony to the increased professionalism required of directors of public companies whether they are executive or non-executive. This is a long way from the cult of gifted amateur or amiable lunatic who was once so readily accepted even in large companies.[92]

---

88 Case 1:12-cv-04156-TWT, Thomas W. Thrash, JR. United States District Judge, in The United States Distict Court for The Northern District of Georgia Atlanta Division at p 10. 25/11/ 13

89 LaCroix K, *Are Bank Directors and Officers Entitled to Less Business Judgment Rule Protection Than Other Corporate Directors and Officers?*, December 3 2013, at www.dandodiary.com. Federal Deposit Insurance Corporation as receiver for The Buckhead Community Bank v R. Charles Loudermilk, SR., et al. Case 1:12-cv-04156-TWT, Thomas W. Thrash Jr. United States District Judge, in The United States Distict Court for The Northern District of Georgia Atlanta Division at p 10. 25/11/ 13:

> There is every reason to treat bank officers and directors differently from general corporate officers and directors. In general, when a business corporation succeeds or fails, its stockbrokers bear the gains and losses. The business judgment rule is primarily applied in Georgia *because* 'the right to control the affairs of a corporation is vested by law in its stockholders – those whose pecuniary gain is dependent upon its successful management'. (citation omitted). But when a bank, instead of a business corporation fails, the FDIC and ultimately the taxpayer bear the pecuniary loss. The lack of care of the officers and directors can lead to bank closures which echo throughout the local and national economy. To some extent, the failure of bank officers and directors to exercise ordinary care led to the very financial crisis that continues to affect the national economy. By all accounts, the loose lending practices alleged by the FDIC in this case were rampant within Georgia's community banks.

90 LaCroix, op cit.

91 *Asic v Healey* [2011] FCA 717.

92 Ashe M, *Reasonable Care, Skill and Diligence*, Comp. Law. 2012, 33(2), 33–4.

CONCLUSIONS

The need for efficient NEDs is paramount if a financial institution purports to build a solid and trustworthy business. It is essential for banks to retain consumers' and investors' trust and confidence in the financial system, and one way to achieve this is by implementing a better and more efficient board structure, where the duties of both executive and non-executive directors are not only distinguished but thoroughly followed.

NEDs are appointed with a single objective in mind, which is guaranteeing that executive directors follow the rules for the sake of the company (bank) and everybody who depends on its business follows the fortunes of corporate decisions. Thus, NEDs are vitally needed for the wellbeing of both national and international banking.

The non-executive position comes with some concerns and difficulties that existing and/or prospective candidates may like to consider. First, it is well established that NEDs owe their duties to the corporate body and not to outsiders, nevertheless, the way in which the body of recent judicial decisions is developing, suggests that this approach is changing, in the sense that by guaranteeing the soundness of the corporate body, social welfare is protected.

Secondly, and regardless of the reality that the UK adopts a one or two-tier corporate body structure, there exists the need to clearly identify the scope of NEDs' duties as separate from executives. The UK Companies Act 2006 does not distinguish between executive's duties and non-executive's duties, hence it is probably time to suggest that this needs some consideration and revision. Harmonising banking corporate governance, especially for banks that offer services in more than one jurisdiction, will result in better and more reliable services. Banks as much as other corporate bodies may overcome the burdensome task of dealing, for example, with different standards of the duty of care or duties and liabilities not recognised by the UK legal system.

Third, the standard of care, skill, and diligence required from NEDs has been raised and will continue to be so. The body of judicial decisions considered in this chapter suggest so. NEDs should understand that what is now required from them, as members of the board in financial institutions, is not less than utmost diligence. The business judgement rule which effectively works for executive directors in jurisdictions like the US, may no longer be of assistance for NEDs. Efficiency in discharging office starts by understanding the business structure and devoting enough time to their role.

Lastly, everything which has been covered in this short piece of research would make no sense if NEDs fail to exercise their judgement with absolute independence and objectivity. They should not have personal interest (including insurance) in the company nor close business relations with members of the executive board.

Undoubtedly, careful and skilful NEDs are very much needed in financial institutions, and the better NEDs are, the more financially sound banks would be. However, do not forget that being a NED is a very serious business.

13. The relationship between investors and corporations after the financial crisis

*Anita Anand**

> The most advanced justice system in the world is a failure if it does not provide justice to the people it is meant to serve. Access to justice is therefore critical. Unfortunately, many Canadian men and women find themselves unable, mainly for financial reasons, to access the Canadian justice system. . .Their options are grim: use up the family assets in litigation; become their own lawyers; or give up.
>
> Chief Justice Beverley McLachlin, Supreme Court of Canada[1]

1. INTRODUCTION

Investors are consumers. They purchase a good called a 'security' in a market. Although the security carries value or potential value, it is intangible. The consumer may never see evidence of the security itself, especially if he or she executes the purchase through a dealer or other intermediary. Nevertheless, this consumer has at least one purpose in mind, to turn a purchase into a profitable investment. When numerous consumers purchase and sell such securities, a capital market is born.

In Canada, investing is a widespread phenomenon. Approximately 50 per cent of all working Canadians are directly or indirectly invested in the securities market (IIAC, 2007)[2] and 55 per cent of Canadians own securities outside a retirement savings plan (such as a company-managed

* The author extends her appreciation to Grant Bishop, Vlad Calina and Parsa Pezeshki for very helpful research assistance.

1 Beverley McLachlin, 'The Challenges We Face: Remarks of the Right Honourable Beverley McLachlin, P.C.' (Presented at the Empire Club of Canada, Toronto, 8 March 2007) <http://www.scc-csc.gc.ca/court-cour/judges-juges/spe-dis/bm-2007-03-08-eng.aspx> accessed 16 August 2014.

2 The Investment Industry Association of Canada (IIAC) is a national self-regulatory body of the Canadian securities industry. Investment Industry

pension plan, RRSP or RRIF (CSA, 2012)).[3] In the United States (US), about 49.9 per cent of all family-owned securities in 2010 are invested in similar retirements savings plans.[4] In continental Europe, the proportion of households estimated to be investing in the stock market ranges from 15 to 20 per cent (Guiso et al, 2002). Similar proportions of stock market participation exist across other developed market economies.[5]

The scale of investment participation and its attendant risks compel us to consider the legal remedies available to investors. What remedies should investors have when a public corporation violates the law – be it securities law, corporate law or criminal law? Currently, the scheme of remedies available to investors is broader on the private than on the public side. Wronged investors have more options for initiating private actions than even the securities regulator. This imbalance has the effect of favouring plaintiffs with deep pockets and those who are able to undertake the lengthy process involved in private litigation. Investors who rely on public remedies are unlikely to see their investment returned; public remedies usually have no provision for restitution for injured investors and regulators may not exercize powers of restitution even when they have them.

This chapter argues in favour of a remedy that ensures that investors are paid back a percentage of any amounts obtained by the regulator as a result of disgorgement of funds from the defendant. The argument counters the views of traditional law and economics scholars (e.g. Easterbrook and Fischel, 1985) who argue that investors should not be compensated for securities fraud. They contend that active investors with diversified portfolios will have their losses arising from fraud netted out against their legitimate gains. But if we accept that some

Association of Canada, 'Representing Canada's Investment Professionals' <http://www.iiac.ca/welcome-to-iiac/about-us/who-we-are/> accessed 16 August 2014.

[3] In May 2012, the Canadian Securities Administrations (CSA) engaged Innovative Research Group to conduct an in-depth national survey to gauge Canadians' investment knowledge and behaviour, finding that 55% manage their investment portfolios, where 21%, or 38% of the 55%, are active investors while 34%, or 62% of the 55%, are passive. Innovative Research Group, '2012 CSA Investor Index' (16 October 2012), 11 <http://www.securities-administrators.ca/uploadedFiles/General/pdfs/2012%20CSA%20investor%20Index%20-%20Public%20Report%20FINAL_EN.pdf> accessed 10 January 2013.

[4] The SCF Chartbook published by the Federal Reserve describes the trajectory of US family stock holdings. Federal Reserve, *SCF Chartbook*, 506 <http://www.federalreserve.gov/econresdata/scf/files/2010_SCF_Chartbook.pdf> accessed 10 January 2013.

[5] Norway has 0.93 million (21%) households investing in the stock market, Denmark 1.2 million (23%), Japan 36.8 million (29%), UK 17.7 million (30%) and Australia 7.75 million (41%).

investors' portfolios are not diversified, we may more readily accept an argument in favour of a restitutionary right for investors. Egregious conduct is more likely to be efficiently deterred if third-party regulators set monetary penalties at an amount that allows investors to receive restitution.

To be clear, this chapter does not deny the importance of 'buyer beware' and it does not relate only to cases of fraud. Rather, it addresses the following question: when an investor is wronged for breach of fiduciary duty or other violations of corporate or securities law, what remedies should he or she have? Part 2 reviews the law relating to private remedies, focusing on remedies for breach of fiduciary duty, before turning to examine public remedies. Part 3 then focuses on the relative efficacy of private versus public remedies and the importance of the latter in the overall remedial regime available to investors. Part 4 concludes.

Any discussion regarding remedies for corporate malfeasance should be placed in the context of the 'nexus of contracts' conception of the corporation as being an entity comprised of many contracts with various stakeholders (Jensen and Meckling, 1976). The nexus of contracts idea, however, is not determinative with respect to remedies. That is, the remedies to which stakeholders are entitled tend to be found in common law or in statutes rather than in their individual contracts with the corporation. The strange fact is that a mere violation of one's fiduciary duty does not automatically entitle those who bear the consequence of this violation to a remedy. In many cases, the remedies are difficult, not to mention expensive to pursue, as will be discussed below.

2. PRIVATE AND PUBLIC REMEDIES

Shareholders have certain remedies available when corporations or their boards of directors violate the law. 'Private remedies' refer to the ability of individual litigants to bring suit on their own against the corporation or its members, such as its directors and officers. 'Public remedies' involve a third party, usually a governmental body or regulator, that brings suit in the public interest for the alleged wrong.[6] Thus, private remedies are personal whereas public remedies have a societal element. These two types of remedies will be discussed in turn, using Canadian and UK law as the basis for the discussion.

---

[6] The 'public interest' is not a well-defined term. See e.g., Securities Act (Ontario), RSO 1990 c S5 (as am) [OSA], s 127.

(a) Private Remedies

Private remedies for investors span various areas of law, particularly securities regulation and corporate law. The main securities law remedy is civil liability for misrepresentation in a prospectus or continuous disclosure document. In Canada, this remedy exists in statute and is less onerous to prove than the similar right that exists in tort at common law; the plaintiff does not need to prove reliance because the statute contains a 'deemed reliance' provision.[7] The civil remedy in securities law is rarely used, perhaps because of the associated litigation expenses involved as well as extensive defenses available to boards of directors and other parties.[8]

By contrast, a host of corporate law remedies exist for breach of 'fiduciary duty', which differ by jurisdiction. The US operates under a shareholder primacy doctrine (also referred to as a 'norm'), which, at its core, holds that directors must act in the best interests of shareholders of the corporation over which they preside. The doctrine is reflected in various shareholder rights, including the right to elect directors, approve the financial statements, appoint auditors and approve fundamental changes (Gordon, 1998). Boards of directors are required to make decisions in the best interests of shareholders and they have an explicit responsibility to maximize shareholder value.[9] In reviewing whether directors' decisions conform to these rules, courts will apply the business judgement rule, presuming that directors are motivated by a bona fide regard for the corporation's interests.

In the UK, directors' duties have been codified since 2006.[10] While it is still necessary to consider the duties of directors under common law and equity,[11] many duties are codified as being owed to the company. Under the UK *Companies Act, a* director's fiduciary duty is to run the company 'for the benefit of its members as a whole, [but] in doing so have regard' to other interests including the environment and the employees of the company.[12] Directors must act within powers granted by the company's constitution for the purposes conferred;[13] to promote the success of

---

[7] See OSA, s 130. See also Securities Act of 1933, 15 USC § 77a, s 12 for the American provision.

[8] OSA, n 6, s 130.

[9] See the line of cases beginning with *Hedley Byrne & Co Ltd v Heller & Partners Ltd* [1964] AC 465; *Queen v Cognos Inc*, [1993] 1 SCR 87.

[10] UK Companies Act 2006, c 46, s 170 [UKCA].

[11] ibid, s 170.

[12] ibid, s 172.

[13] ibid, s 171(a)–(b).

the company;[14] to exercise independent judgment;[15] to exercise reasonable care, skill and diligence;[16] to avoid conflicts of interests;[17] to refuse benefits from third parties;[18] and to declare interests in proposed transactions.[19] The director's duty to promote the success of the company includes considering a 'long-term increase in value' of the company (Goldsmith, 2006, column 254).

The statutory provisions in the UK render it clear that the duty of a UK board is not solely to maximize shareholder value. In making their decisions, directors are to take into account a series of factors, including the likely consequences of any decision in the long term; the interests of the company's employees; the need to foster the company's business relationships with suppliers, customers and others; the impact of the company's operations on the community and the environment; the desirability of the company maintaining a reputation for high standards of business conduct; and the need to act fairly as between members of the company.[20] Thus, directors must consider the competing interests of all stakeholders in the corporation, though it is entirely within their discretion to determine a particular course of action, considering the interests of investors beyond shareholders alone.

Canada stands closer to the UK than the US in terms of fiduciary duties owed by boards of directors. Directors' basic statutory duty is as follows: 'Every director and officer of a corporation in exercising their

---

14 ibid, s 172(1). Note that s 171(3) says that the duty 'imposed by this section has effect subject to any enactment or rule of law requiring directors, in certain circumstances, to consider or act in the interests of creditors of the company.' The explanatory note states that this provision should be taken to mean that bankruptcy law governs in this context.

15 ibid, s 173(1)–(2).

16 ibid, s 174. It is worth noting in passing that the codification of this rule and its traditional common law form are not substantively different.

17 ibid, s 175.

18 ibid, s 176.

19 ibid, s 177.

20 ibid, s 172(1)(a)–(f). There is no guidance given as to the relative weight of these factors. The governing principle is suggested by the UK legislature as one of maximizing 'enlightened shareholder value' (i.e. value for a shareholder who takes into account the considerations of other stakeholders when making decisions). The Explanatory Note Commentary accompanying the legislation is useless for guidance, as it only says that: 'The duty requires a director to act in the way he or she considers, in good faith, would be most likely to promote the success of the company for the benefit of its members as a whole and, in doing so, have regard to the factors listed.' Explanatory note to the UK Companies Act 2006, s 172 Duty to promote the success of the company, [325].

powers and discharging their duties shall (a) act honestly and in good faith with a view to the best interests of the corporation; and (b) exercise the care, diligence and skill that a reasonably prudent person would exercise in comparable circumstances.'[21] In the recent *BCE* decision, the Supreme Court of Canada explained that the duty is not owed to any one particular stakeholder group in the corporation, including the shareholders. Rather, 'the directors owe a fiduciary duty to the corporation, and only to the corporation . . . [I]t is important to be clear that the directors owe their duty to the corporation, not to stakeholders . . .'[22] Thus, unlike in the US, shareholder value maximization is not the law in Canada.

In terms of remedies, in the US, a plaintiff does not have an automatic remedy for breach of fiduciary duty (Rothschild, 2013). The remedies available depend, in part, on state law. A plaintiff can seek an injunction against the impugned conduct or damages (Black, 2001). In many states, the plaintiff can also seek and recover punitive damages, particularly if the plaintiff proves that the defendant's breach was due to fraud (Lawinfo, 2009). As a remedy to be claimed, damages are most common, particularly where transactions are approved by non-interested directors. This remedial approach may result from the reluctance of US courts to intervene in transactions that have been approved by the board (Black, 2001) because of the business judgement rule. Thus, plaintiffs may turn to other remedies to recover against conduct that they perceive to be wrong, including a derivative action for damages.

In the UK, shareholders are entitled to bring a derivative action against the directors on behalf of the company in certain circumstances.[23] While the statute does not seek to replace the common law rules, it attempts to create 'a new derivative procedure with more modern, flexible and accessible criteria for determining whether a shareholder can pursue an action' (Law Commission Report, 1997, [6.15]). Under the UKCA, a court must refuse permission where a person acting in accordance with the duty to promote the success of the company would not seek to continue the claim.[24] Further, before granting permission to continue, the court must evaluate the importance that a person acting in good faith would ascribe to continuing the action, whether an individual

---

[21] Canadian Business Corporations Act, RSC 1985 c C-44, s 122 [CBCA].

[22] *BCE Inc v 1976 Debentureholders* 2008 SCC 69 [2008] 3 SCR 560, [66] [*BCE*].

[23] UKCA, ss 178, 260.

[24] ibid, s 263(2)(a). For an application, see e.g. *Franbar Holdings Ltd v Patel* [2008] EWHC 1534 (Ch).

shareholder would have a personal action available and whether the act or omission complained of is likely to be or has been authorized before or ratified after occurring.[25]

Legal remedies for oppressive conduct exist under UK common law and statute. In particular, conduct that is 'unfairly prejudicial to the interests' of members or shareholders[26] permits a broad range of remedies, including any orders fit for providing relief, regulation of company affairs, injunctive relief and compulsory buy-backs of shareholders' stocks, among others. This ability of plaintiffs to recover for being treated oppressively derives from the common law[27] and a remedy of corporate dissolution is available under the UK Insolvency Act.[28]

The derivative action in Canada, as in the UK and the US, is a representative action brought in the name and on behalf of the corporation. Thus, any remedy granted accrues directly to the corporation rather than the litigants who brought the action on the corporation's behalf. An individual plaintiff requires leave of the court to proceed and so must satisfy the court that he or she has given notice and is acting in good faith. The court must also be satisfied that it is in the interests of the corporation that the action be brought.[29] Once leave is granted and the action proceeds, the plaintiff can reasonably expect that his or her costs will be recovered on a solicitor-client or substantial indemnity basis.[30]

The second statutory action is called the 'oppression remedy', a remedy unique to Canada and the UK. Unlike the derivative action, under the oppression remedy, a plaintiff can bring an action because of a wrong suffered by him or her personally. In granting a remedy, the court must be satisfied that the powers of the directors of the corporation or any of its affiliates are or have been exercised in a manner that is 'oppressive or unfairly prejudicial to or that unfairly disregards the interests of any security holder, creditor, director or officer'.[31] If a court finds that this provision has been violated, it can make an interim or final order as it

---

25 The only case to have moved forward beyond the second stage was recognized by the court to be a 'classic case' of a derivative action at common law: *Parry v Bartlett & Anor* [2011] EWHC 3146 (Ch).

26 UKCA, s 172(1).

27 *Ebrahimi v Westbourne Galleries Ltd* [1973] AC 360.

28 See UK Insolvency Act, 1986, s 122(1); Sandrak Miller, 'How Should U.S. and U.K. Minority Shareholder Remedies for Unfairly or Oppressive Conduct be Reformed?' (1999) 36:4 *Am Bus LJ* 579, 580–2.

29 CBCA, s 239(2).

30 *Primex Investments Ltd v Northwest Sports Enterprises Ltd,* (1995) 2383 (BCCA) cited in Cohen et al, 2011.

31 CBCA, s 241.

thinks fit.[32] In interpreting the wording of the statute, the courts require that directors consider the reasonable expectations of other parties when making decisions.[33]

Where does the concept of fiduciary duty fit in interpreting and awarding a remedy under the derivative action or oppression remedy? Historically, the courts have shied away from characterizing the substantive duties created by the oppression remedy as fiduciary in nature. In Canada, it was not until *BCE* that it became clear that an oppression claim exists for breaches of fiduciary duty and that constituents other than shareholders can bring the action (in this case, creditors).[34] In this case, the Supreme Court of Canada reiterated the statutory obligation of boards of directors to act in the corporation's best interests.[35] The result of *BCE* is vague (Lupa, 2011) and indeterminate (Iacobucci, 2009); what does it mean to say that directors owe their duty to the 'corporation'? The *BCE* decision does not provide directors with clarity regarding how and to whom specifically their duties are owed. The concept that a duty is owed to 'the corporation' when in fact the corporation is a legal fiction is highly ambiguous (Anand, 2004).

By contrast, on its formulation of the oppression remedy, the Supreme Court was relatively clear. It outlined two related inquiries for an oppression claim to be found. First, the court would determine whether the evidence supports the reasonable expectation asserted by the claimant. Second, the court would determine whether the evidence establishes that the reasonable expectation was violated by conduct falling within the terms 'oppression', 'unfair prejudice' or 'unfair disregard' of a relevant interest contained in the statute (*BCE*, [68]). In the court's view, the oppression remedy 'focuses on harm to the legal and equitable interests of stakeholders affected by oppressive acts of a corporation or its directors' (*BCE*, [45]).

---

32 ibid, s 241. As suggested above, the oppression remedies of the corporations acts of Alberta (ABCA, s 242), Saskatchewan (SBCA, s 234), Manitoba (MCA, s 234), New Brunswick (NBBCA, s 166), Nova Scotia (NSCA, Third Schedule, s 5) and Newfoundland (NCA, s 371) are substantially similar to that of the CBCA.

33 See *Westfair Foods Ltd v Watt* (1991), 79 DLR (4th), 48 (Alta CA); *Ebrahimi v Westbourne Galleries Ltd* [1973] AC 360; *Naneff v Con-Crete Holdings Ltd* (1995), 23 OR (3d) 481 (CA), 487.

34 As the court stated, 'the reasonable expectation of stakeholders is simply that the directors act in the best interests of the corporation'. *BCE*, n 22, [66].

35 CBCA, s 122. The basic statutory duty is as follows: 'Every director and officer of a corporation in exercising their powers and discharging their duties shall act honestly and in good faith with a view to the best interests of the corporation; and exercise the care, diligence and skill that a reasonably prudent person would exercise in comparable circumstances.'

Plaintiffs welcome the *BCE* judgment since it explicitly allows the consequences of breach of fiduciary duty to be characterized as oppressive conduct. This characterization benefits plaintiffs since the oppression remedy offers a broader substantive cause of action – one based on fairness and reasonable expectations rather than breach of trust and good faith conduct. Furthermore, the remedies available under the oppression remedy are broader than those available in an action for breach of fiduciary duty (historically a restitutionary-type remedy, damages or accounting of profits). There are thus numerous reasons that the *BCE* decision is plaintiff friendly, at least from a remedies' standpoint.

Despite the availability of the oppression remedy when a breach of fiduciary duty occurs, a separate question arises as to the likelihood that plaintiffs will pursue an oppression remedy or other private cause of action when corporate law has been violated. Private law remedies are generally difficult to pursue given the costs involved in the litigation (lawyers' fees and opportunity costs, for example). The plaintiff pays the costs associated with pursuing an oppression claim because, unlike a derivative action, the oppression claim is personal. He or she will only be entitled to recover costs if they are awarded at the end of the proceeding. Even if one is successful in the action, the precise 'remedy' is still at the discretion of the court and certainly may not amount to the monies paid for the investment or the profit lost.

(b) Public Remedies

A defining feature of the private remedy in securities and corporate law is that the remedy – indeed any remedy granted – accrues to the individual alone if directors have breached their fiduciary duty to act in the best interests of the corporation. But corporate law generally does not contain public remedies, unlike securities legislation where, depending on the jurisdiction, the action is brought by a third party (Crown, regulator or prosecutor) on behalf of the public at large. The third party is typically a securities commission that has jurisdiction under securities legislation to act in the public interest[36] in fulfilling the mandate of securities legislation to protect investors and to maintain fair and efficient capital markets.[37] Thus the remedy by and large seeks to benefit the public at large by deterring future conduct from occurring again.[38]

---

[36] See eg, OSA, s 127. 'The Commission may make one or more of the following orders if in its opinion it is in the public interest to make the order or orders. . . .'

[37] ibid, s 1.1.

[38] *Cartaway Resources Corp (Re)*, [2004] 1 SCR 672, 2004 SCC 26 [*Cartaway*].

The term 'public interest' is undefined in the statute. The OSA states: 'The Commission may make one or more of the following orders if in its opinion it is in the public interest to make the order or orders.'[39] These include orders that a person cease trading in any securities, a person or company be reprimanded, a director or officer resign or a person be prohibited from acting as a director or officer, a person or company pay an administrative penalty of not more than $1 million for each failure to comply, and a person disgorge to the commission any amount obtained as a result of non-compliance with the law.

The securities commission will not pursue cases of breach of fiduciary duty on investors' collective or individual behalves. The commission will refrain from adjudicating fiduciary duty questions because fiduciary duty falls under corporate law and is outside the commission's purview. Case law specifies that the purpose of such public interest remedies in securities law is to protect the public interest by removing from the capital markets those individuals whose conduct is so abusive as to warrant apprehension of future conduct detrimental to the integrity of the capital markets.[40] Further case law holds that the public interest jurisdiction is not compensatory or punitive but should be applied as necessary to prevent harm to the capital markets. Prevention may include considerations of deterrence, both general and specific (*Cartaway*). The former refers to deterrence aimed at society to prevent wrongdoing from taking place; the latter refers to deterrence aimed at the individual wrongdoer to prevent her from repeating the wrong (*Cartaway*, [52]).

A further public remedy that exists in some jurisdictions, particularly in Canada, is for the securities commission to bring quasi-criminal actions against defendants for violations of securities law. The actions are brought in courts rather than in administrative bodies (i.e. securities commissions). The explicit purpose of this type of action is to punish the defendant. The penalties in this type of action are accordingly more severe and can range from fines to five years less a day in prison.[41] A court can also order the defendant to provide restitution to investors.[42]

In a majority of cases brought within securities commissions in Canada,

---

[39] OSA, s 127.

[40] *Committee for the Equal Treatment of Asbestos Minority Shareholders v Ontario (Securities Commission)* [2001] 2 SCR 132, 2001 SCC 37, [43] [*Asbestos*].

[41] Note that in Canada, certain constitutional issues can arise in relation to the size of administrative monetary penalties in the securities commission. *Rowan v Ontario Securities Commission*, 2012 ONCA 208 [*Rowan*].

[42] See OSA, s 122.1(1). 'If a person or company is convicted of an offence under this Act, the court may, in addition to any penalty, order the convicted

investors do not receive restitution or compensation for lost funds. The relevant statutes contain no explicit right to restitution for investors in cases where the securities regulator brings an action in the public interest via an administrative proceeding. Admittedly, where commission staff members choose to pursue disgorgement of profits as a sanction, they may, if successful, dispense funds to investors. But this regulatory distribution of disgorged funds occurs at the regulators' discretion rather than by any right of recovery that accrues directly to the investor per se.

By contrast, under the 'Fair Funds' provision in the Sarbanes-Oxley Act of 2002, the US Securities and Exchange Commission (SEC) has the ability to place moneys received from defendants under a court order or settlement in a fund which can be used to compensate injured investors.[43] The SEC has no obligation to compensate victims but the ability and discretion to do so exists by virtue of the fund. The creation of this fund is unprecedented among Western jurisdictions including Canada, the UK and Australia.

3. REBALANCING REMEDIAL RIGHTS?

La Porta et al (2006) have studied private and public remedies extensively.[44] They analyzed the securities laws of 49 countries and found that financial markets do not prosper when left to market forces alone. Both disclosure rights and liability standards were positively correlated with larger stock markets, whereas public enforcement, such as having an independent securities regulator, played a modest role in the development of stock markets. Although their research has been criticized (Siems, 2008; Spamann, 2010), their findings at least suggest that securities laws have the greatest impact on market efficiency, and thereby on capital market performance, by providing default contract terms, ensuring minimum disclosure and enabling stakeholder participation in corporate governance. But La Porta et al also found that extensive disclosure requirements and standards of liability facilitating investor recovery of losses are associated with larger stock markets.

This section builds on the empirical findings of La Porta et al (2006) and

---

person or company to make restitution or pay compensation in relation to the offence to an aggrieved person or company.'

[43] Public Company Accounting Reform and Corporate Responsibility Act (Sarbanes-Oxley), 15 USC §7264 (2011), s 308.

[44] Note that the work of La Porta et al (2006) has been criticized on a variety of fronts. See La Porta et al (2006).

suggests that private contracting as well as public enforcement are integral to a comprehensive remedial regime. In short, public enforcement matters as a means to ensure that investors have confidence in the capital markets. The starting point for the discussion is to recognize that while investors have the ability to seek a private remedy under the oppression remedy or derivative action, they have no analogous ability to be compensated in the public domain except in the quasi-criminal sphere, as described above. The rationale for the absence of compensation for individual investors in the public sphere is that the securities regulator acts on behalf of the investing public, ensuring that capital markets operate with integrity. As case law has explicitly set forth, the regulator's foremost task is to maintain the public interest by deterring prospective misconduct rather than compensating victims or ensuring restitution.[45]

The absence of a right to restitution in the public sphere, however, presents an incongruity between the private and public spheres that is difficult to comprehend. Why shouldn't investors be entitled to compensation or restitution in the public sphere when a third-party regulator brings an action on their behalf? It stands to reason that investors who have suffered financially because of the defendant's violation of the law should have a right to be compensated or to receive restitution for the defendant's unjust enrichment. Such a right is fundamental to the idea that capital markets operate with integrity; investors will know that if their legal rights are violated, they will have a remedy. They will have greater confidence in the disclosure documents that they review and in placing their money in the capital markets on the basis of this information. Without remedies, investors will question the potential reliability of the disclosure they receive, which undermines the point of the disclosure regime.

The distinction between protecting capital markets on the one hand and ensuring that investors are compensated on the other is outmoded. Securities are goods. Just as consumers who purchase faulty products may be compensated, investors who purchase faulty securities should be able to be repaid funds that have been taken from them illegally. Investors' rights should be no different from consumers who purchase faulty goods. For example, when I inspect and purchase a box of raspberries at the grocery store and find at home that they are rotten, I take them back to the store and have the price of the raspberries returned. Similarly, when I

---

[45] One could argue that a deterrence-compensation distinction exists generally between the public-private realms: e.g. absent victim compensation provisions, a tort action for an assault injury is separated from the criminal process. Similarly, in competition law, cartel penalties are not paid to victims (although they may separately sue under a statutory right of action).

purchase a new computer, and bring it home only to find out that it does not function properly, I can return and exchange the good or receive my money back. Indeed, consumer protection legislation typically provides a remedy – rescission or damages – in the face of unfair practices.[46] There is seen to be something wrong with the quality of the good that warrants reimbursement.

One could argue that there is a public interest in preventing consumers from purchasing defective goods, including allowing the market for such goods to operate with integrity. Consumers of securities, i.e. investors, should be entitled to a restitutionary remedy, available because they enter into transactions in which 'buyer beware' is insufficient to protect their interests. The consumer of raspberries is not, in law, responsible for inspecting each berry to ensure its high quality; there are some things consumers cannot know at the time of purchase. Similarly, an investor in securities may not know at the time of purchase that the corporation in which he or she is investing will violate the law and that the security will then decrease in value.

Ultimately, one must question why securities are treated differently from other, tangible goods especially when the harm arising may be significant. One could argue that there is even a heightened basis on which to allow investors to receive restitution in cases of fraud or other violation of securities law. A key characteristic of securities markets is information asymmetry as between insiders of the corporation and unrelated shareholders. Such information asymmetry has historically augured in favour of the disclosure-based model currently in place in Canada, the US and the UK. Information asymmetries inherent in securities markets justify greater remedies, given that there is inability for consumers to 'inspect' their goods. Relative to traditional buyers and sellers of tangible goods, the greater the asymmetry in information between investors and management, the more the restitutionary remedy for violation of the fiduciary obligation or other law is warranted.

This argument counters traditional law and economics scholars who argue that investors holding diversified portfolios are as likely to be on the losing side of transactions as on the winning side (Easterbrook and Fischel, 2007). Their expected losses will therefore match their expected gains so they should not be compensated for securities fraud

---

[46] Ontario's Consumer Protection Act, SO 2002, c 30, Sched A provides that in the face of unfair practice consumers are entitled to rescind their agreement, under s 18(1), or if rescission is not possible, consumers are entitled, under s 18(2), to recover damages or the difference between their payment and value derived from good or service, or both.

losses. Other scholars challenge the traditional view, arguing that the undiversified investor suffers uncompensated harm as a result of fraud where there is a lack of disgorgement of wrongful gains from the perpetrators of the fraud (i.e. the violating company's management or its board) (Thakor et al, 2005). In particular, Davis Evans (2007) argues that, 'because there is measurable harm from fraud, there is a basis for granting compensation to its victims' because many retail investors do not diversify and some will buy and hold an undiversified portfolio for the long term. She favours providing compensation through an investor compensation fund whereby a portion of the purchase price payable to the selling shareholder on a securities transaction would be placed into an investor compensation fund that will provide victims of the fraud restitution.[47]

The restitutionary remedy advocated here is slightly different. It relates to a regulatory power to award restitution akin to the US Fair Funds provision. The difference between the current proposal and the Fair Funds provision, however, is that under Fair Funds, the SEC has no legal obligation to compensate victims of securities violations. Rather, it has the discretion to do so if it obtains a court order or settlement against a defendant (Connolly, 2007) and it may choose whom to compensate.[48] The argument put forth here, however, is that, absent an explicit statutory right to restitution, individuals should be entitled to a portion of the funds obtained by the securities regulator where it seeks and obtains disgorgement of profits in a regulatory hearing. This would become a legal obligation of the securities regulator that arguably is not contrary to the objectives of securities regulation.

As we know, the securities commission's public interest jurisdiction is aimed at protecting the interests of the investing public on a prospective basis. It is also charged with maintaining investor protection generally.[49] Unless investors are confident that they will receive restitution in the case

---

[47] In addition, a moral hazard problem should be noted: this proposal taxes well-governed corporations in favour of compensating for bad corporations, relieving those who make risky investments and increasing the capital costs for 'good' corporations which could lead to inefficient outcomes.

[48] *Official Committee of Unsecured Creditors of WorldCom, Inc v Securities and Exchange Commission*, 467 F3d 73 (2nd Cir 2006) <http://images.jw.com/com/publications/837.pdf> accessed 16 August 2014. Here, the SEC proposed to distribute the settlement funds only to certain interest holders of WorldCom. Specifically, the SEC's proposal to distribute $750 million excluded a number of interest holders, including those who recovered 36 cents or more on the dollar under the chapter 11 reorganization plan.

[49] OSA, s 1.1.

of securities fraud or legal wrongs, their interests will remain unprotected and their trust in the capital market will be correspondingly reduced. Less well-off and less sophisticated investors will be discouraged from the capital markets altogether because they do not have the knowledge or the resources to diversify. Investors lose because their wealth will not grow as quickly. Markets lose because fewer individuals will invest their wealth.

Furthermore, the egregious conduct will not be efficiently deterred. Capital market participants may suffer a type of fraud discount: if fraud increases, diversified and undiversified investors alike will be harmed (see Park, 2009, pp. 323, 341), not to mention public corporations that operate above the law. With a restitutionary remedy in place, investors will be more confident in making larger investments in individual securities without discounting such purchases by the probability that the stock price is fraudulent (Goshen and Parchomovsky, 2006). They will share the risk of fraud with all investors, knowing that if they happen to purchase securities inflated by fraud, they will be placed in the same position as those shareholders who did not.

A restitutionary remedy will better balance private and public remedies, allowing investors who do not have deep pockets to still recover if they are victims of corporate malfeasance. One may argue that 'balance' itself is unimportant, especially because investors have remedial rights that, as La Porta et al (2006) may argue, are already comprehensive. On the contrary, the addition of a restitutionary remedy tweaks the currently available panoply of investor remedies and it is necessary for both investor protection and efficiency reasons, as described above.

4. CONCLUSION

This chapter examined remedies that are available for breach of fiduciary duty. It also analyzed the broader remedial scheme consisting of both public and private remedies. When one considers the availability of compensation for breach of fiduciary duty and other wrongs in the private sphere, it seems reasonable to expect that restitution would be available to investors in the public sphere also. The proposal extends beyond the Fair Funds provision in the US to include a mandatory obligation for securities regulators to provide restitution to investors of a corporation of any disgorgement obtained from a defendant. Providing such restitution would deter breaches of fiduciary duties and violations of securities regulations, thereby bolstering investor confidence and enhancing the efficiency of capital markets.

REFERENCES

Anand A, 'Supreme Ambiguity' (2004) *The National Post* (18 November 2004) (op ed).

Black BS, 'The Principal Fiduciary Duties of Boards of Directors' (2001) (Presentation at Third Asian Roundtable on Corporate Governance) <http://www.oecd.org/daf/ca/corporategovernanceprinciples/1872746.pdf> accessed 19 February 2013.

Cohen TM, Pontin TM & Graeme Hooper. 'Distinguishing Oppression Claims and Derivative Actions: Shareholders Remedies – 2011 Update' (2011) Continuing Legal Education Society of British Columbia <http://www.fasken.com/files/Event/2508039d-8edf-46ac-a158-52dad507f6d6/Presentation/EventAttachment/572b7f22-e024-4e6b-8243-5362e5197614/53611_2_CohenPontin.pdf> accessed 19 February 2013.

Connolly J, 'Fair Funds and the Future of Securities Fraud Remedies' (2007) <http://papers.ssrn.com/sol3/papers.cfm?abstract_id=1004766> accessed 19 February 2013.

Davis Evans A, 'The Investor Compensation Fund' (2007) 33:1 J Corp Law 101, 103.

Easterbrook FH & Fischel R, 'Limited Liability and the Corporation' (1985) 52 University of Chicago LR 89.

Goldsmith PH, *Lords Grand Committee* (Grand committee meeting held at 6 February 2006).

Goshen Z & Parchomovsky G, 'The Essential Role of Securities Regulation' (2006) 55:4 Duke LJ 711.

Guiso L, Haliassos M & Jappelli T, 'Household Stockholding in Europe: Where Do We Stand and Where Do We Go?' (2003) 18:36 Economic Policy 123 <http://www.ecb.int/events/pdf/conferences/haliassos.pdf> accessed 11 January 2013.

Iacobucci E, 'Indeterminacy and the Canadian Supreme Court's Approach to Corporate Fiduciary Duties' (2009) 48 Can Bus LJ 232.

Jensen MC & Meckling WH, 'Theory of the Firm: Managerial Behaviour, Agency Costs and Ownership Structure' (1976) 3 J Fin Econ 305.

La Porta R, Lopez-De-Silanes F & Shleifer A, 'What Works in Securities Laws?' (2006) 61 J Finance 1.

UK Law Commission, *Shareholder Remedies: Report on a Reference under 3(1)(e) of the Law Commissions Act 1965* (Law Com No 246 Cm 3769, 1997) (London, Stationery Office).

Lawinfo, 'A Breach of Fiduciary Duty' (2009) <http://resources.lawinfo.com/business-law/a-breach-of-fiduciary-duty.html> accessed 19 February 2013.

Lupa P, 'BCE Blunder: An Argument in Favour of Shareholder Wealth Minimization in the Change of Control Context' (2011) 20 Dal J Legal Stud 1.

Park JJ, 'Shareholder Compensation as Dividend' (2009) 108:3 Mich L Rev 323.

Rothschild KR, 'Breach of fiduciary duty claims don't automatically create individual remedies' (2013) <http://www.lexology.com/library/detail.aspx?g=4e8924ed-1efe-4312-8654-0ce38d937560> accessed 19 February 2013.

Siems MM, 'What Does Not Work in Comparing Securities Laws: A Critique on La Porta et al.'s Methodology' (2008) International Company and Commercial L Rev 300.

Smith DG, 'The Shareholder Primacy Norm' (1998) 23:2 J Corp L 277.

Spamann H, 'The 'Antidirector Rights Index' Revisited' (2010) 23:2 Rev Financ Stud 267.

Thakor AV, Nielsen JS & Gulley DA, 'The Economic Reality of Securities Class Action Litigation' (2005) US Chamber Institute for Legal Reform 1 <http://www.nytimes.com/packages/pdf/business/27suit.pdf> accessed 16 August 2014.

Index